Indian Film Stars

Indian Film Stars

New Critical Perspectives

Edited by

Michael Lawrence

THE BRITISH FILM INSTITUTE
Bloomsbury Publishing Plc
50 Bedford Square, London, WC1B 3DP, UK
1385 Broadway, New York, NY 10018, USA

BLOOMSBURY is a trademark of Bloomsbury Publishing Plc

First published in Great Britain 2020 by Bloomsbury
on behalf of the
British Film Institute
21 Stephen Street, London W1T 1LN
www.bfi.org.uk

The BFI is the lead organisation for film in the UK and the distributor of Lottery funds for film. Our mission is to ensure that film is central to our cultural life, in particular by supporting and nurturing the next generation of filmmakers and audiences. We serve a public role which covers the cultural, creative and economic aspects of film in the UK.

Copyright © Michael Lawrence, 2020

Michael Lawrence has asserted his right under the Copyright, Designs and Patents Act, 1988, to be identified as author of this work.

For legal purposes the Acknowledgements on p. xv constitute an extension of this copyright page.

Cover design by Louise Dugdale
Cover image: myLoupe/Universal Images Group via Getty Images.

All rights reserved. No part of this publication may be reproduced or transmitted in any form or by any means, electronic or mechanical, including photocopying, recording, or any information storage or retrieval system, without prior permission in writing from the publishers.

Bloomsbury Publishing Plc does not have any control over, or responsibility for, any third-party websites referred to or in this book. All internet addresses given in this book were correct at the time of going to press. The author and publisher regret any inconvenience caused if addresses have changed or sites have ceased to exist, but can accept no responsibility for any such changes.

A catalogue record for this book is available from the British Library.

A catalog record for this book is available from the Library of Congress.

ISBN: HB: 978-1-8445-7855-9
       PB: 978-1-8445-7854-2
       ePDF: 978-1-9112-3993-2
       eBook: 978-1-8445-7857-3

Typeset by Integra Software Services Pvt. Ltd.
Printed and bound in India

To find out more about our authors and books visit www.bloomsbury.com and sign up for our newsletters.

For Om Puri (1950–2017) and Sridevi (1963–2018)

Contents

List of Illustrations — ix

Contributors — xi

Acknowledgements — xv

Introduction *Michael Lawrence* — 1

1. Shanta Apte and the unexpected *Anupama Kapse* — 15

2. Confessions of Indian cinema's first woman superstar: Kanan Devi's memoirs, film history and digital archives *Ranita Chatterjee* — 31

3. Star's 'dust': Miss Kumari and the fossilized memory of the 'first Malayalam female star' *Darshana Sreedhar Mini* — 45

4. In the wink of an eye: The comedic universe of Johnny Walker *Radha Dayal* — 59

5. Dharmendra Singh Deol: Masculinity and the late-Nehruvian hero in Hindi cinema *Anustup Basu* — 73

6. Rajkumar and the Kannada-language film *M. K. Raghavendra* — 87

7. The feudal lord reincarnate: Mohanlal and the politics of Malayali masculinity *Meena T. Pillai* — 99

8. From Gandhi to Jinnah: National dilemmas in the stardom of Rattan Kumar *Salma Siddique* — 109

9. From *Son of India* to teen king: Sajid Khan and transnational stardom *Meenasarani Linde Murugan* — 125

10. Harbhajan Maan: The transnational migrant success story of Punjabi cinema *Harjant S. Gill* — 137

11	Helen: The Chin Chin Chu girl *Sudesh Mishra*	151
12	'She's everything that's unpardonable': Hema Malini, dream girl on a motorbike *Rosie Thomas*	163
13	Sridevi, queen of farce: Comedy, performance and star persona in popular Hindi cinema *Nandana Bose*	181
14	The irresistible badness of Salman Khan *Shohini Ghosh*	193
15	Shah Rukh Khan starring as Shah Rukh Khan: Performance style, audience expectation and self-parody *Charlie Henniker*	205
16	The curious case of Katrina Kaif: NRI stardom and ethnicity in Bollywood *Midath Hayder*	219
	Index	232

Illustrations

1.1 Shanta Apte and Shahu Modak, pictured together in the booklet for *Shyam Sundar* (1932). 17
1.2 Durga Khote, Shanta Apte and Vasanthi in *Amar Jyoti* (1936). Public domain. 18
1.3 Shanta Apte as Niru. Booklet cover for *Duniya Na Mane* (1937). 23
1.4 'The Adventure of the Stick'. Cartoon in *The Times of India*, 7 August 1937, p. 18. 25
1.5 'Shanta Saves a Soul'. Advertisement in *The Times of India*, 7 August 1937, p. 18. 25
1.6 Apte pictured with a whip in the booklet cover for *Swayamsiddha* (1949). 27
1.7 Shanta Apte and M. S. Subbulakshmi in *Savitri* (1941). 28
3.1 Miss Kumari in *Anavalarthiya Vanambadi* (P. Subramanyam, 1960). 50
4.1 *Naya Daur* (New Times, Baldev Raj Chopra, 1957). 63
4.2 *Pyaasa* (The Thirsty One, Guru Dutt, 1957). 66
4.3 *Pyaasa* (The Thirsty One, Guru Dutt, 1957). 66
4.4 *Pyaasa* (The Thirsty One, Guru Dutt, 1957). 69
7.1 Mohanlal. 100
8.1 'Star Profile', *Filmfare*, 16 September 1954. 113
8.2 Poster of *Jagriti* (1954), *Filmfare*, 4 February 1955. 116
9.1 Sajid Khan as Raji in *Maya* (John Berry, 1966). 126
9.2 Sajid Khan performing 'Getting to Know You' on *American Bandstand* (ABC, 27 July 1968). 131
10.1 Harbhajan Maan with his wife Harminder Kaur Maan at a publicity event for his 2009 film *Heer Ranjha*. 138
10.2 Maan being interviewed on PTC Punjabi News Channel at a publicity event for his 2009 film *Heer Ranjha*. 139
10.3 Guggu Gill (left) and Yograj Singh (right) faceoff in a revenge-themed Punjabi film *Anakh Jattan Di* (Ego of Jats) from 1990. 141
11.1 *Gumnaam* (Raja Nawathe, 1965). 158
11.2 *Don* (Chandra Barot, 1978). 162
12.1 Postcard of Hema Malini bought on Bombay streets in 1980. 164
13.1 Sridevi's memorable impersonation of Charlie Chaplin's *The Tramp* in Shekhar Kapur's *Mr. India* (1987). 185
13.2 Unusual, decentred edge-of-frame composition of a female star that showcases her expressive range in a song picturization from *Roop Ki Rani Choron Ka Raja* (Satish Kaushik, 1993). 186
14.1 Salman Khan. 196

15.1 A genuine Tag Heuer advertisement featuring Shah Rukh Khan is used as a backdrop for a fictional character, played by Shah Rukh Khan, in *Om Shanti Om* (Farah Khan, 2007). 209
15.2 A film star arrives for a film shoot surrounded by fans and security: Shah Rukh Khan plays Sahir Khan, whose background is communicated through other movie posters and scenes from Shah Rukh Khan's career in *Billu* (Priyadarshan, 2009). 215
16.1 *Bombay Talkies* (Karan Johar, Dibakar Banerjee, Zoya Akhtar, Anurag Kashyap 2013). 229

Contributors

Anustup Basu is Associate Professor in English, Media and Cinema Studies, and Criticism at the University of Illinois at Urbana-Champaign. He is the author of *Bollywood in the Age of New Media: The Geo-televisual Aesthetic* (2010) and the co-editor, with Rajinder Dudra, Sangita Gopal and Amit Rai, of *InterMedia in South Asia: The Fourth Screen* (2012) and, with Meheli Sen, of *Figurations in Indian Film* (2013). His essays on film, media, culture and politics have appeared in journals such as *boundary 2, Journal of Human Rights, Postscript, South Asian History and Culture, PostModern Culture* and *Critical Quarterly*. As a film producer, he made the Bengali feature *Herbert* (2005), which won the Indian National Award for the Best Regional Film.

Nandana Bose is Associate Professor at the Department of Humanities and Languages at the Foundation for Liberal Arts and Management Education (FLAME University). She was previously Associate Professor of Film Studies at the University of North Carolina Wilmington, where she worked from 2009 to 2017. She is the author of the monograph *Madhuri Dixit* (2019). Her essays have appeared in journals such as *Cinema Journal, Celebrity Studies, Velvet Light Trap, Studies in South Asian Film and Media, Feminist Media Studies* and *Journal of the Moving Image*, and in Aysha Iqbal Viswamohan and Vimal Mohan John (eds), *Behind the Scenes: Contemporary Bollywood Directors and Their Cinema* (2017), Meheli Sen and Anustup Basu (eds), *Figurations in Indian Film* (2013) and Daniel Biltereyst and Roel Vande Winkel (eds), *Silencing Cinema: Film Censorship Around the World* (2013). She has won awards and grants from such scholarly associations as the Society for Cinema and Media Studies (2008) and the Association of Asian Studies (2014).

Ranita Chatterjee is Lecturer in Film at the University of Exeter. Her research interests include film history; nineteenth- and twentieth-century screen cultures; Indian cinema; colonial film; cinema industries and transnational film circulation. Previously she held a Leverhulme Early Career Fellowship at the Centre for Research and Education in Arts and Media (CREAM), University of Westminster (2012–2015). She is currently working on a manuscript on early cinema in Calcutta with a focus on the regional, national and transnational networks of film in South Asia before the Second World War. Her publications include 'Film History Through Fragments: The Aurora Archive and the transnational travels of early Indian cinema' in *BioScope: South Asian Screen Studies* (2014) and 'Cinema and the Colonial City: Catering for Calcutta's Multiple Audiences' in Ian Christie (ed.), *Audiences: Defining and Researching Screen Entertainment Experience* (2012).

Radha Dayal holds a master's degree in Film from King's College London. She previously studied and worked as an architect in India before completing a liberal arts postgraduate degree from Temple University, Philadelphia. Her academic interests include 1950s Bombay films, fringe characters, comedy, cultural theory and the city and architecture in film. She currently teaches in India with ongoing research projects in both film and architecture.

Shohini Ghosh is Sajjad Zaheer Professor at the AJK Mass Communication Centre, Jamia Millia Islamia (Central University) in New Delhi. She is the director of *Tales of the Nightfairies* (2002) a documentary about the sex workers' rights movement in Calcutta and the author of *Fire: A Queer Classic* (2010). Ghosh has been Visiting Professor in a number of universities within and outside India and has had a long association with the Sexuality, Gender and Rights Institute. Ghosh writes on contemporary media, speech and censorship, popular cinema, documentary and issues of gender and sexuality. Her current work is titled *Violence and the Spectral Muslim: Action, Affect and Bombay Cinema at the Turn of the 20th Century*.

Harjant Gill is Associate Professor of Anthropology at Towson University, Maryland. His research examines the intersections of masculinity, modernity, transnational migration and popular culture in India. Gill is also an award-winning filmmaker and has made several ethnographic films that have screened at film festivals, academic conferences and on television networks worldwide including the BBC, Doordarshan (Indian National TV) and PBS. His films include *Roots of Love*, which looks at the changing significance of hair and turbans among Sikh men in India and *Mardistan (Macholand)*, which explores Indian manhood focusing on issues of sexual violence, son preference, homophobia, toxic masculinity and patriarchy. His latest film *Sent Away Boys* examines how provincial communities across northern India are transformed by the exodus of young men giving up farming to seek a better future abroad. Gill co-edits the Multimodal Anthropologies section of the journal *American Anthropologist*. His website is www.TilotamaProductions.com.

Midath Hayder is a doctoral candidate at the University of Sussex. His PhD thesis considers issues of stardom and transnationalism in contemporary Bollywood culture.

Charlie Henniker is Head of Film Production at the LEGO Agency and is based in Århus, Denmark. He holds a master's degree in South Asian Area Studies from SOAS, University of London, where he specialized in Indian cinema and undertook fieldwork in India and East Africa. His chapter 'Pink Rupees or Gay Icons? Accounting for the Camp Appropriation of Male Bollywood Stars' appeared in Russell Meeuf and Raphael Raphael (eds) *Transnational Stardom* (2013). Charlie's research focuses on stardom, performance and subcultures.

Anupama Kapse is Associate Professor at the School of Film and Television in Loyola Marymount University. Her work has appeared in *Film, Fashion and the 1960s* (2017); *Figurations in Indian Film* (2013); *Framework*; *South Asian Popular Culture* and is forthcoming in *Cinema Journal, Film Quarterly* and *Film History*. She is currently completing a book on emotion and embodiment in pre-independence Indian cinema. She serves on the editorial board of *Journal of Cinema and Media Studies*.

Michael Lawrence is Reader in Film Studies at the University of Sussex. He is the author of *Sabu* (2014) and the co-editor, with Laura McMahon, of *Animal Life and the Moving Image* (2015), with Karen Lury, of *The Zoo and Screen Media: Images of Exhibition and Encounter* (2016) and, with Rachel Tavernor, of *Global Humanitarianism and*

Media Culture (2019). His work on Hindi cinema has appeared in Corey K. Creekmur and Linda Y. Mokdad (eds), *The International Musical* (2012), Iain Robert Smith and Constantine Verevis (eds), *Transnational Film Remakes* (2015), Sabrina Qiong Yu and Guy Austin (eds), *Revisiting Star Studies: Cultures, Themes and Methods* (2017) and Stephanie Hemerlryk Donald, Emma Wilson and Sarah Wright (eds), *Childhood and Nation in Contemporary World Cinema: Border and Encounters* (2017).

Sudesh Mishra is the author of two critical monographs, including *Diaspora Criticism* (2006), five volumes of poetry, two full-length plays and several short stories. His research papers have appeared in *New Literary History, Meanjin, Subaltern Studies, Australian Humanities Review, Continuum, Social Text, Borderlands, Emergences, Oxford Literary Review, The Journal of Pacific History* and *The Contemporary Pacific*. His most recent contribution to diaspora studies is a long entry on the subject for the second edition of *The Oxford Encyclopedia of Aesthetics*. Having previously taught at universities in Australia and Britain, he presently holds the position of Professor in the School of Language, Arts and Media at the University of the South Pacific.

Meenasarani Linde Murugan is an Assistant Professor in the Department of Communication and Media Studies at Fordham University. Her research focuses on television history and theories of race and visuality, with special attention to popular music, fashion and diaspora. Her essay 'Maidenform: Temporalities of Fashion, Femininity, and Feminism in Mad Men' appeared in Scott F. Stoddart (ed.), *Analyzing Mad Men: Critical Essays on the Television Series* (2011). She has written on contemporary Asian American pop culture aesthetics and politics for the *Los Angeles Review of Books* and *The Platform*. Her book, *Gender and Race in Postwar Variety Television: Colourful Performance*, is forthcoming.

Meena T. Pillai is the Director of the Centre for Cultural Studies at the University of Kerala. She has been a Fulbright Fellow at Ohio State University, a Shastri Fellow at the Mel Hoppenheim School of Cinema at Concordia University and a Commonwealth Fellow at the Media Studies Centre, University of Sussex. She is the editor of *Women in Malayalam Cinema: Naturalizing Gender Hierarchies* (2010) and the author of 'Matriliny to Masculinity: Performing Modernity and Gender in Malayalam Cinema' in the *Routledge Handbook of Indian Cinemas* (2013). She has been published widely and her areas of interest include gender, film and cultural studies.

M. K. Raghavendra received the National Award (the Swarna Kamal) for best film critic in 1997. Since then he has authored three volumes of academic film criticism: *Seduced by the Familiar: Narration and Meaning in Indian Popular Cinema* (2008), *Bipolar Identity: Region, Nation and the Kannada Language Film* (2011) and *The Politics of Hindi Cinema in the New Millennium: Bollywood and the Anglophone Indian Nation* (2014) as well as two volumes of popular film criticism, *50 Indian Film Classics* (2009) and *Directors Cut: 50 Major Filmmakers of the Modern Era* (2013). Two of the above books have been named by FIPRESCI as among the best books on cinema worldwide. Two of his books are also being published as Russian translations in 2019. His book *The Oxford India Short Introduction to Bollywood* was published in 2016 and his edited anthology *Beyond Bollywood: The Cinemas of South India* in 2017. His essays have appeared in numerous volumes on film published by Oxford University Press, Sage and Routledge, among others.

Salma Siddique is a filmmaker by training and completed her doctoral thesis 'Between Bombay and Lahore: A partition history of cinema in South Asia (1940–1960)' at the University of Westminster, London in 2015. Currently, she is a postdoctoral research fellow at Freie University, Berlin.

Darshana Sreedhar Mini is a PhD Candidate at the Cinema and Media Studies Division, University of Southern California. Her dissertation explores transnational circulation of media artefacts such as low-budget films produced in India and the informal economy that it sustains. Her work is supported by the Social Science Research Council. Her research interests include feminist media, gender studies, South Asian Studies and Media Ethnography. She has published articles in *Bioscope: South Asian Screen Studies*, *South Asian Popular Culture*, *Journal for Ritual Studies* and *International Journal for Digital Television*.

Rosie Thomas is Professor of Film, founding director of the Centre for Research and Education in Arts and Media (CREAM) and Co-director of the India Media Centre at the University of Westminster. She is co-founder and co-editor of the journal *Bioscope: South Asian Screen Studies*. Her early research as a social anthropologist was on the Bombay film industry and, since 1985, she has published widely on Indian cinema. Her current research is on the history of Indian stunt and Islamicate cinema, as well as documentary filmmaking. Her monograph *Bombay Before Bollywood: Film City Fantasies* was published in India in 2013 and in the United States in 2015.

Acknowledgements

I would like to thank the contributors, for their patience; the staff at the BFI, for their assistance; my partner, John David Rhodes, for his support; and my parents, Vic and Toni, for their love.

Introduction
Michael Lawrence

In the United Kingdom, in the spring of 1999, there was a great deal of surprise when an Indian actor, Bollywood icon Amitabh Bachchan (1942–), regarded by many Indian film fans as a living legend and synonymous with the popular Hindi cinema produced in Mumbai (Bombay), was voted 'the greatest actor of stage or screen' in an online poll organized by the BBC (British Broadcasting Corporation) held to mark the millennium (Laurence Olivier came second). The following year, Bachchan became the first Indian actor to be represented at the Madame Tussauds waxworks museum in London.[1] While Bachchan is one of a number of Bollywood stars who have become increasingly familiar to the general public in the West (he subsequently made a special appearance in Baz Lurhmann's 2013 film *The Great Gatsby*), the vast majority of the most significant and successful stars of Indian cinema remain largely unknown in the West, except to fans of Indian cinema or to Indian cinema specialists, despite many of them having over the years acquired international audiences.[2] Historically, Hindi cinema (or Bollywood) may have enjoyed the greater global visibility, but Telugu cinema (based in Hyderabad) boasts several stars whose level and longevity of fame might eclipse that of Amitabh Bachchan, at least for audiences in India. The Telugu actor N. T. Rama Rao (Nandamuri Taraka Rama Rao, 1923–1996), a huge star who worked predominantly in mythological films during the 1950s and 1960s, is barely known to non-Indian audiences, even though he was voted the greatest male actor in Indian cinema in a poll launched by CNN-IBN to celebrate the centenary of Indian cinema.[3] In the early 1990s, another Telugu actor, Chiranjeevi (Konidela Siva Sankara Vara Prasad, 1955–), popularly known as 'Mega Star', was reported to have become the highest-paid star in Indian cinema, and was subsequently dubbed 'Bigger than Bachchan' by the popular media (but probably couldn't have been named by the global audiences who in their millions watched him perform when the so-called 'Indian Thriller' video (a song-sequence from *Donga* [A. Kodanarami Reddy, 1985]) went viral). And another Telugu star, Brahanandam (Brahanandam Kanneganti, 1956–), celebrated for his work in comedy, currently holds the Guinness World Record for the

---

[1]'Bollywood star tops the poll', 1 July 1999, online at: http://news.bbc.co.uk/1/hi/entertainment/381017.stm (accessed 12 February 2016).
[2]As Dhondy (1985: 131) and Rajagopalan (2008) have shown, popular Hindi cinema stars such as Raj Kapoor [Ranbir Raj Kapoor, 1924–1988], Nargis [Fatima Rashid, 1929–1981] and Mithun Chakraborty [Gourang Chakraborty, 1950–] were extremely popular throughout the Arab world and Africa, and the Soviet Union; similarly, Dimitris Eleftheriotis (2002: 194) reminds us of the popularity of Madhubala [Mumtaz Jehan Dehlavi, 1933–1969] in Greece).
[3]'NTY greatest actor in India: CNN-IBN Poll survey', IBNLive, 9 March 2013, online at: www.ibnlive.com/news/india/ntr-greatest-actor-in-india-cnn-ibn-poll-survey-595559.html (accessed 12 February 2016).

most screen credits for a living actor (867 roles as of 2007).[4]

If film stars such as N. T. Rama Rao, Chiranjeevi and Brahanandam remain largely unknown to audiences in the West, the massive scale of film production in India, which Ashish Rajadhyaksha memorably described as the 'sheer gigantomania of India's film factories', is, by contrast, very likely to be known (Rajadhyaksha and Willemen [1994] 1999: 10). The diversity of India's film culture, comprising over a dozen regional industries making films in various languages, led Paul Willemen to argue that it should be compared to the production landscape in Europe rather than to that of any other nation state (Willemen and Gandhy 1980: 38). The challenges involved in adequately and inclusively representing this national cinema are obvious and manifold, and given the incontrovertible centrality of the star to the film industries in India, a scholarly collection about Indian film stars could have easily become (and arguably should have been) a multi-volume enterprise.

A negative view of the centrality of the star to (commercial) Indian cinema was to some extent sanctioned by the publication in 1963 of *Indian Film* by Erik Barnouw and S. Krishnaswamy ([1963] 1980), the first major study of Indian cinema to be published in English, and which was promptly and rather pointedly praised by reviewers (who likely had seen very little if any Indian cinema, except perhaps *Pather Panchali* [Dir. Satyajit Ray, 1955]) for its lucid account of 'the extraordinary rise of the Indian film-star to godlike fame in a land given to deification' (Woodcock 1964: 330); for its 'clear and dismal' portrait of the 'particular difficulties' that have 'molded' the Indian film, chief among them the 'virulent star system' (Harrison 1963: 61); and for accurately apportioning due blame to 'a star system which makes ours look like the height of rationality' for producing 'a system theoretically incapable of having permitted a Satyajit Ray to have emerged professionally' (Hazard 1963: 65).[5] While mainstream Indian films are now taken seriously as the subject of critical inquiry, as indeed are film stars, the serious study of Indian film stardom is a project that inherits a dual prejudice (against commercial entertainment, and against celebrity systems) that has often been perpetuated specifically in order to devalue, deride and dismiss Indian film culture. Such a project would begin with legendary figures such as K. L. Saigal (Kundan Lal Saigal, 1904–1947), the original 'singer superstar' of Indian cinema, who appeared in both Hindi and Bengali films, first in Kolkata (Calcutta) during the 1930s (most famously he played the lead in P. C. Barua's *Devdas* [1935])

---

[4] "Guinness record for Brahmanandam", *The Times of India*, 15 December 2007, online at: http://timesofindia.indiatimes.com/entertainment/bollywood/news-interviews/Guinness-record-for-Brahmanandam/articleshow/2622862.cms?referral=PM (accessed 12 February 2016).

[5] The study of stars has often suggested connections between stardom and religion or mythology (see also recent books by Williams [2012] and Burr [2012]). Edgar Morin's seminal account of the 'cult of stardom', for example, emphasizes 'the process of divinization that the movie actor undergoes ... that makes him the idol of the crowds' (2000 [1957]: 30). A few years earlier, in her examination of Hollywood, the anthropologist Hortense Powdermaker compared contemporary attitudes towards films stars with those of 'primitive people's relationship to their totemic heroes', observing rather acidly: 'Certainly no folk hero or god has ever been known so intimately by his admirers as are the movie stars. But, of course, none of the ancient gods had publicity departments' (1950: 248, 249). Behroze Gandhy and Rosie Thomas have argued 'the parallels between Indian stars and the gods of the Hindu pantheon are frequently remarked upon: both are colourfully larger than life, their lives and loves, including moral lapeses, the subject of voyeuristic fascination and extraordinary tolerance, and stars accept, on the whole graciously, an adoration close to veneration'; they also concur that 'the position stars command today – both economically and in the popular imagination – is the result of an idiosyncractic economic system that has accorded them more absolute power than even their Holywood counterparts' (1991: 107).

and subsequently in Mumbai during the 1940s. It would then track the numerous stars who have played important roles in the various regional Indian popular and 'parallel' film traditions that developed over the subsequent six decades, before concluding with representative recent stars, whose careers, like so many Indian film stars before them, encompass distinct regional and international industries, and whose popularity and appeal traverse and transcend various cultural differences. But such a project should not restrict itself to a proscriptive pantheon of illustrious screen legends and 'superstar' icons (such as Bengali cinema's Suchitra Sen [Roma Dasgupta, 1931–2014], Hindi cinema's Rajesh Khanna [Jatin Khanna, 1942–2012], Malayalam cinema's Mammooty [Muhammad Kutty ismail Paniparambil, 1951–], Kannada cinema's Malashri [Sri Durga, 1973–], Tamil cinema's Rajnikanth [Shivaji Rao Gaekward, 1950–] or Telugu cinema's Pawan Kalyan [Konidela Kalyan Babu, 1971–]) and instead should offer an expansive account that would accommodate figures as diverse as the wrestler-actor star Dara Singh (1928–2012) as well as the many stars who have either 'crossed over' from or remained popularly associated with the various regional cinemas' B- and C-grade output (such as Shakti Kapoor [Sunil Sikanderlal Kapoor, 1953–], Silk Smitha [Vijayalakshmi, 1960–1996], Shakeela [C. Shakeela Begum, 1991–] and Sapna Tanveer).

Indian film stars can become international film stars when either the Indian films in which they star reach international audiences or when they work in films produced for international audiences by industries outside India.[6] Indian film stars, particularly those associated with popular Hindi cinema, have often worked in English-language cinema: in Hollywood, they were typically cast as exotic villains (for example Kabir Bedi [1946–] in *Octopussy* [John Glen, 1983] and Amrish Puri [1932–2005] in *Indiana Jones and the Temple of Doom* [Stephen Spielberg, 1984]), while in British films, Indian actors were cast mainly in historical heritage dramas set during the colonial period or comedy dramas exploring post-war multicultural society in the UK: Saeed Jaffrey (1929–2015), for example, in *The Man Who Would Be King* (John Huston, 1975), *Gandhi* (Richard Attenborough, 1982), *A Passage to India* (David Lean, 1984) and *My Beautiful Launderette* (Stephen Frears, 1984), and Om Puri (1950–2017), in *My Son the Fanatic* (Udayan Prasad, 1997) and *East is East* (Daniel O'Donnell, 1999). By contrast, Bollywood actors Anupam Kher (1955–), Irrfan Khan (Sahabzade Irrfan Ali Khan, 1967–) and Aishwarya Rai Bachchan (1973–) have recently worked across a more diverse range of films, including films in which their being Indian is not necessarily or explicitly relevant to their character's narrative function: Kher appeared in *Bend It Like Beckham* (Gurinder Chadha, 2002) and *Bride and Prejudice* (Gurinder Chadha, 2004) but also *Silver Linings Playbook* (David O. Russell, 2012) and *You Will Meet a Tall Dark Stranger* (Woody Allen, 2010); Khan appeared in *The Darjeeling Limited* (Wes Anderson, 2007), *Slumdog Millionaire* (Danny Boyle, 2008) and *Life of Pi* (Ang Lee, 2012), but also *The Amazing Spider-Man* (Marc Webb, 2012) and *Jurassic World* (Colin Trevorrow, 2015); Rai Bachchan appeared in the aforementioned *Bride*

---

[6] The first Indian actor to become an international star was Sabu [Selar Sheik Dastigir, 1924–1963], whose career began with the lead role in Robert Flaherty's *Elephant Boy* (1937) and who subsequently worked on British imperial films such as *The Drum* (Zoltan Korda, 1938) *The Jungle Book* (Zoltan Korda, 1940) and *Black Narcissus* (Michael Powell and Emeric Pressburger, 1947) and Hollywood fantasy adventures such as *Arabian Nights* (Walter Wanger, 1942) and *Cobra Woman* (Robert Siodmak, 1944) (see Lawrence 2014).

and Prejudice, The Mistress of Spices (Paul Mayeda Berges, 2005) and *The Provoked* (Jag Mundhra, 2006), but also *The Last Legion* (Doug Lefler, 2007) and *The Pink Panther 2* (Harald Zwart, 2009). This presence provides a different context for the recent turn by Anil Kapoor (1956–), who also featured in *Slumdog Millionaire*, as the villainous media mogul in *Mission Impossible: Ghost Protocol* (Brad Bird, 2011).[7] In his recent introductory guide to the field of star studies, Martin Shingler suggests that the stardom systems of Hollywood and Bollywood 'appear to be converging in the twenty-first century', proposing that 'the ways in which they are increasingly occupying common ground have much to tell us about the history of film stardom' (2012: 6). Indeed, Indian film stars are increasingly attractive options for commercial filmmakers working in Hollywood: at the time of writing, for example, there is a great deal of buzz across online media platforms and forums about Bollywood star Priyanka Chopra (1982–) playing a lead role in *Baywatch* movie (Seth Gordon, 2017), alongside Dwayne 'The Rock' Johnson (who described her on his Instagram account as 'one of the biggest stars in the world'), and Telugu actor Prabhas (Prabhas Raju Uppalapati, 1979–), star of the Telugu/Tamil epic blockbuster *Baahubali: The Beginning* (S. S. Rajamouli, 2015) – reportedly both the most expensive and successful film ever made in India – who may or may not be starring with Jackie Chan in an upcoming Hollywood action film (like Chan, Prabhas has legions of fans across China).[8]

There has been a marked increase in the number of academic books about Indian cinema published during the last two decades, reflecting and contributing to a growing interest in India's various film cultures. While popular Hindi cinema, or Bollywood, has received the most attention – appropriately enough for the Indian cinema with the largest global audience – there have also been several studies of other regional film industries.[9] Despite this welcome increase, however, there is a relative dearth of critical scholarship addressing the significance of the *film star* for the production and reception of Indian cinemas, despite the development of star (and more recently celebrity) studies across the fields of film and media studies since the publication of foundational works by Richard Dyer ([1979] 1998, 1986) and Richard deCordova ([1990] 2000) and important collections edited by Christine Gledhill (1991) and Jeremy

---

[7] Nitin Govil has discussed the 'inter-industry contact … affirmed and celebrated' via a photograph showing Kapoor and Tom Cruise shaking hands before the Taj Mahal, in which the actors 'stand in for the *real* star of the scene: the connection between Hollywood and Bombay cinema' (2015: 12). In a conversation about the recent Hollywood roles of Irfan Khan and Anil Kapoor, Corey Creekmur argues that such major Indian film stars become secondary figures when they move from 'leading man category' into a 'character role' or a 'cameo part' in a Hollywood film, and observes that 'it would almost be an embarrassment for these idolized stars to move into a Hollywood film and play a kind of sidekick role'; Sangita Gopal is doubtful that Bollywood stars 'whose main star text isn't anchored in action would succeed' in Hollywood (Beltran, Creekmur, Gopal and Raphael 2013: 22, 25).
[8] Jonhson's comments, online at: www.instagram.com/p/BB2m-ZeIhzW/ (accessed 12 March 2016).
[9] A representative list of recent scholarship on popular Hindi cinema would include Gopalan 2002; Mishra 2002; Virdi 2003; Kaur and Sinha 2005; Bose 2006; Dudrah 2006; Lal and Nandy 2006; Mazumdar 2007; Velayutham 2008; Kavoori and Punathambekar 2008; Raghavendra 2008; Rai 2009; Rajadhyaksha 2009; Basu 2010; Gehlawat 2010; Dywer and Pinto 2011; Mehta 2011; Raghavendra 2011; Dudrah 2012; Gokulsing and Dissanayake 2013; Punathambekar 2013; Joshi and Dudrah 2014; Thomas 2014; Dayal 2015; Joshi 2015; Mahadevan 2015; Mubarki 2016; Krämer 2017; Sen 2017. For Bengali film, see Gooptu 2011 and Mukherjee 2016; for Malayalam film see Pillai 2010; for Kannada film see Raghavendra 2011; for Tamil film see Velayutham 2008; for Telugu film see Srinivas 2013.

G. Butler (1991).¹⁰ As Sumita S. Chakravarty has suggested, 'In the expanding field of Indian film studies, stars are a taken-for-granted aspect of Bollywood, but compared with other aspects of the institution and its products, they have been given less attention' (2013: 180). One notable exception is Neepa Majumdar's *Wanted Cultured Ladies Only! Female Stardom and Cinema in India, 1930s–1950s* (2009), which provides analyses of several actresses (including Sulochana [Sulochana Latkar, 1928–], Fearless Nadia [Mary Ann Evans/Wadia, 1908–1996] and Nargis) as part of its exploration of stardom in Indian cinema from the silent era to the post-Independence period. Majumdar states at the beginning of her book that 'stardom as a subject of inquiry in Indian cinema is better represented in popular discourse than in scholarly work' and describes critical scholarship on Indian film stars as an 'attenuated field of study' (2009: 11). There has been a handful of book-length studies of specific Indian film stars as well as articles about individual stars published in academic journals and in various edited collections, suggesting a growing awareness of the importance of stars (and star studies) for understanding India's cinema.¹¹ Introductory guides to popular Hindi cinema or Bollywood typically include a discussion of either the star system or individual stars or both (for example, Ganti 2004: 115–36; Fay 2011: 45–80, 91–102; Varia 2013: 95–110), as do the more advanced academic studies (for example, Dwyer and Patel 2002: 32–5, 183–92; Mishra 2002: 125–56; Virdi 2003: 137–44; Vasudevan 2011: 150–62; Ganti 2012: 207–13; Bhattacharya 2013: 110–25); there are also anthologies of essays about and interviews with stars by Indian film critics (for example, Pinto 2011; Saari 2011; Patel 2012; Kabir 2014). Furthermore, the critical discussion of Indian film stars (at least those associated with popular Hindi cinema) is increasingly to be found in more general introductory guides to both star studies (for example, the aforementioned Shingler 2012, the cover of which is adorned by a photograph of Aishwarya Rai as Paro from *Devdas* [Sanjay Leela Bhansali, 2002]) and film studies (for example, Etherington-Wright and Doughty 2011). But there is as yet no single edited collection that brings together a

---

¹⁰While Karen Hollinger suggests 'Star studies have always been a poor second cousin within the family of film studies' (2006: 35) there has been a recent and welcome increase of interest and scholarship – now routinely described as an 'explosion' – devoted to films stars, building on and moving beyond the sociological and semiological approaches associated with Dyer, which focused on the 'structured polysemy' of the star 'text' ([1979] 1998: 3). For a survey of star studies 'before' and 'after' Dyer's *Stars*, see Shingler (2012: 8–36). Notable recent interventions include the launch in 2010 of the journal *Celebrity Studies*, the *Film Stars* series of monographs on international stars published by the British Film Institute (2012–) and the *Star Decades* series of edited collections about American stars published by Rutgers University Press (2010–2012). See also the recent work on Hollywood stardom by Austin and Barker (2003), Basinger (2007), Williams (2012) and McDonald (2013), and collections on cult stardom (Egan and Thomas 2013), transnational stardom (Meeuf and Raphael 2013) and stardom and longevity (Bolton and Lobalzo Wright 2016).

¹¹For examples see books (both critical and popular) about Hindi cinema stars such as Pran (Pran Krishen Sikand, 1920–), 'Indian cinema's most memorable villain' (Bunny 2005), Amitabh Bachchan, 'India's greatest star-actor' (Dasgupta 2006; Hines 2007; Singh 2017), Shah Rukh Khan, 'King of Bollywood' (Chopra 2007), Helen (Helen Jairag Richardson, 1938–), (Pinto 2005), Rajesh Khanna, 'India's first superstar' (Usman 2014), Meena Kumari (Mahjabeen Bano, 1932–1872), 'Indian cinema's greatest tragedienne' (Mehta 2013), and Telugu 'Mega Star' Chiranjeevi (Konidela Siva Sankara Vara Prasad, 1955–) (Srinivas 2009). An international academic conference devoted to Shah Rukh Khan recently resulted in an edited collection focused on the Bollywood superstar's relationship with globalization (Dudrah, Mader and Fuchs 2015). For examples of articles and chapters on various Indian stars (mainly popular Hindi cinema stars), see Gandhy and Thomas 1991; Sharma 1993; Vichani 1999; Prasad 2004; Thomas 2005; Roy 2008; Vasudevan 2010; Rajagopalan 2011; Gehlawat 2012; Mazumdar 2012; Mishra 2012; Basu 2013; Bose 2013; Mitra 2013; Bose 2014; Shingler 2014; Viswamohan 2014; Dwyer 2015; Lawrence 2017; Bose 2019.

range of original essays concerned with assessing the cultural, industrial and political significance of India's film stars past and present.[12] Recent work has moved beyond traditional frameworks for examining stars and considered, for example, the impact of television and the internet on 'the changed landscape of stardom of stardom in India in the period of globalization' (Mazumdar 2012: 833) and suggested 'a mediological approach that sees stars as part of larger historical formations and technological transformations (Chakravarty 2013: 198). *Indian Film Stars* seeks to contribute to the development of Indian cinema star studies by looking back at the history of stardom in India from a variety of perspectives that emphasize stars' relationship to the formations and transformations that constitute the changing mediacultural landscape.

This book is neither a dictionary nor an encyclopaedia of Indian films stars (there are hundreds of informative entries devoted to stars in Ashish Rajadhyaksha and Paul Willemen's *Encyclopaedia of Indian Cinema* [(1994) 1999]; instead, the chapters presented in this volume offer detailed critical analyses of a selection of stars that, while relatively generous given the constraints of a single volume, is clearly and inevitably partial. It should be admitted at the outset, then, that *Indian Film Stars* does not cover all the regional film traditions that constitute the cinema of India (the book doesn't discuss stars of Telugu or Tamil cinema, for instance). There are, inevitably, famous and important stars conspicuous by their absence in the current collection, and yet compiling and including a list of the stars who aren't discussed here would likely simply reproduce in miniature the more general state of omission being acknowledged. The chapters that are collected here examine a range of stars associated with several of the major Indian film industries, including Hindi cinema (or Bollywood, the largest and by far the most well-known outside India), as well as the Malaylam, Bengali, Kannada and Punjabi cinemas, and include studies of transnational stars whose careers traversed political borders and cultural boundaries.

The first three chapters examine actresses who are associated with the establishment of regional cinemas (Hindi, Marathi, Bengali and Malayalam) during the 1930s, 1940s and 1950s, and who are regarded as central to these cinemas' popularity with audiences. In 'Shanta Apte and the unexpected', Anupama Kapse discusses the career of the singing sensation Shanta Apte (1916–1964), one of the foremost actresses working in Hindi films during the early sound era and before the emergence of the playback system. Kapse examines Apte's dynamic and distinctive screen femininity, and in particular her skilful yoking of her voice to her body, and addresses her innovations as a performer in relation to the defiant actions that contributed to her 'firebrand' persona. In 'Confessions of Indian cinema's first woman superstar: Kanan Devi's memoirs, film history and digital archives', Ranita Chatterjee considers Shanta Apse's contemporary Kanan Devi (1916–1992), a major but now forgotten star of the Bengali cinema produced in Kolkata (Calcutta) during the 1930s and 1940s, and known as 'the first woman superstar' of Indian cinema (she was the leading actress at the New Theatres studio). Chatterjee turns to Devi's autobiographical writings in order to complicate our understanding of the star's relation to the 'new woman' discourses of the time. In 'Star's "dust": Miss Kumari and the fossilized memory of the "first Malayalam

---

[12] The relative obscurity of Indian film stars in the West is suggested by the publication of several collections concerned with stars from East Asia (for example Farquhar and Zhang 2010; Leung and Willis 2014; Funnell 2015).

female star"', Darshana Sreedhar Mini explores the career of Miss Kumari (Thresiamma Thomas, 1932–1969) and her relationship with the Kerala studios to explore how she was constructed as both a studio artist and a 'domestic custodian of native films'. The chapter concludes with a reflection on the ways Miss Kumari has been recollected and recuperated since her death, focusing on the physical and memorial traces her career has left on the Malayalam industry.

The following four chapters address male stars working in the Hindi, Malayalam and Kannada language cinemas in the decades following Independence, and consider their relationships to the ideological work of popular cinema and the politics of masculinity in mainstream entertainment. Radha Dayal's chapter, 'In the wink of an eye: The comedic universe of Johnny Walker', considers the most iconic comic actor of 1950s Bombay cinema. Unlike other comic actors of the period, Johnny Walker (Badruddin Jamaluddin Kazi, 1920–2003) was a privileged presence in his films, granted solo songs and substantial romantic scenarios; Dayal focuses in particular on the latter to argue that Walker's characters often disrupted, decentred or 'disarranged' the ideological work associated with the Bombay socials in which he appeared. Continuing this exploration of the star's function in the cinema's relationship with its political context, Anustup Basu's chapter 'Dharmenda Singh Deol: Masculinity and the late-Nehruvian hero in Hindi cinema', examines the 'durable' stardom and 'malleable' screen persona of Dharmendra (1935–), in relation to how mainstream Hindi cinema's representations of heroic masculinity reflected the shifting sociopolitical climate of the 1960s and 1970s. Carefully comparing Dharmendra to his contemporaries, such as Dilip Kumar and Amitabh Bachchan, Basu also considers why he was largely excluded when Hindi cinema morphed into the contemporary Bollywood culture industry. In 'Rajkumar and the Kannada-language film', M.K. Raghavendra addresses Rajkumar (Singanalluru Puttaswamayya Muthuraju, 1929–2006), who dominated Kannada-language cinema for several decades following his rise to fame in the 1950s. Raghavendra argues that Rajkumar should be understood as a mnemonic icon of the former Princely State of Mysore (the region of Karnataka most explicitly addressed by Kannada cinema) who was instrumental in the attempt to address the rest of the Kannada-speaking state (Greater Mysore); Rajkumar emerged as a star as Princely Mysore was becoming defunct politically, and his subsequent stardom reflected efforts to keep the state's memory alive for audiences in Mysore and beyond. In 'The feudal lord reincarnate: Mohanlal and the politics of Malayalam masculinity', Meena T. Pillai interrogates the politics of masculinity in Malayalam cinema via an analysis of the rise of Mohanlal (Mohanlal Viswanathan Nair, 1960–) to 'superstar' status in the 1980s and 1990s. Pillai argues that Mohanlal's popularity reflects a 'feudal nostalgia' that during these decades transformed the ideological work and visual iconography of Malayalam cinema, and that the star's screen image should be understood in the context of the liberalization of the Indian economy, which linked images of masculinity to popular consumption.

There follow three chapters that focus on film stars whose careers are defined by migration. In 'From Gandhi to Jinnah: National dilemmas in the stardom of Rattan Kumar', Salma Siddique considers the career of the quintessential child star of 1950s popular Hindi cinema, Rattan Kumar (1943–), who left India for Pakistan in 1956, nearly a decade after the partition. Siddique examines Kumar's failure to replicate his stardom in Pakistan, focusing on how his migrant star image was elaborated in his earliest films, and discusses his association with double roles and remakes in relation to the divisions and disavowals produced by the partition. In 'From *Son of India* to teen king: Sajid Khan and transnational stardom', Meenasarani Linde Murugan looks at the transatlantic stardom of Sajid Khan (1953–), who shot to fame after playing the young Birju in *Mother India* (Mehboob Khan, 1957), and subsequently worked on American films and television, before enjoying a brief career in the United States as a teen heartthrob and pop singer sensation. Exploring how Khan became 'an arbiter of cultural exchange', Murugan argues that his incorporation into white American culture was aided by a more general fascination with India amongst American youth during the late 1960s; while his stardom was predicated on a rehashing of Orientalist fantasies as hip fashion, his performance of Indian-ness nevertheless engaged a cosmopolitan modernity. In 'Harbhajan Maan: The transnational migrant success story of Punjabi cinema', Harjant S. Gill discusses Harbhajan Maan (1965–), one of the most celebrated actors in contemporary Punjabi cinema, whose popular film portrayals of diasporic and migrant subjects have proven particularly meaningful for young Punjabi men who regard transnational mobility as the only route to economic success. Gill argues that Maan embodies a new model of idealized masculinity in Punjabi cinema, one that reflects major shifts in notions of nationhood, citizenship and belonging.

The next three chapters address several of the most popular and significant actresses to establish their careers in the pre-Bollywood era of the 1960s, 1970s and 1980s. In 'Helen: The Chin Chin Chu girl', Sudesh Mishra reassesses the screen performances and public image of the Anglo-Indian/Burmese star Helen (Helen Jairag Richardson, 1938–), a figure of 'unassimilable' and 'incurable' otherness who appeared in dozens of dancehall dramas in the 1960s and 1970s. Mishra argues that Helen typically functioned as a 'sacrificial foil' in these films, a 'non-masquerading other' whose presence was necessary for the films to maintain their programmatic disavowal of the inexcusable and the intolerable. Continuing the exploration of the female star's relation to fantasies of tradition and modernity, Rosie Thomas's chapter addresses Hema Malini (Hema Malini Chakravarty, 1948–), the 'undisputed queen of Bombay cinema' during the 1970s and early 1980s. In '"She's everything that's unpardonable": Hema Malini, dream girl on a motorbike', Thomas suggests that the star's success was due to her apparent encompassing of values both traditional and scandalously modern. Thomas explores how these contradictions were negotiated by the popular press and across her more notable screen performances, and proposes that Malini played a significant role in the industry's acceptance of independent female characters. In 'Sridevi, queen of farce: Comedy, performance and star persona in popular Hindi cinema', Nandana Bose offers an evaluation of the performance style and public image of Sridevi (Shree Amma Yanger Ayyapan, 1963–2018), and suggests that her distinctive persona was shaped by the perceived disjunctures between her traditional beauty, her funny voice and her flair for boisterous physical comedy. For Bose, the infantilized image produced for Sridevi sought to make the provocative potential of her riotous on-screen behaviour less threatening to mainstream audiences.

The final three chapters consider current personalities from Bollywood. Megastar Salman Khan [Abdul Rashid Salim Salman Khan, 1965–] is the focus of the first chapter, by Shohini Ghosh. In 'The irresistible badness of Salman Khan' Ghosh addresses the star's on-screen performances (and particularly his roles in action films) and his off-screen reputation as the enfant terrible or bad boy of Bombay cinema. Ghosh argues that unlike the other Khans (Shah Rukh Khan [Shahrukh Khan, 1965–] and Aamir Khan [1965–]) Salman, 'the king of single screens', has for more than two decades appealed to largely non-metropolitan Muslim subalterns, for whom the star's body (and its association with on-screen and off-screen violence) functions affectively to embody their own impossible and utopian dreams. Bollywood icon Shah Rukh Khan is the subject of the penultimate chapter: in 'Shah Rukh Khan starring as Shah Rukh Khan: Performance style, audience expectation and self-parody' Charlie Henniker examines SRK's successful self-branding and his symbiotic relationship with audiences by considering his acting as it has developed during his rise to megastar status, with a particular focus on his roles in *Devdas* (Sanjay Leela Bhansali, 2002) and *Billu* (Priyadarshan, 2009). Henniker argues that Khan's particular dramatic and comic skills and performance style are as intrinsic to his success as his commercial acumen. The collection concludes with a study of the actress Katrina Kaif (1983–). In 'The curious case of Katrina Kaif: NRI stardom and ethnicity in Bollywood', Hayder explores how a public idea of Kaif's unstable 'otherness' – her foreign background and parentage, her 'European' beauty, and her heavily-accented Hindi – has been both explained and exploited in her more successful screen roles (such as the non-resident Indian characters she regularly plays) and endorsement work (for example her association with India's first Barbie doll) and yet are simultaneously debated with derision in the mainstream media. Hayder compares Kaif to earlier 'exotic' and 'foreign' stars of Hindi cinema (such as Helen) to argue that Kaif's appeal for post-liberalization audiences depends on the careful cultivation of a modern and Western, yet sexually non-threatening image.

Together the chapters offer original insights and important reappraisals that contribute to improving our understanding of film stardom in India from the early talkie era of the 1930s to the contemporary period of global blockbusters. The collection presents a substantial intervention in the endeavour to excavate and evaluate the development of film star cultures in India during the twentieth and twenty-first centuries. *Indian Film Stars* seeks to inspire and inform further inquiries into the histories of film stardom – the industrial construction and promotion of star personalities, the actual labouring and imagined lifestyles of professional stars, the stars' relationship to specific aesthetic cinematic conventions (such as frontality and song-dance) and production technologies (such as the play-back system and post-synchronization), and audiences' investment in and devotion to specific star bodies –across the country's multiple centres of film production and across the overlapping (and increasingly international) zones of the films' distribution and reception. The star images, star bodies and star careers discussed in the chapters that follow are examined in relation to a wide range of issues, including the negotiation and contestation of tradition and modernity; the embodiment and articulation of both Indian and non-Indian values and vogues; the representation of gender and sexuality, of race and ethnicity and of cosmopolitan mobility and transnational migration; innovations and conventions in performance style; the construction and transformation of public persona; the star's association with film studios and the mainstream media; the star's relationship with historical, political and cultural change and memory; and the star's meaning and value for specific (including marginalized) sectors of the audience.

Works Cited

Austin, Thomas and Martin Barker, eds (2003), *Contemporary Hollywood Stardom*, London: Arnold.
Barnouw, Erik and S. Krishnaswamy ([1963] 1980), *Indian Film*, 2nd edn, Oxford: Oxford University Press.

Basinger, Jeanine (2007), *The Star Machine*, New York: Alfred A. Knopf.

Basu, Anustup (2010), *Bollywood in the Age of New Media: The Geo-Televisual Aesthetic*, Edinburgh: Edinburgh University Press.

Basu, Anustup (2013) '"The Face that Launched a Thousand Ships": Helen and Public Femininity in Hindi Film', in Meheli Sen and Anustup Basu (eds), *Figurations in Indian Film*, 139–57, Basingstoke: Palgrave Macmillan.

Beltran, Mary, Corey Creekmur, Sangita Gopal and Raphael Raphael (2013), 'A Panel Dicussion on Transnational Stardom', in Russell Meeuf and Raphael Raphael (eds), *Transnational Stardom: International Celebrity in Film and Popular Culture*, 19–30, New York: Palgrave Macmillan.

Bhattacharya, Nandini (2013), 'The Man Formerly Known as the Actor: When Shah Rukh Khan Reappeared as Himself', in *Hindi Cinema: Repeating the Subject*, 110–25, London: Routledge.

Bolton, Lucy and Julie Lobalzo Wright, eds (2016), *Lasting Screen Stars: Images that Fade and Personas that Endure*, New York: Palgrave Macmillan.

Bose, Derek (2006), *Brand Bollywood: A New Global Entertainment Order*, London: Sage.

Bose, Nandana (2013), 'From Superman to *Shahenshah*: Stardom and the Transnational Corporeality of Hrithik Rohsan', in Meheli Sen and Anustup Basu (eds), *Figurations in Indian Film*, 158–78, Basingstoke: Palgrave Macmillan.

Bose, Nandana (2014), 'Bollywood's "Fourth Khan": Deconstructing the "Hatke" Stardom of Vidya Balan in Popular Hindi Cinema', *Celebrity Studies*, 5 (4): 394–409.

Bose, Nandana (2019), *Madhuri Dixit*, London: British Film Institute.

Bunny, Reuben (2005), *… and Pran: A Biography*, New Delhi: Harper Collins.

Burr, Ty (2012), *Gods Like Us: On Movie Stardom and Modern Fame*, New York: Knopf Doubleday.

Butler, Jeremy G., ed. (1991), *Star Texts: Image and Performance in Film and Television*, Detroit, MI: Wayne State University Press.

Chakravarty, Sumita S. (2013), 'Con-figurations: The Body as World in Bollywood Stardom', in Meheli Sen and Anustup Basu (eds), *Figurations in Indian Film*, 179–201, Basingstoke: Palgrave Macmillan.

Chopra, Anupama (2007), *King of Bollywood: Shah Rukh Khan and the Seductive World of Indian Cinema*, New York: Warner Books.

Dasgupta, Susmita (2006), *Amitabh: The Making of a Superstar*, New Delhi: Penguin.

Dayal, Samir (2015), *Dream Machine: Realism and Fantasy in Hindi Cinema*, Philadelphia: Temple University Press.

deCordova, Richard ([1990] 2000), *Picture Personalities: The Emergence of the Star System in America*, Urbana: University of Illinois Press.

Dhondy, Farukh (1985), 'Keeping Faith: Indian Film and its World', *Daedalus*, 114: 125–40.

Dudrah, Rajinder (2006), *Bollywood: Sociology Goes to the Movies*, New Delhi: Sage.

Dudrah, Rajinder (2012), *Bollywood Travels: Culture, Diaspora and Border Crossings in Popular Hindi Cinema*, New York: Routledge.

Dudrah, Rajinder, Elke Mader and Bernhard Fuchs, eds, (2015), *SRK and Global Bollywood*, New Delhi: Oxford University Press.

Dwyer, Rachel (2015), '"I Love You When You're Angry": Amitabh Bachchan, Emotion and the Star in the Hindi Film', in Andrea Bandhauer and Michelle Royer (eds), *Stars in World Cinema: Screen Icons and Star Systems Across Cultures*, 13–23, London: I.B. Tauris.

Dwyer, Rachel and Divia Patel (2002), *Cinema India: The Visual Culture of Hindi Film*, London: Reaktion Books.

Dwyer, Rachel and Jerry Pinto (eds) (2011), *Beyond the Boundaries of Bollywood: The Many Forms of Hindi Cinema*, New Delhi: Oxford University Press.

Dyer, Richard ([1979] 1998), *Stars*, London: British Film Institute.

Dyer, Richard (1986), *Heavenly Bodies: Film Stars and Society*, Basingstoke: Macmillan.

Egan, Kate and Sarah Thomas (eds) (2013), *Cult Film Stardom: Offbeat Attractions and Processes of Cultification* (New York: Palgrave Macmillan)

Eleftheriotis, Dimitris (2002), *Popular Cinemas of Europe: Studies of Texts, Contexts and Frameworks*, New York: Continuum.

Etherington-Wright, Christine and Ruth Doughty (2011), *Understanding Film Theory*, New York: Palgrave Macmillan.

Farquhar, Mary and Yingjin Zhang, eds (2010), *Chinese Film Stars*, New York: Routledge.

Fay, Garrett (2011), *Studying Bollywood*, Leighton Buzzard: Auteur.

Funnell, Lisa (2015), *Warrior Women: Gender, Race, and the Transnational Chinese Action Star*, New York: State University of New York Press.

Gandhy, Behroze and Rosie Thomas (1991), 'Three Indian Film Stars', in Christine Gledhill (ed.), *Stardom: Industry of Desire*, 107–31, London: Routledge.

Ganti, Tejaswini (2004), *Bollywood: A Guidebook to Popular Hindi Cinema*, New York: Routledge.

Ganti, Tejaswini (2012), *Producing Bollywood: Inside the Contemporary Hindi Film Industry*, Durham, NC: Duke University Press.

Gehlawat, Ajay (2010), *Reframing Bollywood: Theories of Popular Hindi Cinema*, Los Angeles: Sage.

Gehlawat, Ajay (2012), 'The Construction of 1970s Femininity, or Why Zeenat Aman Sings the Same Song Twice', *South Asian Popular Culture* 10 (1): 51–62.

Gledhill, Christine, ed. (1991) *Stardom: Industry of Desire*, London: Routledge.

Gokulsing, K. Moti and Wimal Dissanayake, eds (2013), *Routledge Handbook of Indian Cinemas*, New York: Routledge.

Gooptu, Sharmishta (2011), *Bengali Cinema: An Other Nation*, London: Routledge.

Gopalan, Lalitha (2002), *Cinema of Interruptions: Action Genres in Contemporary Indian Cinema*, London: British Film Institute.

Govil, Nitin (2015), *Orienting Hollywood: A Century of Film Culture Between Los Angeles and Bombay*, New York: New York University Press.

Harrison, Edward (1963), '*Indian Film* (Review)', *Film Quarterly*, 17 (4) (Summer): 61–2.

Hazard, Patrick D. (1963), '*Indian Film* (Review)', *Annals of the American Academy of Political and Social Science*, 350 (November): 165–6.

Hines, Jessica (2007), *Looking for the Big B: Bachchan, Bollywood and Me*, London: Bloomsbury.

Hollinger, Karen (2006), *The Actress: Hollywood Acting and the Female Star*, London: Routledge.

Joshi, Priya (2015), *Bollywood's India: A Public Fantasy*, New York: Columbia University Press.

Joshi, Priya and Rajinder Dudrah, eds (2014), *The 1970s and its Legacies in India's Cinemas*, New York: Routledge.

Kabir, Nasreen Munni (2014), *Conversations with Waheeda Rehman*, New Delhi: Penguin.

Kaur, Raminder and Ajay J. Sinha, eds (2005), *Bollyworld: Popular Indian Cinema through a Transnational Lens*, New Delhi: Sage.

Kavoori, Anandam P. and Aswin Punathambekar, eds (2008), *Global Bollywood*, New York: New York University Press.

Krämer, Lucia (2017), *Bollywood in Britain: Cinema, Brand, Discursive Complex*, New York: Bloomsbury.

Lal, Vinay and Ashis Nandy, eds (2006), *Fingerprinting Popular Culture: The Mythic and the Iconic in Indian Cinema*, New Delhi: Oxford University Press.

Lawrence, Michael (2014), *Sabu*, London: British Film Institute.

Lawrence, Michael (2017), 'Darsheel Safary: Globalisation, Liberalisation and the Changing Face of the Bollywood Child Star', in Sabrina Qiong Yu and Guy Austin (eds), *Revisiting Star Studies: Cultures, Themes and Methods*, 125–44, Edinburgh: Edinburgh University Press.

Leung Wing-Fai and Andy Willis, eds (2014), *East Asian Film Stars*, New York: Palgrave Macmillan.

Mahadevan, Sudhir (2015), *A Very Old Machine: The Many Origins of the Cinema in India*, Albany: State University of New York Press.

Majumdar, Neepa (2009), *Wanted Cultured Ladies Only! Female Stardom and Cinema in India, 1930s–1950s*, Urbana: University of Illinois Press.

Mazumdar, Ranjani (2007), *Bombay Cinema: An Archive of the City*, Minneapolis: University of Minnesota Press.

Mazumdar, Ranjani (2012), 'Film Stardom after Liveness', *Continuum: Journal of Media and Cultural Studies*, 26 (6): 833–44.

McDonald, Paul (2013), *Hollywood Stardom*, Malden, MA: John Wiley.

Meeuf, Russell and Raphael Raphael (eds) (2013), *Transnational Stardom: International Celebrity in Film and Popular Culture*, New York: Palgrave Macmillan.

Mehta, Monika (2011), *Censorship and Sexuality in Bombay Cinema*, Austin: University of Texas Press.

Mehta, Vinod (2013), *Meena Kumari: The Classic Biography*, New Delhi: Harper Collins.

Mishra, Sudesh (2012), 'Yahoo! Shammi Kapoor and the Corporeal Stylistics of Popular Hindi Cinema', *Continuum: Journal of Media and Cultural Studies*, 26 (6): 815–32.

Mishra, Vijay (2002), *Bollywood Cinema: Temples of Desire*, New York: Routledge.

Mitra, Sreya (2013), 'From Heroine to "Brand Shilpa": Reality Television, Transnational Cultural Economics, and the Remaking of the Bollywood Star', in Russell Meeuf and Raphael Raphael (eds), *Transnational Stardom: International Celebrity in Film and Popular Culture*, 187–206, New York: Palgrave Macmillan.

Morin, Edgar ([1957] 2000), *The Stars*, trans. Richard Howard, Minneapolis: University of Minnesota Press.

Mubarki, Meraj Ahmed (2016), *Filming Horror: Hindi Cinema, Ghosts and Ideologies*, New Delhi: Sage.

Mukherjee, Srimata (2016), *Women and Resistance in Contemporary Bengali Cinema: A Freedom Incomplete*, New York: Routledge.

Patel, Bhaichand (2012), *Bollywood Top 20: Superstars of Indian Cinema*, New Delhi: Penguin Books.

Pillai, Meena T., ed. (2010), *Women in Malayalam Cinema: Naturalising Gender Hierarchies*, Orient Blackswan.

Pinto, Jerry (2005), *Helen: The Life and Times of an H Bomb*, New Delhi: Penguin Books.

Pinto, Jerry, ed. (2011), *The Greatest Show on Earth: Writings on Bollywood*, New Delhi: Penguin Books.

Powdermaker, Hortense (1950), *Hollywood: The Dream Factory – An Anthropologist Looks at the Movie-Makers*, Boston: Little, Brown.

Prasad, M. Madhava (2004), 'Reigning Stars: The Political Career of South Indian Cinema', in Lucy Fischer and Marcia Landy (eds), *Stars: The FILM Reader*, 97–114, New York: Routledge.

Punathambekar, Aswin (2013), *From Bombay to Bollywood: The Making of a Global Media Industry*, New York: New York University Press.

Raghavendra, M. K. (2008), *Seduced by the Familiar: Narration and Meaning in Indian Popular Cinema*, New Delhi: Oxford University Press.

Raghavendra, M. K. (2011), *Bipolar Identity: Region, Nation and the Kannada Language Film*, New Delhi: Oxford University Press.

Rai, Amit (2009), *Untimely Bollywood: Globalization and India's New Media Assemblage*, Durham, NC: Duke University Press.

Rajadhyaksha, Ashish (2009), *Indian Cinema in the Time of Celluloid: From Bollywood to the Emergency*, Bloomington: Indiana University Press.

Rajadhyaksha, Ashish and Paul Willemen, eds ([1994] 1999), *Encyclopaedia of Indian Cinema*, London: British Film Institute.

Rajagopalan, Sudha (2008), *Leave Disco Dancer Alone! Indian Cinema and Soviet Movie-going After Stalin*, New Delhi: Yoda Books.

Rajagopalan, Sudha (2011), 'Shahrukh Khan as Media Text: Celebrity, Identity and Emotive Engagement in a Russian Online Community', *Celebrity Studies*, 2 (3): 263–76.

Roy, Parama (2008), 'Figuring Mother India: The Case of Nargis', in Rajinder Dudrah and Jigna Desai (eds), *The Bollywood Reader*, 109–21, Maidenhead: McGraw Hill.

Saari, Anil (2011), *Indian Cinema: The Faces Behind the Masks*, New Delhi: Oxford University Press.

Sen, Meheli (2017), *Haunting Bollywood: Gender, Genre, and the Supernatural in Hindi Commercial Cinema*, Austin: University of Texas Press.

Sharma, Ashwani (1993), 'Blood, Sweat and Tears: Amitabh Bachchan, Urban Demi-God', in Pat Kirkham and Janet Thurmin (eds), *You Tarzan: Masculinity, Movies and Men*, 167–80, New York: St. Martin's Press.

Shingler, Martin (2012), *Star Studies: A Critical Guide*, London: British Film Institute.

Shingler, Martin (2014), 'Aishwarya Rai Bachchan: From Miss World to World Star', *Transnational Cinemas*, 5 (2): 98–110.

Singh, Sunny (2017) *Amitabh Bachchan*, London: British Film Institute.

Srinivas, S. V. (2009), *Megastar: Chiranjeevi and Telugu Cinema After N.T. Rama Rao*, New Delhi: Oxford University Press.

Srinivas, S. V. (2013), *Politics as Performance: A Social History of Telugu Cinema*, Rankhet: Permanent Black.

Thomas, Rosie (2005), 'Not Quite (Pearl) White: Fearless Nadia, Queen of the Stunts', in Raminder Kaur and Ajay J. Sinha (eds), *Bollyworld: Popular Indian Cinema through a Transnational Lens*, 35–69, New Delhi, Thousand Oaks, CA: Sage.

Thomas, Rosie (2014), *Bombay Before Bollywood: Film City Fantasies*, New Dehli: Orient Blackswan.

Usman, Yasser (2014), *Rajesh Khanna: The Untold Story of India's First Superstar*, New Delhi: Penguin.

Varia, Kush (2013), *Bollywood: Gods, Glamour and Gossip*, London: Wallflower.

Vasudevan, Ravi (2010), 'Father India and the Emergence of the Global Nation', *Contributions to Indian Sociology*, 44 (1–2): 11–32.

Vasudevan, Ravi (2011), *The Melodramatic Public: Film Form and Spectatorship in Indian Cinema*, New York: Palgrave Macmillan.

Velayutham, Selvaraj (2008), *Tamil Cinema: The Cultural Politics of India's Other Cinema*, New York: Routledge.

Vichani, Lalit (1999), 'Bachchan-alias: The Many Faces of a Film Icon', in Christiane Brosius and Melissa Butcher (eds), *Image Journeys: Audio-Visual Media and Cultural Change in India*, 199–230, New Delhi: Sage.

Virdi, Jyotika (2003), *The Cinematic ImagiNation: Indian Popular Films as Social History*, New Brunswick, NJ: Rutgers University Press.

Viswamohan, Aysha Iqbal (2014), '*Haute Couture* and the Discourses of Stardom in Globalized Times: Sonam Kapoor as Hindi Cinema's Representative Fashion Icon', *South Asian Popular Culture*, 12 (2): 73–88.

Willemen, Paul and Behroze Gandhy, eds (1980), *Indian Cinema*, London: British Film Institute.

Williams, Michael (2012), *Film Stardom, Myth and Classicism: The Rise of Hollywood's Gods*, New York: Palgrave Macmillan.

Woodcock, George (1964), '*Indian Film* (Review)', *Pacific Affairs*, 37 (3) (Autumn): 330–1.

Chapter 1

Shanta Apte and the unexpected
Anupama Kapse

Shanta sings

With their enhanced realism, talkies sealed the fate of male actors who played female parts on stage and in early Indian silents. The Gandharva Natak Mandali, which established Bal Gandharva as a celebrated female performer put up its last show on December 31, 1934 (Nadkarni 1987: 111). By the 1930s, educated young women from high-caste, high-class families broke the taboo on acting and became key attractions of the talkies. Women such as Durga Khote were given top billing in both advertisements and reviews that began to appear in English language dailies such as *The Bombay Chronicle* and *The Times of India*. Along with journals such as *Filmland* and *Film India*, newspapers that covered mostly political events began to include regular columns on major studios such as Prabhat, New Theatres and Bombay Talkies. Stars such as Devika Rani (Bombay Talkies) and features such as *Devdas* (P. C. Barua, 1935, New Theatres) were of particular interest. A *Times of India* review applauds Durga Khote's work as Saudamini, pirate queen of Prabhat's *Amar Jyoti/The Eternal Flame* (1936), thus: she 'gives to the picture its strong *virility*. … She speaks and acts with appropriate *force* and dignity' [my emphasis] (Anon. 1936: 7).

Durga Khote's own role model, the celebrated male actor Bal Gandharva was, however, known for being far more feminine in his theatrical performances. His 'seductive' facial expressions and hand gestures made him a perennial favourite in Goa and Maharashtra during the teens and the twenties. Theatre-goers admired his ivory, 'porcelain smooth' hands, their 'sleek, curved shape [and] … the closing and opening of the actor's tapering fingers'; the 'feminine charm' with which he shook his lower lip (Nadkarni 1987: 93, 100). Khote remembers the 'indescribable' beauty of his hands, 'whether they were carrying a garland at [Rukmini's] *swyamwar*, Sindhu's hands holding the wooden stick of the stone grinding mill, Draupadi's piteously pleading hands spread before Krishna for help, or even a courtesan's hands lovingly offering a paan' (Khote [1976] 2007: 44, cited in Kosambi 2015: 271).

Bal Gandharva went to great lengths to make his female appearances convincing. He would lighten his skin with specially ordered makeup from Max Factor and wear custom wigs designed by an Italian saloon named 'Fucile', located in Bombay (Nadkarni 1987: 93). Gandharva's popularity rested upon the enhancement of femininity, while Khote's performance was lauded for its regal gravitas, an attribute of male monarchs in traditional theatre. Critics praised her stately, authoritative bearing to the extent that any male actor cast against her risked being overshadowed and needed to differentiate the register of his performance. In *Ayodhyecha Raja* (V. Shantaram, 1932), Prabhat's first talkie and Khote's second, Khote appeared in the role of Queen Taramati. A stage actor named Gole (first name unknown) was initially cast as her husband, the selfless, long-suffering King Harishchandra. Gole found Khote's proximity so unsettling that he had to be replaced by music director Govind Rao Tembe, a well-known actor and composer who was able to match Khote's 'imposing' stature (Godbole 2015: 71).

Khote was not literally 'manly'; rather, the talkies' new patrons were impressed by her muted femininity. In contrast, the extravagant Bal Gandharva once complained about wearing plain cotton saris as his brocades had become unaffordable after Mahatma Gandhi launched his *swadeshi* campaigns. He began to drench his saris in eau-de-cologne to make them cling to his body (Nadkarni 1987: 80, 99). Meera Kosambi observes that 'no respectable woman would have draped the sari tightly enough to reveal the contours of her body. … A man dressed as a woman could take liberties that women themselves were not allowed' (2015: 271). Khote thus embodies the transformations that well-born women underwent when they embraced acting, traditionally a male profession. As a first-generation actress who had crossed over from elite to a relatively mofussil underclass, she was required to 'dignify' acting through subtle gradations in screen femininity. She could appear majestic, but if she appeared too feminine she risked travestying the heightened codes of femininity established by male performers.

I begin with Khote in an attempt to outline the specific contributions Shanta Apte (1916–1964) made to song performance and acting during this era, as Khote's contemporary and successor. If Khote was forceful, then her twenty-year-old co-star Apte was 'captivating' and 'enchanting'.

Khote excelled at playing a 'difficult' role while Shanta Apte was praised for 'carrying the picture on her shoulders … her singing is … one of the major beauties of [this] production' (*Times of India*, 26 June 1936: 7). Apte started her career as a child star in Bhalji Pendharkar's mythological *Shyam Sundar* (1932).[1] Christian-born Shahu Modak co-starred as Krishna in a joint debut (Figure 1.1). Modak was lauded for his remarkable singing talent while Apte was barely noticed in her first film (*South China Morning Post*, 10 February 1934: 12). Nevertheless, the picture ran for twenty-five weeks, a record run that echoed the new craze for talkies. It became the first film to add a song sequence by popular demand *after* its release (Godbole 2015: 51).

Amar Jyoti established a firm reputation for Shanta Apte as a vivacious singing star. In *Rajput Ramani* (Keshav Rao Dhaiber, 1936) Apte once again played second lead, this time to Nalini Tarkhad. However, reviews singled Apte out for carrying the film on her shoulders: 'the picture really belongs to Shanta Apte, who steals it entirely by her vivid personality, her wonderful singing [and] the naïve naturalness of her acting' (*Times of India*, 13 November 1936: 9). Elements of her work as a child star were thus recast in the mould of an effervescent child-woman, a trait enhanced by her light singing style. Although she played second lead to Khote in *Amar Jyoti*, Apte's virginal charm was widely appreciated in her adult roles (Durga Khote was separated from her husband but was often referred to as 'Mrs Khote'). If Apte was an ingénue, Khote was admired for her majesterial qualities, which were 'charming by contrast' (9): too much sexuality was inadmissible for

---

[1] Apte would revisit the role of Radha as Prabhat's most salable star in *Gopal Krishna* (V.Damle and S. Fattelal, 1937). Shahu Modak shot to fame as a police inspector who falls in love with a prostitute in Prabhat's *Aadmi/Man* (V. Shantaram, 1940) and would later immortalize *Sant Dyaneshwar* in a career-defining performance (V.Damle and S. Fattelal, 1941).

Figure 1.1 Shanta Apte and Shahu Modak, pictured together in the booklet for *Shyam Sundar* (1932). Courtesy of the National Film Archives of India, Pune.

both. Together both stars personified the complementary elements of screen femininity in the early talkie, of which *Amar Jyoti* remains the best example (Figure 1.2).

To be sure, Apte's star appeal depended on her ability to sing *and* act at the same time. Close associate, friend and lyricist Shantaram Athavale describes this transition as one fraught with intense disagreement and doubt. Prabhat's reputation grew with the success of director V. Shantaram's early talkies, *Ayodyecha Raja/ Ayodhya Ka Raja, Jalti Nishani/Agnikankan* (Branded Oath, 1932) and *Maya Machchindra* (Illusion, 1933), which were released in Hindi and Marathi versions. Shantaram started his career as an assistant photographer under the master scenarist Baburao 'Painter', who founded the Maharashtra Film Company in Kolhapur in 1929. The Prabhat team included Painter's disciples V. Damle, who did the sound with a newly bought Audio Camex machine, and S. Fattelal, who designed the massive sets and elaborate costumes. Keshavrao Dhaiber joined Prabhat as the principal cameraman, with Keshvarao Bhole as the music composer. Ashish Rajadhyaksha and Paul Willemen describe the early Prabhat features as neoclassical ([1994] 1999: 178). Themes were drawn from mythological stories and historical epics, while the sets often featured elaborate plaster of Paris statues and columns. The ornamental grandeur of the sets and Shantaram's astute stewardship were crucial to the studio's success.

Figure 1.2 Durga Khote, Shanta Apte and Vasanthi in *Amar Jyoti* (1936). Public domain.

On par with its competitors Bombay Talkies and New Theatres, Prabhat was known for its decorative realism and stylized treatment of nationalist themes, not to mention its reputed actors. Publicity materials describe the 175 feet long, 80 feet broad and 55 feet high studio as a mammoth film city or 'Prabhat Nagar' (*Times of India*, 8 October 1934: 14). Newspapers argued that the talkies ensured a 'rosy' and profitable future for Prabhat, which drew large audiences across the country and participated in international film festivals with *Amar Jyoti*'s release. The studio controlled every aspect of film production including the hiring of stars, distribution and publicity, and agendas that were meticulously documented in deeds and contracts.[2] A documentary, *Prabhatche Prabhatnagar* (V. Shantaram, 1935) was made to promote its films and show off the studio's state-of-the art cameras, lighting and costume departments, and sets and machinery; attractions displayed to visitors invited to marvel at Prabhat as a 'museum' of the talkies.

Amrit Manthan/The Churning of Nectar (V. Shantaram, 1933) was Prabhat's first major, all-India hit, with Nalini Tarkhad as a just princess who attempts to overthrow a sacrificial cult. Shanta Apte plays her aide: her ghazal 'Raat aayi hai naya rang jamane ke liye' (Night fall ushers new colors) attracted large crowds in Punjab, a major centre in the talkie circuit that extended Prabhat's reach further north to Lahore. Like Bombay Talkies' founder Himansu Rai, Shantaram visited UFA studios in Germany to supplement the Indian elements gleaned from his guru Baburao Painter. Following this visit, *Amrit Manthan* marks a distinct shift towards expressionism: Shantaram's most famous shot is an extreme close up of the 'eye of evil' taken with a telephoto lens. Evoking megalomania and tyranny, it doubled as a veiled reference to British colonialism. Audiences went wild for Apte, now hailed as 'a singing siren' (*Times of India*, 7 August 1937: 18), but she would again be cast as second lead to Leela Chitnis in *Vahan* (Beyond the Horizon, K. Narayan Kale, 1936). Shantaram thought that Apte could sing but had little knowledge of acting, while music director Keshav Rao Bhole felt that her singing style was 'too classical'. Worse, Keshav Rao Dhaibher, director of *Rajput Ramani* (Prabhat's first solo Hindi release) was attracted to Nalini Tarkhad, and favoured her over Apte. In spite of being sidelined, Apte's songs rescued an otherwise unremarkable film (Athavale 1965: 151).

---

[2] For a discussion of how the studio system gentrified movie-going, see Mukherjee 2011.

John Belton has argued that 'sound recording and mixing lack the authenticity of the photographic image, which guarantees the authenticity of reproduction … The microphone records an invisible world—that of the audible, which consists of different categories of sound—dialogue, sound effects, and music … regularly broken down into and experienced as different elements' (1985: 64). There are several extant accounts of the frustrations accompanying Prabhat's attempts to normalize sound. As a hero, Govindrao Tembe did not stop singing while *Ayodyecha Raja* was being filmed. The camera had to continue rolling (Godbole 2015: 69) until he stopped. When he was finally cast in a male role in *Dharmatma* (1935), Bal Gandharva could not follow Shantaram's directions. It was hard to break his performance into shots that broke the linear temporality and continuity of stage performance (Athavale 1965: 135). The audience was invisible. Instead of requests for encores, Gandharva had to contend with demands for retakes. Used to hearing rather than reading prompts, the thespian forgot his lines. More unfortunately, he could not find the right pitch for the microphone as he was partially deaf in one ear (Athavale 1965: 171; Kosambi 2015: 333). The film incurred losses that *Amar Jyoti* more than made up for.

Upon viewing the rush print of *Ayodyecha Raja* the day before its release, Damle discovered that the sound was out of sync (Godbole 2015: 68). As in early sound films elsewhere, the Audio Camex equipment picked up far too much ambient sound. Prabhat built a soundproof studio to fix this. Musicians who would sit in front of the stage now sat behind the camera and 'background' music was performed onsite so as not to interfere with spoken dialogue. If, as John Belton notes, the coming of sound often 'bec[a]me unreal in [its] quest for realism' (1985: 67–68), then there were important differences that revolved around the use of songs in the Indian context. Playback was introduced in 1935 (Pande 2006; Majumdar 2009) but Prabhat stuck to synchronized songs – technically, they were cheaper. Non-naturalistic forms of theatre were slowly being brought in line with fresh conventions of realism as the actor performed without a live audience in front of a camera, microphone and studio technicians. To this end *Kunku/The Unexpected/Duniya Na Mane* (V. Shantaram, 1937), which I examine in my next section, included a background score that was shot without any musical instruments: sound was produced on the set by props such as cups, clocks and canes, which were integral to its visual design.

As a matter of fact, sonographic realism assumed greater significance over and above photographic authenticity, a preference unique to Indian talkies. The presentation of songs became the primary yardstick for evaluating talking pictures. In songs, photographic verisimilitude took its cues from a *mise en scène* that was, in the first instance, auditory. All visual cues were derived from an aural source of performance rather than the other way around. Further, if theatrical and classical performance repertoires were modified to suit the requirements of the talkies, that transition posed fewer problems for male singing stars. Actors who started out in female roles continued to sing in an androgynous voice. Nadkarni states emphatically that Bal Gandharva 'did not have a falsetto voice'. Rather, 'he had a singing voice that could be said to be midway between that of a man and a woman' (1987: 118), a trait common to other Marathi actor-singers such as Bhaurao Kolhatkar, Keshavrao Bhosle and most famously Vishnupant Pagnis, whose performance as Tukaram was noted for its transcendental softness (1937).

Women who faced the camera had to contend with the fact that it was no longer possible to locate femininity at a site of a *deliberate* enunciation. The actress had to be 'natural' – a trait that *The Times of*

India's Filmfan [*sic*] notices repeatedly in the reviews quoted above. Ease of performance would define audience expectations and acceptance. Bal Gandharva's voice continued to be revered for its 'restrained pathos and eroticism' (Nadkarni 1987: 117), but the gramophone had delinked his voice from the image, allowing for an appreciation that fell outside film performance. Even after he grew old, the gramophone preserved the youthful popularity of his songs, as they became available to listeners who were too young to remember his stage performances.[3] Film actresses, on the other hand, had to create an alternative, 'screen-ready' singing style, marked by the brevity of the film song, and a naturalism that was seen as the hallmark of screen performance. Such a style would become a major factor in distinguishing the thirties from the forties, when playback became the norm and actresses could focus on acting rather than singing.[4] Apte was one of the finest practitioners of the new, light performative register characteristic of the early talkie.

In her memoirs, Khote describes her vocals as 'nothing to write home about … [the music director] somehow made it acceptable' ([1976] 2007: 60). She attributes her success to the cinematography rather than her voice. It is not surprising that Khote readily concedes the lack of singing ability: she prided herself upon her education and lineage. Musically trained women were the exception, not the norm. Apte was classically trained, which helped, but viewers preferred an accessible singing style that was not too heavy. Ashish Rajadhyaksha and Paul Willemen write that, in addition, Apte infused her performance with a new 'gestural spontaneity' ([1994] 1999: 44) that went hand in hand with her arguably 'modern' singing style. While Bhole's compositions favoured a classical method, they crippled Apte's innovative style. Her potential was fully realized when Bhole gave way to the more contemporary Master Krishnarao. Krishnarao helped Apte to extend her creative output as Prabhat shifted its focus to current topics through the social. Coincidentally, cameraman Dhaiber walked out of the Prabhat contract and was replaced by Shantaram's brother, V. Avadhoot, and became his preferred cinematographer. Apte also learned to swim, ride a horse, and dance (Apte 1939: 2; Maladkar 2015). She developed a professional notation system that allowed her to write music (Athavale 1965: 156). These efforts endowed her with tremendous physical mobility, technical skill and musical dexterity, lending credence to a technique that was both easier to understand and suitable for the three-minute duration required by gramophone discs. The conditions were ripe for creating a dynamic, smooth singing style that transformed Apte into one of the foremost actresses of the early sound era. Apte sang – and moved – *for* the movies.

Shanta saves a soul

According to Gerry Farrell,

> The first recordings of Indian musicians, made on Saturday 8th November 1902, were of two *nautch* (dancing) girls called Soshi Mukhi and Fani Bala of the Classic Theatre. They sang extracts from popular theatre shows of the time such as *Sri Krishna, Dole Lila, Pramode Ranjan* and *Alibaba* … According to Gaisberg they had 'miserable voices' … [that were] unappreciative of chords and harmonic treatment. (1993: 34–5)

---

[3] Several viewers describe their disappointment upon meeting him in old age but describe his music as untarnished (Athavale 1965; Nadkarni 1987; Kosambi 2015).
[4] For detailed comments on the introduction of playback singing, see Majumdar (2009: 185–92).

Their 'miserable' voices and the lack of harmony give us a sense of the lack of familiarity of recorded sound in its first instantiations. Within the space of a few years Gauharjan (c. 1875–1930), 'doyenne of the Calcutta *kothis* [brothels]' became a major recording artist for the Gramophone Company (34–5).

By the thirties, the radio and the gramophone had found their way into many Indian homes as new sound media, and the film industry quickly realized their value for promoting talkies. Apte's songs from *Amar Jyoti* became so popular that Shantaram cut a separate disc for *Kunku*'s songs, popularizing a trend that released film music individually on gramophone discs. He left the Gramophone Company of India (GCI) because of its dwindling financial prospects (Joshi 1988: 150). Shantaram was a prominent shareholder in His Master's Voice (HMV), the most successful gramophone company of its time. The switch proved beneficial to HMV, which capitalized on Shantaram's clout as well as his directorial fame. *Kunku* is Apte's best-remembered film, and the gramophone is an important symbol of her popularity. The gramophone is featured prominently on *Kunku* publicity booklet, while film ads would refer to the songs released on gramophone discs and invite viewers to watch them on screen.

Apte plays Niru, a young, well-born orphan raised by her aunt and uncle. Like Apte, she is musically trained. *Kunku* opens with a sequence from *Sangeet Sharda*, a well-known music drama that satirized the practice of marrying off young girls to old widowers. The play within the film opens with a mock performance riddled by failure as the children forget their lines, and the little heroine refuses to marry an old man. Abandoning the play, the children listen to Niru as she sings about a king and his abiding love for his sweetheart (ek tha raja): a dream-scenario of mutual love that takes the place of a forced May–December marriage, the subject of *Kunku*. The children create an innocent *mehfil* where the female singer is surrounded by adoring eyes that, like the heroine, dream of a happy ending.[5] Niru's performance is supported by a portable gramophone, a cherished gift from her deceased parents. Apart from being a symbol of her cultural inheritance, the gramophone also provides 'live' musical accompaniment as Niru performs for her foster sisters, brothers and friends. The home becomes a theatre, and the children become ideal spectators who see and hear with fresh eyes as they leave the cultural baggage of the stage and the *kotha* (brothel) behind.

Theatre historian Anuradha Kapur has defined frontality as a grouping strategy that positions actors directly towards the audience to create intimate contact between performer and spectator; a 'relationship [where there] is no dissembling between the two—the actor looks at the audience and the audience looks at the actor' (1993: 92). In the words of James Naremore, film, however, 'creates a boundary between performer and audience unlike any other ... the physical arrangement is permanently closed, and it cannot be opened even if the performer speaks to us directly' (1990: 27, 29). Kunku takes advantage of this so-called gap between performer and audience. Apte abandons speech for song here: *Kunku* reconstitutes the basic parameters of theatrical frontality in favour of a mediated frontality structured by song sequences. Unlike the relatively static stars of music drama, Apte augments the voice with a new repertoire of gestures: eye and hand movements complement lyrics that invoke a libidinal space as she gazes off screen while her voice soars. Rather

---

[5] A *mehfil* is an intimate coterie audience, usually men, who surrounded the courtesan in the *kotha*; also, a circle of patrons who would listen to recitations of poetry by eminent litterateurs.

than standing still, she moves ecstatically in the interior of her home, inciting her young audience to dance like her.[6] Apte looks at *her* audience, while the emotional tenor of her voice ensures heightened 'contact' between her and the listener, in ways that transcend the diegetic and the theatrical. The song ends with an outburst of movement as the camera circles around the animated group in a lively crescendo. The camera's circular movement refuses to contain the action within the picture-frame aesthetic typical of proscenium-style music dramas such as *Sangeet Sharada*. *Kunku*'s circular motifs are dizzying in the symbolic burden they carry: the entire group dreams of consensual marriage in a free and equal society.

Kunku is based on Narayan Hari Apte's Marathi novel *Na Patnari Goshta* (The Unacceptable Incident, 1923); the author also wrote the film's screenplay (Apte [1923] 1944). While the novel highlights the heroine's purification (the novel's subtitle is *Chittashuddhi*, or soul-purification), the film includes a more militant focus on rebellion. Niru/Apte never sings in front of her husband (in the novel, her husband is aroused by the sound of her voice). Shankutala Paranjape, daughter of the Cambridge-educated ambassador R. P. Paranjape was cast as Niru's grown up stepsister. Paranjape was one of the earliest women to file for divorce in Maharshtra and was known for her activism since she was a student at Ferguson College, Pune (*Times of India*, 11 June 1937: 5).

Paranjape's casting was essential for strengthening *Kunku*'s progressive social vision. Sushila is a figure imbued with the spirit of freedom; a former widow, she embodies the free spiritedness of a social activist and reformer who has successfully challenged patriarchy. When we first see her, she is seen in a dull *khadi* (cotton) sari and no jewellery except for a watch. She carries a book, an umbrella and a purse – signs of travel and proximity to the streets. She appears, in other words, in the iconography of a female politician or Gandhian *satyagrahi* (activist). When she arrives, Niru gives her a hero's welcome, offering specially cooked food and incense. This sequence represents an obvious dramatic contrast to the violence that erupts whenever Niru encounters figures of authority in her household: her uncle, father, stepson and her domineering aunt-in-law (who asks the aging Kakasaheb to beat Niru into having sex with him).[7]

The film's best-known sequence shows Niru singing Henry Wadsworth Longfellow's 'Psalm of Life' to the accompaniment of the gramophone as Sushila watches, enraptured. Once again, a 'live', homely performance takes the place of a public, theatrical rendition. Apte performs for Sushila, in an intimate setting that mirrors the relation between the filmic songstress and her extra-diegetic audience. Niru's voice liberates her, though she remains culpable in the eyes of her immediate family. Unlike the subjects of public litigation whose cases were taken to court after women were ill-treated by their husbands (Sarkar 1993: 1869), Niru 'fights' her husband – a lawyer by profession – by singing in her own voice. Her repeated protests – which, other than saying 'no' to sex take the form of saying 'no' to being photographed, cooking and dressing up – are acts that earn curses from those she crosses: *kutiya* (bitch), *rakshasi* (demon), *chudail* (witch), *bazaari aurat*: words that cut female protest to size

---

[6]These improvisations successfully adapted music drama's conventions into a cinematic style that was not only easier to understand but also suitable for the three-minute duration that gramophone discs required.
[7]The aunt (Kaki) uses the Hindi words *laga de* (literally affix, couple). The film pointedly conflates the additional meanings of *laga de* as 'to beat' or 'have sexual intercourse'.

by equating it with the *kotha* (brothel). Against this oppressive backdrop, Niru sings Longfellow to Sushila, 'Life is real! Life is earnest! And the grave is not its goal … Not enjoyment, and not sorrow, Is our destined end or way; But to act, that each to-morrow, Find us further than today.' Gramophone spinning in the background, it is a scenario where the act of performance is equated with liberation and self-expression as the two faces of public femininity – the performer and the feminist – come together. As the song reaches its climax, tears roll down Niru's cheeks as she looks towards the skies. Throughout the film, mostly shot indoors, Niru looks away from the camera towards some other space, one free and more sacrosanct. Here, too, theatrical frontality is reconfigured in cinema within the logic of the almighty and the sacred, as a gaze that desires the unattainable.[8] The film's central image – used in its poster – shows Niru applying *kunku*, the red dot that all married women wear, against a mirror whose reflection she turns away from, in search of a higher reality (Figure 1.3).

By turning away from herself, Niru turns towards freedom as a space that she can sing about but cannot envision, a feeling that is mimed ecstatically in *Kunku's* opening scenes and through the hypnotic turning of the gramophone,

Figure 1.3 Shanta Apte as Niru. Booklet cover for *Duniya Na Mane* (1937). Courtesy of the National Film Archives of India, Pune.

---

[8]For a discussion of melodrama's extreme stylization of gesture in *Daera* (1953) and *Devdas* (1955) see Bhaskar 2012.

to which we are introduced in the opening credits. In Naremore's words, 'technology allows us to take control of such moments' through a *fort da* game of presence and absence that lets us '[dismantle] the ideological self-identity of … routine social behaviour' (1990: 31). Rick Altman traces the sacral power of sound all the way back to the Greek oracle (which could only be heard and not seen) (2004: 5–6). *Kunku* sacralizes the female voice to expose the emptiness of traditional, rule-bound authority: the mirror reflects a void that Niru looks away from.[9] This pivotal image, like the one where Niru performs for Sushila, structures new forms of contact between performer and audience to 'frontalize' the female voice against a foreclosed, recorded moving image performance. The extraordinary yoking of voice to suffering, and of suffering to suffrage, would create an aura and cult value around Apte's firebrand star-image that people would return to again and again.

Niru fits the description of what John Cawelti calls the 'good bad girl': a protagonist who spearheads action against 'bad social institutions … a regenerated flapper who faces down the villain and so shames him that he is forced to leave the territory' (1991: 40, 43). *Kunku* was an all-India hit, and letters and fan mail poured in to congratulate Apte on creating a character who had a positively real impact on society. 'Shanta Saves a Soul!' screamed a headline in *The Times of India* (January 29, 1938: 5) as a contrite father thanked Apte for preventing him from the grave injustice of marrying his daughter to a wealthy widower. In June 1938, *Film India* firmly ensconced *Kunku* as a filmic landmark by republishing *The Times of India* story to applaud its powerful impact on society.

Niru's knowledge of English, and her rendition of Longfellow's 'The Psalm of Life' takes the place of a traditional duet sung by the hero and heroine. It joins other numbers Niru sings with her niece and female neighbours that are remarkable because of the absence of any men. However, a role that was so transgressive was not without its detractors. One newspaper review called Apte's English rendition of Longfellow's 'The Psalm of Life' a 'terrible misfit'. Shantaram himself would satirize the Anglicized accents of Anglo-Indian film actresses in his next venture *Aadmi* (Man, 1939). That said, Niru's ease with English parodies the educated female protagonists of films such as *Indira MA* (N. Jaswant Lal, 1934) and *Dr. Madhurika* (Sarvottam Badami, 1935) who are inept at housework and remain selfish rather than socially committed. Here the English-educated Niru, instead of caring for her elderly aunt-in-law, gets *her* to cook and clean for her in order to resist her abuse. As the film's English title suggests, the excitement revolves around watching such unexpected incidents (in another scene Niru beats her lascivious, grown stepson) that depict the sorry fate of obnoxious, abusive men (Figures 1.4, 1.5).

'Known as the "stormy petrel" of … Indian films … [o]n screen and in life, Shanta defied many conventions', writes Mrinal Pande (2006: 1652). Apte was the first female star to protest against salary cuts in the Prabhat Studio system, leading to allegations of a breach of contract (Majumdar 2009: 42–43). Sumati Gupte describes Apte's long hunger strike as nothing less than a female '*satyagraha*'. What we have here is an act of suffrage that fell outside government legislation. Ironically, child marriage was seen as a just cause for political reform, but lower pay for film

---

[9] P. K. Nair characterizes this moment as one of hesitation (2002: 23). While Niru is limited by her social standing, Apte's performance transforms this moment into a rejection of Niru's wifely ritual, marked by a shaking of her head and then a turning away.

Figure 1.4 'The Adventure of the Stick'. Cartoon in *The Times of India*, 7 August 1937, p. 18.

Figure 1.5 'Shanta Saves a Soul'. Advertisement in *The Times of India*, 7 August 1937, p. 18.

actresses fell outside what counted as suffragist agitation. Shantaram dismisses Apte's protest as mere pretence in his autobiography *Shantarama*, saying that she was drinking milk while pretending to have water (1987: 231). What's more, he accuses her of throwing her arms around him while pretending to faint as he tried to persuade her to return to work. He refused to cast Apte in his next film *Admi*, telling her that she would be the wrong choice to play a prostitute. The two would never work together again.

The hunger strike was widely documented by newspapers worldwide, though the complete details are usually suppressed in favour of Prabhat's public image as an avuncular, family-friendly studio. In fact, Apte was not required to shoot on the days in question and left for a tour of Southern India, for which her pay was cut (Shantaram 1987: 231). While Shantaram marginalizes the importance of Apte's protest, Apte's strike intervenes in the paternalistic functioning of the studio and its regulation of the female actress' labour and image. As Neepa Majumdar points out, 'Apte's hunger strike is one of those small events out of which the vaster network of women's film history is constituted' (2015: 181).

Not satisfied with the treatment meted out by the studio, Apte wrote in *The Mirror* about how hard she had to work to earn her admittedly high salary of two thousand rupees. Critiquing the studio's authority and the director's tyranny, she writes,

> We are at the mercy of directors and have to do the role that is assigned to us … If an actress fails to do justice to her role, these worthies will heap on them showers of nasty adjectives. On the other hand, if they come out with flying colours in their roles, the credit invariably goes to the director! (Apte 1939: 2)

The Mirror later carried the full text of her speech (Majumdar 2015: 189), outlining in detail the reasons for her protest, while *The Times* released a director's statement expressing their confusion (22 July 1939: 18).

In reality the discourse of the studio as a family was a cover for its careful regulation of any 'performance' (work that could generate extra income) that did not conform to its contractual rules. Apte's choice of the studio veranda as her main platform was a clear indication of this spatial breach. Her clothes – she slept on the veranda dressed in trousers and shirt – represented a sartorial violation that refused to conform to the unofficial dress code for female employees, usually a sari. They also reveal the limitations of extending the tactics of Gandhian *satyagraha* to a hostile studio system. Apte's revolt becomes entangled with details from the star's personal life that were common knowledge in the public imaginary: her brother Baburao had tricked her into acting in the movies and, worse, lived off her income (Jasraj 2015: 133). Ironically, Apte's personal life told a story of victimization, while her on screen roles told a story of powerful dissent. V. Shantaram was not alone in undermining Apte's character by calling attention to her forward behaviour: Raj Kapoor's cinematographer Radhu Karmakar alleges that, like all actresses, she may have had 'liaisons' with cameramen – although not with him. Instead, he writes about how she would 'wink' at him in a mischievous manner that was both attractive and threatening to him (Karmakar 2005: 62, 63). Such 'wink-nudge' innuendos tarnish the sartorial and performative power of her strike. Ultimately, the multiple narratives of the strike reveal the inadequacy of the studio's stance. In turn, they transform Apte's star image into a cluster of unresolved but productive contradictions. Rather than being separate, these diverse elements become mutually constitutive in a configuration where extra-diegetic information about Apte's life as a forward and 'fiery' (Majumdar 2015: 1879) woman is mapped on to the recognition of Niru/Apte as an unexpected practitioner of *satyagraha*, a narrative that resonated with the public and found support outside the directors' circle to produce visible social effects; so much so that Shanta could 'save a soul'.

Conclusion

If Apte's early screen career was defined by her ingénue charm, in her later years she was known primarily for defying convention. While her gramophone discs 'continued to sell in thousands' for Prabhat, she quit the studio in search of greater independence. From there on, she worked in Tamil, Marathi and Bengali and Hindi in socials such as *Swayamsiddha* (self-made, 1949) and in films that continued to do well and maintained her public image as an iconoclast and nonconformist (Figure 1.6).

Apte was involved in further legal battles in the forties and fifties, again in the context of dates and remuneration (Kumari Shanta Apte vs Sailapati Chatterji, 31 July 1945). The second involves the possession of liquor bottles during prohibition, when Apte was arrested along with her brother Baburao (Kumari Shanta Govindrao Apte … vs The State of Madhya Pradesh, 30 July 1956).[10] This incident is largely responsible for a second defamation of the last few years of her life as an alcoholic (Pande 2006; Kosambi 2015), although she was acquitted both times. Fans and scholars alike need to recognize Apte's contributions to film acting along with the erotic iconoclasm of her activist image. Apte's daughter Nayana Apte has written about her effort to establish schools to provide education for women, particularly actresses (Maladkar 2015). These accounts are accompanied by descriptions of the long hours of vocal practice (Apte 1939: 2; Maladkar 2015), recollections that underscore the unusual regional paths she undertook in her long career as a singing star.

Apte's work in the Tamil mythological *Savitri* (1941) marks her nationwide popularity as 'the bulbul of India', well before the term was applied to Lata Mageshkar. She sings in Tamil with 'the nightingale of the South' M.S. Subbulakshmi, or M.S., who appeared in the male role of Narada in a popular, ingeniously cast, cross-dressed 'duet' (Figure 1.7). While both performed in their female voices (M.S. does not sing in a masculine voice although she is in male attire). Apte provides a dynamic contrast to M.S., who is photographed in close-ups or mid shots and hardly ever dances or moves while she sings. Like Lata Mangeshkar, Apte was specially invited to perform by Prime Minister Jawaharlal Nehru, reputedly her admirer (Maladkar 2015).

Apte was a major star of the thirties and forties: someone who could sing, act, write, ride a horse and perform a *satyagraha* for women's rights. Her marriage became the subject of intense speculation; it is rumoured that she

Figure 1.6 Apte pictured with a whip in the booklet cover for *Swayamsiddha* (1949). Courtesy of the National Film Archives of India, Pune.

---

[10]Kumari Shanta Apte vs Sailapati Chatterji on 31 July 1945, online at: https://indiankanoon.org/doc/847608/ and Kumari Shanta Govindrao Apte vs The State of Madhya Pradesh on 30 July 1956, online at: https://indiankanoon.org/doc/891209/.

had an incestuous relationship with her brother Baburao (Jasraj 2015: 133; Sathe, n.d.). The most damning of all the insinuations is that Baburao fathered her child. That she chose not to reveal details of her marriage when she was otherwise so outspoken is yet another form of 'telling' whose rebellion we need to be attuned to. Apte's self-published 1940 autobiography *Jau mi cinemat* (Should I go to the Movies?) represents one of the earliest accounts of film acting by women, and outlines the discrepancies between labour and fame (Apte 1940). Her autobiographical writings do more than end gossip: they reflect on film acting as work that exceeds the parameters of morality or fame. Apte worked and lived on her own terms, and it is now more important than ever that historians attend to her pioneering work both on- and off-screen as well as the unexpected directions it took.

Works Cited

Altman, Rick (2004), *Silent Film Sound*, New York: Columbia University Press.

Anon. (1936), '*Amar Jyoti* sets fans raving at Ahmedabad', *The Times of India* (1861–current); 13 November 1936; ProQuest Historical Newspapers: The Times of India, 9.

Apte, Narayan Hari ([1923] 1944), *Na Patnari Goshta*, 2nd edn, Pune: Vasudev Ramchandra Pendse.

Apte, Shanta (1939), 'Films are not my Goal But a Means to an End', *Mirror*, 14 May, pp. 2–4.

Figure 1.7 Shanta Apte and M. S. Subbulakshmi in *Savitri* (1941).

Apte, Shanta (1940), *Jau Mi Cinemat/Should I go to the Movies?*, Mumbai: B. Govind, Shanta Apte Concerns.

Athavale, Shantaram (1965), *Prabhat Kaal*, Pune: Venus Publications.

Belton, John (1985) '"Technology and the Aesthetics of Film Sound', in Elisabeth Weis and John Belton (eds), *Film Sound: Theory and Practice*, 63–72, New York: Columbia University Press.

Bhaskar, Ira (2012), 'Emotion, Subjectivity and Desire: Melodrama and Modernity in Bombay Cinema, 1940s-50s', in Christine Gledhill (ed.), *Gender Meets Genre in Post War Cinema*, 161–76, Chicago: University of Illinois Press.

Cawelti, John (1991), 'The Evolution of Social Melodrama', in Marcia Landy (ed.), *Imitation of Life: A Reader on FIlm and Television Melodrama*, 33–49, Detroit, MI: Wayne State University Press.

Farrell, Gerry (1993), 'The Early Days of the Gramophone Industry in India: Historical, Social and Musical Perspectives', *British Journal of Ethnomusicology*, 2: 1–53.

Godbole, Mangala (2015), *Damlemama: Charitrapat ani Chitrapat*, Damle Uncle: Cinema and Life; Pune: Rajhans Prakashan.

Jasraj, Madhura Pandit (2015), *V. Shantaram: The Man Who Changed Indian Cinema*, New Delhi: Hay House.

Joshi, G. N. (1988), 'A Concise History of the Phonograph Industry in India', *Popular Music in India*, 7 (2): 147–56.

Kapur, Anuradha (1993), 'The Representation of Gods and Heroes: Parsi Mythological Drama of the Early Twentieth Century', *Journal of Arts and Ideas*, 23–24: 85–107.

Karmakar, Radhu (2005), *Radhu Karmakar: Painter of Lights*, Prafulla: Orissa Publications.

Khote, Durga ([1976] 2007), *I, Durga Khote*, trans. Shanta Gokhale, New Delhi: Oxford University Press.

Kosambi, Meera (2015), *Gender, Culture and Performance: Marathi Theater and Cinema Before Independence*, London: Routledge.

Majumdar, Neepa (2009), *Wanted Cultural Ladies Only! Female Stardom in India 1930s–1940s*, Chicago: University of Illinois Press.

Majumdar, Neepa (2015), 'Gossip, Labor and Female Stardom in Pre-independence Cinema: The Case of Shanta Apte', in Christine Gledhill, Jane Gaines and Julia Knight (eds), *Doing Women's Film History: Reframing Cinemas, Past and Future*, 181–92, Chicago: University of Illinois Press.

Maladkar, Sagar (2015), 'Kraantikaari ani Samvedansheel Abhinetri Shanta Apte' (The Revolutionary and Sensational Actress Shanta Apte), online at: www.marathisrushti.com/articles/revolutionary-and-sensitive-marathi-actress-shanta-apte/ (accessed 25 July 2015).

Mukherjee, Debashree (2011), 'Letter from an Unknown Woman: The Film Actress in Late Colonial Bombay', *Marg*, 62 (4): 54–64.

Nadkarni, Dyaneswar (1987), *Bal Gandharva and the Marathi Theatre*, Bombay: Roopak Books.

Nair, P. K. (2002), 'A Close Look at Director V. Shantaram's Prabhat Film *Kunku/Duniya Na Mane* (The Unexpected)', *South Asian Cinema*, 1 (3–4): 19–35.

Naremore, James (1990), *Acting In Cinema*, Berkeley: University of California Press.

Pande, Mrinal (2006), '"Moving beyond Themselves": Women in Hindustani Parsi Theatre and Early Hindi Films', *Economic and Political Weekly*, 41 (17): 1646–53.

Rajadhyaksha, Ashish and Paul Willemen ([1994] 1999), *Encyclopedia of Indian Cinema*, Revised edition, London: British Film Institute; New Delhi: Oxford University Press.

Sarkar, Tanika (1993), 'Rhetoric Against Age of Consent: Resisting Colonial Reason and Death of a Child-Wife', *Economic and Political Weekly*, 28 (36): 1869–78.

Sathe, V. P. (n.d), http://cineplot.com/shanta-apte-profile/ShantaApte.

Shantaram, Rajaram Vankudre (1987), *Shantarama*, Mumbai: Rajkamal Prakashan.

Chapter 2

Confessions of Indian cinema's first woman superstar: Kanan Devi's memoirs, film history and digital archives

Ranita Chatterjee

On 15 August 1947, the day India celebrated its independence from British rule, the programme at India House, the High Commission in London, consisted of flag hoisting, speeches and songs by Kanan Devi. During 1947 Kanan Devi also appeared in newspaper advertisements for Lux soap in several mainstream Indian newspapers.[1]

These two divergent appearances allow us an insight into the wide resonance of Kanan Devi's star appeal: the privilege accorded to her as the face and voice of the new Indian nation on that momentous occasion in London points to the potency of her star image with the establishment. The Lux advert, on the other hand, was – and remains – a veritable marker of the popularity of female film stars in India. Kanan Devi's presence as a Lux girl points to her resonance with the masses.

Neither of these apparently inconsequential trivia comes to us from received film history. We know of the advert through Lux's promotional film that has found renewed circulation online and of the India House performance through Devi's memoir. A leading star of the Indian screen in the 1930s and 1940s, Kanan Devi ([?] 1916–1992) is barely present in official histories of Indian cinema, and we certainly do not get a sense of her stardom from official history. Kanan Devi's disappearance from subsequent versions of Indian film history is not unique; rather it is symptomatic given the scattered, selective and limited nature of the archive on Indian cinema. This was even more so in the case of the 'other' cinemas, that is, the cinemas not originating from Bombay. Nevertheless, her omission is surprising given that she is not altogether absent from the canon, appearing in photographs with male stars or mentioned as part of the star cast in classic films from the period, but never on her own merit (Barnouw and Krishnaswamy [1963] 1980; Majumdar 2009: 179–82).

This chapter is not going to dwell on the inadequacies of received film history in India, for that has been collectively said many times over by contemporary scholars. Indeed, over the last few years new film history in India has been complicated, its gaps opened up, by a renewed turn to the archives and a move beyond the film archive to explore parallel archives. Using a media archaeological approach, this chapter turns to a number of such archives, including the film archive, to excavate the star text of Kanan

---

[1] See, for example, *Times of India*, 4 July 1947, p. 3; 10 November 1947, p. 10.

Devi, a major but now forgotten superstar of Indian cinema – the 'new woman' of Calcutta cinema, but not quite, as I argue. A key source, and indeed a starting point for this endeavour, is Kanan Devi's memoir *Shobare Ami Nomi* (I Bow to All, [1973] 2001) written in Bengali. This chapter explores how such 'autobiographical disclosures' (Hansen 2011) by actresses complicate the standard history of Indian cinema and challenge the discourse of the 'new woman' as it played out in Calcutta in the studio era. It goes on to ask how women's writing in general, and the opening up of such 'archives of the self' (Chatterjee 2006: xxix), add to our understanding of the rich past of Indian cinema and, further, the ways in which the proliferation of digital archives open up new modes of doing film history.

Kanan Devi

Kanan Devi was the proverbial 'first lady' (Singh 1992) of Calcutta cinema in the heydays of the studio era, from the mid-1930s and through the 1940s, and the top female star of the iconic Indian studio New Theatres, from 1937 to 1941, after which she turned independent. Indeed, she was characterized as the 'first woman superstar' of Indian cinema,[2] working across the Bombay and Calcutta industries. A highly successful and popular 'singing star' and a fine actress, she was paired opposite the biggest male stars of the day, including K. L. Saigal (Kundun Lal Saigal, 1904–1947), P. C. Barua (Pramathesh Chandra Barua, 1903–1951) and Ashok Kumar (Kumudial Ganguly, 1911–2001). It is rumoured that she was the only major female star in Calcutta to command a guaranteed box office draw, a rare feat even today. Little surprise then that she was much in demand by studios across India, including in Bombay and Lahore.

Kanan Bala, as she was known in the early days of her career, came from a poor and questionable background: she was allegedly an illegitimate child and joined the silent film industry as a child artiste to make ends meet after her father (or adoptive father according to some sources) died. She made her debut at the age of 10 in *Joydeb* (Jyotish Banerjee, 1926) and made a successful transition to the talkies with *Jore Barat* (Jyotish Banerjee, 1931). Thereon she quickly rose to the top, playing the leading lady by the early 1930s. *Sree Gouranga* (Prafulla Ghosh, 1933) for the Calcutta-based Radha Studio was her first hit film and her performance as a modern fashionable lady in *Maa* (Prafulla Ghosh, 1934) brought her much acclaim. The release of *Manmoyee Girls' School* (Jyotish Banerjee, 1935) made her a household name in Bengal and firmly established her as the leading female star in Calcutta. She achieved fame across South Asia after the runaway hit devotional, *Vidyapati* (Debaki Bose, 1937), produced by the celebrated Calcutta studio, New Theatres, and a string of all-India superhits followed with the New Theatres' 'double-versions': *Mukti* (Pramathesh Barua, 1937), *Sathi/Street Singer* (Phani Majumdar, 1938) and *Parichay/Lagan* (Nitin Bose, 1941). After walking out of New Theatres she was approached by Barua for another 'double-version', *Sesh Uttar/Jawab* (Pramathesh Barua, 1942) and thereafter she remained independent, starring in a number of Bengali and Hindi films through the 1940s.

Kanan Devi was also a very successful singer and, at the height of her singing career, she reportedly received royalties worth the princely sum of 25,000 rupees quarterly just from the sale of her

---

[2]Obituaries in *The Times of India*, 19 July 1992, p. 7; *The Guardian*, 12 August 1992, p. 33.

music records.³ She turned producer in 1949, producing a number of films until 1959, largely adaptations of celebrated Bengali novelist Sarat Chandra Chatterjee's social realist novels. She cut down on her acting and singing career in the 1950s, only performing in films she co-produced with her husband. Her last film as an actor was in 1959. She was awarded the Dadasaheb Phalke award, the country's highest award in cinema, in 1977 and became a highly respected senior figure within the Bengali film industry in later years. Kanan Devi also made a significant contribution towards improving working conditions in the Bengali film industry, setting up a charity to help senior women artistes, and perhaps this is a major reason why she is remembered with respect within the older generations of the Calcutta industry if not in film history or public memory.⁴

Kanan Bala's stardom derived from her beauty, performance and from her songs. She played both traditional and modern female characters with equal ease, portraying several roles as a fashionable, modern woman as well as more traditional roles of the village girl: notably, her screen characters were always strong women. This image of the strong woman resonates across Kanan Devi's memoir as well, and while public personas, star texts and the represented self in memoirs are always shades of a complex 'authentic' self, popular accounts suggest that Kanan Devi was indeed a strong, independent woman in her personal and professional life. In her memoir she comes across as a remarkable personality: fiercely independent, graceful, with a sharp cultivated mind – a woman who worked hard to improve herself, educating herself in the arts, literature and music, the quintessential 'new woman': strong, confident, modern yet firmly rooted in tradition.

The 'new woman' of modern India

At the time Kanan Devi entered films, a rigid moral code operated on women in public spaces. Indian women in general were not seen in public and women performers were frowned upon, likened to prostitutes and socially shunned by 'respectable' society. As public women, actresses held an uncertain social status, celebrated for their performances but simultaneously remaining outside legitimized social domains. While the demand for women performers in theatre and film in Calcutta saw theatre managers and studio producers introduce talented performers from the red-light district, courtesan families and poorer marginal communities (including Jews, Anglo-Indians and Armenians) on the stage and screen, a number of young Indian women from poor and disadvantaged backgrounds also entered the profession. However, prevailing moral norms, along with the presence of performing women of so-called disreputable backgrounds, led to the popular perception of theatre and screen worlds as a space where vice, immorality and corruption prevailed. While this negatively impacted the legitimacy of the cinema in particular, and its acceptability in middle-class Bengali society, it also created problems for new entrants to the industry, including young male actors, directors and crew who were deemed tainted by association.⁵

---

³To put this in perspective, the reigning male star of Indian cinema, K. L. Saigal, also a singing star, received around a fifth of that per quarter as his salary in 1940.
⁴Here it is worth contrasting her place in film history with her counterpart in Bombay, Devika Rani (Devika Rani Chaudhuri, 1908–1994), generally celebrated as the 'first lady' of Indian cinema in the studio era.
⁵See, in particular, memoirs of Ahindra Choudhury (1962) and Dhiraj Bhattacharya (1954).

Concerns around respectability proved to be a double whammy for women in film and served as a barrier for women from respectable families entering the cinema.

At the same time, a counter force was in play in Bengali society. Nineteenth-century efforts at modernizing Bengal had seen much of the impetus of both Bengali intellectuals and the colonial administration focus on women's upliftment and education.[6] From very early on in the history of feature film production in Calcutta the 'new woman' becomes central to the cinema both as actor and as character, largely because it was the educated youth of Bengal, schooled in nationalist ideas of advancement, who took to filmmaking in the early years.

In the burgeoning Calcutta film industry of the 1920s and 1930s educated young filmmakers made a concerted effort to introduce educated 'cultured ladies' (Majumdar 2009) from respectable families, including their own families, into the cinema to counter its low reputation and bring legitimacy to the beleaguered industry.[7] As Neepa Majumdar asserts, 'By the late 1920s … the class composition of actresses associated with the cinema became the single most important issue for redefining the moral status of cinema, with the greatest emphasis on education and well-known families' (2009: 61).

By the advent of the talkies in 1931, filmmakers and the intelligentsia also argued that these educated ladies of high society were better able to play complex roles and thereby improved the tenor of screen characters, in line with the preferred ideals of the 'new woman'. This discourse is prevalent in film and theatre journals where industry personnel canvass repeatedly for the need for educated, respectable women in the industry.[8] By the 1930s a remarkable trend can be observed: actresses start to write articles in these journals expounding their positive experience in the industry and praising the high ideals of the cinema towards a higher (nationalist) cause.

---

[6] As Partha Chatterjee and others have pointed out, women were crucial to the nationalist discourse within colonial India and took on the burden of representing the nation. By the 1920s the woman's question had been resolved through its identification in the nationalist project, whereby the acceptable norm of the modern Indian woman lay in her rootedness in a nineteenth-century reconstitution of Indian 'tradition'; a composite characterization that would distinguish her from the 'Western' woman: 'The "new woman" was to be modern, but she would also have to display the signs of national tradition and therefore would be essentially different from the "Western" woman' (Chatterjee 1994: 9). The 'new woman' was to 'improve' herself along these lines and 'improvement' was further equated with modern education. This rhetoric was vigorously mobilized in Calcutta, the seat of the so-called Bengal Renaissance in the nineteenth century, where the nationalist impetus was particularly strong. 'One of the recurrent rhetorical practices in this discourse of improvement was the claim that the state of the nation was reflected in the state of its cinema' (Majumdar 2009: 54).

[7] See, for example Dhiren Ganguly's introduction of his wife on screen in the first so-called 'Bengali' film, *Bilet Pherat* (England Returned, Dhiren Ganguly, 1921). Also see Modhu Bose's efforts at introducing friends and family on stage and the screen in the late 1920s and early 1930s.

[8] There was a prevailing understanding that uneducated actresses from marginalized backgrounds were unable to understand and effectively portray the complex characterizations and convey the 'high ideals' embodied in the 'new woman' roles that were increasingly being written for the Bengali screen, or indeed carry off the role of an upper-class woman. On the whole, the women were perceived as vulgar and lacking the grace, poise, gestures, expressions and understanding to work across a range of female characterizations. This was seen as a serious limitation since the nationalist agenda required the 'new woman' to be represented on screen in all her various incarnations – mother, housewife, modern urban woman, village girl, devotee, mythological heroine, historical queen. The inclination to conflate the biographies of actresses with their screen characters has been described by Majumdar as a tendency towards 'autobiographism'.

Actresses, autobiographical disclosures and cinema journals in the 1930s

A good number of articles published in theatre and film journals in the 1920s and 1930s dealt with the question of 'good cinema' and the possibilities this new medium offered in education and social uplift of the modernizing nation. By the 1930s, journals such as *FilmLand* and *Dipali* regularly published pieces written by actresses advocating the merits of cinema, underlining its educative qualities, in what was, arguably, a deliberate move that furthered efforts towards legitimating the cinema as a respectable institution.

A regular contributor to English-language journals published from Calcutta, Sabita Devi, is introduced in her articles as an educated 'society' lady.[9] She argues for the prescient need to produce good cinema, portraying 'high ideals' and how much her own mind had 'improved' by playing such roles: 'As a screen actress I have benefited immensely in my personal life from studying these noble ideals. I think the artist's mind comes alive and develops greatly inspired by these grand ideals' (Devi 1932). On another occasion she lists the qualities of various characters she has played, proclaiming: 'Her ideals high to lift and inspire, / Just to live in roles like these / Is my prayer, my one desire - ... / Ah! My "Silver Sheet" that holds me, / May I never idle rest, / But with noble screen portrayals / Give you of my humble best' (Devi 1932).

Another celebrated New Theatres actress, Chandravati Devi, highlights the 'sublime mission' of film, stressing the complex characterizations she has portrayed:

> Leaving aside the question of entertainment, we have a mission – far more sublime and pure. I speak of its ethical side – the moral and educative aspect of the screen. In my screen life, I had the fortune of playing two great roles both of them substituting two mighty characters from the pages of our National History and most revered mythology. They were subtle, penetrating and full of complexities to the extreme. (Devi 1935)

Such first-person avowals of the merits of cinema were responding to the widespread critique of immorality, corruption and vice that shrouded the institutions of the stage and screen, also to be found in other articles published in the very same journals. In such 'autobiographical' declarations of the educative aspects of the cinema the actress's identity is constructed as one with her screen persona, leaving no room for any construction of the self beyond her public image. Such articulations serve as a manifesto for the nationalist cause for improvement and reiterate the dominant rhetoric.

As Tharu and Lalita underline, in the mid-nineteenth and early twentieth centuries, women authored an extraordinary number of autobiographies, especially in Bengali and Marathi (1993: 160). With the rise of print culture and women's literacy in Bengal in particular, a number of autobiographies were published after 1850 written by 'the unheralded women of the inner quarters'; that is, women from respectable households as well as by the so-called 'disreputable' actresses, the public women of Bengali theatre (Hansen 2011: 32). Tanika Sarkar argues that it was largely 'women from lesser-known circles', the Bengali housewives and actresses, who used self-narration to bring back agency and counter their 'low social esteem' (1999: 131). The

---

[9] Sabita Devi was the screen name of Iris Gasper, an Anglo-Indian actress.

proliferation of nineteenth-century print culture had ensured that Bengal had an established culture of journals and little magazines that were consumed by middle-class Bengali households and profusely read by educated women of these households. These journals regularly published articles by theatre actresses although, as Rimli Bhattacharya points out, not all the articles were written by women: many were actually penned by men who fabricated first-person accounts of '*actress-like* figures' (1998: 22, emphasis in original). Furthermore, as Majumdar recognizes in her study of Bombay stars, extra-cinematic materials do not add very much to our knowledge of film stars and merely reproduce their professional identities (2009). Yet, I would argue that, despite adding to the dominant rhetoric, such writings also perform a distinct function that plugs into the discourse around respectability – a crucial concern in discussions around nation building (Chatterjee 1994). Articles written by, or indeed on behalf of, actresses were consciously mobilized by the authors and the industry to reinforce the cinema as a respectable institution, on a par with other 'high arts'. And in the very act of performing the dominant discourse they served to quell social anxieties and highlight the presence of the 'respectable lady' in cinema, both in terms of her screen image *and* in her star persona, as the author of these articles. In effect then, such articles become another act of 'autobiographism' (Majumdar 2009): indeed 'autobiographism' has come full circle whereby educated actresses who bring their high ideals to screen characters in turn profess their potential to further self-improvement through the cinema and thereby suggest that the audience too would be able to improve themselves through the act of viewing. Writings by actresses therefore become a claim for the much-maligned film industry to be accepted within the home as a progressive art form, in keeping with high-nationalist ideals.

It is in this context that I wish to dwell on the figure of Kanan Devi. In the light of the wider discourse around respectability, as well as associated writings in contemporary journals testifying to the growing respectability of the film industry, Kanan Devi's memoir is a rare insight into the everyday life of a film actress in the 1930s and 1940s and comes as a scandalous revelation.

Whither new woman? From Kanan Bala to Kanan Devi

Kanan Devi's memoir departs from official film history in significant parts to provide insights into the everyday experiences of a woman in the industry, even offering a critique of an iconic studio like New Theatres and larger-than-life stars, such as Barua, in sharp contrast to writings by actresses in contemporary journals. Her insights undercut the widely held belief that the Calcutta industry was a far more progressive and respectable place to work in as compared to Bombay.[10] Her memoir reveals her persistent feelings of helplessness and a deep sense of humiliation at being exploited, especially in her teens but even later at the height of her stardom. She repeatedly recounts her hurt at the way she was treated by colleagues and friends in the industry. Apart from what today could only be seen as harassment in the workplace – including sexual harassment – she felt she did not gain the respect she deserved by her peers. She cites several incidents when she was socially snubbed, even insulted. On one occasion she

---

[10] See for instance Wilford Deming's article 'Talking Picture in India', in *American Cinematographer* (1932) and Barua's own characterization of Bombay as a 'bazaar' (cited in Dasgupta *c.* 1981: 52).

describes greeting one of her co-actresses in a famous Calcutta hotel only to be snubbed. Her explanation for this snub is as follows: 'After all, this actress was from an elite family and did not think my low calling merited acknowledgement in Calcutta society' (Devi [1973] 2001: 50). Clearly, a class hierarchy was in operation and Kanan Bala was from the wrong end of the social spectrum.

Despite being a top-rated star, she repeatedly states that she had little control over her own roles. She was not allowed to read detailed scripts and had little say in costumes, how much she could reveal – especially in her younger days when she was a rising star with Radha Studio – how she could be portrayed and had no say in whom she could star with, even with a progressive studio like New Theatres that repeatedly espoused high-nationalist ideals about women's emancipation. This testimony is in sharp contrast to the experiences of actresses from high society, such as Devika Rani and Sadhona Bose. Kanan Devi also reveals that women in the 1930s were not allowed to read contracts: they simply signed without detailed scrutiny and were not allowed to take the contracts home to get advice. This goes totally against the grain of the rhetoric around the 'new woman' and pronouncements by the Calcutta industry, which prided itself as being much more progressive than Bombay. She also reveals that she was approached by star actor-director Barua, then with New Theatres, to play the role of Parvati in *Devdas* (1935) in what was to become an iconic role, and one that would certainly have ensured her place in Indian film history. She was unable to accept, however, due to her contractual obligations with rival studio Radha and was threatened with legal action if she dared leave. It was much later that she discovered that her contract with Radha had actually ended by that time and she could have negotiated an exit deal (Devi [1973] 2001: 27).

Kanan Devi's story transcends the inclination towards 'autobiographism'. Her questionable background had little impact on the type of roles she was cast in and she successfully played the 'new woman' several times over. Yet in her personal life few people overlooked her low calling, and her screen image did little to uplift her social status. In a particularly cruel anecdote she recalls that pamphlets were distributed outside her house by protesters loudly condemning her wedding to Ashok Maitra in 1940, and the public outcry that followed put an irreversible strain on their marriage. Although she expresses gratitude to Maitra for giving her the social respectability she so craved, in the public mind the shift from *bala* to *devi*, that is, from girl to revered lady, was yet to be.

At the height of her career with New Theatres, Kanan Devi claims that she asked for a raise and, although she does not explicitly state so, she was asking for a salary that would be at par with her male co-star, Saigal.[11] Unsurprisingly for the time, she was refused. A lesser woman would have stayed on, but Kanan Devi was angry and humiliated at not getting her due and she left New Theatres to embark on a career as an independent star.

In many ways Kanan Devi's experiences suggest that here was an ideal candidate who was a living embodiment of the new woman – she *was* the new woman both on and off screen – a woman who had improved herself immensely through hard work, talent and discipline. In his discussion of the 'new woman' of nineteenth-century

---

[11] Saigal was her co-star in runaway New Theatres hits such as *Street Singer* (Phani Majumdar, 1938) and *Lagan* (Nitin Bose, 1941).

Indian nationalism, Partha Chatterjee contrasts her simultaneously with lower-class female characters and the parody of the westernized woman found in nineteenth-century literature. Chatterjee argues that,

> The 'new' woman was quite the reverse of the 'common' woman, who was coarse, vulgar, loud, quarrelsome, devoid of superior moral sense, sexually promiscuous, subjected to brutal physical oppression by males …. It was precisely this degenerate condition of women that nationalism claimed it would reform, and it was through these contrasts that the new woman of nationalist ideology was accorded a status of cultural superiority to the Westernized women of the wealthy parvenu families spawned by the colonial connection as well as to common women of lower classes. Attainment by her own efforts of a superior national culture was the mark of woman's newly acquired freedom. (1994: 127)

Chatterjee's observations have an uncanny resemblance to Kanan Devi's own assertions in her memoir about improving herself against all odds, in her efforts to master Hindustani classical music and study Sanskrit literature, in using her memoir to negotiate, challenge and counter unpleasant public constructions of herself in the past, in highlighting her struggles against patriarchal oppression, in her breaking away from the shackles of the studio and reinventing herself as an independent star, in her gaining education, learning English and travelling abroad to understand and network with the film industry in Hollywood and the music recording industry in London, in her interactions with elite society in India and abroad …. In fact, one can see resonances of Chatterjee's claims with Kanan Devi's assignation in the role of the new nation's songstress on that eventful celebration in August 1947 at the High Commission in London.

Kanan Devi had risen above her so-called low-class background and poverty to rise to the very top and, in an industry predicated on economic logic, she was much in demand by the major studios because her films and songs were consistently superhits, drawing large audiences and ensuring ticket sales. Yet, she did not quite attain the respect or the recognition from her peers or from society, even at the height of her stardom. It is ironic that New Theatres, which championed the 'new woman' in so many of its films, chose not to champion Kanan Devi as their star and even let go of her.

Writing her/self

Kanan Devi's memoir reveals much more than the 1930s journal articles, perhaps because it was published in 1973, from the vantage point of posterity, when she was established and could afford to critique iconic studios and stars. The memoir has been reprinted a number of times in more recent years, allowing her currency in public memory in Bengal if not quite in Indian film history. It recasts her persona in a new light renewing its circulation in the cultural domain in Bengal despite her self-imposed withdrawal/exile from active filmmaking in the late 1950s and the fading memory of her films and her songs.

Autobiography can be read as 'a history of selfhood, a paradigmatic narrative through which the subject has learned to know who s/he is' (Anderson 2011: 17). In her introduction to the text Kanan Devi claims that in Sandhya Sen, her ghostwriter, she found an empathetic listener, one who was able to appreciate and bring out the nuances and complexities of her emotions, her dilemmas, anguish and joys. As a result of this connection, she claims, Sen was able to tap into many experiences that Kanan Devi herself had never revealed to anyone. Thus, asserts Kanan

Devi, 'I have found myself in my life-story, as have my readers' ([1973] 2001, n.p.).

This particular life-story, however, manages to move beyond an easy 'narrative of the self' to allow crucial insights into working conditions of actresses and one that splinters the discourse of the 'new woman' as it played out in the studio era and associated myths of the 'glorious years' of the Calcutta studios. Kanan Devi's memoir is striking in the distance she is prepared to go in discussing everyday conditions and the text offers critiques of larger-than-life icons such as New Theatres and Barua. Here, it may be apposite to draw parallels with the autobiography of one of her contemporaries from Bombay cinema, Durga Khote (1905–1991), which is a crisp, direct narrative, primarily descriptive and steering clear of critical interventions about the industry and personnel.[12] It is apparent from the text that Kanan Devi felt strongly about the working conditions of women and worked towards their improvement in Calcutta, and this perhaps bestows her with the required authority to comment at a time when she had gained nationalist legitimacy, social standing and respect from the industry.

'Writing "I" has been an emancipatory project for women, and a crucial one in the evolution of contemporary American feminism' (Perreault 1998: 191). Kanan Devi's efforts at writing this memoir can be seen as an act of reclaiming her public image and, indeed, correcting past (mis)assertions of herself. Her autobiographical assertion becomes a site for negotiating and challenging difficult, unpleasant public constructions of her/self and therefore brings back control on the narrative of the self or rather how she is represented in public, beyond scandal and hagiography. Her intervention allows for a more nuanced perspective of icons and stars beyond hagiographic histories. A good example of this would be her reflections on Barua the director as opposed to Barua the actor. While she expresses admiration for Barua's creativity and superior directorial abilities, she acutely observes how his ego overpowered his directorial judgement in his arrangement of shots to favour himself and enhance his screen presence at the cost of his co-actors even if the shot did not demand this (Devi [1973] 2001: 40–2).

Autobiographical narratives become a form of witnessing – of experiencing, of being there and thereby leading to the evidentiary nature of the narrative as experienced by the self, often the marginalized self speaking from a position of disadvantage, confessing truths that are not otherwise evident in the dominant narrative and needs to be told by the act of witnessing. The confessional mode is a key element of Western autobiography tracing back to Rousseau's *Confessions* (1782) and indicative of the 'modern' tradition in autobiography. The act of confession is a performative act, a deliberate stance in the autobiography (Anderson 2011: 46–8 citing de Man 1979). This act of telling, as distinct from witnessing, however, becomes problematic in the case of women's writing, argues Lionnet, as the narrating subject and the experiencing self 'can never coincide exactly' (1989: 92). The woman writer therefore resorts to 'alienated communication' as a mode of autobiographical address: 'The female narrator gets caught in a duplicitous process ... because the text is the locus of her dialogue with a tradition she tacitly aims to subvert' (93). Kanan Devi's narratorial persona in the memoir can be read, I would argue,

---

[12]Khote, another top leading lady of the early talkie era, had a long innings in Bombay cinema from 1931. The difference in backgrounds between the two women, however, was great – Khote belonged in elite Bombay society, born and married in renowned and wealthy families.

as a careful adoption of 'alienated communication', and one that primarily borrows from Indian traditions of self-writing. Her narratorial voice shifts continually between strong subjective assertions that go against the grain of established star texts and canons and an overly modest, deferential, religious self. In telling her story Kanan Devi takes on what can be construed as the excessively humble and overtly religious rhetorical stance of a devotee to Gopal, the baby Krishna. The title of the text too evokes this gesture of devotion and humility towards the industry past and present: the Bengali word *nomi* (bow) has connotations of worship, reverence and respect, and is used both in a devotional and a social sense. In her discussion about the autobiography of poet-playwright Narayan Prasad Betab, Kathryn Hansen likens Betab's posturing to 'the conventional self-denigrating stance of the Urdu poet, especially the narrator of the lyric ghazal' and traces a lineage to both Persian and Urdu prose (2011: 317–8). It may be recalled here that Kanan Devi was a singer and schooled in Hindustani classical music. She was influenced by the devotional and love poetry of Hindustani music, the *ghazals* and the *bhajans*. The excessive humility and devotional stance to God was inherent in these genres of Hindustani music, which also borrowed from the Bhakti tradition, in particular Meera's *bhajans*, where the singing voice of Meera dedicated her life to Lord Krishna. Kanan Devi was well familiar with this rhetorical strategy and thus able to mobilize it. The devotional self, especially as a devotee of Gopal, is a familiar mode of being for Hindu women, and, I suggest, allows for the construction of a sincere, spiritual 'I' in Kanan Devi that adds to the truth-value of her narrative persona while simultaneously making her accessible to a middle-class readership.

While literary traditions like the autobiography are firmly rooted in Western modernity, and have strong links to colonialism and nationalism, scholarship on women's writing in India have also traced multiple literary and cultural traditions that permeate these writings (Tharu and Lalita 1993; Sarkar 1999; Hansen 2011). Following on from the seminal works by Tharu and Lalita (1993) and Sarkar (1999), Gayatri Chatterjee points out that women's self-writing in India, like Bahina-bai's seventeenth-century writings in Marathi and Rashsundari Devi's nineteenth-century autobiography in Bengali, can also be placed within the Bhakti tradition, which expresses the spiritual self and 'is all about self-articulation' (2006: xxii–xxiii). Rashsundari Devi's writings, considered the first autobiographical utterances in Bengali, are spun around her love of Krishna, and may well have been accessible to Kanan Devi. And without doubting her sincerity, or her religiosity, I would further venture to suggest that perhaps this humble, spiritual self was a convenient rhetorical stance mobilized to negate the allegations of arrogance that Kanan Devi encountered during the early years of her stardom, and one that ensured that the critique of masters and icons were acceptable amongst her readers.

'Memoir is "personal history that seeks to articulate or repossess the historicity of the self … [it] places the self relative to time, history, cultural pattern and change"' (Hansen 2011: 37, citing Hart 1970: 491). In narrating her life-story, Kanan Devi is able to put her voice forward in an effort to reclaim control over her-story, even while offering fresh insights on her contemporaries, peers and the Indian film industry, complicating hagiographic histories of the studio era. Perhaps it is worth underlining that Kanan Devi's narratorial persona is a carefully constructed star text, directly aligned to the 'new woman' that she played with such ease on Bengali and Hindi screens. Her humble self in her memoir may be a 'ruse' for exposure (Anderson 2011: 46–7 citing de Man 1979: 286), but, unlike Rousseau's exhibitionist stance in the guise of confession, her gaze is turned outwards, to comment on the tensions of a society in transition and the complex, shifting position of women in general and female performers in particular.

And in so doing, Kanan Devi's self-writing reveals much more than received film history and indeed more than articles and the memoirs of her contemporaries. It adds detail to an otherwise sketchy history, a rich narrative of everyday women's lives in the industry, alongside offering insights into the lives of Indian film stars of the early talkies, of herself and others. Given her stature, she can now afford to fight back and voice her subtle appraisal, even critique, of the industry. Kanan Devi is acutely aware of this, recognizing at several points in her narrative that she was not able to articulate her objections, opinions and frustrations during her career and is only now able to do so. And thus this 'alienated' voice becomes crucial in constructions of a critical film history.

Epilogue

Kanan Devi died in 1992. In the early 1990s, HMV released two compilation albums dedicated to male and female singing legends of Indian cinema. Lata Mangeshkar (1929–), the legendary playback singer, and a superstar in her own right, lent her well-known voice to these 'immortal artists', in an act of 'humble tribute'. Volume 2 of *Shraddhanjali* (1994) is dedicated to five women artists of the past and starts with a tribute to Kanan Devi.[13] The tribute starts with an introduction by Lata, then Kanan Devi's singing voice fades in ever so briefly, for just over 30 seconds – faint, distant, with a marked use of reverberation – to technologically simulate Lata's nostalgic remembrance. Lata's voice returns and takes over, first introducing us to this artist and then singing a Kanan Devi song. Shikha Jhingan argues that,

> This engagement with the past, with its memory, re-enacts the erasure of these voices, and their effacement. As soon as we connect with Kanan Devi's voice, it is gone. *Shraddhanjali* can be seen as an archive that relives the journey of the female voice in film songs and its ephemeral quality …. It is ironic that through this device, HMV participated at least symbolically, in the erasure of its own archive. (2013: 109)

If institutions are engaged in erasing and re-inscribing their archives, the internet offers a rich repository of our cinematic heritage thanks to the creative endeavour of fans and enthusiasts who upload their personal collections of music, film and ephemera online and generously share their knowledge of stars. The internet is, arguably, the stimulus for our renewed interlocution with the past of Indian cinema and provides a rich source of material forgotten, in particular fan sites created by cineastes and music connoisseurs through whose collective efforts other archives rise to the surface; new histories become available.

When I searched for this song I found the original film clip with some difficulty. The majority of the first few links went to Lata's 1994 version and the search page was populated with links to video clips of Madhubala, a major star of the 1950s and 1960s. Imagine my astonishment – and confusion – as I stared at a 1950s Madhubala singing a 1930s Kanan Devi song in Lata's 1990s voice, wondering if the original film was remade sometime in the 1950s or the song reused on Madhubala … until I realized that this is a compilation video, a creative remediation by one fan, and the images have no relationship whatsoever to the song. This video is then picked up by others and shared and this is

---

[13] I am grateful to Shikha Jhingan for pointing me to this album.

the clip that is circulating widely on the internet. To add to the confusion the search also includes a soundcloud link, which rather confusingly names this song clip as 'KANAN DEVI … aye chand chup na jana … Madhubala … Dilip Kumar', although the song is the original in Kanan Devi's voice, a fact that would escape the general searcher/surfer unless s/he recognized Kanan Devi's voice – and even then s/he might be forgiven for thinking the song was picturized on Madhubala.[14] This rather muddling encounter on the palimpsest that is the World Wide Web led to my contemplating on the perils and pleasures of 'big data'. Here was Kanan Devi once again facing erasure by generations that followed, not only rendered inaudible by CD culture through another singing star who did not act but now rendered invisible by a film star who did not sing. In an age of creative mechanical reproduction, the archive may be rapidly proliferating but the ephemerality of the filmic artefact looms large and continues to pose a challenge to film-historical excavations into the past. The digital turn must necessarily, therefore, be complemented by the historical turn and it is the expanded archive of the memoir, the still image, the song, the film fragment, their versions and their collective trace on the internet, in print, in living memory that keeps Kanan Devi – and the rich past of Indian cinema – alive today.

Works Cited

Anderson, Linda (2011), *Autobiography*, 2nd edn, Abingdon: Routledge.

Barnouw, Erik and S. Krishnaswamy ([1963] 1980), *Indian Film*, 2nd edn, Oxford: Oxford University Press.

Bhattacharya, Dhiraj (1954), *Jakhan Police Chhilam*, Calcutta: New Age Publishing.

Bhattacharya, Rimli (1998), 'Introduction', in Rimli Bhattacharya (trans. and ed.), *Binodoni Dasi, My Story and My Life as an Actress*, New Delhi: Kali for Women.

Chatterjee, Gayatri (2006), 'Durga Khote: The Contour of a Life and Work', in Shanta Gokhale (trans.), *I, Durga Khote*, xxii–xxiii, New Delhi: Oxford University Press.

Chatterjee, Partha (1994), *The Nation and Its Fragments: Colonial and Postcolonial Histories*, Princeton, NJ: Princeton University Press.

Choudhury, Ahindra (1962), *Nijere Haraye Khunji*, 2 vols, Calcutta: Indian Associated Publishing.

Dasgupta, Chidananda (c. 1981), *Talking About Films*, New Delhi: Orient Longman.

Deming, Wilford, Jr. (1932), 'Talking Picture in India', *The Cinema*, June 1932.

Devi, Chandravati (1935), 'What I Actually Think of the Screen', *Moving Picture Monthly*, Annual Issue 1935.

Devi, Kanan ([1973] 2001), *Shobare Ami Nomi*, 4th edn, Kolkata: M. C. Sarkar & Sons.

Devi, Sabita (1932), *Dipali*, n.p.

Hansen, Kathryn (2011), *Stages of Life: Indian Theatre Autobiographies*, London: Anthem Press.

Hart, Francis (1970), 'Notes for an Anatomy of Modern Autobiography', *New Literary History*, 1 (3) (Spring): 485–511.

Jhingan, Shikha (2013), 'Lata Mangeshkar's Voice in the Age of Cassette Reproduction', *Bioscope: South Asian Screen Studies*, 4 (2) (July): 97–114.

Lionnet, Francoise (1989), *Autobiographical Voices: Race, Gender, Self-Portraiture*, Ithaca, NY: Cornell University Press.

Majumdar, Neepa (2009), *Wanted Cultured Ladies Only! Female Stardom in India, 1930s–1950s*, Urbana: University of Chicago Press.

de Man, Paul (1979), *Allegories of Reading: Figural Language in Rousseau, Nietzsche, Rilke and Proust*, New Haven, CT: Yale University Press.

Perreault, Jeanne (1998), 'Autography/Transformation/Asymmetry', in Sidonie Smith and J. Watson (eds),

---

[14] See Noor S, 'KANAN DEVI .. aye chand chup na jana .. Madhubala .. Dilip Kumar', SoundCloud, online at: https://soundcloud.com/noor-s/kanan-devi-aye-chand-chup-na (accessed 3 September 2019).

Women, Autobiography, Theory: A Reader, 190–6, Madison: University of Wisconsin Press.

Singh, Kuldip (1992), 'Obituary: Kanan Devi', *Independent*, 22 July, online at: www.independent.co.uk/news/people/obituary-kanan-devi-1534655.html (accessed 15 July 2015).

Sarkar, Tanika (1999), *Words to Win: The Making of Amar Jiban: A Modern Autobiography*, New Delhi: Kali for Women.

Tharu, Susie and K. Lalita (eds) (1993), *Women Writing in India*, vol. 1, London: Pandora Press.

Chapter 3

Star's 'dust': Miss Kumari and the fossilized memory of the 'first Malayalam female star'

Darshana Sreedhar Mini

The decade of the 1950s in Malayalam cinema witnessed the efflorescence of film studios based in Kerala along with a burgeoning pool of local talent. Among the locally procured actresses was Thressiama, who in a short time stole the limelight under the screen name 'Miss Kumari' and became one of the most visible faces of the Malayalam Studio films. Miss Kumari's unique popularity allowed her to be one of the first Malayalam actresses to negotiate contractual entitlements with the studio as a lead heroine. Stardom discourses in the context of South Indian cinema have often focused on the popularity of male stars and the interconnectedness of the cinematic and political realms (Pandian 1992; Prasad 1999; Sreenivas 2009). While there have been works on female stardom in Indian cinema, such as those focusing on actresses like Fearless Nadia and Sulochana (Thomas 2005; Majumdar 2009), works that explore the intrinsic connections of female stars with local cinematic practices are few and far between. This is even more so in case of South Indian cinema, where the authoritative male star has remained at the centre of the discourse. Taking a slight detour from prevalent works on stardom in South Indian cinema and female actors in particular, this chapter looks at the star persona of Miss Kumari, the actress whose filmic career and rise to fame was entwined with the success of Merryland studios, one of the foremost studios in Kerala established in 1951. Drawing on archival sources, film texts and interviews, I look at the varied modes through which the figure of the female star emerges in the construction of Miss Kumari as a studio artist. In particular, I examine the discursive modalities employed in the film writing of the 1950s that shape her as a domestic custodian of native films and as the star body that boosted indigenous experimentations with filmic forms and themes. I also examine the mobilization of her absent star body in an array of recollections after her death drawing on her otherwise 'private' persona, even adding new strands to the understanding of how a star persona is recuperated after her death.

The decade of 1950s was a fertile ground for the formative phase of Malayalam cinema. This era was marked by entrepreneurial endeavours to mobilize capital, resources and technical know-how to facilitate the transfer of films and film services to Kerala from Madras in the neighbouring state of Tamil Nadu. Even though linguistic demarcations were not strongly marked out in the Malayalam speaking regions comprised of the princely states of Thiruvithamkoor, Kochi and Malabar in the 1950s, the imagination of an indigenously produced form of cinema remained in the backdrop since the 1930s. But the native topos of Kerala was initially perceived as an impediment in supporting entrepreneurial ventures and attempts to initiate business establishments involving cinema was largely discouraged as there was an ominous sense of failure associated with such projects.[1] To add to this sense of anxiety, there was a simmering sense of dissatisfaction among the exhibitors of travelling cinema in Kerala regarding the loss of revenue owing to paucity of good quality prints. All of these factors contributed to the discussions about the need to improvise film production in the native soil of Kerala. In 1946, Udaya Pictures Private Limited was started by Kunchacko in Alappuzha and this later gave way to Udaya Studios in 1949.[2] In another two years' time, a second studio, Merryland was started by P. Subramanyam on an abandoned school-lot in Nemom, a suburb of Thiruvananthapuram.

Even though the initial phases of both studios were steeped in uncertainties of various kinds, the establishment of both Udaya and Merryland provided solid ground to assemble talent, finance and creative collaborations in Kerala itself. Even while they borrowed generic templates that were deemed commercially successful in the Tamil and Telugu films of the time, these 'native' productions attempted to carve out distinct filmic artefacts that could carry the stamp of autochthony. For instance, even when they aimed to galvanize a base for home productions, both Kunchacko and P. Subramanyam, the founders of the first two Malayalam studios were quite conscious of the need to muster enough support from the distributors based in Madras and Salem who were allocating the business to agents of travelling cinema (Koshy 1968: 20). Permanent exhibition spaces were relatively rare until the 1960s, making film-shows one of the myriad seasonal forms of entertainment that existed alongside folk performances including dance-dramas and travelling circus. Therefore, in this phase, Malayalam cinema had to struggle to find a space for itself.

It is also true that there was a seething contempt for Tamil films that lurked in the backdrop, providing the much-needed fillip to the proposal of indigenous productions based in Kerala (Joseph 2012: 59). Even the proponents of Aikya Kerala, a political group demanding a united Kerala based on linguistic similarity since the independence of India, were in favour of supporting local productions as a safeguard against Tamil films (60). The building of the studios in Kerala and the

---

[1] This anxiety about supporting localized production stemmed from the failures that were associated with the production of the first two Malayalam films. *Vigatakumaran* (J. C. Daniel, 1930), which was shot in a make-shift studio in Thiruvanthapuram, suffered huge financial set-backs and the second Malayalam film *Marthanda Varma* (V. V. Rao, 1933) shot in Thiruvanathapuram did not even see the light of the day as it was caught amidst copyright infringements. After the release of *Prahlada* (K. Subramaniam, 1941), there was a period of latency and there were no films produced in Malayalam from 1942 to 1948, on account of lack of infrastructural and technical support. By and large, the money sourced into production came from the producers who were based outside the space of Kerala, as for instance the Madras-based Annamala Chettiar who produced *Gnanamika* (S. Nottani, 1940) or T. R. Sundaram, the proprietor of Modern Theatres in Salem who produced the first Malayalam talkie, *Balan* (S. Nottani, 1938). In 1948, when P. J. Cherian formed Kerala Talkies Limited with financial support from the Cochin royal family and the general public, the major drive was to make it an all-Malayali cast and crew. This venture resulted in the production of *Nirmala* (P. V. Krishna Iyer, 1948), the fourth talkie in Malayalam, which also saw the introduction of playback singing. But the lack of studios in Kerala had delayed the release of the film, leaving the producer neck-deep in debt.

[2] In fact, the core reason behind collaboration between Kunchacko, the director and producer and K. K. Koshy, the distributor whose joint venture later became Udaya studio, was necessitated by strategic alliances to float a company that could substitute the requirement for advance payment to the distributors and agents based in Madras to book the films.

understanding of self-sustainability that informed the discussions among the proponents of the early studios in Kerala are central to examining the growth and success of Miss Kumari. Counter to the widely held belief that regional film studios were a natural outgrowth that came by and large as an emulation of production, distribution and exhibition systems employed by the studios in Bombay, Pune and Madras, the beginning of the studio system based in Kerala was deliberately cultured to nurture a local base of talent. Often, the modes of publicity were carefully devised by the studios to project their roles as guardians of art and culture and a responsible support-base for artists to realize their full potential. In fact, the emphasis on grooming and mentoring aspirants was deliberately *showcased* as a serious responsibility. The song booklets, lobby display cards and the personal appearance of actors amidst the viewing public during the exhibition of the films were all aimed towards promoting the personal link that the masses would have with the characters they saw on screen, making the studio an interface between the on- and off-screen worlds.

Merryland certainly had an edge over Udaya in devising and implementing novel publicity features during the exhibition of the films, including preview shows before selected guests, as they owned four theatres in Thiruvananthapuram. The endeavours of Udaya and Merryland to break new grounds in film production in Kerala were reflected in the commissioned articles in the film magazines that highlighted the selection of the production team, including scripting, music composition, technical support and cast, months in advance of the scheduled shoot.[3] These articles reinstated their achievements as fruits of brave, and often risk-laden, endeavours. The 'indigenous' films that sprung from these studios were chiselled out with characteristic markers that stood as authorial imprints while concurrently serving as vernacular bases that could cater to the demands of nurturing local talent. The emergence of Miss Kumari as a 'star' figure is therefore connected to the initial travails and necessities of Kerala's studio system.

Emergence of Miss Kumari as a studio artist

Miss Kumari, whose real name was Thressiama, was introduced to the Malayalam screen by Sebastian Kunju Kunju Bhagavatar, one of the practitioners of the song-dance drama of the time. It was her father's interest in drama that came across as a strong support for her entry into films. Reminiscent of the anonymity-to-instant fame narratives of many in the film industry, Miss Kumari's entry was nothing short of an accidental find. When the shooting of a song sequence for *Vellinakshatram* (Silver Star, Felix J. Beyas, 1949), Udaya Studio's first film, was progressing, Thressiamma was noticed by the German director Felix J. H. Beyas who was excited to have found a face that was 'impressive'.[4] Carrying the tricolour Indian flag in her hand and dressed in a Gandhi-cap, the close-up shots featured Miss Kumari's entry, accompanied by a music track beginning '*Thrikkodi Thrikkodi*' ('thrikkodi' meaning tricolour and referring to the Indian flag) sung

---

[3] These articles came in film monthlies of the time such as *Aruna, Cinema Masika* and *Cinema Deepika*.
[4] Interview with T. E. Vasudevan, proprietor of Associated Pictures, given in Ernakulam on 12 March 2014. This is one among many narratives that reiterates Miss Kumari as an unexpected 'find'. In fact, there are counter narratives, including that of Chelangatt Gopalakrishnan that Miss Kumari was unnoticed when she acted in *Vellinakshatram*, but these speculatory pieces do not provide enough justification as to how she became the lead heroine in the next Udaya film.

by Cherai Ambujam. This is the only film in which her name appears in the opening credits as Thressiama.

Hailing from Bharananganam, a small town in the district of Kottayam, Thressiamma's early life was not influenced by film, nor was it geared towards a film career. In fact, some sources claim that she had watched hardly two films before plunging into acting herself (Kottarathumkuzhi 1970: 9). For a brief spell of time she taught at Sacred Heart School in Bharananganam as an English teacher and toyed with the idea of becoming a nun and engaging in social service. Unlike many others who had to struggle to make their presence felt in the initial stages of their career, Miss Kumari's cameo performance in *Vellinakshatram* landed her the titular role in Udaya Studio's next film *Nalla Thanka* (P. V. Krishna Iyer, 1950), which drew on the legend of Nalla Thankal, a popular Tamil folk tale that was adapted widely for music-dance drama of the time. Interestingly, Thressiamma's screen name 'Miss Kumari' was coined by K. V. Koshy, one of the co-producers of K. K. Productions, the production house associated with Udaya Studios. While Koshy's coinage was influenced by a strategic move to foreground Udaya Studio's reputation in introducing new faces, the idea backfired. The name 'Miss Kumari' turned out to be a lucky mascot for Thressiamma, but she soon moved to Udaya's rival studio Merryland when she signed the contract for their first film *Atmasakhi* (Soulmate, G. R. Rao, 1952). This contract, in fact, remains the first known instance of a Malayali actress signing a contract as an artist for a Kerala based studio.[5] It was for the remuneration of 7000 rupees, with an advance payment of 500 rupees, that Miss Kumari made her initial commitment with Merryland. It is interesting to note that in the contract the name of the beneficiary is given as 'Miss Kumari (alias Thressiamma).' Crucially, the phrase '(alias Thressiamma)' has been added in different ink, almost like an afterthought, with 'Miss Kumari' being the main name under which the contract was signed. Therefore, much to the disappointment of Udaya Studios, it was not only Thressiamma who moved to the rival Merryland studios but also the brand-value of her screen-name 'Miss Kumari.' After beginning her stint with Merryland, the name 'Thressiamma' was soon forgotten by the public, leaving only the name 'Miss Kumari' as her reference marker.

Subsequent films such as *Avakasi* (Claimant, Anthony Mitradas, 1954), *Balyasakhi* (Childhood Friend, Anthony Mitradas, 1954), *Harischchandra* (Anthony Mitradas, 1955) and so on added to Miss Kumari's star value and she soon rose to become one of Merryland's foremost studio artistes, who at one time could bargain a price much higher than the lead male actors of the time. The repeated pairing of artists whose on-screen chemistry struck chords with the audience was something that Merrlyand's founder, P. Subramanyam, considered a virtue that could boost the visibility of its artists by conflating their presence with the image of the studio. For instance, the popularity of *Avakasi* made the combination of the star-actor Prem Nazir and Miss Kumari a success formula. This was replicated in subsequent films such as *Balyasakhi* (Anthony Mitradas, 1954)*, Aniyatti* (Sister, M. Krishnan Nair, 1955)*, Manthravadi* (The Sorceror, P. Subramanyam, 1956), *Padatha Painkili* (The Mute Nightingale, P. Subramanyam, 1957), *Jayilpulli* (Convict, P. Subramanyam, 1957) and *Mariakutty* (P. Subramanyam, 1958). In the 1950s,

---

[5]Contract for Miss Kumari offered by Neela Pictures, 30 January 1952. Accessed from the private collection of R. Gopalakrishnan.

almost all the films released by Merryland were directed and produced by P. Subramanyam, with the exception of a few films by Anthony Mitradas and Krishnan Nair. Most of the films directed by Mitradas retained the combination of Nazir and Miss Kumari. When Krishnan Nair, a long-time associate of P. Subramanyam had his directorial debut in *CID* (1955), the first Malayalam film to have experimented with the crime thriller genre, there was a strange request he had to comply with. His interest in casting a new combination was turned down by Merryland, who cited that in order to compensate for the novelty in theme and execution, the combination of Prem Nazir and Miss Kumari should be retained to guarantee box office success, highlighting the immense star value that Miss Kumari commanded at this time. The healthy, and at times cutthroat, competition between Udaya and Merryland studios also bifurcated the technicians and artists to one camp or the other. The exception to this was Prem Nazir, who acted both in Udaya and Merryland films, but became the fulcrum around whom the Udaya studio chiselled its image.[6] On the other hand Miss Kumari soon emerged to become Merryland's ambassador. For Miss Kumari, this came as a blessing in disguise as almost all Merryland films from then on had her as the lead heroine, subsequently making her the most visible face of the 1950s studio films.

Even though Miss Kumari acted mostly in Malayalam films (and a couple of Tamil films), she had a crucial presence in genre films that were produced simultaneously in Malayalam and Tamil. While the commercial success of genre films projected Merryland's fame as an exemplar in creating a pan-South Indian assemblage of sorts, drawing artists across Tamil, Telugu and Malayalam films, it was also a self-validation of the success of Kerala-based studios in broadening their viewer base. To some extent, the import of popular Tamil and Telugu actors in Merryland productions was also to counter the competition with Udaya that spawned copycat productions released during the same time as the original one. For instance, while Merryland's *Bhaktakuchela* (Kuchela the Devout, P. Subramanyam, 1961) and Udaya's *Krishnakuchela* (Krishna the Devout, Kunchacko, 1961) tapped the devotional genre and had similar storylines. *Bhaktakuchela* successfully waded the tide of competition by incorporating a cast that included Telugu actors C. S. R. Anjaneyulu and Kanta Rao, along with the Malayalam cast. When Udaya decided to boost ticket sales by gifting puffed rice to the viewers in the theatre, Merryland adopted door-to-door marketing strategies to win over the viewers. Among Merryland's improvisations with the form of genre films, the one film that stands out is *Anavalarthiya Vanambadi* (Nightingale Brought Up by the Elephant, P. Subramanyam, 1960), that inaugurated the series of 'jungle films' in Malayalam (Figure 3.1). Even though this was not the first jungle film in Malayalam, the first one being *Vanamala* (Garland of the Forest, G. Viswanath, 1951), *Anavalarthiya Vanambadi* was crucial in introducing the indigenous variant of the figure of Lady Tarzan, a character that was popularized through Thavamani Devi's stellar performance in *Vanamohini* (Mohini of the Forest, Bhagwan, 1948). Drawing on the lost and found narrative and sequences shot in the forest, *Anavalarthiya Vanambadi* emerged as a huge box office success, with Miss Kumari's performance

---

[6]It is interesting here to note that Prem Nazir's role in the commercial success of films was exploited by *both* Udaya and Merryland studios, even though he was first and foremost an Udaya star. But he appeared widely in Merryland films of the time as well without facing many injunctions, a rarity that many other actors could not afford.

as the Mowgli-like character Malli being seen as the highlight of the film. Merryland went on to make more jungle films and also came up with the first sequel in Malayalam cinema titled *Anavalarthiya Vanambadiyude Makan* (Son of the Nightingale Who Was Brought Up by the Elephant, P. Subramanyan, 1971), starring Shivaji Genesan. Therefore, for all practical purposes, one could argue that Miss Kumari became central to both the genre productions of the time as well as the inter-studio competition that had to account for the star value of the actress.

The precarious fame of the 'social' star

Associating separate cottages with lead stars was part of the tradition in the studio system of 1950s Malayalam cinema, indicating the policy of creating different tiers among artists and technicians. If Udaya studio prominently named 'Nazir cottage' after Prem Nazir, many film goers of the 1950s still remember Merryland's 'Camp House' – the lodge behind the New Theatre in the East Fort area as being associated with Miss Kumari.[7] The location of 'Camp House' in a prime area that housed three theatres in close proximity to each other also meant that the viewers who were near the vicinity of the theatres could catch a glimpse of the artists who were camping there.[8] By virtue of her association with many amateur drama troupes of the time, Miss Kumari's off-screen visibility in such public spaces shaped the perception of her as someone who was accessible to the fans to interact with and share conversations. In fact, in spite of writing harsh reviews about her, the film critic

Figure 3.1 Miss Kumari in *Anavalarthiya Vanambadi* (P. Subramanyam, 1960).

---

[7]Interview with Sadasivan given in Trivandrum on 2 February 2015.
[8]Interview with Balan given on 27 January 2015. Balan's forefathers ran the tea stall opposite the New Theatre.

Vasudevan Nair co-acted with Miss Kumari in the play staged at the first drama festival organized by Akhila Malabar Kendra Kala Samiti. Radha, one of her co-artists at Merryland recollects: 'The way she carried herself had an air of ordinariness that exceeded her stature as a leading star. Perhaps, her girl-next-door image and her simplicity appealed to the masses. Unlike what is normally expected of a leading actress, she consciously tried to de-glamourize herself by wearing an off-white sari and minimal jewellery.'[9] Until the very end of her career, she played down her status as a star and recounted her successful breakthrough into films as 'luck' more than anything else.

Even though this revelation bespoke of her natural impulse not to foreground her presence more than was absolutely required, it backfired when some film critics such as Vasudevan Nair, who wrote under the pen name of 'Cinic', were quick to take it literally as a confession on Miss Kumari's part about how her success was guided solely by luck and by the Merryland bandwagon. This accounts for the reason why the film writings of the 1950s reveal a strange contradiction in the inscription of Miss Kumari as the first Malayalam female star. On the one hand, the criticism levelled against the genre of studio films and its commercial impulse was deflected on Miss Kumari as she was seen as one of the unqualified beneficiaries of a system that allowed prerogatives and benefits to a few, ignoring many others who were equally or more talented. Most of the reviews by Nair had complaints of inappropriate casting that dissipated the story into fragments, and this could have been one of the reasons why he expressed his anguish against Miss Kumari's 'sophistication', which he felt betrayed the authenticity that the roles demanded (Cinic 1959b: 130). Some of his reviews accused Miss Kumari of misconstruing the emotions so much that 'when she cries, it seems as if she was smiling', making him pronounce the verdict that 'her experience and maturity in the field has unfortunately failed to impress anyone' (Cinic 1959a: 49).

Clearly, Miss Kumari's attempts to chart a new terrain in conceptualizing female stardom had to reel under the unqualified denigration of her as a misfit for the label of a 'star'. In fact, Miss Kumari did not fit the normative criteria outlining the profile of female stars of the time, such as the expectation that an actress should be proficient in dance. Further, Miss Kumari's physical appearance was particularly 'everyday'; as a buxom young woman, she did not have the hourglass figure of other dancer-actresses. In fact, it was her refusal to toe the line that contributed to her fame. First and foremost, Miss Kumari had an unconventional profile for an actress, let alone a star. As a devout Christian she incurred the wrath of the Christian community by starting her career acting in Hindu mythological and devotional films. As opposed to the 'Travancore Sisters', Lalitha, Ragini and Padmini, who had been part of many Udaya and Merryland films, and the ease with which they used the performative dimensions of dance-drama to carve a niche for themselves, Miss Kumari's image was limited by the studio label of Merryland. Her lack of proficiency in dance stood as an impediment that restricted her from being cast in roles involving dance, a limitation that was stressed in most of the film writings of the time.

Yet, on the other hand, Miss Kumari's presence contributed quite a lot to highlighting the space of studio actresses at a time when women's entry to films was looked down upon as anathema to family and domestic life. To deflect the attention from the circulation of gossip centred on actresses and the functioning of the studio system, there was a tendency in many write-ups featuring

---

[9]Interview with Radha given in Chennai on 12 August 2013.

Miss Kumari to emphasize her personal traits as her marks of distinction. Her description as 'fair skinned, humble, cultured and with a demeanour that can impress anyone' (Kottaruttumkuzhi 1969: 11; 1970: 9) was rehashed in one article after the other as a defence mechanism to uphold the integrity and transparent dealings involved in casting. Miss Kumari also used her visibility as a star to voice her opinions about social issues, such as the suitable age for marriage for girls. Her decision to get married therefore evoked such a stir among readers that the Sunday supplement of *Malayala Manorama*, published a special article on Miss Kumari in 1963. Titled 'A life steeped in belief and moral values: Stepping into a happy domestic life', the article gave a roundup of Miss Kumari's professional career and her parting from the industry in her own words. It is interesting to note here that there were questions about how her decision to stay in the acting field until the age of twenty-eight, and her subsequent exit, was framed as a transition to new responsibilities. When asked if her marriage would mean the end of her career, she sidestepped the question with a rhetorical counter question: 'I personally do not think that family life and an acting career are incompatible. But, the deciding factor is whether the industry would accommodate a married woman to continue in the lead role' (Kumari: 1963).

The short shelf-life of actresses as compared to actors and the ways this equation reflected in the casting came up in the discussions following Miss Kumari's marriage. *Sreeramapattabhisekham* (The Coronation of Lord Ram, P. Subramanyam, 1962), a mythological film centred on Rama's exile from Ayodhya, came as a prelude to her exit from films. Here Miss Kumari was cast as Kaikeyi, one of the three wives of King Dasarada who demands that her son Bharata be made the heir apparent and her step-son Rama be exiled for fifteen years. Quite ironically, contrary to the expected combination of Prem Nazir and Miss Kumari, it was Shanti, another budding actress, who was paired with Nazir. Miss Kumari did not hide her discomfort with being cast as stepmother to Nazir. But the justification given for her being cast as Kaikeyi was something that fortified her status as a star, boosted her popularity and was clearly not something she could deny: in the studio's rationale, this casting decision was based on Miss Kumari's distinctive *hair*.

Throughout her career, starting from her first film, the most distinguishable facet of Miss Kumari had been her long lustrous hair. In fact, there were even attempts to highlight this in scene composition through freeze frames and focused camera movement. The dishevelled tresses and plaits of Miss Kumari were frequently highlighted by the film critics and writers of the time as an iconic trope in her films. Citing the crucial visual cue of the open hair in the sequence that shows Kaikeyi's sudden transformation, Miss Kumari, who was reluctant to accept the abrupt change of role from Sita to Kaikeyi, was asked to concede to the request.[10] Even though this instance was a perfect exemplar of the ways new faces in the film industry replace the old, the reference to Miss Kumari's hair would reappear in her obituary columns, with her hair becoming metonymic of her lost glory in the history of Malayalam cinema.

Unlike the constraints and regulations that bound artists to studio films, Miss Kumari's popularity and success helped her strike negotiations with Merryland studio, allowing her leeway to do occasional films *outside* the banner of Neela Productions, under which most Merryland

---

[10]Interview with S.Kumar, son of P. Subramanyam given on 12 February 2014.

films were produced. For instance *Neelakuyil* (The Bluebird, P. Bhaskaran and Ramu Karyat, 1954), the film that brought her to the pinnacle of success, was produced by Chandrathara productions. This film refashioned her image as a versatile actress who could excel in mythological, social and film adaptations of popular fiction with equal ease. Rooted in the social realist mode, *Neelakuyil* explored caste oppression and social inequalities and became the first Malayalam film to bag the All India Certificate of Merit in 1954. The casting of Miss Kumari in the role of Neeli, a Dalit girl who gets impregnated by an upper-caste schoolteacher and subsequently ostracized from society, came across as something radical for the time, as it proved to be a herculean task for the production team to find an actress who was willing to take up the role.[11] The political edge of the film in exposing social inequalities and caste hierarchies, set in a social milieu with which viewers could easily identify, made it immensely popular, and Miss Kumari was subsequently cast in more films that drew on the themes of feudal landlordism and bonded labour.

It is true that her association with Merryland had given her the standing of a studio artist, but this identity also shaped the perception of her earlier films, creating a separation between her Udaya and Merryland phases. For instance, before Miss Kumari became an artist of Merryland she had starred in *Navalokam* (The New World, V. Krishnan, 1951), but the film was forgotten and left out in her later appropriation as the Merryland star. Coming in the interregnum between her stint with Udaya and Merryland, *Navalokam* was remarkable in offering a powerful depiction of the perils of the *zamindari* system alongside the need for women's liberation, and was heavily censored by the newly constituted Censor Board for its pro-labour position (Vijayakumar 2008). The role of Neeli gave Miss Kumari a popular appeal that was exploited to publicize more films that highlighted the issue of exploitation of peasants and underprivileged sections of the society. *Randidangazhi* (Two Measures, P. Subramanyam, 1958), adapted from the novel by Thakazhi Sivasankara Menon and exposing the perils of bonded labour in Kuttanad, was one such social film. The film adaptation of *Mudiyanaya Putran* (The Prodigal Son, Ramu Karyat, 1961), which carried on the legacy of the plays staged by the Kerala Progressive Writers Association (KPAC), was backed by a strong political message and highlighted Miss Kumari's screen image as a star whose presence could evoke intertextual resonances in the viewers.

Moreover, there were extra-diegetic factors that contributed to her association with social films. Her political leanings towards the Congress Party and her support for nationalist causes were reflected in the political meetings where she spoke of the responsibilities invested with the masses to protest against power-laden structures. Some reminiscences, for instance, recount Miss Kumari's public appearance in a *Khadi* sari, sharing the dais with political leaders such as Kamraj and Asok Mehta, translating their speech from Hindi and English to Malayalam.[12] Through the strategic use of contexts from the social films, and by occasionally gesturing towards the characters she had enacted on screen, whether Neeli, Chellamma (*Mudiyanaya Putran*) or Chirutha (*Randidangazhi*), Miss Kumari exhibited a unique acumen to mobilize cinematic reality for political mileage. Considering that, unlike Tamil Nadu and Andhra Pradesh, cinema and politics were

---

[11]Interview with R. S. Prabhu, ex-manager of Chandrathara Productions given in Chennai on 5 September 2013.
[12]Telephone interview with Balachandran Chulikkadu on 16 February 2015.

not yet deeply enmeshed in Kerala, the presence of Miss Kumari in the realm of political mobilization reflects how her star persona stood as a contemporary marker, where the *presentness* of the moment was mediated through cinematic realism and character identification. The success of the social films and Miss Kumari's presence as a star even forced Udaya to cast her in *Kidappadam* (Dwelling, R. S. Mani, 1955) after she had become a contractual artist of Merryland. Drawing inspiration from the Hindi film *Do Bigha Zamin* (Bimal Roy, 1953), *Kidappadam* explored the plight of the dispossessed peasant family and their last effort to retrieve their land from being lost to a feudal landlord.

Even though Miss Kumari's stardom and its relationship to the genre of social films were integrally connected, her appearance in social films cannot be seen as singlehandedly responsible for her stardom. Neepa Majumdar (2009) identifies a circular, but necessary, relationship conjoining social films and stardom in the 1930s, with the genre of social films being essential to the emergence of stars and vice versa. But in Miss Kumari's case, social films were only incidental to her stardom, as her appearance in social films merely added to her versatility as a star. Citing the realistic drift in social films, there were reviews that raised objections to Miss Kumari being cast as a Dalit woman in *Neelakuyil*, citing it as an appropriation of Dalitness diluting the strength of the narrative. For instance, in his critique of *Neelakuyil* published in *Mathrubhumi*, Nair's scathing review goes: 'If they looked around, the production team might have found someone who had experienced the severity of caste inequalities and could have portrayed the character of Neeli much more forcefully than Kumari' (Cinic 1959b: 134). Thus, even her stardom was precariously placed, allowing for questions of authenticity to crop up time and again. On the one hand, the dedication shown by Miss Kumari towards her profession as an actress was recognized as compelling enough to draw the interest of the viewers. There were write-ups on how she risked being run over by a train during the shoot of *Neelakuyil* (Sabu 1969: 3) or that she was ready to rehearse as many times as possible for the perfection of the character. But on the other hand, suspicious remarks were cast on her inadequate performance of certain roles, to the extent of even alleging that her off-screen persona was so 'forceful' that it curtailed her from doing justice to the roles.

Even when Miss Kumari was at the peak of her fame, there was severe opposition to her profession as an actress. To many conservative elements, Miss Kumari's acting career came across as an aspiration that went contrary to the moral ethos of the Syrian Christian community. There was severe pressure on her family and even threats that the church might be forced to pronounce *Mehroon* (excommunication) against her for taking up acting. The pressures and oppositions she had to negotiate to stay in films had a filmic variant as well. The role of the popular stage actress Miss Kumari enacted in *Chechi* (Sister, T. Janakiraman, 1950), a film adaptation of the play staged by Ochira Parabrahmodayam Nadana Sabha, comes as a striking depiction of the ostracization of stage actresses. As a social film, *Chechi* also becomes a self-reflective mirror of a society that thrives on the rumour and gossip that accompanies the popularity of actresses.

Miss Kumari's stint in the cinema was rather short, lasting just ten years, but she had more than *fifty* films to her credit. Her marriage was a much-anticipated event and fans thronged in their thousands to the Metropolitan church in Ernakulam where the marriage was solemnized. To prevent the crowd from causing a stampede, the roads adjoining the church had to be blocked by the police to regulate traffic congestion

(Gopalakrishnan 2012: 21). As the marriage convention demanded that the first part of her screen name 'Miss' be avoided in the wedding invitation, it was her second name 'Kumari' that was used. 'No one even bothered much to fuss about her real name then as everyone recognized her by her screen name Kumari', said Miss Kumari's brother when asked about the transition from Thressiamma to Miss Kumari.[13] If Miss Kumari was the fulcrum around which the films of Merryland studio found their feet, her parting from professional commitments as an actress was also coloured by a cinematic trace. The special wedding reception held at Bolgatty Palace, the Dutch-built palace on an island in Kochi, turned out to be a high-key event, with the whole proceedings being shot on film by Merryland studio to honour their prestigious studio artist. 'It was not a farewell in the strict sense of the term. It was a public event attended mostly by film personalities. The film-like hype which it had was primarily because the invitee list had almost all the key figures who then decorated the Malayalam cinema industry', reminisced P. Subramanyam's son, S. Kumar.[14]

Re-packaging Kumari: Stardom and memorialization

Miss Kumari's stardom and her untimely death in 1969 became moments that were invoked in film writings of the time, giving a new layer to her cinematic exit. Her demise at the young age of thirty-seven triggered a memorialization that reinstated her as someone who left the screen before her time. There was a strange way in which her cinematic exit and her subsequent death became interconnected, primarily because it was the absence of the star from 'real life' and the lacuna it created that triggered an explosion of memory around her 'absent' star body. Song sequences were central to the screen-presence and star value of Miss Kumari, so much so that even now it triggers intergenerational cinephilia. To a great extent, the contemporary remembrances of Miss Kumari have been mediated through the sonic and affective charge of song sequences.

Today, extracted song sequences from 'Miss Kumari films' are repacked as markers of nostalgia for an imagined classical canon of Malayalam cinema. In June 2013, *Old Malayalam Cinema*, a leading blog dedicated to the history of Malayalam cinema, carried an image of Miss Kumari in the custom header with the text 'arguably Malayalam's first actor-star'. Over the years, the blog has published write-ups that have triggered a collective remembrance of the production and reception of old Malayalam films, including those starring Miss Kumari. By using the occasion of her birth anniversary as a moment to look back at her films and the decade of the 1950s, the tribute to Miss Kumari reminded the readers of her contribution as 'a legacy never to be forgotten'.[15]

Among the different modes of memorialization with which Miss Kumari's posthumous memory was mediated, most striking is the opening of a theatre in her hometown – the 'Mini Theater', which initially screened *only* her films in the 1970s and subsequently became a nostalgic screening spot for old Malayalam films until 1995 when it was finally shut down. Other instances include the naming of the stadium in her hometown as 'Miss Kumari Memorial Mini Stadium' and the branding of the state-level Best Actress

---

[13]Telephone interview with Miss Kumari's brother, Jacob Thomas Kollamparampil on 20 January 2015.
[14]Interview with S. Kumar, son of P. Subramanyam given in Trivandrum on 5 January 2013.
[15]Skype interview with Biju Ebenezer owner of the blog, *Old Malayalm Cinema*, on 9 March 2015.

Award as the 'Miss Kumari Award'. Even though this and the naming of the best actor award as the 'Satyan Award' in 1971 were discontinued after a year, it still remains the last instance when the state awards were instituted in memory of bygone actors. This is an instance to be noted because acknowledgement to J. C. Daniel, the maker of the first Malayalam film *Vigatakumaran* (The Lost Boy, 1930) also came long after his death, with the institution of J. C. Daniel Award as a lifetime achievement award for contribution to Malayalam cinema. In fact, there were demands to name the best state actress award the 'P. K. Rosy Award' in memory of the Dalit actress P. K. Rosy who acted in *Vigatakumaran* and had to face the ostracization of society for donning the role of a Nair character. In 2019, P. Bhaskaran foundation named its annual Yuva Prathibha Puraskaram (Youth idol award) the Miss Kumari Award, in memory of the fiftieth anniversary of her death.

Death, obituary and the 'fossilized' memory of Miss Kumari

Miss Kumari's death was invoked time and again in film writings of the time and it was even coloured by speculations about whether her death could have been an extension of the many sorrowful characters she had enacted in her films. Chelangatt Gopalakrishnan, one of the film journalists of the time, offers Miss Kumari's cinematic exit as a tragic episode, foretelling her death itself. In his collection of film writings titled *Annathe Nayikamar* (Actresses of the Yesteryears, 2012), Gopalakrishnan begins his section on Miss Kumari by citing her fascination with Marilyn Monroe and how emotionally affected she was on hearing about Monroe's death. Gopalakrishnan writes: 'Death at the peak of one's fame was something unimaginable for Kumari, but when her death came, it was as if it she had already awaited it and was at ease with it' (19).

There is also a strange way in which Miss Kumari's reminiscences of her stint as an actress is addressed in her obituary columns. Miss Kumari had plans to pen her memoir and it was also widely publicized in the film monthlies of the time. It somehow did not attain fruition. But *Cinema Masika*, one of the prominent film monthlies in Malayalam, with a high circulation, published an experiential account of Miss Kumari titled *Ente Chalachitra Anubhavangal* (My Film Experiences). Commissioned as a series on Miss Kumari, it was C. R. Omanakuttan, a BA student then who was also doing occasional reviews for *Cinemamasika*, who became the ghost-writer for Miss Kumari. While Omanakuttan prepared the series after extensive interviews with Miss Kumari, the series was published as an autobiographical account, giving the semblance of it being written by the actress herself. Coming immediately after she had announced her decision to quit acting after marriage, the timing of the series was much anticipated and it became part of the narrative of transition from prominent actress to homemaker. Reminiscing on the writing of the series Omanakuttan says: 'Perhaps, it was the first ghost writing in autobiographical mode in Malayalam film writing. But no one except the editors knew that the account was "kettezhuthu" (ghost-written).'[16] Coming after the series on Sophia Loren and Elizabeth Taylor, this series became so popular among the readers that it was published for the next sixteen weeks, with regular fan letters seeking clarification about

---

[16]Interview with Omanakuttan on 10 January 2015.

which parts were published or seeking Miss Kumari's signed photographs as a part of the subsequent issues (Thyagarajan 1969: 89).

Apparently, the deaths of Miss Kumari and K. V. Koshy were reported together in most of the magazines and newspapers of the time, recollecting their individual contributions to the growth of Malayalam cinema (Anon. 1964; Nair 1969). *Cinemamasika* used this occasion to foreground their role as pioneers in breaking new ground in Malayalam film journalism by publishing the experiences of prominent cinema personalities through their columns. The carefully crafted title 'Koshy Sir, Miss Kumari and *Cinemamasika*' stresses the personalized touch given by Koshy and Kumari through their autobiographical accounts serialized in *Cinemamasika*. Excerpts from the account published in *Cinemamasika* even made their way into other obituary columns (Kottaruttumkuzhi 1969: 11). Reports of her death became a chronicle of sorts, where Miss Kumari as an actress was invoked through varied modes of recollections. While the reports of *Malayala Manorama* mobilized the memory of Koshy and Kumari as 'The Lost Stars', *Cinerama* carried the responses of the film fraternity to the shocking news of her death. The report begins with the detailed description of how the news of her death was received by the shooting units in Madras and details the condolence meeting convened by the Malayala Chalachitra Parishad (an organization of film actors, directors and producers), to mourn her loss.

But perhaps Miss Kumari's most 'haunting' presence today is *physical*. As mentioned earlier, her lush hair was commended not only in her heydays but also in the obituary columns, where hair became the metaphor invoked to mourn her loss. For instance, in the report titled 'The Death Anniversary of Miss Kumari' published in the June 1970 issue of *Keralabhoosahanam*, the columnist recollects Miss Kumari's career trajectory by referring to the hair as powerful enough to create waves in the theatres alongside the Merryland logo (Kottaruttumkuzhi 1970: 9). Her hair, which refused to be contained within plaits because of its thick texture, became a unique reference, a lasting marker of an era of films and her indomitable spirit to stay in films. More than an attractive feminine virtue, its forceful presence ripped open the contradictions that accompanied Miss Kumari's stardom. Curiously, her hair is actually preserved in the Kottayam Medical College where her body was taken after death. As a nine-year-old child who had gone to visit the Medicos Exhibition in 1974 as a part of a study tour, Johny Thaliath, Miss Kumari's son, was left with an uncanny sense of loss when he visited the Kottayam Medical College. He recollects: 'It was an eerie experience to see my mother's remains preserved as an exhibit alongside skeletons and preserved embryos inside the glass jars.'[17] Crucially, the text on the plaque in the medical exhibit read: 'The ribs and hair of one of the foremost Malayalam film stars', marking even her last remnants with a cinematic reference (Raghunath 2013: 49). In a strange way, it is as if Miss Kumari the star's body has undergone a somatic death, yet the shape of its fossilized imprint can still be seen in the film-going public. Perhaps, in Miss Kumari's instance, this is what is meant by 'star-dust' – the physical and memorial trace left by her career on the surface of Malayalam film history.[18]

---

[17] Telephone interview with Johny Thaliath on 1 February 2015.
[18] I would like to thank Babu Thaliath, Johny Thaliath, R. Gopalakrishnan and C. R. Omanakuttan for opening their personal collections and memories to me for this chapter. I would also like to thank Anirban Baishya for his suggestions and comments.

Works Cited

Anon. (1964), 'Manmaranjupoya randu Vellinakshatrangal', *Malayala Manorama*, 17 June, p. 4.

Cinic (1959a), 'Atmashanti', in *Malayala Cinema*, vol. 1, 41–9, Trichur: Mangalodayam Private Limited.

Cinic (1959b), 'Neelakuyil,' in *Malayala Cinema*, vol. 1, 127–35, Trichur: Mangalodayam Private Limited.

Gopalakrishnan, Chelangatt (2012), *Annathe Nayikamar*, Kottayam: D. C. Books.

Joseph, Jenson (2012), *Industry, Aesthetics, Spectatorial Subjectivities: A Study of the Malayalam Cinema of the 1950s*, PhD dissertation, University of Hyderabad.

Koshy, K. V. (1968), *Ente Cinema Smaranakal*. Kottayam: SPSS.

Kottaruttumkuzhi, Jose Mathew (1969), 'Vellinakshatram', *The Deepanalam Weekly*, 11 (24): 10–12.

Kottaruttumkuzhi, Jose Mathew (1970), 'Kumariyude Charamadinam Innu' (Today is Kumari's Death Anniversary), *Keralabhushanam*, 9 June 1970, p. 9.

Kumari, Miss (1963), 'Daivabhayavum sanmargabodavum thaliridunna 'Santoshakaramaya Kudambajeevitham', *Malayala Manorama* Sunday Supplement, 6 January, p. 1.

Majumdar, Neepa (2009), *Wanted Cultured Ladies Only! Female Stardom and Cinema in India, 1930s–1950s*, Urbana: University of Illinois Press.

Nair, Madhavan (1969), 'Chalachitrarangattu Velicham chorinja Anargha Jyothis', *Cinemamasika*, 22 (8) (August): 70–5.

Pandian, M. S. S. (1992), *The Image Trap: M. G. Ramachandran in Film and Politics*, New Delhi: Sage.

Prasad, M. Madhava (1999), 'Cine Politics: On the Political Significance of Cinema in South India', *Journal of Moving Image*, 1: 37–52.

Raghunath. Rashmi (2013), 'Neelakuyilinte Ormayku', *Mangalam varika*, 13 May, pp. 48–50, online at: www.mangalamvarika.com/index.php/en/home/index/87/48 (accessed 5 January 2015).

Sabu, A. C. (1969), 'Parannakanna Neelakuyil' (The Blue Cuckoo which Flew Away), *Cinerama*, 3 (11): 1–3.

Srinivas, S. V. (2009), *Mega Star Chiranjeevi and Telugu Cinema after N.T Rama Rao*, New Delhi: Oxford University Press.

Thomas, Rosie (2005), 'Not Quite (Pearl) White: Fearless Nadia, Queen of the Stunts', in Raminder Kaur and Ajay J. Sinha (eds), *Bollywood: Popular Indian Cinema through a Transnational Lens*, 35–69, New Dehli, Thousand Oaks, CA: Sage.

Thyagarajan, Kazhakutam (1969), 'KoshySirum Miss Kumariyum Cinemamasikayum', *Cinemamasika*, 22 (8): 85–93.

Vijayakumar, B. (2008), 'Navalokam', *The Hindu*, 24 May, online at: www.thehindu.com/todays-paper/tp-features/tp-metroplus/article1417249.ece (accessed 20 December 2014).

Chapter 4

In the wink of an eye: The comedic universe of Johnny Walker

Radha Dayal

Main Bambai ka babu naam mera anjaana
Englis dhun mein gaaun main Hindustani gaana
…
Aaya hoon main bandhoo Roos aur Cheen mein jaa ke
Kaam ki baat bata di comedy gaana ga ke
(I'm a gentleman from Bombay, no one knows my name,
I sing Hindustani songs set to English tunes …
My travels have taken me to Russia and China
In a comic ditty, my friends, I can say what needs to be said) (my translation)

These lyrics from a song in *Naya Daur* (New Times, Baldev Raj Chopra, 1957) provide a subjective self-introduction to the character performing the song, a journalist (played by Johnny Walker) who remains unnamed in the film. Cultural and regional descriptors mark the character as a *babu* (educated gentleman) from Bombay and a well-travelled person, while other references – such as the mention of socialist countries Russia and China – bring into play the ethos of postcolonial Indian nationalism that scholars have identified as one of the most powerful constitutive frameworks for understanding cinematic narratives of the 1950s (Chakravarty 1993: 8). The iconic decade of the 1950s in Bombay cinema largely consists of epic narratives that focus on the promises and pathos of postcolonial nationalism, and simultaneously imbue films with mirth and merriment through obligatory comedy tracks played by stock comedians (Prasad 1998: 31). Walker was undoubtedly one of the most popular comedians of the fifties and the song from *Naya Daur* discursively and playfully highlights some of the themes that are central to understanding his star text in this period: the framework of the nation and India's post-independence socialist ideology in producing a discourse of Indian subjectivities, the conflicting paradigms that seek to establish the identity of male characters especially between the contradictory forces of the Anglicized 'gentleman' and the 'Hindustani' (Indian), and most importantly the decentred position of the comedian that offers a different perspective from the principal characters in these debates. This chapter discusses some of Walker's most popular film roles of this period and the way in which his fictional characters challenge and problematize nationalist perspectives embodied by the films' principal characters and narrative trajectories.

Born Badruddin Jamaluddin Kazi (called Badru) on 11 November 1924, Walker belonged to a traditional Muslim family and his early childhood was spent in Indore (a small industrial town in central India). He always wanted to work in films like his idol Noor Mohammed 'Charlie' (Narwekar 2005: 86) and cheekily claimed he was 'delighted' when his father lost his job as a textile worker and moved the family to Bombay.[1] He had to work many odd jobs such as selling vegetables and performing in local fairs (Ghose 1997). Success came through a chance encounter with actor Balraj Sahni on a local Bombay bus where Badru was working as a conductor. Sahni, who was co-writing the script of *Baazi* (A Turn of Dice, Guru Dutt, 1951) with newcomer Guru Dutt, was struck by Badru's ability to make passengers laugh with impromptu comedic acts and invited him to meet Dutt. At Sahni's suggestion Badru made an unannounced entrance onto the set pretending to be drunk and Dutt almost had him physically evicted, believing him to be a disruptive miscreant (Ghose 1997). Sahni intervened and Dutt, who had been on the lookout for a comedian to play a small role in his film, rewrote the miniscule part in *Baazi* as a drunk and cast Badru in it.[2]

Walker's debut scene in *Baazi* is barely fifteen seconds long but in this unbelievably short span of time he gave a performance that brought him overnight success and became the template for his most beloved and oft-repeated fictional character, that of the drunk. A teetotaller, he nevertheless took Johnny Walker (after the whiskey brand 'Johnnie Walker') as his screen name, 'so that when people thought of a drunkard they would think of me.'[3] His excessively thin body, clinched-at-the-waist belted trousers, large head perched on a long neck, 'pencil-thin moustache, facial grimaces and [high-pitched] nasal drawl' (Rajadhyaksha and Willemen [1994] 1999: 239) created a comedic effect unlike any other comedian of that time. Lalitha Lajmi, Guru Dutt's sister, later said of Walker's uniqueness: 'When Guru Dutt gave him a small role in *Baazi*, he developed a very original body language and a manner of speaking. It had a freshness that wasn't imitative of Charlie Chaplin or anyone, so he just clicked' (Shedde 2003).

Walker's stellar career consists of more than three hundred films that span over four decades. From petty pickpockets to upper-class aristocrats, taxi drivers to journalists, his lovable characters cover a range of religious, cultural and social identities. Though not exclusively, most of these come from the fringe communities of India's social demographics in the 1950s and, as I show in this chapter, it is these marginal figures that are key to Walker's high popularity index. In addition, his narrative pairing with female partners and eager love pursuits provided him with an unusually high visibility for a secondary character and attest to his value as a star performer in the 1950s. This is true also of the solo song performances that he was regularly privileged with and his presence on publicity material like film posters, song booklets, lobby cards and more. In this chapter I will show that through his playful acts and the uneven way in which his characters were integrated into the narrative architecture of the films Walker released a host of uncontrolled or only partially controlled affects and unresolved energies into the film that provided the necessary twists and balances to the emotional, affective and psychosocial workings of the narratives. Seen through the lens of the dominant ideology of the narratives these loosely structured and lively deviations staged a covert critique of the status quo and make Walker's characters far more complex than they have so far been given credit for in academic discourses.

Walker's roles and performances have broadly been defined as para-narrative units that function as a parallel track to the main narratives, 'not

---

[1] This anecdote is taken from Rosie Thomas's unpublished field notes from February 1980 that she generously shared with me.
[2] Walker's son Nasir Kazi confirmed this story to me in a personal interview in Bombay on 28 April 2010.
[3] From Rosie Thomas's unpublished field notes, February 1980.

merely a part of the narrative continuum' but 'to create parallel pleasures and perhaps to problematize the work of the narrative' (Vasudevan 1989: 31). As a secondary character in a comedic role these figures usually fall outside the rigid ideological frameworks of the narratives and foreground the fault-lines of Indian society along the lines of patriarchy, class, caste, gender and religion, issues that intersected with key nationalist discourses that were central to Bombay film narratives in the era following India's independence. Through his differently charged performances Walker compels a rethinking of nationalist ideologies by foregrounding an imagination of very different Indian male subjectivities from those of the principal characters, which have largely been obscured in the epic debates that dominate the discourse of 1950s' cinema. This chapter is an attempt to recover some of them.

Disarranging nationalist narratives

Walker's star text requires an understanding of the 1950s and the films and themes that dominated the Indian imagination during this period when his popularity achieved an unusually high index. In the wake of Indian independence in 1947, a powerful national mood pervaded the Indian republic that can broadly be defined as anti-colonial and the search for a distinctive Indian subjectivity (Prakash 1999: 201–26). It was perhaps only natural that modernity, viewed primarily as an empire-building enterprise, began to contradict with popular perceptions about 'Indianness' (Chakravarty 1993: 8).[4] The multiple foci of Indian nationalism on the one hand sought to retain existing social structures based on ancient fault-lines of class, caste, gender, religion and ethnicity, while on the other attempted to reconfigure them into a more technological, scientific and rational enterprise. The contradictory vision of nationalism critiqued specific aspects of Western modernity while retaining others. It remained ambivalent towards certain divisive aspects of Indian tradition but continued to aim for a more unified nation-state through a new, constructed ideology of the nation (Prakash 1999: 213–34).

In the 1950s, films attempted to create a largely homogenized 'national' fiction by positioning, often problematically, India's myriad heterogeneous regional, ethnic, social, religious and cultural identities in subordinate terms to an 'overarching north Indian, majoritarian Hindu identity' (Vasudevan 2006: 296–7). By mapping these identities in a specific hierarchy popular cinema was involved in creating a symbolic national space (297) in which the identities of the 'southerner', the Parsi, Muslim or Christian, occupied subordinate positions in the narrative universe dominated by the north Indian, Hindu identity (296). By taking on identities that projected, however comically, disenfranchised social communities, and some form of religious, class or caste marginalization, Walker was positioned on the fringes of society that merged with his narrative marginalization. However, through his delightful performances and unique embodiment of the most marginalized of characters, Walker sublimated the abjectness and possible tragedy of these characters into quirky roller-coaster performances of linguistic twists and muscular dexterity to create delightful deviations from the project of nationalism. Through the comedic track and principally through the figure of Johnny Walker in the 1950s, Bombay

---

[4]Chakravarty takes the term from South Asian scholar Edwin Gerow who uses it as a way to define a national Indian consciousness that came about as a response to a growing awareness about other nations/civilizations.

cinema surreptitiously, and perhaps inadvertently, nurtured the staging of a very different Indian male subjectivity.

Following this shifting framework, the imaginative landscapes of the films of this decade produced different, often contradictory, articulations of tradition and modernity[5] through dislocated subjectivities, socially and ideologically diverse characters, and multilayered storylines, putting into motion a number of conflicting paradigms, some of which eventually cohered, while others remained irreconcilable or only loosely aggregated, with the offered narrative resolution. Even though independence was seen as a force of modernity that would erase the ills of past traditions (such as social inequality, communal unrest and so forth) the notion of tradition as 'appended to morality' persisted in narratives themes such as rules of kinship and family, destiny and religion (Thomas 2006: 289). It is seen that these frameworks were not as incumbent upon comedians like Walker, which left him free to occupy multiple and contradictory identities that were sustained in a peripheral universe without upsetting the ideological thrust of the protagonists and main narratives.

In this context, a return to the narrative of *Naya Daur* reveals that Walker's character is uniquely positioned to propose a middle ground in the film, the contours of which are staged throughout but remain only loosely defined even at the end of the film. The film presents its central conflict as a polemical divide between the values espoused by the urban and the rural communities of India in the 1950s. Embodying these binary positions are the village dweller-protagonist-hero Shankar (Dilip Kumar) and a villainous, greedy man who has been educated in the city Kundan (Jeevan) with the moral force of the film clearly supporting Shankar. Walker complicates the positions of both the hero and the villain by acting as a catalyst, and in the process foregrounds a nuanced definition of modernity and tradition as well as muddling the film's principal point of view of presenting the city as a place that spawns evil and greed, while the village as a symbolic space remains innocent.

The film sets up its main plot around a conflict between Kundan and the villagers. Kundan, whose urban education has made him aware of machinery and modern systems, is keen to modernize the village by replacing human labour with machines, but he remains callously unmoved by the destruction his act will cause to the traditional livelihoods of the villagers. Shankar, representative of the villagers' plight, voices their concern to Kundan and when he remains unheard escalates the conflict to the point where a wager suggested by one of Kundan's men becomes the only way to settle the matter: a truck (representative of machinery and driven by Kundan) will race against a bullock-cart (representative of human and bestial labour, driven by Shankar). Whoever wins the race will chart the course of progress for the village.

Walker enters this unusual conflict as a neutral newspaper reporter. From his first scene the film sets up a complication to the codes that have been set up until then. Walker's speech and sartorial choices set him up as an outsider to the village community. His printed shirts, loose trousers, large cap, a rucksack swung over one shoulder and a camera hung around his neck visually code him as an urban dweller (Figure 4.1). Since a film's costume communicates, through well-understood tropes, about moral character, instigating actions and responses to people who wear them (Wilkinson-Weber 2014: 3), it is important to note

---

[5] For a more detailed discussion on these terms, see Das 2000: 167; and Mishra 2002: 4.

Figure 4.1 *Naya Daur* (New Times, Baldev Raj Chopra, 1957).

that Kundan is the only other figure in the film who dresses in Western attire in sharp contrast to the villagers' more traditional *dhoti* and *kurta*. This seems to create a narrative alignment between him and Walker. In addition, Walker initially speaks in English and only later on in Hindi, but always interspersed with English words and phrases that are suggestive of Western-styled education that was only found in the metropolitan cities of India in the 1950s. Kundan speaks with a strongly accented Hindi that also suggests a similar education.

The film soon begins to unravel this initial alignment between Kundan and Walker. Walker joins the villagers in their wager against Kundan by helping them to build a road on which their bullock cart can run better; he records their efforts by taking photographs of their activities; and he acts as a mediator to end a traditional caste feud with their rival community. Most importantly for the film, he writes a story about the wager that is published in several English, Hindi and regional language newspapers across India and garners support for the villagers from across the country. It is through the publication of this story that the benevolent village headman, who is ironically Kundan's father and who is away on a pilgrimage, comes to know of the plight of his village and decides to return and rein in his son's excesses. Although Shankar has already won the race, the headman's return satisfactorily concludes the reconciliation between technology and human labour. Indian modernity, in which opposites often 'exist side by side with the history of their untidy complicities and intermixtures' (Prakash 1999: 234), is given a voice in the film through Walker, whose embodiment of the positive forces of technology (notably, the circuits of modern communication like the newspaper) enables a reformulation of the traditional village community. Though it is the values espoused by the villagers that dominate at the end of the film Walker's character complicates the initial point of view of the film that reposed unmitigated evil in the city dweller. Walker stands for a different kind of urbanism, one that does not seek to destroy but to ameliorate the village.

At its conclusion the film stands for merging 'the past [world of humanist values that is] not dead but alive, open to the modern age and ready to give moral direction to science and technology' (213), a merger that is most strongly embodied by the figure of Walker. Madhava Prasad has defined Walker's role in *Naya Daur* as that of a 'subaltern' figure, an 'anonymous citizen', 'witnessing the drama on behalf of ... the Nation' (2004: 88). The Nehruvian vision of empowering the village into a model of self-development represented in the basic 'socialist thematics' of the film's 'reformist [tale] of class conflict' (88) is configured through the ideological positioning of this 'anonymous citizen'. Despite his secondary position in the narrative it is Walker who gently and comically eases some of the obstacles that Shankar, with his deep entrenchment in social and cultural systems, is unable to. By referencing his travels in the song 'Main Bambai ka babu' (I'm a gentleman from Bombay) Walker self-suggests the contours of his own subjectivity, primarily that he has become a world citizen: he is from everywhere and nowhere, a hybridity of cultures, manners and language, a truly modern figure who can be at home in any environment. The song also addresses the *bandhoo* (friends), which could possibly refer to the villagers to whom the song is being sung within the diegesis of the film. Yet, at the end of the song, when Walker looks straight at the camera and breaks with classical narrative conventions and the diegetic world of the film, he expands the comedic figure into an extra-diegetic sphere in which the *bandhoo* that he refers to could also be the citizenry of India, or the film's audience who are seated in the space of the theatre, or the camaraderie between different social groups that is imagined as the dream of a utopian community yet to be realized in the newly formed sovereign nation-state. He highlights the gaps in the scholarship on Indian cinema to foreground a new kind of subjectivity, one that blurs the boundaries of tradition to a less nostalgic mode of address and makes claim to a modernity that overlooks class, region and language barriers to suggest a more egalitarian, international and individualistic version of Indian subjectivity, setting him apart from all other characters in the film as he dismantles and complicates one of the most popular narrative tropes of the 1950s that almost always sets up the urban in a negative as compared to the rural. Neither completely heroic nor villainous, his character foregrounds a unique imagination of Indian subjectivity that does not entirely cohere with the cinematic staging of popular nationalist ideology.

Critiquing the family

Walker's critique of the nation was not restricted to films that staged a nationalist conflict. In films that focused on individuals, community and social struggles, his characters continued to challenge other 'national' frameworks, that of the family and the heterosexual couple. While characters occupying the central structure of cinematic discourse within the nationalist framework were defined by their 'rigid commitment to a moral project' the comedy track and comedians such as Walker remained free to represent 'ordinary life situations' that were less elevated in principle and sentiment (Prasad 1998: 71). One of the sites that emerged as a key focus for several films of the fifties was a preoccupation with the fate of the homeless and the disenfranchised sections of society. Several films of the 1950s, notably those made by Guru Dutt and Raj Kapoor, were written around protagonists that were inadvertently cast out from or deprived of the comfort of their biological family, class and caste privileges. In being forced to forge new relationships outside traditional zones their journeys served to '[dramatize] the contemporary sense of social flux' (Vasudevan 1994: 93) and invited the spectator to invest emotionally in the 'difficulty that assails those lacking power' and who were 'assailed by doubt as to the possibilities of ethical meaning and individual and social fulfilment in the world presented to us by the fiction' (Vasudevan 2010: 24). The relationship of 'centre to periphery' (Doraiswamy 2008: 8–9) became a complex terrain negotiated through several discursive and visual strategies. Modernity became one of the principal vehicles for advancing social change and through it the emergence of new possibilities began to cause a breakdown of traditional regional, class and caste barriers. Walker emerges at this nexus of old and new as more mobile, nimble, a figure who is able to move between different, sometimes contradictory, constructs of ideology; a study of his roles helps to illuminate positions that are contrary to the established canon and help to excavate other, more marginal, nodes of narrative meaning.

In the 1950s, the restoration and reformulation of the middle-class family was the ultimate goal of several cinematic narratives. A microcosm of the nation, the family itself was staged as a flawed institution, setting limits to the freedom of the films' protagonists and subjecting them to its controlling mechanisms. Its symbolic place at the centre of the social structure confirmed its importance, but its failure to live up to its promise as the locus of moral, spiritual and physical sanctuary for the protagonists set up the conflict in which protagonists were often forced to leave the safe and familiar environment of their biological home to find other, alternate, sources of intellectual, emotional and physical support and expand their experiences through identification with a wider social existence (Vasudevan 1994: 95). The narrative movement of leaving and then returning back to the zone of middle-class respectability necessarily involved a figure from another, often lower, class and caste that was often played by Walker, who became an enabler in providing support to the protagonists in their return to the ideological centre of society.

In no film does the supportive role played by Walker acquire greater philosophical and dramatic tension than in the enigmatic *Pyaasa* (The Thirsty One, Guru Dutt, 1957) in which his role as Abdul Sattar, a Muslim head masseur, whose friendship with the film's poet-protagonist Vijay (Guru Dutt) and a prostitute Gulabo (Waheeda Rehman) creates a complex set of relations for the film's position on labour and gender roles. The film uses irony as an expressionistic device to accentuate the juxtapositions between the three main characters. Walker consolidates the status quo of the film through his intervention in the narrative while remaining outside its controlling frameworks.

The lyrics of the song that introduces Walker to the film, 'Sar jo tera chakraaye' (If your head is reeling) emphasizes the value and social matrix of labour that is one of the central themes of the film and sets up the primary relationship between him and the film's protagonist. The beginning of the song shows Sattar wandering the streets at night with a bottle of oil and a portable chair, calling out 'Maalish, tel maalish' (massage, oil massage) in his unique high-pitched voice. His subaltern status is recognizable primarily through his name and sartorial choices, and later through his accent. A skullcap, the overall dark texture of his long shirt and the pattern of his *dhoti* identify his religion as Muslim, and unkempt strands of oily hair sticking out from under his cap speak to his underclass status. The melody gives way to the song:

> Sar jo tera chakraaye ya dil dooba jaye,
> Aaja pyaare paas hamaare
> kaahe ghabraaye, kaahe ghabraaye
> (If your head is reeling or your heart is sinking
> Come to me, my friend
> No point fretting, no point fretting) (Kabir 2011: 46)

Figure 4.2 *Pyaasa* (The Thirsty One, Guru Dutt, 1957).

Walker's slow dance-like walk to the beat of the calypso music and enticing glances towards potential customers to try his head massage energizes the narrative frame and creates the film's first hint of hope and cheerfulness (Figure 4.2). His wide grin, sparkling eyes and drum-like finger tapping on a customer's head while performing a massage further foregrounds the lovable quirkiness of his character. The song's lyrics emphazise his 'special' wares – 'this oil of mine has perfume, curing baldness and dandruff … this oil has great healing powers; It cures a thousand ailments'[6] – and labour – 'once my hands begin to whirl, your fate won't look so rough' and 'a touch of this strong hand will dissipate all woes'[7] (Kabir 2011: 48). Close ups of Walker strenuously massaging a man's head, pouring out the oil, twisting the man's neck to loosen up the muscles accompanied by

Figure 4.3 *Pyaasa* (The Thirsty One, Guru Dutt, 1957).

corresponding musical sounds emphasize physical labour as central to his identity (Figure 4.3). Ironically, however, we learn that it is the intellectual Vijay who has penned the frivolous lyrics of 'Sar jo tera chakraaye', lyrics that Sattar claims have

---

[6]Original lyrics in transliteration: 'Tel mera hai mushki, ganj rahe na khuski … Is champi mein bade-bade gun / Lakh dukhon ki ek dawa hai' (Kabir 2011: 48).
[7]'Jis ke sar par haath phira doon chamke qismat uski' (Kabir 2011: 48).

brought him 'great success' while leaving the author of the words penniless and homeless. This irony is emphasized in another stanza from the song that light-heartedly mocks society's perception of status: 'Be you a servant, be you a master; Be you a leader, or one of the led, King or soldier, to me all bow their head' (Kabir 2011: 48). These lines emphasize the 'superiority' of the masseur since leaders, kings and soldiers have to bow their heads before him (in order to get a massage). The irony is sharp primarily because Vijay's disillusionment throughout the film rests principally on the fact that his labour – his poetry – has not found its proper place in society and he has on occasion derided those who have failed to recognize its value. Vijay epitomizes the fall of a doomed nation that is unable to prevent 'its brightest talents from becoming either "respectable" or outcast whores' (Creekmur 2009: 110). On the other hand, Sattar's cheerfulness and seeming nonchalance towards his poverty and lack of class privileges creates a strong dialectic on the issue of the value of labour and its creation of identity. The contradictory position that the film creates through the value of physical labour versus intellectual labour sets up the divide in the otherwise strong friendship between the poet and the masseur.

Pyaasa depicts the family (in its broadest definition including blood relations and others of the same class, status and community) as an unreliable, almost evil, institution. Vijay's brothers, friends and college sweetheart all desert him and he is forced to find support outside his social and class structure, namely among society's marginalized characters, Sattar and Gulabo. While Vijay's brothers and friends collude with a greedy publisher to get Vijay locked up in an asylum for the insane it is Sattar who rescues him, enabling Vijay to confront his oppressors and claim justice against their hypocrisy. This is Sattar's first major plot intervention in the film.

The second is Sattar's assistance to Gulabo in leaving prostitution as she has fallen in love with Vijay. Through most of the film Vijay maintains a respectful distance from her and seems to be different from the conventional male gaze that either desires her sexually or rejects her as a disreputable outcast. A closer examination of the film's narrative trajectory reveals that even Vijay is circumscribed by the film's tacit ideological boundaries around gender and morality. He remains indifferent to Gulabo's charms when he first meets her and she tries to seduce him (in the song 'Jaane kya tune kahi' [Who knows what you spoke]). Later, though better acquainted, he remains unaware of her growing attraction for him (which she expresses through the song 'Aaj sajan mohe ang laga lo' [My beloved, take me in your arms today]). Sattar plays a crucial role in bringing about the transformation required by the narrative for the coming together of the lead couple. After hearing that Gulabo no longer wishes to practise prostitution because she has fallen in love with Vijay, Sattar confronts her pimp and in a farcical display of strength and intimidation forces him to leave Gulabo alone. The film's climax shows Vijay accepting her as his partner and leaving the city together towards an unknown future. Sattar's intervening act highlights the agency that is reposed in secondary comedic characters even though it consolidates the status quo of gender positions that Vijay's character otherwise seems to disavow. Although the film takes many risks by showing the coming together of the hero and a prostitute, its implicit stand on morality, especially of female sexuality, remains conservative when viewed through the principal couple. Gulabo's love and appreciation of Vijay's poetry is not enough; the narrative demands she give up prostitution to be 'worthy' of his love.

Pyaasa effectively negates the value of the family as a moral register for reconciliation, 'the relations of paternal authority and maternal nurture, of filial respect, duty, and emotional attachment' (Vasudevan 2010: 48). Through Sattar, who steps into the void left by Gulabo's absent family and Vijay's ineffectual one, the film challenges the notion of the family as the emotional and moral locus of the protagonist's world. His marginal status operating from the fringes of society stages a complex alternative to the family and, together, the unlikely triumvirate of the poet, the whore and the masseur, rejected and neglected outcasts of society, come together to provide emotional, physical and intellectual sanctuary to each other and present an oppositional moral superiority to the world of the allegedly 'respectable'.

Challenging the formation of the couple

Walker was perhaps the only comedian in the 1950s who was regularly privileged with a vibrant romantic pairing with a female partner that foregrounded his position in the narrative by providing him with a romantic trajectory 'that ran parallel to the main narrative' (Prasad 1998: 72). Although siphoned off as comedy, his comedic partnerships and eager love pursuits staged a different imagination of the modern couple in India that was starkly different from the framework within which the lead couple operated. The formation of the (heterosexual) couple in the 1950s was not just about a romantic, conjugal union as 'the modern state [was] present as only one of several patriarchal authorities competing for domination' and the couple was 'repeatedly reabsorbed into the parental patriarchal family and [was] committed to its maintenance' (95). Though the narrative trajectory of the principal couple involved an initial protest against the forces of tradition to stage hope of a new individuality, sexual and social relations, the films' and the protagonists' ideological matrix did not allow them to fully affirm themselves in this position (67).

Walker's romantic pairings led to a very different imagination of the modern couple. A scene from the thriller *C.I.D.* (Raj Khosla, 1956) shows him in the police station unhappily having to explain his presence at a newspaper office late at night. He is a petty thief who had hoped to steal a few typewriters but instead becomes the sole witness to a gruesome murder. He is in the middle of concocting an elaborate tale about being there to put in a matrimonial advertisement when his paramour (Kumkum) walks in and overhears him. Belligerent, she wastes no time in giving him a loud scolding while also attempting to beat him. He, in classic slapstick style, runs around the police desk, trying to protect himself while trying to extricate himself from his staged duplicity. One fist on hip, *sari* hitched up to her knees in the style of working-class women, her high-pitched voice screaming with little regard for the appropriateness of place or time, Kumkum is every bit the '"common" woman … coarse, loud, vulgar, quarrelsome' that nationalist discourses had identified as belonging to India's past that needed to be written out of the nationalist framework that was being formulated for the new, educated, domestic woman (Chatterjee 1997: 244). Walker, as a lying thief and publicly terrified of his lover, also presented a less-than-heroic figure. Together the pair stood for a comical but unique imagination of the everyday working-class couple, people who were trying to find ways to make ends meet, and who in the process sometimes found themselves on the wrong side of the law. Disparagingly written out from the nationalist discourse, these lower-class, working men and women surreptitiously re-entered the cinematic frame through the comedic track to challenge the idealized gender roles formulated through the principal couple to articulate more quotidian positions on love, romance, desire and sexuality.

In *Pyaasa* Sattar's romantic pursuit of Juhi (Kumkum), who is Gulabo's friend and a prostitute, forms a parallel structure with the Vijay–Gulabo romance. The film shows two encounters between Sattar and Juhi, in both Sattar trying to persuade Juhi to marry him. His sentimental and idealistic romantic overtures, in a rare reversal of conventional gender perspectives, are met with Juhi's cold, hard pragmatism. More than her refusal of his proposal it is their performances that invert normative gender expectations. Juhi's confident body language is exhibited in her pert, straight walk, the firm toss of her head as she dismisses Sattar and her crackling sharp voice that reprimands him for his foolishness. Sattar's pursuit, while ardent, is accompanied by a hesitant and embarrassed demeanour, and his 'proposal' of marriage is delivered while shyly and coyly biting his lower lip and demurely lowering his eyes (Figure 4.4). The dismantling of gender through performance inserts fissures in the nationalist perspectives that idealized women as educated but demure homemakers while men were expected to be the organizers and controllers of the public sphere (Chatterjee 1997: 233–53). Unlike the lead couple, Sattar and Juhi's gender definitions do not change as the film progresses. Their story remains incomplete but, because of its absence within the moral frameworks that eventually encircle the film's main couple, it becomes possible to imagine a space outside the film that possibly supports a more equitable gender relationship.

C.I.D., Pyaasa and several other films leave Walker's romantic trajectory incomplete. A rare exception to this is *Mr and Mrs 55* (1955), a film that plays with the themes of feminism, divorce, a marriage of convenience and love and stages the critique of a law that, for the first time, enabled the divorce of a Hindu marriage in 1955. The principal couple, Preetam (Guru Dutt) and Anita (Madhubala) have a marriage of convenience so that she may inherit her fortune according to the conditions stipulated by her father's will, but under a legal agreement that he

Figure 4.4 *Pyaasa* (The Thirsty One, Guru Dutt, 1957).

will divorce her at the end of one year. Anita's 'feminist' spinster aunt (Lalita Pawar) spearheads this project although Anita herself doesn't seem to mind being domesticated. Preetam and Anita, although seeming to challenge social norms by accepting an unconventional pact in an area usually considered sacrosanct, eventually move towards a resolution that is not only socially and culturally normative but one in which their embracing of the notions of conventional marriage and hard work 'enable them to function effectively and productively within the respected bourgeois Indian society they had previously contested' (Cooper 2005: 68). Preetam manages to convince Anita of his true love and of the benefits of marriage before the stipulated year is over and Anita settles into the docile role of a traditional Hindu housewife, submissively extolling the virtues of a wife and homemaker over all other female roles at the end of the film to silence her aunt's disappointment.

Preetam's friend Johnny (Walker)'s pursuit of Juhi (Yasmin), an attractive stenographer in his office, introduces a very different set of modernist challenges to the film. While the principal couple engage and disengage with the question of divorce, the secondary couple quietly stages an inter-religious alliance. Unlike Preetam and Anita, Johnny's Hindu identity and Juhi's Christian one does not cause any conflict in their relationship. The film's climax shows them arguing over whether to get married in church or in the registrar's office, not a conflict over their respective religious rituals. Although not definitive, this comes as close to a narrative resolution for Walker as any. The defiant couple leaves the narrative with the excitement that is part of the flux of social change, the dream of gender equality and an individuality that does not subscribe to nationalist ideology, all changing debates within the nation but rarely examined by cinematic narratives.

Walker's romantic pursuits open up space in the national imaginary for an alternative to the ideal couple of nationalism. The 'failure' of some of these pursuits, the incomplete stories and the doubt left in some of the narrative trajectories, signals a crisis of heroism and a failed masculinity that is denied by the rigid traditions of a patriarchal nationalism. Through Walker's designated trajectory of comedy, the repeated failure to form the couple, ambiguous love pursuits and unconsummated love relationships, the films introduce fissures to the dominant patriarchal framework and by embodying and refracting multiple post-independence Indian subjectivities Walker effectively fractures the homogenization attempted by the narratives as well as the nationalist project.

Conclusion

Barely representative of Walker's extensive oeuvre, the films discussed in this chapter aim to highlight his representation of the subaltern figure in the most iconic films of the 1950s. Marginalized and neglected in academic discourse, these figures stage a critique to the dominant nationalist imagination. By focusing on these epic narratives, the positions of the lead protagonists and a relational analysis of the intervention staged by Walker, this chapter provides an overview of the way Walker dismantled the principal nationalist structure in films to foreground different, playful, quirky and even contradictory positions of the epic ideological frameworks.

Works Cited

Chakravarty, Sumita S. (1993), *National Identity in Indian Popular Cinema 1947–1987*, Delhi: Oxford University Press.

Chatterjee, Partha (1997), 'The Nationalist Resolution to the Women's Question', in Kumkum Sangari and

Sudesh Vaid (eds), *Recasting Women: Essays in Colonial History*, 233–53, New Delhi: Kali for Women.

Cooper, Darius (2005), *In Black and White: Hollywood and the Melodrama of Guru Dutt*, Calcutta: Seagull Books.

Creekmur, Corey (2009), 'Pyaasa / Thirst', in Lalitha Gopalan (ed.), *The Cinema of India*, 106–12, London: Wallflower Press.

Das, Veena (2000), 'The Making of Modernity: Gender and Time in Indian Cinema', in Timothy Mitchell (ed.), *Questions of Modernity*, 166–88, Minneapolis: University of Minnesota Press.

Doraiswamy, Rashmi (2008), *Guru Dutt: Through Light and Shade*, New Delhi: Wisdom Tree.

Ghose, Sagarika (1997), 'Return of the Wit', *Outlook*, 11 June, online at: www.outlookindia.com/magazine/story/return-of-the-wit/203681 (accessed 10 August 2016).

Kabir, Nasreen Munni (2011), *The Dialogue of Pyaasa: Guru Dutt's Immortal Classic*, New Delhi: Om Books International.

Mishra, Vijay (2002), *Bollywood Cinema: Temples of Desire*, New York: Routledge.

Narwekar, Sanjit (2005), *Eena Meena Deeka: The Story of Hindi Film Comedy*, New Delhi: Rupa.

Prakash, Gyan (1999), *Another Reason: Science and the Imagination of Modern India*, Princeton, NJ: Princeton University Press.

Prasad, M. Madhava (1998), *Ideology of the Hindi Film: A Historical Construction*, New Delhi: Oxford University Press.

Prasad, M. Madhava (2004), 'Realism and Fantasy in Representations of Metropolitan Life in Indian Cinema', in Preben Kaarsholm (ed.), *City Flicks: Indian Cinema and the Urban Experience*, 83–99, Calcutta: Seagull.

Rajadhyaksha, Ashish and Paul Willemen, eds ([1994] 1999), *Encyclopedia of Indian Cinema*, London: British Film Institute; New Delhi: Oxford University Press.

Shedde, Meenakshi (2003), 'Walker developed his own unique brand of humour', *Times of India*, 29 July, online at: http://timesofindia.indiatimes.com/entertainment/hindi/bollywood/news/Walker-developed-his-own-unique-brand-of-humour/articleshow/101573.cms (accessed 15 August 2016).

Thomas, Rosie (2006), 'Indian Cinema: Pleasures and Popularity', in Dimitris Eleftheriotis and Gary Needham (eds), *Asian Cinemas: A Reader and Guide*, 280–94, Edinburgh: Edinburgh University Press.

Vasudevan, Ravi S. (1989), 'The Melodramatic Mode and the Commercial Hindi Cinema: Notes on Film History, Narrative and Performance in the 1950s', *Screen*, 30 (3): 29–50.

Vasudevan, Ravi S. (1994), 'Dislocations: The Cinematic Imagining of a New Society in 1950s India', *Oxford Literary Review*, 16 (1): 93–124.

Vasudevan, Ravi S. (2006), 'Addressing the Spectator of a Third World National Cinema: The Bombay Social Film of the 1940s and 1950s', in Dimitris Eleftheriotis and Gary Needham (eds), *Asian Cinemas: A Reader and Guide*, 295–316, Edinburgh: Edinburgh University Press.

Vasudevan, Ravi S. (2010), *The Melodramatic Public: Film Form and Spectatorship in Indian Cinema*, Ranikhet: Permanent Black.

Wilkinson-Weber, Clare M. (2014), *Fashioning Bollywood: The Making and Meaning of Hindi Film Costume*, London: Bloomsbury.

Chapter 5

Dharmendra Singh Deol: Masculinity and the late-Nehruvian hero in Hindi cinema
Anustup Basu

Introduction

I intend to use the durable stardom of Dharmendra Singh Deol (1935–), particularly his early years, as a tracking device to make a few genealogical observations about masculine figures in late-Nehruvian Hindi cinema. The actor, for the most part, has been a 'gun for hire' for more than five decades, featuring in close to three hundred films. Even in his peak years, this major leading man did not seriously explore an entrepreneurial path to congeal and nurture a fixed screen persona. He did not 'plan' his career like some of his contemporaries, even after acquiring the cultural capital to do so. He was, by his own admission, not too selective in terms of scripts, production houses or directors (see Anon. 1965; Anon. 1969). He refrained from using a home production banner to cultivate and sustain a particular screen image through made-to-order projects as in the cases of Raj Kapoor (the tramp), Dev Anand (the urban Romeo/rogue) or Manoj Kumar (the patriotic Mr Bharat). Dharmendra was a mass actor whose aura was not founded on rarity of screen appearances or exclusivity of films.[1] The errant departures as well as accidental consolidations that mark his overall career therefore illustrate the nodal shifts and chaotic experiments in the terrain of Hindi cinema itself.

As a star for all seasons, Dharmendra has been widely eclectic in terms of personas, genres and indeed industries, moving from A-list blockbusters to B- and C-grade potboilers aimed at rural belts of the north and then, later in his career, to prestige, multiplex projects such as *Johnny Gaddar* (Sriram Raghavan, 2007) and *Life in a Metro* (Anurag Basu, 2007). In the post-independence, post-studio decades dominated by fly-by-night producers, some family firms such as the Chopras or the Kapoors, and a dictatorial distributor class, he has been one of the prolific lead players with more than half a dozen annual releases during peak years. There have been other actors such as Jeetendra, Shashi Kapoor, Mithun Chakravarty or Govinda with such dizzying numbers. However, unlike them, Dharmendra was not, until the decade of the 1980s, called upon to settle on a singular, predominant screen persona that could be exploited with assembly-line tenacity in formula pictures.

This is not to say that Dharmendra has never been slotted into heroic typologies. The most paradigmatic one is indeed that of the 'Garam Dharam' – the action star of the angry 1970s with perhaps the first consciously sexualized male body of the Indian

---

[1] Dharmendra never directed a film; apart from the odd *Satyakam* (Hrishikesh Mukherjee, 1969), as a producer he has been largely focused on establishing and then periodically reviving the careers of his sons Sunny and Bobby Deol.

screen. But there have been others. Dharmendra's screen presence retained a malleable quality (especially during the first two decades of his career) that allowed him to switch personas from film to film in a synchronous manner and also to evolve diachronically and fit into the next sociopolitical climate, cult of masculinity and filmic trend. It could actually be argued that he ended up playing a greater spectrum of heroic types and with greater frequency than any of his peers, even more than Dilip Kumar (interspersing 'tragedy king' duties with comic swashbucklers such as *Aan* [Savage Princess, Mehboob Khan, 1952]*, Azaad* [Sriramulu Naidu SM, 1955] and *Kohinoor* [S. U. Sunny, 1960]) or Amitabh Bachchan (the 'Angry Young Man' films as well as mass comedies and social melodramas such as *Amar Akbar Anthony* [Manmohan Desai, 1977] and *Abhimaan* [Pride, Hrishikesh Mukherjee, 1973]).[2] Apart from the unplanned nature of his career, this was also due to Dharmendra's surprising range of melodramatic expression, which seems to have been recognized only in retrospect.[3] When it was called for he could turn on an effortless urban naturalism in front of the camera marked by, amongst other things, a clean-cut, conventional handsomeness, muscularity, clear Hindusthani/Urdu diction and sharp comic timing, and this was exploited in a series of urban middle-class reformist socials by directors such as Bimal Roy and Hrishikesh Mukerjee. In other films, sometimes of the same period, he could convincingly deliver the lowbrow, high-voltage expressive melodrama riding heterosexual appeal and agrarian machismo that was solicited by makers such as Manmohan Desai and Rajkumar Kohli.[4]

Dharmendra has therefore delivered *major* critical and box-office successes across an amazing spectrum of genres: the woman-centred melodrama (*Bandini* [Prisoner, Bimal Roy, 1963] and *Phool Aur Patthar* [The Flower and the Stone, O. P. Ralhan, 1966]), the literary reformist social (*Devar* [Brother-in-law, Mohan Sehgal, 1966], *Majhli Didi* [The Middle Sister, Hrishikesh Mukherjee, 1967] and *Naya Zamana* [New Age, Pramod Chakrovorty, 1971]), the war film (*Haqeeqat* [Reality, Chetan Anand, 1964] and *Lalkaar* [Clarion Call, Ramanand Sagar, 1972]), the suspense thriller (*Shikaar* [The Hunt, Atma Ram, 1968] and *Kab? Kyoon? Aur Kahan?* [When, Why? And Where? Arjun Hingorani, 1970]), the feudal family romance *(Aya Sawan Jhoom Ke* [Monsoons, Raghunath Jhalani, 1969], *Anupama* [Hrishikesh Mukherjee, 1966] and the Bond-inspired spy film (*Aankhen* [Eyes, Ramanand Sagar 1968], *Yakeen* [Conviction, Brij, 1969] and *Keemat* [Price, Ravikant Nagaich, 1973]), the dacoit film (*Mera Gaon Mera Desh* [My Village, My Country, Raj Khosla, 1971], *Sholay* [Embers, Ramesh Sippy, 1975] and *Pratigya* [Promise, Dulal Guha, 1975]), *Dream Girl* [Pramod Chakravorty, 1977]), the folklorish costume drama (*Dharam Veer,* Manmohan Desair, 1977), the caped crusader adventure (*Jugnu* [Spark, Pramod Charkravorty, 1973] and *Khatron ke Khiladi* [Play with Danger, T. Rama Rao, 1988]), the portmanteau-style lost and found entertainer (*Yaadon ki Baraat* [Procession

---

[2]This of course pertains to Bachchan's career up to the mid-1990s as a conventional leading man. He has played a greater variety of roles as a character actor in the multiplex era.
[3]For an insightful appraisal see Kesavan 2008.
[4]More than anything else, it is this exchange between a bourgeois realism and the snarling, high-pitched theatrical mode that was on display in the real person/star dialectic in Mukherjee's middle-brow ethnographic look at the Hindi film industry in *Guddi* (1970). This was a film in which Dharmendra plays himself, as a star gamely helping to cure a young fan's obsession with his screen image. He 'appears' as his own self in the naturalistic style and switches to the mass-actorial mode in the 'filming within the film' scenes where he is seen to be shooting.

of Memories, Nasir Hussain, 1973] and *Chacha Bhatija* [Uncle and Nephew, Manmohan Desair, 1977]), comedies high- and lowbrow (*Chupke Chupke* [The Prank, Hrishikesh Mukhejee, 1975] and *Naukar Biwi Ka* [The Wife's Servant, Rajkumar Kohli, 1983]), the western (*Jagir* [Estate, Pramod Chakravorty, 1984]), the underworld film (*Qayamat* [Apocalypse, Raj N. Sippy, 1983] and *Hathyar* [Weapon, J. P. Dutta, 1989]) and, indeed, dozens of populist actioners that dominated the years leading up to and following the Emergency, from the 1968 superhit *Aankhen* to 1989's *Elaan-E-Jung* (Call of War, Anil Sharma). As a matter of fact, apart from teenage love stories, the horror film, Muslim socials and generic musicals, where his infamous lack of dancing skills would have been a hindrance, there has hardly been a major template of Hindi commercial cinema that the Jat actor has not touched successfully.

And yet, this perennial star was never the defining screen persona of an age, the way Raj Kapoor or Dilip Kumar were emblematic of the Nehru era, Amitabh Bachchan of the angry Emergency period, and Shah Rukh Khan the primal face of the psychosis, the irascibility and the awry energies of globalization. Dharmendra remained a major star without ever creating a 'wave' like the ephemeral hysteria around Rajesh Khanna in the early 1970s or the 'rebel' run of Shammi Kapoor a decade earlier. Another noteworthy feature about this 'long distance' and multifaceted stardom is the fact that it was achieved without any special critical recognition of actorial powers at the time. Dharmendra was never seriously regarded as a thespian, either by the film industry itself or by the press. He never won an acting award in his entire career; he rarely received specially designed 'author-backed' scripts to showcase larger-than-life star performances as happened with the megastars Dilip Kumar and Amitabh Bachchan, and even with stars with lesser wattage but greater acknowledged acting credentials, such as Sanjeev Kumar.

The many avatars

Dharmendra's entry into the world of Hindi films is stuff of legend, much akin to the 'girl next to the soda fountain' story of the rise of Lana Turner from ordinary obscurity to classic movie stardom.[5] Unlike the thousands of young men and women who have come to the city of Mumbai down the ages to lead the life of the proverbial industry struggler, Dharmendra was discovered.[6] He was born in Ludhiana in the year 1935 and grew up in a small village called Sahnewal in East Punjab. His strict school headmaster father disapproved of movie culture and Dharmendra thus saw his first film when he was well into his teens. But by the time he had passed his college intermediate examinations and was working as an assistant driller in an American tubewell company, Dharmendra was strongly taken up by the desire to act. He confided in his mother who, blissfully unaware of the industry's modes, advised him to send an 'application' for the job. That, in essence, was what happened. In 1959, the 24-year-old Dharmendra visited a professional photographer to take some pictures of him and then replied to an advertisement

---

[5] See Dyer, for instance, on the soda fountain girl ([1979] 1998: 42). The mythography of 'rags to riches' as a distinctly American theme of course does not apply here punctually as a credo, since, as I elaborate further, the class ascension and wealth that comes with cinema are also seen to be alienating and corrupting.

[6] This story has been recounted many times by the star himself, in his earliest press interviews as well as recent television engagements. See, for instance, Anon. 1961; Anon. 1963; and Anon. 1971.

for a national talent search published in *Filmfare*. Dharmendra won the contest and was sent a first-class ticket to come to the city then known as Bombay. He was featured on the cover of *Filmfare* (20 November 1959) along with four other star aspirants. Within a short time, the young man was working in the Bombay industry, despite doubts about whether he was too muscular and brawny to fit into the then dominant 'soft and poetic' cast of the Hindi film hero.[7] It was also quite well known from the onset that the fresh new romantic hero of Hindi cinema was already a married man with children.[8]

There are a few interesting sides to this particular genesis story. That is, if we keep in mind how social origins of a spectral screen persona have traditionally been tailored and sometimes fabricated. This perhaps has been all the more true for cultural, ethnic or class 'outsiders', be it the former chain-gang member with a dangerous depression-era childhood who became the face of film noir in Robert Mitchum; the son of a Jewish emigre 'ragman' from Belarus who changed his name from Issur Danielovich to Kirk Douglas; or Yul Brynner, who touted his fictitious Mongol parentage to the Hollywood press. For Dharmendra, it was an abiding insistence on his *Dehati* son-of-the-soil roots, reiterated in thousands of press stories and interviews across the decades and indeed, most famously, in Mukherjee's *Guddi*. In an early cover story interview to *Filmfare* in 1964, for instance, Dharmendra announces his feeling of alienation not just towards the industry, but the city itself, which he finds artificial and stifling. Rather than suggesting a continuity between reality and the screen image, the article points out that it was a rather 'placid' and 'lumbering' man who transforms into a 'dynamic, strikingly agile person' in front of the camera (Anon. 1964). In another interview the following year the 'shy, unsophisticated, somewhat inarticulate peasant boy' who was by then a bona fide box office sensation declared that driving a car made him feel more like a mechanic than a prince (Anon. 1965).

Despite the general habitation of his screen figure in the alluring but profane mise en scènes of the modern, it is this ontological pull of a pastoral naissance that perhaps restores Dharmendra to a state of pristine innocence all the time. It is supposed to absolve the man on screen from his urban embroilments and the many prodigal narratives he wanders into. The man-child relentlessly returns to the wheat fields of Punjab only to step into the artifice of the city and the film yet again. If cine stardom can indeed be understood to some extent in terms of a Weberian political charisma (Dyer [1979] 1998: 30–1) or the notion of a

---

[7]See for instance Raheja 2002. Raheja mentions that in those early days a director apparently looked at the screen test of the hero and advised him that he would be better off playing hockey.

[8]I cite this biography in a spirit of partial allegiance to Dyer's classic study. I am sympathetic to his critiques of Barry King, Herbert Marcuse and others of a culture industry of stardom in which the phenomenon is understood in terms of a pure liberal democratic increase of social mobility into positions of expressive power wholly unconnected to sacred institutions and the concomitant production of a marketable human emptiness ([1979] 1998: 8–13). Indeed, stars cannot be totally manufactured. Instead, stardom is a perpetual set of exchanges between the star as real person and the star as image. This is a complex process in which scandal (Fatty Arbuckle, Ingrid Bergman) can eviscerate or actually deepen the image. However, for reasons I do not have the space to elaborate on here, I find Dyer's admirable and necessary attempts to integrate a sociological understanding of stardom with the semiotic one a bit formalistic in the final instance. Neepa Majumdar's *Wanted Cultured Ladies Only!* (2009) is an insightful study about how the cultural technology of stardom was different in India. For a long time it did not involve scandals, elaborate fashion industries or conspicuous consumption as it did in the West. The star text in India had to be a discourse of 'surface' rather than any 'inner essence' of the performer. See Majumdar 2009: 1–8 and esp. 139–40 for an elaboration of this difference.

psychological automaton that Deleuze memorably borrowed from Bergson and Benjamin, this origin aura is a key feature of the Dharmendra phenomenon. It is inherent in the manner in which his screen image was shaped over the decades and in the way it was reinforced by celebrity culture. It was a composite real/virtual figure that was capable of eternal returns. The spectral *Dehati* served as an ontological constant in hundreds of movie adventures across a profane world and its staggering and estranging paraphernalia. He was the son-of-the-soil who could be trusted to make the unhappy yet historically inevitable journey through the modern. This aura of the boy from Sohnewal sometimes accorded the star figure extreme licenses in elemental moral fables, especially when he played murderers and rapists in *Karishma Kudrat Kaa* (Miracle of Nature, Sunil Hingorani, 1985) or *Paap Ki Aandhi* (Storm of Sin, Mehul Kumar, 1991).

A feature that is concomitant to the agrarian innocence and patrimony of the village school master's son is the relative silence about his education and cultural training seen from the vantage point of the modern. That is, it was never spelled out to what extent his intermediate education was tied to an urban-industrial pedagogy of nationalist becoming in the Nehruvian era or to what degree he was prepared to deal with the sophistry and circumspection of the wider world. In an era in which the film industry was trying to gain bourgeois respectability, this was in stark contrast to film magazines touting Raj Kapoor or Dilip Kumar's British public-school education, or Dev Anand and Sunil Dutt's college degrees as markers of lineage, urbanity and culture. Dharmendra, unlike Shashi Kapoor or Rajesh Khanna, did not boast of any professional or amateur experience on stage. There were no photo features about him and his intellectual pursuits, like Ashok Kumar and his paintings, chess or homeopathy, or Bharat Bhushan inside his legendary library.

It was as if the Bombay star was immaculately born in the heartland of the nation. This emanation remained constant, even though Dharmendra made a career out of playing vanguard professionals, intellectuals and bureaucrats of Nehruvian development: the doctor (*Bandini*), engineer (*Satyakam; Aadmi Aur Insaan* [Man and Humanity, Yash Chopra, 1969]), barrister (*Mamta*, [Affection, Asit Sen, 1966]), chartered accountant (*Mere Hamdam Mere Dost* [My soulmate, My Friend, Amar Kumar, 1968]), banker (*Jeevan Mrityu* [Life and Death, Satyen Bose, 1970]), psychiatrist (*Baharon Ki Manzil* [The House of Spring, Yakub Hassan Rizvi, 1968]), professor (Botany in *Chupke Chupke*, Sanskrit in *Dillagi* [The Affair, Basu Chatterjee, 1968]), publisher (*Begaana* [Alien, Sadashiv Rao Kavi, 1963]), newspaper editor (*Baharen Phir Bhi Aayengi* [Springs Still Return, Shaheed Latif, 1966]), poet (*Ek Mahal Ho Sapnon Ka* [Let There be a Mansion of Dreams, Devendra Ogel, 1975]), novelist (*Anupama; Naya Zamana* [Pramod Chakravorty, 1971] and *Phagun* [Rajinder Singh Bedi, 1973]), and then entrepreneur (*Akashdeep* [Phani Majumdar, 1965]) as well as the labour leader (*Resham Ki Dori* [The Thread of Silk, Atma Ram, 1974]). When it came to defending the nation, apart from the soldiers, secret agents mentioned above and a legion of police officers, Dharmendra essayed the customs officer in *Dil Kaa Heera* (Diamond of the Heart, Dulal Guha, 1979) and the forest ranger in *Kartavya* (Duty, Mohan Sehgal, 1979). Apart from a few exceptions, the occupational trappings of these men were not decorative; they were essential to the thrust of epic reformist sagas about the coming into being of not just institutions but also the postcolonial state itself. In *Pratigya* he inaugurates the police station in a landscape of lawlessness; in *Kartavya* it is the forest office.

Occasional elite sniggers about his English accent notwithstanding, Dharmendra was 'accepted' in these roles over the decades.[9] That is, for the most part, it was acknowledged by the industry and the press, as well as by middle-class audiences that the portrayals of nation-building characters had crossed a critical threshold of being 'sincere' and 'believable'. Yet the general acknowledgement of 'authenticity' came with a rider of indulgence. There was an endearing duality in the performance: it was, in the final instance, unmistakably a 'shy, unsophisticated, somewhat inarticulate peasant boy' playing the urban, sometimes foreign-returned Nehruvian hero (see Anon. 1965). This sense of 'play' between actor and character – between a 'pan-Indian' industrial progressivism of the new order and its earthy, regional inflexion – was crucial to the Dharmendra charm. It was a brave new naturalizing proximity between two worlds but also a necessary working separation in the locus of the performance itself between the ethical mass of the *volk* and the works of an often distant Anglophone state.[10]

Meanwhile the off-screen Dharmendra of gossip tabloids and the general public realm remained a resolute bulwark of 'tradition' amidst the profanity of show business. The women of the extended Deol family that he headed were never allowed to step into the limelight. On this matter as well as other sundry things such as whether his sons should have arranged marriages or whether his daughters should act in films, he continued to espouse chauvinistic caste-based Hindu values. During the early 1970s, especially after the appearance of the tabloid *Stardust*, the Hindi film gossip industry evolved from what Majumdar has called the 'innuendo' format of the past, perhaps best exemplified by vernaculars such as *Mayapuri* and Baburao Patel's *Filmindia* (see Majumdar 2009: esp. chs. 1 and 2). This was the period in which film journalism changed from a dry, proto-bourgeois shepherding of culture to scoops, sensational exposes and stronger innuendos in terms of sleaze count. The public star-image of Dharmendra thus transformed from the squeaky-clean country boy with suits and Impalas to the hard-drinking Lothario. The gossip columns were agog with rumours of his many affairs. And yet, even his famous second marriage to co-star Hema Malini and a reported conversion to Islam to facilitate the union could not quite eclipse the aura of the *Dehati* from Sohnewal.

The films dominated by women

Dharmendra began his career in the early 1960s working primarily in reformist socials. He was a late Nehruvian hero, following not so much the footsteps of the iconic triumvirate Raj, Dilip and Dev but tracing a more studied Bengali literary modernism epitomized in the earlier decade by Balraj Sahni and the two Dutts, Guru and Sunil.[11]

---

[11]By this notion of literariness I do imply a certain realistic-sociological template of storytelling, a certain gesture towards interiority, autonomy and motivation in drawing up characters – indeed, a brave novelization of the universes of legend and theodicy, but not necessarily brought home and confined within a stable ego and perspective of the individual subject.
[9]This observation, of course, in an age of limited television and radio reach, pertains only to the literate classes.
[10]Prasad's exemplary reading of the South Indian male stardoms of M. G. Ramachandran, N. T. Rama Rao and Raj Kumar among others speaks of an affectional pushback against the 'Trojan horse' of the Anglophone state by the colonial class and 'identification' based on an aspirational/utopian politics rather than one based on real interests (2014: 28–78). Prasad calls this living without 'traditional leadership' in a new post-independence dispensation where the king is gone and the new state is distant. Prasad's political reading is thus quite different from what Dyer discusses and critiques as 'compensation' in a commodity form and a Horatio Alger effect ([1979] 1998: 28).

Dharmendra's work as the idealist crusader can be broadly divided into two phases. In the first one he featured in a series of 'women-centred' melodramas in which established actresses such as Mala Sinha, Waheeda Rehman, Nutan and the peerless Meena Kumari – undoubtedly the queen of this genre – played the principal protagonists. *Bandini, Phool Aur Patthar* and *Anupama* would be the noteworthy films in this set. In the second phase, Dharmendra, a bigger star by the late 1960s, featured in a series of reformist socials where he played the main character himself. In this series one could include films such as *Izzat* (Honor, T. Prakash Rao, 1968), *Satyakam, Sharafat* (Courteousness, Asit Sen, 1970), *Naya Zamana* and *Dost* (Friend, Dulal Guha, 1974).

The figure of the woman, as supreme ethical instantiation of nationhood, is rendered imperiled and devoid of shelter in the films where the narrative has her at the centre. She is either caught between forces of capitalist transition and feudal recidivism, between law and custom, or in the middle of a generational conflict between the old and the new that takes unrest from the public sphere to the heart of domesticity itself. The matter of contention could be female literacy (*Anpadh* [The Illiterate, Mohan Kumar, 1962]), female infertility (*Chandan Ka Palna* [The Sandalwood Cradle, Ismail Memon, 1967]), dowry (*Shaadi* [Marriage, Krishnan-Panju, 1962]), bigamy (*Bandini*), marital compatibility (*Devar*), bloodline and caste (*Ganga Ki Lehren* [The Tides of the Ganges, Devi Sharma, 1964], *Mamta* and *Satyakaam*), premarital sex and pregnancy (*Begaana* [Ambrish Sangal, 1986]), justice and restitution for rape victims (*Dulhan ek Raat Ki* [Bride for a Night, D. D. Kashyap, 1967] and *Satyakam*) or the question of widow remarriage (*Purnima* [Narendra Suri, 1965] and *Phool aur Patthar*). These narratives take place in an elemental landscape where the errant powers of the historical test, suspend or weakly affirm promises of mythic restitution. The institutions of old fathers decay and lose their sacred natures and gods seem to be in twilight; enterprises of new sons bear promises of radical change but they too are embroiled in a profane that spells agoraphobia and anxiety. Elsewhere I have theorized this form of melodrama as *assemblages* in which emotional and discursive diagrams of 'tradition' and modernity enter into dynamic arrangements of conflict, mutation, attraction or recoil (see Basu 2010: esp. ch. 1). There are indeed restoring powers of Dharma at play in a historical field of problems, just as there are weak administrations of the state, but the sensationalist, catalyzing forces *in between* come in awry forms: accidents, amnesia, madness, *doppelgängers*, eruptive violence, natural catastrophes, orphanhood, dereliction and death. These are often matters that neither Dharma nor man-made law can thread into a stable narrative of constitution.[12] A general apocalyptic temporality – Bhaskar Sarkar has insightfully theorized this as a delayed psychosis of loss, mourning and homelessness pertaining to the primal event of the Partition – tends to inform movements and rites of passage (2009).

There are a few crucial qualities about the performance of the male supporting player in the woman-centred melodrama. The hero who is sensitive and sympathetic to the 'new' travails of the woman has to lodge himself in the very fissures of a patriarchal edifice undergoing customary decay as well as reconstruction. His stance is that of a principled endurance of pain and timely absorption of anxiety. Yet, if melodrama is

---

[12]I am, of course, alluding to the notion of *sutra* as a cosmic principle.

about a theatre of retreat into an inner sanctum of homeliness in the face of public perils, in classical Hindi cinema this recoil is to the sphere of community or the extended family rather than to the psyche of the individual subject or the private domain of the couple. The interplay between propositions and affectations thus has to be on the 'surface' and cannot be jettisoned into the confines of the autochthonous mind where traumas, pathologies or drives take over, as happens in Fritz Lang, Alfred Hitchcock or Douglas Sirk films. The 'internal' storm has to surface at every step in the form of flashbacks, nightmares, reveries, delusions, doublings, utopian or dystopian musical departures and simply extended imaginary scenarios. Apart from the usual *Awaara* (Vagabond, Raj Kapoor, 1951)-style totemic song sequences, scenes of characters expressing internal conflict by talking to their mirror images in *Andaaz* (Style, Mehboob Khan, 1949) and *Shree 420* (Gentleman Cheat, Raj Kapoor, 1955) or the classic star 'doubles' in *Anhonee* (The Uncanny, K. A. Abbas, 1952) or *Ram Aur Shyam* (Chanakya, 1967), here one can recall rarer but even more radical devices such as the extended climax of *Teen Devian* (Three Ladies, Amar Jeet, 1965) where the hero (Dev Anand), in consecutive sequences, imagines married life with each of the three women he is courting.[13]

This surface registering of principled endurance and negotiated acceptance of change, the constant melodramatic movement from the actual to the virtual, calls for a special idiom of performance and indeed different terms of engagement when it comes to measuring authenticity or the (subjective) integrity of the character drawn up. In the 'woman's picture' Dharmendra usually played educated, sensitive individuals who purportedly served as resonating devices or lightning rods for the sufferings, voices, as well as the silences of the female protagonist. Within the auspices of this melodramatic dispensation, this masculine figure had to respire under a divided sky of meaning. It was a world marked by split temporalities between fathers and sons. The hero had to absorb counteracting memories and gravitations pertaining to ethics and feeling. The Dharmendra persona had to endure the all-too-human or society-impelled frailties of the woman, the fatal and absolutist historical blindness of older generations as well as crippling dilemmas that were his own. The 'truthful' and candid presentation of such conundrums, as I have suggested earlier, for the most part, did not involve the internalization of these tensions (knowledge, cognition, law and disaffection) and their external manifestation as psychological or behaviourist signatures of method acting.[14] Rather, it involved the immersion of the self into an entire cosmology of naturalist and expressive forces.

Consider, for instance, the climax of *Begaana* (Sadashiv J. Row Kavi, 1963), one of the early Dharmendra starrers. Seema is a young girl who is rendered pregnant by her lover Deepak, who subsequently goes missing. She delivers a son who is then given up for adoption. Bowing to family pressures, Seema then gets married to Prakash

---

[13]See Ravi Vasudevan's reading of the 'mirror conversation' in *Andaz* (1989: 42–3) and Virdi's elaboration of the same in *Shree 420* (2003: 94–5). See also Basu 2010: 40.

[14]Christine Gledhill (1991) understands this as a special mode of stars in the West functioning as rhetorical systems that work as melodrama. Critically transposing the works of Thomas Elsaesser and Peter Brooks among others, she points out that while melodrama invents emblematic personages that incarnate ideological conflicts and, in the process, domesticate them within the realm of private emotions, it is an 'internalization' that is necessarily made external. The tribulations of the private have to be made external so that they can take over the affectional and discursive space. Paradoxically, therefore, as Peter Brooks puts it, there is no psychology in melodrama, rather it is always a melodrama of psychology. See Majumdar's discussion of this theme (2009: 139–40).

(Dharmendra), an idealist young publisher. Seema is happy in her marriage, but because of a series of fateful coincidences, both her long lost son and lover re-enter her life. She comes to know that Keshu, the adoptee of the family next door, is actually her own. Deepak turns out to be an old friend of her husband's. He is given a job as well as shelter by Prakash. The melodrama moves with the usual workings of triangulated desire, Seema's feelings of anxiety and guilt and Prakash's increasing suspicions.

In the end, Prakash devises a method to test the loyalties of his wife and friend. He tells Seema that he is leaving for Delhi for a few days and leaves the house. His departure is followed by a sequence in which Seema, by now at the end of her tether, has a nightmare. It begins with a shot of her asleep in bed while some past sentences uttered by her husband fill the soundtrack. Many of these statements were enigmatic ('You should lead a free existence for a while', 'One should never live in fear', 'Wish you best of luck') but originally delivered in a genial, everyday manner. Here they increase in sharpness, volume, urgency and ironic accentuation. Seema then dreams that she confesses her past to Prakash. Prakash is stunned by the revelation. His face hardens; he tellingly turns his back on Seema and exits the frame. The frame closes in on Seema, holding her in a tightened close-up. A despondent Seema accuses her husband of being close-minded. She says that in modern times even courtesans, widows and rape victims could, with love and sacrifice, enter the sacred relationship of marriage.

Seema then wakes up to realize that she had been dreaming. Following that, her former lover Deepak arrives in the scene. He declares that Prakash is Seema's husband only by law and convenience. It is he who is her true and original love. In the altercation that follows, Seema declares that it is only her husband Prakash who has rights over her; no weight of the past can sever their bonds of marriage. Then, in a remarkable departure from usual conventions of motherhood, she reveals to Deepak that Keshu is his son. She tells him that he should leave forever and take *his* son with him.

This conversation is overheard by Prakash when he returns, presumably to catch Seema and Deepak red-handed. After the revelation, Prakash slaps Deepak, goes to the next room and flails his arms, throwing down his cigarette. He stands in front of an open window. The elemental turmoil in his being is by then already externalized in a classic form of Hindi film melodrama. A storm rages outside and hits Deepak's face, largely turned away from the camera in a mid-long shot. It is an absorption/introspection image that assembles a figure as well as a tempestuous cosmology. It is a caesura in the melodramatic flow; it is a pause for the maturation and settling of emotions. However, this actual moment of repose before the denouement has already imbibed ethical pressures from the virtual dream sequence seen earlier, where Seema makes a passionate plea for a more tolerant and understanding patriarchal order. The dream was not a part of Prakash's subjective world, but both the virtual and actual movements that contribute to an exorcism of the past belong to the same cosmology of being.

After Deepak's exit, Seema enters the room and asks for forgiveness in a much more muted manner compared to the dream. Prakash tells her that she has done him a grave injustice by not telling him earlier so that he could have allayed all her fears and protected her from suffering and anxiety. He says that she had selfishly monopolized all the pain while extending love and happiness to others. He decides to adopt the suffering orphan Keshu and raise him as his own son.

More often than not, there is thus no actual voice of the woman in the woman's film. What she enunciates is the ventriloquism of the softer, eternally evolving and tolerating patriarchy. Standing between her and more inclement fathers, the heroic task of the understanding man is thus to let this ghostly voice passing through the figure of the possessed and disconsolate woman seep into his being. He has to either make it his own or reveal that it was already his own. This has to occur by way of stormy absorption and endurance before it can be ratified and accepted in a new familial arrangement.

In terms of star performance, it is necessary to play out the extremes of patriarchal reaction. Dharmendra has to set up the hydraulics of the melodrama by enacting both parts sequentially – the inclement, absolutist husband in the dream, as well as the sensitive and understanding one in real life. The virtual role he assumes in the nightmare, his actual stormy moment of stoic absorption and the final acceptance of an irrevocably novelized temporal scenario (the wife is steadfastly committed to the strictures of tradition at present; she is, what old tradition would call, a fallen woman). This dualism of a historical post-independence masculinity, as well as passages of poetic endurance, is central to Dharmendra's performances in the reformist social. In differential measures therefore, all such roles are essentially 'double' roles because they involve a staging of the patriarchal bipolar and not an assimilation of the conflict into an integrated subjectivity. This can be seen in various forms in films such as *Bandini* (where his beloved, a convicted murderer, leaves him for her bigamous husband), *Majhli Didi* (where his wife attempts to walk out on him and the extended family to nurture an abandoned child) or *Dulhan Ek Raat Ki* (an adaption of Thomas Hardy's *Tess of the d'Urbervilles*, with Dharmendra essaying the character based on Angel Clare). Among other things, the task of absorption required a critical femininization of a male figure with an evidently powerful physical presence.[15] This was perhaps most apparent in the half a dozen or so films Dharmendra did with the thespian Meena Kumari in the 1960s. She was a much bigger star whose 'screen age' was much greater than his by the time they were cast together. There was a strong Oedipal undercurrent in the pairing, between the nurturing woman who possesses an ethical being that is steadfast and yet severely tested by the historical, and the greenhorn who listened, absorbed and transformed. In *Phool Aur Patthar*, perhaps their most commercially successful film, Meena Kumari plays an abandoned widow who has been sheltered by a petty criminal called Raka (Dharmendra). At one point in the film she slaps him for his crimes and his drunkenness. Raka endures the slap and laments the fact that he, as an orphan, never had a mother to punish him when he was picking up bad habits as a child.

The twilight of the late-Nehruvian

The same stance of endurance and 'soft' navigation between the old and the new can be seen in the later reformist socials of Dharmendra's career, such as *Anupama, Satyakam, Resham ki Dori, Jwar Bhata* (The Tides, Adurthi Subha Rao, 1973) or *Dost*. In these films, unlike the earlier ones, Dharmendra plays more of the principal protagonist rather than the keen absorber of the female voice.

---

[15]Majumdar talks about early stardom in the Indian context as essentially gendered and feminine in relation to wider national cultural politics, including, for instance, that of K. L. Saigal. Cinema had to be feminized in and of itself because it had to be moral (2009: 10, 61–2). Interestingly, Sumita S. Chakravarty also says that the emblematic hero of the 1950s had an androgynous quality (1993: 146).

The 'lateness' of his Nehruvianism – in the years following Nehru's death, the wars with China and Pakistan, the abiding agrarian crisis, Maoist insurgencies and the great dismantling of that post-independence consensual base Rajni Kothari (1970) called the 'Congress' System – can be felt in many ways. Enduring the vicissitudes of the historical becomes a stoic, unforgivingly dark undertaking in most films, in sharp contrast to the sunny post-independence optimism that is eventually affirmed (even after detours through crime or starvation) in Raj Kapoor or Dev Anand's landmark works of the 1950s. In contrast, the Dharmendra figure acquires an almost schizophrenic dimension in his commitment to truth in a film such as *Satyakam*. Unlike his cinematic ancestors – even the lovable rogues in *Shree 420*, *Kalabazaar* (Black Market, Vijay Anand, 1960) or *House No. 44* (M. K. Barman, 1955) – who have vibrant street communities around them, his is a battle that is stark and lonely. It ends with defeat in all worldly affairs, cancer-induced aphasic silence and eventually death. In *Jwar Bhata*, the late-Nehruvian is declared insane and hauled to court. In *Dost*, the hero Manav lives up to his name and professes a universal humanism that integrates the visions of the major faiths. Driven to utter despondency by starvation and unemployment, he attempts suicide.

This abjectly isolated latecomer to a Nehruvian ethos is also denied axiomatic powers of reconnaissance and diagnosis. That is, he is unable to participate in a kind of wide-eyed moral anthropology of the nation that was often the hallmark of the merry tramp-like figure popularized by Raj Kapoor in films such as *Shree 420*, *Jagte Raho* (Stay Awake, Amit Maitra and Shambhu Mitra, 1956), *Anari* (The Simpleton, Hrishikesh Mukherjee, 1959) or *Shriman Satyawadi* (Mr Truthteller, S. M. Abbas, 1960). In *Jis Desh Mein Ganga Behti Hai* (Land of the Ganges, Radhu Karmakar, 1960), the classic Nehruvian hero Gangaprasad begins from a position of absolute political innocence – a degree zero of national being, if you will – and finds out whether the brigands he chances upon really want to bring 'socialism' to the country. It is particularly significant that Gangaprasad's moral stocktaking applies to the police as well as the dacoits. In his many adventures as the protagonist of reform, Dharmendra is never accorded this singular privilege. His story is almost always that of a comparatively isolated but principled survivalism in the city or the exemplary sacrifice of life itself. Unlike the tramp, he is never the cheerful wayfarer but the embroiled professional whose conscience as a citizen is always at odds with his practical realities. Unlike Gangaprasad, he is not endowed with the magical powers to effect an instant musical deterritorialization of endemic social conflicts. He cannot dissolve phrases and norms in dispute under the utopian horizons of affect that are suddenly ushered in with the songs. What is thus dissolved momentarily is the question of the state and the social contract; warring parties are instead invited to reach a covenant of brotherhood under the spectral sky of the nation. The pacifist in *Jis Desh Mein Ganga Behti Hain* literally sings his way through the hardened hearts of both cops and robbers. Dharmendra's dealings, on the other hand, are with a world that is much more prosaic and unforgiving. The acting out of the late Nehruvian also follows a different pattern from the singsong stylization of speech in Kapoor's films of the 1960s. It is everyday humdrum naturalism (office work in *Satyakam*, the employment exchange in *Dost*) interspersed by occasional dramatic rises in the gradient of melodrama when the frontal broadcast of the ethical statement takes place. The otherworldly utterance has to rise above the clamour of the world. It is usually delivered in close-up, with the gaze rising above eye-level, as if to invoke a covenant greater than man-made law, one that has been written out since eternity.[16] The broadcast of the Dharmic statement by the fallible human being – beset by poverty, hunger or disease but stubbornly refusing to take a bribe or steal – requires a voice and intonation that soars slightly above the ordinary. It is a dying gesture of epic naturalism in a world already rendered woefully disenchanted.

Yet it must be acknowledged that the star image of the early Dharmendra inevitably brought a pronounced heterosexual masculinity to roles that called for poetic affirmations of an ideal world. One of his earliest reviews in *Filmfare* describes this as a special 'tautness', the feeling of 'an immense fire held in check'. The most emblematic screen moment of this sexualization of the male body comes in *Phool aur Patthar* when the drunk, bare chested Raka totters into the bedroom of the sleeping widow played by Meena Kumari, only to cover her with a blanket. In *Satyakam* too, the idealist Brahmin engineer's decision to marry the low-born rape victim Ranjana is not purely an ethical decision. Their growing chemistry, including a sequence where they are forced to spend a night in the same room, is depicted in poignant sequences preceding the tragic rape of Ranjana. The candid admission of sexual attraction makes the subsequent inter-caste marriage all the more resonant in its ambiguities. It is never clear whether it is consummated, despite a strong melodramatic emphasis on the spiritual and ethical love shared by the couple.

Here once again we can cite Raj Kapoor as a counter-example. After the end of his association with Nargis, Kapoor's Nehruvian figure had to evolve and discard the frank, often bravura sensuality that we see in films such as *Barsaat* (Raj Kapoor, 1949), *Awaara* or *Shree 420*. The new tramp was quite self-consciously desexualized and marked by an increasingly pious infantilism *while* women in his films were displayed with voluptuous abandon. The artless anthropologist of the nation – the spirit of the *volk* incarnate – could come into being only after discarding the most primal of desires and interests. He also stopped being from the city or at least being at home in it. The country bumpkins in films such as *Jagte Raho, Anari, Jis Desh Mein Ganga Behti Hain, Teesri Kasam* (The Third Vow, Basu Bhattacharya, 1966), *Diwana* (Mad Lover, Mahesh Kaul, 1967) or *Sapnon Ka Saudagar* (Dream Merchant, Mahesh Kaul, 1968) are not just marked by absolute non-affiliation to anything ideological; they are idiot savants capable of moral commentary precisely because they are also sexually naïve.[17] The late version of the tramp was thus a figure of rigorous abstraction; he had to be removed from all obligations pertaining to caste, clan, women or property. In order to articulate an essence in troubled times that was pre-political, he also had to be pre-libidinal.

Dharmendra on the other hand, was the keen cinematic interlocutor of a late Nehruvianism that had, by then, very much settled into a bureaucratic rather than a mobilizing form (see Kaviraj 1992). Unlike his predecessors, he was often cast as an ideal functionary that the state needed not just for its ground operations (the professor, the doctor, the forest ranger) but to politically call itself into being in the first place. The aura of the assiduous reformer, as I have indicated earlier, was consolidated by a special quality of expressive and candid vernacularization of the modern enterprise; there

---

[16] I extract this idea from Ashish Rajadhyaksha's general work on the epic melodrama.
[17] They are not *Jitendriyas* displaying a Gandhian overcoming of sexual desire. They apparently have no sexual desire in the first place. The 'love' they speak of incessantly is thus an austere concept that is only related to a utopian politics of a proposed organic national community.

was spiritual recompense in seeing the son of Shohnewal shepherding as well as questioning the profane but inevitable industrial order. In other words, this quality, combined with a strong physical presence that was like an 'immense fire held in check', allowed the reformist persona to be inserted into more actionist fantasies in an increasingly turbulent age. The patriotic poet-intellectual could thus morph into various forms of the decidedly post-Gandhian *Jawan-Kisan* (peasant-soldier) assemblages that populated Hindi cinema from the turbulent mid-1960s. He could be not just military men in *Haqeeqat* and *Lalkaar*, or secret agents in *Aankhen* or *Yakeen*, but a warrior arriving as a pure force of nature from any psycho-biographical origins: the petty-thieves who destroy dacoits and deliver villages in *Mera Gaon Mera Desh* and *Sholay* or the truck driver who trains himself to impersonate a dead officer and establish the rule of law in the wild landscape of *Pratigya*.

In the turbulent years during and after the Emergency, Dharmendra became a more hardened moral presence, especially in the increasingly Manichean narratives that dominated the 1980s. That is, while the late-Nehruvian reformist hero became the two-fisted action star of the angry years, in the vendetta films, for the most part, Dharmendra was denied the signs of trauma, a certain latitude of desire and unrest, a volatile irascibility of primal instincts that marked not just Amitabh Bachchan but also the screen personas of screen villains turned heroes such as Vinod Khanna and Shatrughan Sinha. While he joined the brigade of larger-than-life orphans who populated the screen cities, Dharmendra was rarely allowed angry, wilful abnegations of dead fathers and lost villages. He endured tragedy but never bore psychological scars like the tattoo of shame in *Deewar* (The Wall, Yash Chopra, 1975). He rarely played the Durkheimian *anomic* type, the beat hero who simply does not fit in with social norms (see Dyer [1979] 1998: 52).

The meditative late Nehruvian emerged as 'Garam Dharam' when the 'immense fire' hitherto held in check was unleashed. What was also subtracted from the former star-text were the qualities of endurance and absorption, but this was done without the addition of any of the pseudo-anomic angst of the age that defined the Bachchan persona. Dharmendra in the 1980s was therefore reduced to essential physicality in the raw, a violent legal or extra-legal figure of the status quo, utterly devoid of social introspection or political meditation.[18] As a matter of fact, so well defined was this lean and mean persona that it could be instantly introduced and allowed to carry out its functions without character backgrounds in the dozens of multi-starrers of the decade where Dharmendra played short cameos.

What is also significant in this long cinematic journey is that Dharmendra was downsized to poverty-row pictures with the onset of globalization. It was in the early 1990s, with the advent of the NRI films and then eventually the multiplex, that his enduring stardom finally went on the wane. While advancing age could certainly be deemed as one of the natural causes of this eclipse, what was interesting is that Dharmendra, unlike many of his contemporaries such as Amitabh Bachchan, Amrish Puri or Rishi Kapoor could not fit into the prototype of the older, neo-traditional patriarch in the metropolitan dispensation. What was no longer needed in top-drawer films catering to globalizing cities and foreign markets was precisely that wistful vernacular accentuation of the prose of the world. The once major star

---

[18]The roles he played in his trilogy with J. P. Dutta – the Maoist in *Ghulami* (1985), the brigand against caste politics in *Batwara* (1989) and the existentialist Muslim don in *Hathyar* (1989) – would be exceptions.

remained active and prolific but was relegated to B- or C-grade potboilers such as *Mafia* (Aziz Sajawal, 1996), *Loh Purush* (Iron Man, Hersh Kinnu, 1999) and *Daku Bhairav Singh* (Pappu Sharma, 2001) that were often lowbrow parodic approximations of the big-budget genre spectaculars of the previous decade. Dharmendra, therefore, was largely excluded when Hindi cinema was inducted into a transnational Hinglish media ecology popularly known as 'Bollywood'.

Works Cited

Anon. (1961), 'Dharmendra', *Filmfare*, 10 (7) April: 42–3.

Anon. (1963), 'Dharmendra: Maize Fields to Marquees', *Filmfare*, 12 (11) 31 May: 4–6.

Anon. (1964), 'Dharmendra: His Crucial Battle', *Filmfare*, 13 (12), 12 June: 6–8

Anon. (1965), 'Dharmendra: Where is he?', *Filmfare*, 14 (18), 3 September: 6–8

Anon. (1969), 'Dharmendra: Bearing the World's Cross', *Filmfare*, 18 (24), 21 November: 7–9.

Anon. (1971), 'Dharmendra: How those romances started', *Filmfare*, 20 (25), 3 December: 9–11.

Basu, Anustup (2010), *Bollywood in the Age of New Media: The Geo-Televisual Aesthetic*, Edinburgh: Edinburgh University Press.

Chakravarty, Sumita S. (1993), *National Identity in Indian Popular Cinema, 1947–1987*, Austin: University of Texas Press.

Dyer, Richard ([1979] 1998), *Stars*, new edn, London: British Film Institute.

Gledhill, Christine (1991), 'Signs of Melodrama', in Christine Gledhill (ed.) *Stardom: Industry of Desire*, 210–34, London: Routledge.

Kaviraj, Sudipta (1992), 'The Imaginary Institution of India', in Partha Chatterjee and Gyanendra Pandey (eds), *Subaltern Studies VII*, 1–39, Delhi: Oxford University Press.

Kesavan, Mukul (2008), 'No One Writes to the Prison Doctor Anymore', *Outlook*, online at: www.outlookindia.com/article/no-one-writes-to-the-prison-doc-anymore/237463 (accessed 24 May 2015).

Kothari, Rajni (1970), *Politics in India*, New Delhi: Orient Blackswan.

Majumdar, Neepa (2009), *Wanted Cultured Ladies Only! Female Stardom and Cinema in India, 1930s–1950s*, Urbana: University of Illinois Press.

Prasad, M. Madhava (2014), *Cine-Politics: Film Stars and Political Existence in South India*, Hyderabad: Orient Blackswan.

Raheja, Dinesh (2002), 'Dharmendra: All Muscle, All Heart', 24 June, online at: www.rediff.com/entertai/2002/jun/24dinesh.htm (accessed 23 June 2015).

Sarkar, Bhaskar (2009), *Mourning the Nation: Indian Cinema in the Wake of Partition*, Durham, NC: Duke University Press.

Vasudevan, Ravi (1989), 'The Melodramatic Mode and the Commercial Hindi Cinema: Notes on Film History, Narrative and Performance in the 1950s', *Screen*, 30 (3): 29–50.

Virdi, Jyotika (2003), *The Cinematic ImagiNation: Indian Popular Films as Social History*, New Brunswick, NJ: Rutgers University Press.

Chapter 6

Rajkumar and the Kannada-language film
M. K. Raghavendra

The male star in India's popular cinemas

If film stars in world cinema are often associated with specific genres, those in India have other associations largely because of the relative lack of generic differentiation in Indian cinema.[1] Hindi-language popular cinema, which played the role of an unofficial national cinema after 1947, used star personae to address social concerns that come to the fore in each historical era; the same star's persona often transforms in different eras to suit a new sociopolitical purpose. As an example, Dilip Kumar played the urbane man beset by uncertainties in the early 1950s (*Babul* [S. U. Sunny, 1950] and *Jogan* [Female Ascetic, Kidar Sharma, 1950]) furthering an uncharacteristic open-endedness in Hindi films when independent India was confronted with an array of political choices (see Chakravarty 1996: 99; Raghavendra 1996: 106–8). The same actor became known for playing the ebullient rustic later in films such as *Naya Daur* (The New Way, B. R. Chopra, 1957) and *Ganga Jumna* (Nitin Bose, 1961), when India had settled into a stable political system in which rural issues had gained prominence. Since Hindi cinema addressed the national identity and there were several concurrent issues that needed addressing, different stars played their parts to weave a coherent fabric of interdependent narratives.

In contrast to the mainstream Hindi film that addressed national issues, India has also developed a regional-language popular cinema, which can be seen as addressing local identities within India. Unlike Hindi cinema, in which a single star has not dominated because of the variety of issues needing to be narrativized – usually allegorically – each regional-language popular cinema has tended to be dominated by a single male star.[2] The regional-language popular cinemas, by and large, serve much smaller territories[3] and this suggests that there is a distillation of address-worthy issues at any given moment into one or two major ones, with a single star as the vehicle. The fact that their 'constituencies' are concentrated in smaller

---

[1] As instances from Hollywood, John Wayne with the western, Humphrey Bogart and Barbara Stanwyck in *noir*, Gene Kelly with the musical, Bette Davis in a category called 'drama' and Marilyn Monroe in comedy.
[2] Female stars have never dominated any language cinema in India in the same way. This may be attributed to the action in each film narrative revolving largely around the male protagonist and the female lead dominating only in exceptional cases, as in films such as the Hindi *Andaz* (Style, Mehboob Khan, 1949), which had Nargis in the most important role, or the Kannada film *Belli Moda* (Puttanna Kanagal, 1967), which had Kalpana. For a star to dominate a cinema s/he needs to be constantly fed key roles over a significant period and this has not happened with female stars.
[3] They also serve their respective diasporas as, for instance, Tamil cinema, which is consumed by Tamils in Malaysia; but this is not a factor of importance to the Kannada film because Kannada speakers do not constitute a significant part of the Indian diaspora abroad.

territories has also enabled regional film stars to succeed in politics – something that the Hindi film, which is more widely dispersed – does not allow. If regional film stars have sometimes appeared in more than one language cinema, their biggest successes have been confined to one territory demarcated by language.

Rajkumar, the star who dominated Kannada-language cinema for several decades, appeared only in Kannada films. Kannada cinema is nominally consumed across the entire territory where Kannada is the lingua franca (i.e. the Indian state of Karnataka in South India) but in actual practice it addresses only a part of that territory, the part once constituted by the Princely State of Mysore, under indirect British rule. Rajkumar, in fact, can be interpreted as a living icon of former Princely Mysore.

Understanding the milieu

Hindi cinema is intended to appeal to a wide cross-section across an enormous territory and therefore attempts to use a 'non-local' idiom, but since Kannada popular film began by addressing only the citizens of Princely Mysore, the sociopolitical milieu in the state has a large role to play in our understanding of Kannada film convention, if not form, which appears similar to the mainstream Hindi film. That Hindi, Tamil, Telugu and Kannada films are dubbed into other languages implies that the films cannot be formally very distinct, because they are understood by audiences from the other regions as their own cinema.

The key factor to understand about the milieu in Princely Mysore was that it was under indirect rule by the British before 1947. After the break-up of the Vijayanagar Empire (1336–1646) and before the rise of Hyder Ali in the 1760s, the area known as Mysore State was ruled by a network of 'little kingdoms' over which the chieftains who claimed to rule had only a loose suzerainty.[4] The Wadeyar family, the ancestors of the Maharaja of Mysore, ruled over Mysore but it was only under Hyder Ali and his son Tipu Sultan that any genuine consolidation of the little kingdoms under one authority took place. After Tipu's defeat in 1799 the British needed suitable rulers over the dominions that they did not wish to administer themselves and reinstated the Wadeyars, although they ruled indirectly through the dewan (minister), who was (in the initial period) from the Madras presidency.

When the Maharaja resumed power, he was required to raise resources for the British while also restoring the splendour befitting a royal court. If this weakened the Maharaja, it was compounded by other factors. The peasantry had, as may be expected, grievances and there was also the issue of caste dominance. The Wadeyars were Arasus, who were only a few, while the most powerful castes/ sects in the region were the Vokkaligas and the Veerashaivas who constituted the powerful local elite.[5] These factors contributed to the political climate in Princely Mysore and its differences from that of the British-ruled presidencies of Bombay and Madras – though the Maharaja was presented with an administrative structure based on the Bombay and Madras models. As indicated, the British had installed an Indian administrative head (the dewan) with the centralization of power in his hands also as a way of maintaining control. These officials were usually of the highest calibre

---

[4] The chieftains were called *polegars*, local power holders who were normally in charge of twenty villages – a political unit known as *pollam*. See Hettne 1978: 30–1.
[5] According to the census the Arasus numbered less than 1,000 around this time. See *Census of India, 1891* (Bangalore, 1893), xxv, 4, p. 80, cited in Iyer 1928: 47–73.

and Mysore State soon earned the reputation of being among the best-administered native states in India. Since caste will be of some importance in this inquiry it is necessary to note that while Brahmins constituted a small minority in Princely Mysore, of the thirteen dewans of Mysore between 1881 and 1947, nine were Brahmins, most of them from the Madras presidency.[6] The first Mysorean dewan was P. N. Krishnamurthi (1901–1906) and the next was Sir M. Visveswaraiya (1912–1918), perhaps the greatest of the dewans. The dominance of Brahmins in the administration led to an anti-Brahmin movement among the elite classes, but this did not lead to mass mobilization, as had the anti-Brahmin movement in the Madras presidency.

Mysore State was exceedingly fertile and blessed with two rivers, as a consequence of which cheap hydroelectric power could be produced. The state was therefore able to bring off several impressive entrepreneurial schemes. Its performance in areas such as industry and education were so impressive that the government of India rarely interfered in governance either formally or informally. Overall, Mysore was a prosperous state with few of the contrasts of the rest of India. Mysore was a Hindu kingdom, ruled autocratically by a local king with a limited colonial interface. Hinduism was more orthodox and the position of the Brahmin caste and the priests more elevated, although Veerashaivism developed here as a system of protest against Brahmin domination. It is also to be noted that the fact of the state being governed by Muslim rulers from 1761 to 1799 did not change this Hindu characteristic as far as structure was concerned – although in terms of personnel Brahmins and Veerashaivas were largely replaced by Muslims in this period (Hettne 1978: 28–9). The fact that the Mysore regime was virtually created by the colonial power does not mean that it did not strive for autonomy. In fact, the struggle for autonomy became the dominant interest of the Mysore government and the Maharaja even designated his country as a 'nation within a nation' (44).

Caste/sect being a crucial way in which ties were created and maintained, the largest arena within which sustained social interaction occurred was the area across which people from one caste group or sect had established marriage alliances with other families. Being of the same caste/sect was not enough and families sought out links with families of comparable status, some of these ties reinforced by second- and third-generation alliances. The marriage networks overlapped with one another so that over a range of eighty or one hundred miles an entire endogamous unit would be knitted together (Manor 1977: 40–4).

The conventions of Kannada popular cinema

The description of the milieu provided above will explain many of the conventions of Kannada popular cinema that informed the films of the 1950s, which was when Rajkumar entered the scene. The major conventions followed by Kannada popular cinema around the time are as follows (see Raghavendra 2011: xx–xxv):

(a) Where Hindi cinema uses love as the basis of heterosexual attachments, Kannada cinema uses endogamy as the basis and marriages are contracted within the same caste unless

---

[6]According to the census of 1931 Brahmins constituted 3.8 per cent of the population, Veerashaivas 12 per cent and Vokkaligas 20.4 per cent. The category later to be termed 'scheduled castes' constituted 15.1 per cent of the population and Muslims 5.8 per cent. See *Census of India, 1931* (Bangalore, 1931), xxv, 2, p. 230.

specified. Marriage across castes, in defiance of endogamy and for 'love', appears only as an anomaly. The joint family, consequently, is also valourized much more than in Hindi cinema.

(b) Caste hierarchy is much more rigid than in Hindi cinema, although one has to deduce caste identity through names and qualities are associated with the names. Brahmin names connote education and sophistication, and teaching, engineering and medicine are the occupations associated with the caste. But if a person is denoted as a Brahmin because he is a priest, he is usually hypocritical, selfish and opportunistic. Farmers and grain merchants are connoted as Vokkaligas, while traditional businessmen are usually given Veerashaiva names. When 'farmer' comes with sophistication, he is a 'progressive farmer' or coffee planter with Brahmin attributes/names.

(c) There is little evidence of non-Hindu characters in Kannada cinema and their appearance is anomalous.

(d) The code of *dharma* is much more operational in Kannada than in Hindi cinema. As a corollary, there is a hierarchy within the family, with the father treated as lord and master. The ideal father performs his duties towards his wife and children the way a monarch does towards his subjects.

(e) Unlike Hindi cinema, Independence has little or no impact on Kannada cinema. Much more important is the linguistic reorganization of the states in 1956, which enlarged Mysore (renamed as Karnataka in 1973) to include other territories from the Bombay and Madras presidencies, the Nizam's Hyderabad and Coorg.

(f) Magical elements and mythology are absent from mainstream Hindi cinema after 1942–43. Independence was increasingly anticipated from then onwards – after the British reverses against the Japanese. The reform movements of the nineteenth and early twentieth centuries had striven to free the milieu of superstition and this influenced the shape of Indian nationalism thereafter. Kannada cinema does not address the 'progressive nation'; mythology and magic are staple elements until very much later.

(g) The domestic melodrama (or 'social') enters Kannada cinema only in the 1950s and after linguistic reorganization. Until that time virtually every Kannada film included magical elements. The advent of the 'social' introduces generic differentiation between two broad categories – those with costumes (mythological and historical films) and those without (domestic melodramas or 'socials').

Until linguistic reorganization in 1956, Kannada cinema was quite content to address a public in former Princely Mysore. Since the Kannada-speaking areas outside Mysore suffered the most because of their linguistic minority status, it was outside Mysore that the movement for unification of Kannada areas began.[7] Those opposing the linguistic reorganization of Mysore into a new state were largely dominant groups in Mysore who felt that their interests, both cultural and administrative, would suffer in the enlarged state because Mysore was far more prosperous (Muthanna 1980: 89). But Greater Mysore was nonetheless formed and Kannada cinema – nominally – took to addressing the enlarged territory after 1956. Rajkumar came into cinema two years before with *Bedara Kannappa* (1954), which

---

[7] For an account of the agitation for a Kannada-speaking state, see Weiner 1967: 239–55.

allegorizes the prospects of linguistic reorganization from the Mysorean perspective.

Rajkumar and Mysore

Rajkumar was born as Singanalluru Puttaswamayya Muthuraju in 1929 at Gajanur in the Madras presidency. His father was a small-time theatre artiste who played mythological roles on the stage. Rajkumar dropped out of school at the age of eight and started his career as a theatre artiste with his father in a troupe led by Gubbi Veeranna. He was then discovered by a movie producer and played minor characters on the screen until he was twenty-five, when he played his first lead role in H. L. N. Simha's *Bedara Kannappa* (1954).

Awaiting integration

Bedara Kannappa was the first of a series of mythological films made between 1954 and 1956, featuring a strikingly common motif with two other films: *Mahakavi Kalidasa* (K. R. Seetharam Sastry, 1955) and *Bhakta Vijaya* (Triumph of Faith, A. K. Pattabhi, 1956). These films are all about a princely personage grown so arrogant that he is cursed with deprivation of some sort. In *Bedara Kannappa*, the 'prince' is a celestial being cursed by a god and being reborn as a tribal, while in the other two he is a human who has to take up life at a humbler level; but the princely arrogance of the protagonist is unmistakable in all the films. The protagonist is joined each time by his wife who shares his privation without complaining and the man gains a following because of his goodness/devoutness although he remains a common man.

The common motif identified in the three films, the motif of the prince facing deprivation, should be considered in the light of Mysore being a former princely state and the representational habits cultivated under monarchy persisting. 'King' and 'country' are synonymous to subjects in a monarchy and this suggests that the prince's/princess's predicament in the three films has parallels with the predicament of the former Princely Mysore State in the period 1954–1956. That the prince and his wife share the suffering suggests that this is a predicament shared by the king and his subjects rather than the privation being forced upon an individual. This is consistent with my earlier indication of wife and husband being in the analogous position of subjects and monarch. The 'curse' of hardship finds correspondence in the apprehensions of prosperous former Princely Mysore when faced with the prospect of integration with poorer Kannada areas. The fact that it was a 'curse' with no remedy suggests that the people of former Princely Mysore (the constituency addressed by the film) gradually came to realize that they had no option but to submit. The only solace was perhaps that there was a 'higher' benevolent monarch/authority ensuring that the dispensation would not be without recourse. By showing that in the process of dealing with the curse the prince also gains a larger community, the films appeal to the attractions of an integrated Kannada community.

Rajkumar arrived on the scene just when Kannada cinema was contending with a larger Kannada territory that it needed to address. The rest of his career can be fruitfully interpreted as former Princely Mysore finding an icon for itself that could be held up to the other Kannada-speaking areas as well. Rajkumar also became instrumental in addressing all the key issues in the 1960s to engage the Kannada-speaking state – Greater Mysore – as an equal constituent of the Indian nation, the extension of Mysore to include the other territories and Mysore's claim upon modernity.

Greater Mysore and the mythological film

With the linguistic reorganization of the states in 1956, politicians from former Princely Mysore had an obvious advantage over those from the other areas in their efforts to take charge of Greater Mysore. The Kannada-speaking politicians who inherited Princely Mysore were able to approach linguistic reorganization with a considerable organizational advantage over their colleagues in the Kannada-speaking districts outside the state and they were able to garner most power within the enlarged Kannada space (Wood and Hammond 1975: 146). This finds correspondence in cinema, which presumes to speak for the whole of Greater Mysore but uses the idiom employed in addressing the princely state.

Mythological films do not dominate Kannada cinema after 1956 so much as they did earlier, because of the appearance at this time of the family melodrama (the 'social') and the historical film, but two of Rajkumar's mythological films of the period – *Bhookailasa* (K. Shankar, 1958) and *Mahishasura Mardhini* (B. S. Ranga, 1959) – show a change in attitudes. This becomes more striking if the motifs are regarded as a continuation of the motifs in *Bedara Kannappa* and *Bhakta Vijaya*. *Bhookailasa* tells a story about Ravana (Rajkumar) who has grown so arrogant with his prowess that he challenges the gods. Ravana in the film embarks upon penance so severe that the god Shiva has no alternative but to grant him a boon. A key factor in this film is that the god and the king are treated roughly as equals with a democratic transaction between them rather than the unconditional submission of the latter. In fact, the king as 'devotee' has a self-important swagger that is unmistakable. In both films the king responds to a divine visitation (during his penance) as though the god was an expected visitor and this is different from the rapturous way the protagonist receives the gods in *Bedara Kannappa*. The relationship between the king and the god gradually becoming one between equals is consistent with the state becoming part of the nation with full democratic rights. The motif of interrogation of the gods (through Narada, a celestial intermediary) in *Mahishasura Mardhini*, in which the gods conduct themselves wrongly, perhaps finds correspondence in the courtroom scene in Hindi cinema of the 1950s in which the judge is interrogated (*Dhool Ka Phool*, Flower of the Dust, Yash Chopra, 1959) for a wrongdoing (Raghavendra 1996: 129–30).

A different subcategory in the mythological films starring Rajkumar responds to the other side of 'belonging to a larger nation'. In this category a childless couple is divinely blessed with a child and when the child grows up he becomes distant from his family and has thoughts only for God. This motif can be interpreted as a measure of the aspiration on society's part to move away from narrow attachments defined by kinship ties towards higher loyalties. The years up to 1960–1961, as observed by critics, was a period in which optimism over India was made palpable in Hindi cinema (see, for example, Vasudevan 2000: 99–121). It would be expected that such a period of nationalistic optimism would also be the most appropriate moment for narrow loyalties to be abandoned. Two Kannada films of around this period – *Bhaktha Kanakadasa* (Y. R. Swamy, 1960) and *Kaivara Mahathme* (G. V. Iyer, 1961) – display the motif just described. In both films the protagonist moves away from the identity determined by his birth and embraces God, although it involves hardship and being ostracized. A comparable film, *Chiranjeevi* (K. P. Bhave), had appeared in 1936 when there was a move away from 'narrow loyalties' towards nationalism. Nineteen-thirty-six was the crucial year when a movement gathered strength to unify the opposition to princely rule in Mysore and when the Mysore Congress moved away from being a local entity by establishing stronger ties with the Indian National Congress, and the motif was repeated in the 1960s (Manor 1977: 95–104).

Extending Mysore through the historical film

It is acknowledged that historical films partly project the concerns of the present back into the past, and this is true of Indian cinema as well. Kannada cinema, beginning in the late 1950s, also actively engaged in constructing a pan-Kannada nation by appealing to the past – especially empires such as the one in Vijayanagar – and to heroic kings and queens. *Ranadheera Kanteerava* (N. C. Rajan, 1960) is a story of palace intrigue under the Wadeyars and the film begins with a young king who loves pleasure being accosted by his mother, the dowager queen, and his uncle Kanteerava (Rajkumar). The film is preoccupied with defining a Kannada identity and – apart from the opening song eulogizing Kannada – proceeds about it in two ways. On the one hand are Kanteerava's friendly dealings with various chieftains or emissaries who speak different kinds of Kannada. Kanteerava is also allowed to have two wives and the second is a 'romance', signifying the knitting of Kannada areas outside the traditional marriage networks. On the other are Kanteerava's deeds against the Tamils. The chief of these acts is his defeating a Tamil wrestler in Tiruchi. Characters who speak Tamil and Malayalam are placed by the film in the position of Kanteerava's adversaries. After Kanteerava's killing of the Tiruchi wrestler, the wrestler's brother, who is intent upon revenge, attempts to enter into a secret alliance with the crafty minister trying to undo Kanteerava.

Kittur Channamma (B. R. Panthulu, 1961) is a straightforward product of Indian nationalism. *Kittur Channamma* deals with the colonial period and makes an attempt to enlist a national heroine from Belgaum district (Bombay Karnataka) on behalf of the Kannada Nation. The film remains fairly true to the actual story of Rani Channamma of Kittur and explains concepts such as the 'Doctrine of Lapse'. Channamma (B. Saroja Devi) is the second wife of the Raja Mallasarja (Rajkumar), who is captured by Tipu Sultan but escapes – with Tipu duly appreciating his valour. As opposed to the Mallasarja's first marriage, his wedding to Channamma takes place after a 'romance' – once again suggesting a discourse about the knitting of territories not linked by marriage networks as in *Ranadheera Kanteerava*. In praising the kingdom of Kittur the film briefly pours scorn on the rulers of Mysore as lackeys of the British. At the same time, Channamma speaks the Kannada spoken in Mysore while her two ministers/advisors (who are British agents) speak the dialect of Belgaum (in former Bombay presidency). The film is apparently identifying a suitable icon for the Kannada nation while at the same time – through its selective use of different Kannada dialects – privileging Mysore over the other Kannada-speaking areas.

Modernity and the 'social'

The genre to establish the first explicit link between Mysore and the Indian nation was evidently the domestic melodrama, because it invokes the same notion in the late 1950s that Hindi cinema was also invoking – 'modernity'. There were domestic melodramas earlier yet there was also an element of magic, as in *Gunasagari* (H. L. N. Simha, 1953). Magic, however, is eliminated after 1956 with films such as *Rayara Sose* (The Master's Daughter-in-law, K. S. Murthy and R. Ramamurthy, 1957) and *School Master* (B. R. Panthulu, 1958) embracing the modern. In *Rayara Sose*, the doctor played by Rajkumar helps in ushering social justice into a family when the father-in-law demands a dowry from the wife. 'Modernity' in Hindi cinema means eschewing superstition and nation-building, but these are not issues in Kannada cinema, in which modernity in the form of industrialization had been ushered in as early as the 1920s largely through the efforts of Sir M. Visweswaraiya. Social reform including emancipation of women was, however, outside of this 'modernization' and this is what *Rayara Sose* addresses. In *School Master* (in which Rajkumar does not appear) the teacher comes from outside into the corrupt village and cleanses it. 'Outside' may be regarded as outside Mysore, which had been plagued by corruption. Also introduced in *School Master* is the notion of marriage for love outside endogamous circles.

From the 1960s onwards the 'social' undergoes changes and its movement until the end of the decade may be understood as trying to bridge the gap between (Greater) Mysore and India by becoming modern in the Nehruvian sense. After introducing different kinds of spoken Kannada after 1956, the Kannada film increasingly uses a uniform Mysore Kannada, which becomes the standard. Where the Kannada social appears to change most significantly after 1960 is in the way hierarchy is treated and in the denotation of caste. Where, in the earlier films, people were segregated into caste/occupational groups (servants, courtesans, priests, farmers etc.) with little commerce between them, there are fewer signs of it after 1960. It is, however, apparent that hierarchy persists in a subdued way, usually in the comic servant romances through separate subplots. This implies a hierarchical segregation of plot components. As a way of playing down hierarchy without interrogating it, Kannada film narratives of the 1960s deal exclusively with one class – for example a Brahmin class straddling both the village and the city as in *Nandadeepa* (M. R. Vittal, 1963) or a rural landowning Vokkaliga class as in *Chandavaliya Thota* (T. V. Singh Thakur, 1964), both of which star Rajkumar. It is as though the Kannada social was trying to democratize itself (in appearance) to become more Indian.

As the 1960s progress the Kannada social strives harder in this direction with relevant themes. Bangalore, with which Kannada cinema has had an ambivalent relationship because of the city's association with the British and with central government investment after 1947, is increasingly seen as a modern space. A reason was the former chief minister S. Nijalingappa ascending to the post of president of the undivided Congress at the Centre. The 'reformist' films in the period – with Rajkumar as the star – include *Bangarada Hoovu* (Golden Flower, B. A. Arasau Kumar, 1967), in which a good man helps in curing a girl of leprosy and marries her, and *Hannele Chiguridaga* (When a Dry Leaf Turns Green, M. R. Vittal, 1968), in which widowed people marry. The climax of this 'modern' trajectory is reached when Rajkumar plays a spy (CID 999) modeled after James Bond in *Jedara Bale* (Spider's Web, B. Dorairaj, Bhagavan, 1968), a film complete with nightclubs, girls and gadgets.

Mrs Indira Gandhi split the Congress in 1969 and S. Nijalingappa, who had been on the rise for several years, abruptly lost his importance to the Indian nation – at least in the eyes of those in the Kannada state of Mysore. The films coming immediately afterwards are also preoccupied with modernity but in a different way. Instead of making common cause with the Nehruvian variety, it is asserted that modernity knocked at Princely Mysore much earlier than it did at Nehru's India. The key films of this period – representing Rajkumar's most iconic roles – are Dorairaj/Bhagwan's *Kasturi Nivasa* (1971) and Siddalingaiah's *Bangarada Manushya* (Golden Man, 1972). The protagonists of these films have all the qualities idolized in the Brahmin caste (but rarely found in those denoted as Brahmins), which are sophistication and generosity without any hint of selfishness in their acts. They are modern but their Mysorean modernity is contrasted with a more rapacious kind associated with Bangalore – with its British/central government associations. In *Bangarada Manushya* the protagonist (a progressive famer) is explicitly compared to Sir M. Visweswaraiya. Alongside this kind of 'social', as if to complement it, is a historical film extolling a Kannada king who submitted to no outside authority – Rajkumar as *Sri Krishnadevaraya* (B. R. Panthulu, 1970). This is in contrast to *Kittur Channamma* (B. R. Panthulu, 1962) in which the Indian nation is the heroine's object of loyalty.

Mysore fades from memory

By the mid-1970s Princely Mysore was already fading from memory and the renaming of Greater Mysore as Karnataka in 1973 was perhaps the last straw. Kannada cinema tried to hold on to the memory of former Mysore in various ways. A phenomenon of importance is that so many Kannada films of the 1960s and 1970s are based on works of literature, which was not so in the 1950s and before. Popular films found the dramatic novels by writers *from Mysore*, such as Triveni, A. N. Krishna Rao, M. K. Indira, T. R. Subba Rao and Gorur Ramaswamy Iyengar most suitable. As Benedict Anderson proposed, the possibility of the nation depends upon the development of the book, the novel and the newspaper (1983: 14). This implies a reading public capable of using them within a territory and able to imagine themselves as a single community through them. Former Princely Mysore remains inscribed as a territory in Kannada cinema long after it had ceased to exist as a political entity. Although

'Mysore' became defunct as a political entity in 1956, it existed in the place in which it might have existed – in the collective memory of the people of the region, given shape and manifested in the region's literature. If Mysore had not become defunct as a political entity (i.e. it had been 'living' like the nation) adapting literature might have been redundant. 'Mysore' was not only a space but also an ethos that faded as the last generation of Mysoreans passed on. In the mid-to-late 1970s, we already find popular cinema less dependent upon literature. Another way in which Rajkumar's films cope with this approaching demise is to introduce the figure of the sacred mother – in a way reminiscent of Hindi cinema in which the mother allegorizes the nation in films such as *Awaara* (Vagabond, Raj Kapoor, 1951), *Mother India* (Mehboob Khan, 1956) and *Deewar* (The Wall, Yash Chopra, 1975). But where the mother in Hindi cinema needs to act and make sacrifices to deserve the adulation, the mother in Rajkumar's films of the 1970s is loved for her position. This is consistent with what she represents – former Mysore – being defunct as a political entity, only being remembered for what she was – while the nation-as-mother is a functioning entity.

Rajkumar had a series of hits in the mid-to late 1970s, but the person who really came to the fore in the period culturally was the director Puttanna Kanagal – who had made *Sakshathkara* (Witness, 1971) with Rajkumar earlier, a film which has the same motifs as *Kasturi Nivasa* and *Bangarada Manushya*. Kanagal made his mark with women's melodramas but he had a big success in *Nagara Haavu* (Cobra, 1972) in which the unruly youthful male protagonist has two teachers – the one he reveres being associated with Kannada cultural figures and the one he despises and insults having pictures of national leaders on his wall (see Raghavendra 2011: 53–4). Rajkumar's films from the later 1970s are not of much cultural importance today because they are largely vehicles for his histrionic abilities. The star's presence is dependent on its invocation of Mysore – an entity that was losing its significance, not least because Mrs Gandhi's doings at the centre had found a proponent in Greater Mysore/Karnataka Chief Minister D Devaraj Urs. Mysore's cultural identity – as standing apart from that of the Indian nation – was weakened by this.

Conclusion

Rajkumar's career continued well after the 1970s but it was a career kept alive by a hysterical fan following and, in my view, not of much significance culturally to Karnataka. Overall, one could say that the star came into prominence when Mysore was at the point of becoming defunct politically and his career represents an attempt not only to keep Mysore's memory alive among the people of the region but also to hold up its traditions to a Kannada-speaking public outside former Mysore. But one question remains: why did Rajkumar, as a powerful icon, not enter politics – as his contemporaries in Tamil Nadu (M. G. Ramachandran) and Andhra Pradesh (N. T. Rama Rao) did? The explanations offered have generally been of a personal nature – his simplicity, his Gandhian beliefs and so on. But the most plausible solution to the problem lies elsewhere. For someone to stand for a political principle, he must identify the principles he is against and therefore also be clear about his political adversaries. What an icon represents only means something in relation to the forces or ideas it is against, and in Rajkumar's case it is difficult to identify them because (being a 'good man') he was 'for everyone', he was the 'ethical hero'.

As suggested earlier, the milieu in which Kannada cinema originated had not had the benefit of mass mobilization and this tended to accentuate the effects of 'one party dominance'. The Congress came to power in India not as a political party but as a movement for independence and reform. With independence the Congress did not immediately become a political party and it continued to be a 'movement'. The difference was that, having acquired independence from foreign rule, it now took upon itself the task of building a nation and it tried to achieve its ends through a consensus (Kothari 1964: 1166–7). In Mysore, 'one-party dominance' meant a virtual absence of political polarization. Although there had been a non-Brahmin movement in the state, it was not based on mass mobilization but was simply the manifestation of the non-Brahmin elite trying to secure for itself privileges (within an authoritarian system) that were enjoyed by the Brahmins. When the Congress came to power in Mysore the absence of any opposition also meant the absence of clear-cut political programmes. It has been recorded that in the pre-Independence period the only programme that the Congress leaders offered to the public was that the Congress-Raj would be a 'panacea to all public ills' (Manor 1977: 168).

I would like to argue here that the 'ethical hero' represented by Rajkumar comes out of a milieu in which there was little political polarization. Rajkumar in the later films of the 1960s is the voice of the 'good' and his adversaries are not identifiable as traders, landowners, the upper-castes or servants of the state and so on (which are all *political* categories) but simply as 'bad people' who do things that are not legally and ethically correct. 'Incorrect' is initially going against *dharma*, but it also takes other shapes gradually – such as promoting superstition as in *Bangarada Hoovu* or forging currency as in *Jedara Bale.* Unlike Raj Kapoor's films or those of M. G. Ramachandran, which always have a political agenda, Rajkumar's have none, and this has an evident parallel in the bland pronouncements of the first Congress government in Greater Mysore. It was perhaps for these reasons that Rajkumar did not become the political icon that he might have been.

Works Cited

Anderson, Benedict (1983), *Imagined Communities: Reflections on the Origin and Spread of Nationalism*, London: Verso.

Chakravarty, Sumita S. (1996), *National Identity in Indian Popular Cinema, 1947–1987*, New Delhi: Oxford University Press.

Hettne, Björn (1978), *The Political Economy of Indirect Rule: Mysore 1881–1947*, London: Curzon Press.

Iyer, Ananthakrishna (1928), *The Mysore Tribes and Castes*, vol. 2, Bangalore.

Kothari, Rajni (1964), 'The Congress "System" in India', *Asian Survey*, 4 (12) (December): 1161–73.

Manor, James (1977), *Political Change in an Indian State: Mysore 1917–1955*, New Delhi: Manohar.

Muthanna, I. M. (1980), *History of Modern Karnataka*, New Delhi: Sterling.

Raghavendra, M. K. (1996), *Seduced by the Familiar: Narration and Meaning in Indian Popular Cinema*, New Delhi: Oxford University Press.

Raghavendra, M. K. (2011), *Bipolar Identity: Region, Nation and the Kannada Language Film*, New Delhi: Oxford University Press.

Vasudevan, Ravi S. (2000), 'Shifting Codes, Dissolving Identities: The Hindi Social Film of the 1950s as Popular Culture', in Ravi S. Vasudevan (ed.), *Making Meaning in Indian Cinema*, 99–121, New Delhi: Oxford University Press.

Weiner, Myron (1967), *Party Building in a New Nation*, Chicago: Chicago University Press.

Wood, Glynn and Robert Hammond (1975), 'Electoral Politics in a Congress Dominant State, Mysore 1956–1972', in John Osgood Field, F. Frankel, Mary F. Katzenstein and Myron Weiner (eds), *Studies in Electoral Politics in the Indian States*, vol. 4, 112–56, Delhi: Manohar.

Chapter 7

The feudal lord reincarnate: Mohanlal and the politics of Malayali masculinity
Meena T. Pillai

This chapter seeks to interrogate the representational politics of stardom and masculinity in Malayalam cinema, one of the most prolific of the regional film industries in India, with special reference to the rise of Mohanlal as a 'superstar' (Figure 7.1). The entry of Mohanlal (Mohanlal Viswanathan Nair, 1960–) into Malayalam cinema as a villain in the early 1980s, his much-praised energetic and performative prowess in a succession of highly successful roles in light-hearted romantic social comedies, and his gradual transformation into the ultimate icon of Malayali masculinity in the 1990s, mark a paradigm shift in the ideology and visual iconography of Malayalam cinema. Post-liberalization Malayalam cinema is characterized by the return of highly feudal and patriarchal registers. Its earlier preoccupations with social, secular, Renaissance ideals are transformed to reveal the consumerist, individualistic and revivalist bases of its popular appeal. This engenders a re-feudalization of spaces on screen and points to the nostalgia for an earlier 'hegemonic order'. This curious phenomenon was set into motion by two Mohanlal movies in the late 1980s: *Rajavinte Makan* (The Son of the King, Thampi Kannanthanam, 1986) and *Irupatham Noottandu* (Twentieth Century, K. Madhu, 1987). From the 1990s this feudal nostalgia reached its pinnacle in Mohanlal movies such as *Devasuram* (The God-Demon, I. V. Sasi, 1993), *Spadikam* (Prism, Bhadran, 1995), *Aaraam Thampuran* (The Sixth Lord, Shaji Kailas, 1997), *Narasimham* (The Lion Man, Shaji Kailas, 2000) and *Raavanaprabhu* (Ravana the Lord, Ranjith, 2001). These movies foreground the idea of hegemonic masculinity embodied through the 'superstar' image of Mohanlal.

Kerala is a little strip of a state in India located on the southwestern tip of the Indian subcontinent. Like most other regions in India, until the last decades of the nineteenth century Kerala was also a feudal society marked by various caste markers and rituals. And as in other parts of India, Kerala's encounter with modernity, especially colonial modernity under the British rule, was marked by multiple rationalities and disparate and often contradicting understandings of the experiences of modernity, based on caste, class and gender. As with other Indian modernities it was also characterized by a kind of temporal warp, where the modern was itself dependent on and defined by the premodern, with the latter creating political and historical disjunctures in the former while striving for a sense of seamlessness and continuity that complicates social imaginaries. It has been pointed out that the

Figure 7.1 Mohanlal. Getty Images.

process of modernization of Kerala society has different phases:

> The modernisation process in Kerala society in the early decades of the present century can be seen as the product of a three-fold transformation. In the first place, the anti-colonial, anti-feudal struggle radically transformed the social order and paved the way for profound changes in class relations and societal norms. In the second place, the reform movements which sought to cleanse the society of evils like untouchability, social segregation on the basis of caste, polygamy and so on, dealt a death blow to the oppressive ancient regimen with its rigid caste stratification, female servitude and reprehensible practices meant for its perpetuation. In the third place, the struggle against the feudal mores led to a thorough restructuring of the family, not only among the oppressed classes but among the privileged strata. (Ramachandran 1995: 118–19)

It is into this kind of a tenuous terrain that cinema arrived in Kerala in the early decades of the twentieth century. Early Malayalam cinema was believed to be largely social, in stark contrast to the mythologicals that constituted the cinematic enterprise in other parts of India. One can see in this trend a popular desire for modernity and a staunch belief in the capability for modernization of the individual and society. Moreover, cinema itself as an instrument of modernity was linked to scientific objectivity and rationality and therefore committed to the ethics of building modern subjectivities and fostering democratic ideals in a world where feudalism was being eased out, yielding place to more democratic and secular, and therefore more 'modern' social institutions. One can see here how early cinema in Kerala became easily woven into the project of modernity, in fact becoming the most popular icon of the social, cultural and aesthetic expressions of modernity, both intrinsically in the nature of its apparatus and extrinsically in what it sought to represent. However, this chapter argues that after liberalization this progressive egalitarian base of Kerala's development paradigms in the twentieth century underwent radical shifts with a resurgence of caste and communal affinities, a consolidation of overarching patriarchal structures and the criminalization of politics. This in a sense strangled the emancipatory potential of the earlier reform impulses and progressive movements, leading to what can be called regressive modernities. T. K. Ramachandran calls it an ultraconservative backlash in Kerala society and states that it is characterized by 'pronounced anti-progressive, anti-left stances', an 'unabashed idealisation of the feudal past', 'belligerent apolitical posturing', 'unconcealed male-chauvinistic and sexist bias', a 'pathological dread of people's movements' and a 'strident revivalist rhetoric' (1995: 110).

Contemporary discourses on the modern state of Kerala evince a pendular swing from proclamations of it as 'a first world state in a third world country' and clichéd tourist advertisements such as 'God's Own Country', to tirades against its high levels of casteist, communalized politics, largely patriarchal structures in spite of a matrilineal past and an intensely commodified society. This chapter aims to study the star persona of Mohanlal, lauded first as a 'superstar' and later as a 'megastar' by the media and industry, as a site on which is played out many of the tendencies of this 'ultraconservative' backlash in Kerala society. The inscription of the symbols of hegemonic masculinity on Mohanlal's body coincides in significant ways with the eclipsing of the mass base of Kerala's social revolutions and marks an apogee of the processes of marginalization of its women. In seeking to concentrate on the films of Mohanlal I will focus mostly on Kerala society during the last two decades of the twentieth century and the first decade and a half of the twenty-first. This was an age, especially the late 1980s and early 1990s, when cataclysmic changes were happening all over India specifically with regard to the satellite television boom and the liberalization of the economy. Thus, both the skies and the market had opened up to new players

and new iconographies, and Mohanlal's entry into filmdom in the 1980s and his transformation in the 1990s embody the most significant changes that took place during this phase of Kerala's social history. Caroline and Filippo Osella have claimed that 'Mohanlal's flexibility suggests qualities of mutability permitting him to embody a variety of interesting and alluring imaginary positions with which to play, while always remaining safely anchored to a stable and recognizable core identity as "Mohanlal"' (2004: 255). This chapter argues that Mohanlal's rise to 'superstardom' was partly propelled by the liberalization of the Indian economy, which in a sense narrowed down the distance between the civil society and the market and linked the new masculine imagery to popular consumption, in the process privileging a re-traditionalization of intimacy and a communalization of the public sphere. Cinema becomes, from this period onwards, a purely commercial industry, which through a gendered commerce mediates the production and circulation of new representations of masculinity. The ideological discourses of 'superstardom', as played out in the movies of Mohanlal, thus project masculinity both as a consumable object of pleasure and as a trope validating caste, class and gender hierarchies.

It was in 1980 with the film *Manjil Virinja Pookkal* (Fazil) that Mohanlal made his serious entry into Malayalam cinema by playing the role of an antagonist who disrupts the romantic love between the hero and the heroine. Over the last three and a half decades, since the runaway success of this movie, Mohanlal has become a household name, representing everything that Kerala and the Malayali inhabitants of this small state have lived and aspired for. Thus, Mohanlal is a trope for Kerala, with its complex contemporary sociocultural and political histories and its inherent paradoxes. Through his films he seems to have been able to construct a complicated yet homogenous regional identity for the heterogeneous groups of people from diverse castes, classes, religions and ethnicities that Kerala houses. In the 1980s, when Kerala was struggling with rising unemployment and the Gulf dream was showing signs of breaking open at the seams, Mohanlal enacted roles that consisted largely of underprivileged, marginalized upper-caste, asexual males who were struggling with the material and existential dilemmas of life. Movies such as *Visa* (Balu Kiriyath, 1983) emblematize the woes of the unemployed young men of Kerala who are waiting in the wings to procure a visa to go to the Gulf countries but end up being cheated by agents. *Iniyengilum* (I. V. Sasi, 1983) and *Akkare* (K. N. Sasidharan, 1984) are movies that carry forward this theme of the Malayali dream of being the prosperous migrant. This dream, by the time it reaches a cult classic such as *Gandhinagar Second Street* (Sathyan Anthikad, 1986) has transmogrified into a nightmare where the young man played by Mohanlal is willing to do any work to support himself. *Naadodikkattu* (The Vagabond Wind, Sathyan Anthikad, 1987) presents another phase in the life of this unemployed man in which he hopes to sell his lands and set his house in order. *Varavelpu* (Welcome, Sathyan Anthikkad, 1989) narrated the bursting of the Gulf bubble and had the disillusioned young man arriving back from his migrant locations to be further disillusioned by the socio-economic factors that have transformed his native land into a nightmare. This was the phase when Mohanlal was an actor but not a 'star'.

However, the quintessential Malayaliness that Mohanlal's 'stardom' came to represent was accumulated during this phase. This was the time when he was identified and believed to possess those qualities and cultural traits that made his characters, the playful prankster, the simpleton struggling in a bad world, the unemployed youth fighting to keep his family above board, all so endearing to Malayali audiences. Thus, the myth to be born accumulates its cultural capital in the numerous movies that endeared him to his audiences, such as *Chithram* (The Picture, Priyadarshan, 1988), *Kireedam* (The Crown, Sibi Malayil, 1989) and *Bharatham* (Sibi Malayail, 1991). These films also included not only mainstream ones but the likes of Padmarajan's renowned *Namukku Parkkaan Munthirithoppukal* (Vineyards for Us to Dwell in, 1986) and *Thoovaanathumbikal* (Dragon Flies in a Drizzle, 1987), and Bharathan's *Kattathe Kilikkoodu* (A Nest in the Wind, 1983) and *Thaazhvaaram* (The Valley, 1990), which are considered 'middle cinema', delicately poised between the arthouse and the commercial. Thus, Mohanlal's later celebration of extraordinariness is born out of the ordinariness that is so much a part of the characters that he embodied in this first stage.

The factor common to many of the characters of this phase is their charming boyishness and a rather consistent indifference to political ideologies, except for a vehement assertion of the rights of the common man. It is only in movies such as *Lal Salam* (Red Salute, Venu Nagavalli, 1990) that we have an openly political character. But even here he renounces his Communist Party affiliations to move on to a more romantic, capitalistic and individualistic mode of personal politics that is highly critical of the institutionalization of leftist politics in the state. Mohanlal thus side steps political affiliations, unlike many other stars, so as to keep his films strictly on the level of entertainment. In a movie such as *Thandavam* (Shaji Kailas, 2002) he spells this out clearly with a snide comment that one should tilt neither to the Right nor the Left but should be able to question both, critiquing Kerala's binary politics of right-wing congress and left-wing communist parties.

Mohanlal is regarded as a consummate actor; for many, his success is attributed to his innate sense of rhythm. He possesses a rare combination of grace and fluidity, which creates a charisma unparalleled in Malayalam cinema. Even with a stout body, his song and dance sequences have made him one of the most endearing actors in Malayalam cinema. Critics have suggested, furthermore, that '[the] possibility of the actor, especially the dancing actor, using the whole body as phallus is … explored in Lal's playful dance and aggressive flirtatious teasing' (Osella and Osella 2004: 252).

Post-1990s, even in the macho masculine/feudal lord images, Mohanlal does not completely sever his ties with the earlier phase in that the 'lovable little rascal' and mischievous 'forever boy' trope continues into the serious roles he enacts across the decade. This makes him highly popular among women audiences especially. One can see a repeated tapping into the sensual energies of the 'Unnikannan' (little Lord Krishna) myth. Sudhir Kakar has pointed out that as one of the incarnations of Vishnu, Krishna is one of the most popular of Gods: 'in Krishna's iconography and in his representation in religious poetry and song, he is either a toddler – with the child's attributes of freedom, spontaneity and delight in self … or an eternal youth with either his lover Radha at his side or playing the Divine Flute in the middle of a dancing circle of young women' (1978: 143–4). While little Krishna as the embodiment of infinite wisdom and eternal love is the source of *bhakthi*, or devotion, he is also capable of spawning cross-sexual and libidinal energies in his incarnation as the sensuous trickster who can garner the complete attention of both his mother and the infinite number of *gopikas* who always surround him. In psychoanalytic terms Krishna 'encourages the individual to identify with an ideal primal self, released from all social and super ego constraints. Krishna's promise, like that of Dionysus in ancient Greece, is one of utter freedom and instinctual exhilaration' (142). It is interesting, therefore, to note that there are numerous internet sites filled with gossip and banter about Mohanlal's sexual prowess. Such gossip, whether planted or not, created for Mohanlal the myth of a libertine with unlimited capacities into which the notion of 'superstardom' can fit in easily given the contemporary anxieties around masculinity in Kerala in the wake of numerous women's emancipation and empowerment projects there. Many movies have portrayed this aspect of Mohanlal, foregrounding a virile masculinity and women's fervent quest for his attention, the best example being *Casanova* (Rosshan Andrews, 2012) in which he quite literally plays the modern-age version of the eponymous and amorous count Giacomo Casanova. This image was launched by some of the early slapstick comedy movies of Mohanlal such as Priyadarshan's *Boeing Boeing* (1985) and *Aram + Aram = Kinnaram* (1985). What is significant in the post-1990s Casanova images of Mohanlal is, again, the onscreen mixing of a libertine excess with a dignified social stature. However, it has to be emphasized that, as befitting a star, his onscreen desire is always predicated upon reciprocity. Thus, the Casanova image is predicated solely on the pleasure principle and not on any kind of victimization or possession. Moreover, if in his earlier comic Casanova roles he was a lovable roguish pauper with only sex appeal as his capital, in his later avatar there is a paradigm shift.

Though there are no studies to prove the point, the 1990s was the time when Kerala architecture, for example, started reflecting a feudal nostalgia, with people building palatial feudal-style mansions replete with *poomukham*, *chuttu* verandah, paneled walls, wooden pillars, *nadumuttam* (central courtyards), *aambalkulam* (waterlily ponds) and *chaarupadi* and *aattukattil* (wooden seats and swings). Brass utensils such as *kindi*, *montha* and *nilavilakku* are all part of this feudal-style interior décor. It is also significant that Mohanlal in his off-screen persona donned the mantle of a 'connoisseur of art' during this period, accumulating expensive art pieces from around the world and thus bridging the gap between the luxuriant locales of his films and those of his personal life. That the star's domestic décor was no different from those of his screen roles marked Mohanlal's metamorphosis into the extraordinary and unique 'star'. Richard Dyer has pointed out the inherent conflict between the perception of stars as both ordinary and special (1979). Simon Dixon has suggested, '[this] ambiguity in status creates the paradox whereby individuals whose very profession is performance and whose primary goal is public recognition soon yearn for anonymity and privacy. As the subject of a photo shoot, the star's home, no longer a refuge, takes on a peculiar rhetoric that places it somewhere between promotion and publicity' (2003: 82). Mohanlal's body and his domestic décor thus take on a certain stylization that limits his screen persona to certain kinds of roles. The ordinary has now become out of bounds and his masculinity ideal. His public image and his private self are both as stylistically constructed as a shooting set and subsequently take on a kind of vulnerability that easily becomes the butt of ridicule in the intellectual circles in Kerala. For example, one joke went that if someone had to bash up the hero on screen it could not be anyone less than a Bollywood celebrity villain. Mohanlal is the one star to have smoothly effected the rather ambiguous transition from 'star-as-ordinary' to 'star-as extraordinary' in tune with the shifting paradigms of Kerala's socio-economic structures.

But even as the star body revalidates tradition, it also emphasizes modern consumption with a clear underlining of lifestyle and consumer choices. Mohanlal's post-1990s movies, while characterized by landscapes of feudal nostalgia, are nevertheless also dotted with new geographies of consumption. There is an increasingly capitalist concern with the production of images, signs and sign systems that focus on new patterns of consumption. Taken together, his movies and advertisements of late have endorsed choice and variety in experiences as well as commodities, even while offering style manuals for the what and how of consumption/desire. In 2007, Mohanlal provoked a furore when he started appearing in adverts for a prominent brand of whisky. The BBC reported:

> Alcohol advertising is banned in India. Brewers have used different methods to get around the ban, sometimes promoting non-alcoholic drinks with near-identical labels to the alcoholic ones. In this case, television advertisements, billboards and hoardings have come up across Kerala which feature the four-time award-winning actor asking the question: 'What's up this evening?' The actor is shown munching on banana chips, a favourite snack with tipplers, and hurling the loaded question at whoever he meets on the walk. (Mary 2007)

In a state that tops the scale for per-capita liquor consumption in the country (the same report sites statistics pointing out that the average Kerala resident consumes 8.3 litres of liquor every year, which is the highest rate in India and three times the national average) one has again to take note of how the actor taps into his populist mass appeal and the libertine hero ideal. The augmentation of the myth of masculinity is evident in this advertisement. But what is more glaring is the invocation of the entire repertoire of Mohanlal films that glorified drinking, such as *Spadikam, Hallo* (Rafi Mecartin, 2007)*, Chotta Mumbai* (Anwar Rasheed, 2007)*, Chandrolsavam* (Ranjith, 2005), among numerous others, invoked here to offer easy answers to the questions of what constitutes Malayali masculinity. In the Kannan Devan Tea advertisement, which features an initiation rite, a younger inexperienced man is taught how it feels to scale unparallel heights by the successful star himself. The advert casts Mohanlal in the initiation ritual, helping novices attain a smoother and easier passage into masculinity by revealing to them its secret formulas. One sees here the deeply intertwined relationship between celebrity, star image and Malayali male individualism and subjectivity. Mohanlal's competitor for stardom in the Malayalam film industry is Mammooty (Muhammad Kutty Ismail Paniparambil, 1951–), a star whose image is congruent with community and a selfless devotion to the family, as epitomized in movies such as *Valyettan* (Shaji Kailas, 2000). Mohanlal's cultural significance is more discursively anchored to the rise of a Malayali individualism and thus reflects upon the ideological tensions of Kerala society in the throes of globalization. The manipulated individualism, so much a characteristic feature of traditional societies caught up within neoliberal corporate agendas and diasporic elites who create visions of liberal individualism and power, is very much a germane idea in the early Mohanlal movies of the 1980s such as *Akkare Akkare Akkare* (Priyadarshan, 1990), *Gandhinagar 2nd Street* (Sathyan Anthikad, 1986) and *Varavelppu* (1989), which offer the promise of a changed society where individuals will be more free from societal interventions and incursions. This promise is then delivered in later movies, which evince generic traits of the celebration of the rise of a new individualism, one which calls for not only the reinvention of the self but also the need for new moralities and new standards of values and judgements and especially a new male code. For example, in a re-mythification tale of the Ramayana in *Raavanaprabhu*, the Mohanlal avatar is not a modern version of the gentleman Rama but Lord Ravana, who invents his own codes of morality in a changed world and is licensed to behave in the most boorish and uncouth manner to the female protagonist. This holds true for most of his post-1990s movies. Mohanlal is thus the star to most clearly mediate globalization and its anxieties to Malayali audiences. His onscreen hegemonic masculinity combines feudal power with global capital. The 'polysemic' (Dyer 1979: 72) possibilities of Mohanlal's star image thus foreground tradition while masking globalization, in effect creating a seamless union of the two, which is imperative in traditional societies such as Kerala.

Having established himself as ordinary rather than glamorous in the 1980s, Mohanlal had already tapped into the potentials of viewer identification and desire because his was the body with which the average Malayali male could identify without incumbent anxieties regarding the impossibility of achieving it. With a not-so-perfect body, a most ordinary face, and no pretensions whatsoever to glamour or beauty, Mohanlal was as unlike the cinematic ideal hero as was the ordinary spectator himself and therefore elicited more desire in terms of identification. Osella and Osella, for example, note that 'Malayali fans at once revel in Lal's imperfections and claim him as their own *doppelgänger*. While young men repeat dialogue and copy hairstyles, follow *fillum* fashions and modify their walks, they maintain a sense that this is all play, a matter of aesthetics and surfaces' (2004: 256).

The hegemonic masculinity that Mohanlal creates post-1990s has a solid and sensitive base in the roles he enacted in the 1980s. His masculinity is more earthy, raw, in a sensuous way. The subsequent transformation of the comic, gentle and often vulnerable sexuality of movies such as *Appu* (Dennis Joseph, 1990), *Chithram*, *Mithunam* (Priyadarshan, 1993) and *His Highness*

Abdullah (Sibi Malayil, 1990), and of the innocent, wide-eyed, blundering masculinity of *Minnaram* (Priyadarsan, 1994), *Naadodikkattu* (1987), *Akkare Akkare Akkare, Mukunndetta Sumithra Vilikkunnu* (Priyadarsan, 1988) and *Sanmanassullavarkku Samadhanam* (Sathyam Anthikkad, 1986) into a surge of male sexual power fuelled by a feudal sexual economy seems almost like an initiation or rite of passage.

Post-1990s we see Mohanlal in roles where his promiscuity exceeds bodily desires and spills into unlimited cultural and economic markers, fetishistic objects on screen that represent luxury and pleasure. A number of movies have him play the feudal lord/don, such as *Devasuram, Aaraam Thampuran, Raavanaprabhu, Narasimham* and *Thandavam,* where we see him surrounded by cultural artefacts that resonate with a fetishistic value, in the process melding commodity fetishism with culture capital. Thus, aspects of a feudal culture become imbued with desire and are exhibited and celebrated as cultural commodities. The feudal *tharavad*, or ancestral home, with its numerous artefacts of hegemonic value becomes a spectacle that attempts the legitimization of capitalism (neo-feudalism) through a reorientation of cinematic representation and *mise en scène*. Elevated cameras, sensual movements and accentuated lighting, and other stylistic and cinematic techniques, are used to objectify and eroticize the feudal mansion, its wood paneled interiors, antique furniture, elephant tusks and other significant feudal symbols. The camera in fact pauses, caresses and admires these images, and the eroticization of feudal signifiers enhances the fetishized pleasures of the cinema of this period. One can see here a link between cultural forms and the psychic structures of audiences. The ontological crisis, which is essentially a male crisis, is resolved at the end of *Aaraam Thampuran*, for example, when the villagers invest the hero, played by Mohanlal, with 'feudal lordship', and he conducts a ritualistic temple festival after fighting the villain, thus resolving the psychosocial and historical anxieties that signify the cultural conflicts of globalization and liberalization.

Mohanlal's feudal masculinity is here hand in glove with the erotic complicity of the audience, which in a sense establishes the terms of spectatorship as voyeuristic in both cultural and psychic terms. The audience is thus caught in a *mise en scène* that mirrors their own desires and feudal nostalgia. The cracks and fissures in the project of modernity are revealed in numerous Mohanlal films of this era, which explicate how the ontologically incomplete feudal past has not effectively been repressed or buried, but rather returns to haunt us through our inexplicable ties to it that modernity clearly has not been able to sever. One can link this idea to the 'ontological insecurity' felt by people in traditional societies under threat from the forces of globalization, and to Anthony Giddens's formulations regarding 're-traditionalization' (1991). At a time when global economies bring into currency new values and ethics and drastic changes in customs and practices, there is an oppositional identitarian movement that overemphasizes culture and tradition and valorizes masculinity and power. It is this moment of 'ontological insecurity' in Kerala during the liberalization era that popular culture so eminently resolves through the figure of Mohanlal. As Osella and Osella argue, Mohanlal 'assuages young men's anxieties about identity by offering the spectacle of stability which can assimilate changes without threat to self'; Mohanlal is 'held to be flexible yet stable … treading an ideal path through the modern world: neither reluctant nor too-eager to embrace modernity' (2004: 255–6).

It is also significant that during this phase Kerala society at large entered into a cultural over-investment in traditional architecture and in polishing and preserving objects and artefacts that create a romanticized aesthetic environment of the past. Temple festivals were revived, religious identities were resuscitated and food and environments were deliberately tuned to create an abundance of nostalgic affect. This exemplifies what Christopher Pinney calls 'the collapse of the social into the aesthetic' (2004: 11). Houses started having elaborate *puja* rooms crafted on the models of miniature temples.

The embellished and aestheticized women, both beautiful and trained in the classical arts to entertain her man, as seen in films such as *Devasuram* and *Aram Thamburan*, is also a fetish that substitutes for the feudal economy. Freud equates the fetish object with the penis, stating that the function of the fetish is '[to endow] women with the characteristic [the phallus] which makes them tolerable as sexual objects' (1977: 353). Most of Mohanlal's women in these movies, whether the semi-destitute Bhanu in *Devasuram* (played by Revathy), or the orphan Unnimaya in *Aaraam Thampuran* (played by Manju Warrier), are castrated women in that they are signified through a lack. However, in Freudian terms, as fetishes they also serve a double function in that they are both lack and excess, helping the hero Mohanlal to mobilize his libidinal energies and facilitating the redirection of his masculine virility to the male narcissistic function of preserving 'tradition' and, therefore, his own identity.

Another significant facet of the Mohanlal erotic aesthetic is that though adept in the art of lovemaking he is yet as innocent as an adolescent in each of his conquests, forcing the woman into a masochistic, servile bond and never allowing her to sever his ties with the Oedipal mother. This Oedipal tryst features in successful Mohanlal films such as *Kireedam, Devasuram, Vietnam Colony* (Siddique Lal, 1992), *His Highness Abdullah, Gaandharvam* (Sangeeth Sivan, 1993), *Baba Kalyani* (Shaji Kailas, 2006) and *Madambi* (B. Unnikrishnan, 2008), in many of which the actor Kaviyoor Ponnamma plays the role of his mother.

Mohanlal metamorphoses, post-1990s, from his earlier boyish charm into a modern virile manliness combining the aura of the traditional Malayali gentleman hero with the macho-ness and magnetism of the global star. His *mundu* (the white piece of cloth that Malayali men tie around their waists) is traditional but his glasses, watches and sandals are all international brands. The cars he drives and the transnational locales he frequents stamp him as a global citizen with markedly Malayali traits that make him a representative of the thriving diasporic Malayali community all over the world. His success stems from these flamboyant combinations that he is able to effect between the strongly regional and national as well as the transnational, and the cultural spectacles he is able to offer on a visual plane combining dance, music and a virile masculine charm.

Works Cited

Dixon, Simon (2003), 'Ambiguous Ecologies: Stardom's Domestic Mise-en-Scène', *Cinema Journal*, 42 (2): 81–100.

Dyer, Richard (1979), *Stars*, London: British Film Institute.

Freud, Sigmund ([1927] 1977), 'Fetishism', in Strachey (ed.), *On Sexuality*, Pelican Freud Library, vol. 7, 345–8, Harmondsworth: Penguin.

Giddens, Anthony (1991), *Modernity and Self-Identity: Self and Society in the Late Modern Age*, Cambridge: Polity Press.

Kakar, Sudhir (1978), *The Inner World: A Psycho-analytic Study of Childhood and Society in India*, Delhi: Oxford University Press.

Mary, John (2007), 'Trouble Brews Over Alcohol Ads', *BBC News*, 15 February, online at: http://news.bbc.co.uk/1/hi/world/south_asia/6364165.stm (accessed 15 June 2015).

Osella, Caroline and Filippo Osella (2004), 'Young Malayali Men and their Movie Heroes', in Radhika Chopra, Caroline Osella and Filippo Osella (eds), *South Asian Masculinities: Context of Change, Sites of Continuity*, 224–63, New Delhi: Women Unlimited.

Pinney, Christopher (2004), *Photos of the Gods: The Printed Image and Political Struggle in India*, London: Reaktion Books.

Ramachandran, T. K. (1995), 'Notes on the Making of Feminine Identity in Contemporary Kerala Society', *Social Scientist*, 23 (1): 109–23.

Chapter 8

From Gandhi to Jinnah: National dilemmas in the stardom of Rattan Kumar

Salma Siddique

In 1956, after acting in nearly fifty films in the Bombay film industry, the teenaged child star Rattan Kumar (b. 1942?) left India for Pakistan, nearly a decade after the partition of the subcontinent. A letter in a Pakistani film magazine, published seven years after Kumar's arrival, diagnosed the actor's subsequent plummet in popularity following his migration.

> Rattan had done well in *Jagriti* in India. No credit goes to him in *Bedari*. I know when he was a boy of 8 or 10 his acting was excellent and marvellous; I liked his childhood acting very much. I thought that when Rattan would be a young man of 25, he will become the best hero of Indo-Pak subcontinent and will even replace Dilip. But it was an unlucky career for Rattan for joining Pakistani screen. He had done a brilliant tragedy in film like *Baiju Bavra* but now he can't do such type of tragedy roles at all. What he can do is foolish sworing [*sic*].
> (Anon. 1963: 41)

The extract encapsulates the disappointment rife at Kumar's inability to successfully replicate his Indian stardom in Pakistan. If 'no credit' went to him in *Bedari* (Awakening, Rafiq Rizvi, 1957), it was arguably deemed so because the film was a Pakistani remake of the Indian *Jagriti* (Awakening, Satyen Bose, 1954). Such remakes were locally and disparagingly called *charbas*, or replicas, and carried the taint of plagiarism. The other ignominy for Kumar in Pakistan was his appearance in the lowbrow fantasy genre, described here as 'foolish sworing'. There was a considerable overlap between the categories of *charba* and fantasy, the generic constituencies of Kumar's star image in Pakistan. By the age of twenty-one, when this letter was written, the young actor had already managed to shatter the hopes projected onto his mid-twenties self.

While the bulk of the film migration between the cities of Bombay and Lahore took place during late 1947/early 1948, discrete and often discreet relocations continued till the late 1950s, as in the instance of the Muslim family of Kumar, whose real name was Syed Nazir Ali. Kumar's migration has an ideological potency, due to its marginality in Indian accounts and its centrality in Pakistani ones. In these disjunctive national narrations emerges the cultural significance of the child star, identified by Jane O'Connor as a complex figure with inherent powers to generate emotions and embody hope (2008). Starting his film career in independent India, Kumar's career, when compared to other migrants, was outwardly untouched by the disruptions that the appearance of national boundaries effected in pre-national film trajectories. Yet undoubtedly the star's departure must be read within the 'long partition' of the subcontinent (Zamindar 2007), which rendered his star-career as the *kamikaze* of nationalisms in the subcontinent.

In proposing a link between the social order and a star's appeal, Richard Dyer stresses the need to consider 'specific instabilities, ambiguities and contradictions in the culture, which are reproduced in the actual practice of making films and film stars' (1991a: 60). Star charisma, according to Dyer, involves an effective reconciliation of contradictory elements. But contradictions, which in Kumar's case constituted the Rubicon of Indian nationalism, were difficult to condense in a single star image. Kumar's migration sets into motion two distinct modalities of star charisma – an Indian by truncation and a Pakistani by elaboration. Condensing his image to the childhood on screen, a silence is maintained in Indian sources on his migration and later career. In Pakistan, Rattan's migrant star image is elaborated in his earliest films through double roles and the family-produced *charbas* or remakes, both alluding to an Indian past. No longer a child nor an Indian, the star image is set forth in a complicated orbit of disavowal, retaliation and appropriation. Offering a larger vantage point of film enterprise in post-partition Lahore, the *doppelgänger* becomes the privileged form of a reconstituted self, the ultimate embodiment of divided identities.

The departure of the idealized citizen

Becoming the quintessential child of popular Hindi cinema, Kumar played nearly all the key childhood roles in the landmark Hindi films of the early 1950s. Notable among these were neo-realist inspired Bombay films such as *Do Bigha Zameen* (Half Acre Land, Bimal Roy, 1953) and *Boot Polish* (Prakash Arora, 1954); fantasy or 'costume' films such as *Baghdad* (Nanabhai Bhatt, 1952), *Baiju Bawra* (Batty Baiju, Vijay Bhatt, 1952), *Laila Majnu* (K. Amarnath, 1953) and *Bahut Din Hue* (Once Upon A Time, S. S. Vasan, 1954); mythologicals such as *Jai Mahalaxmi* (Hail Goddess Mahalaxmi,1951), *Radha Krishna* (Raja Nene, 1954) and *Ekadashi* (Eleventh Lunar Day, Gunjal, 1955); and socials such as *Sargam* (Music, P. L. Santoshi, 1950), *Afsana (*Lore, B. R. Chopra, 1951) and *Jagriti*. As genres and circuits of Hindi cinema go, this is quite a comprehensive inventory. While Kumar mostly played the childhood roles of the leading heroes, in *Do Bigha Zameen, Boot Polish, Bahut Din Hue* and *Jagriti,* he occupied the key narrative space of a boy protagonist.

With crisp dialogue delivery, a round earnest face and somewhat tubby body, Kumar was regarded as excellent in tragic roles (Anon. 1954: 31). In many of these films, his parents were either dead (*Boot Polish, Baiju Bawra*) or absent and extremely vulnerable themselves (*Do Bigha Zameen, Jagriti, Bahut Din Hue*). Two films in particular, *Do Bigha Zameen* and *Boot Polish*, crystallized Kumar's image as an exceptional child struggling against odds. Regarded as 'landmarks' of national cinema and allegories of the newly independent 'infant' Indian nation (Chakravarty 1993; Rajadhyaksha and Willemen [1994] 1999: 334), both films won popular awards at home and received recognition in international film festivals.[1] Influenced by the neo-realism of post-war Italy, in particular the films of Vittorio De Sica, these Bombay films were part of the realist image that Indian cinema was projecting abroad during the 1950s. Through a self-conscious and selective deployment of neo-realism, these films 'sought to absorb it into the familiar tropes, narrative and

---

[1]*Do Bigha Zameen* won the first Filmfare award for Best Film and Best Director (1954), won the first National Award for the Best Feature Film (1954), won the International Prize at the 7th Cannes Film Festival (1954) and Prize for Social Progress at Karlovy Vary Festival. *Boot Polish* won three awards at the Filmfare Awards (1955) including for Best Film and a special mention for child actress Naaz at the 8th Cannes Film Festival (1955).

performance resources and aesthetic ambitions of an Indian cinema, multiply conceived' (Vasudevan 1997: 154). Crucially, Rattan's stardom was a product of what Neepa Majumdar identifies as the neorealist realignment of Bombay cinema, led by film journalism, involving a shift in emphasis from filmmakers to film stars (2012).

While Kumar was neither an actual street child nor did he look like one, he could well evoke the emotional reaction by embodying the idealized little citizen-boy, clear-complexioned, healthy, clean, well behaved and articulate, facing risks that were real: starvation, neglect and abuse. His physical dexterity, combined with his emotive eloquence, made Kumar the perfect child star for Bombay films, where melodramatic tendencies were more pronounced than in De Sica's films. For *Do Bigha Zameen*, Bimal Roy found his Bruno in Kumar, chubby-faced, pint-sized but also loquacious, who played Kanhaiya, the son of poor farmers, idealized as responsible even if a little spoilt. Acting in a more effective manner than his struggling father, Kanhaiya's character recalls similar child figures in post-war European cinema, which elucidated male lack and stood on 'the ruins of masculinity' (Fischer 2007). One scene in particular, where Kanhaiya's shoeshine friend hurries to watch the new fantasy *Baghdad* at a nearby cinema, functions as an ode to Kumar's star charisma. An intertextual and self-reflexive comment on themes, circuits and stardom, it encapsulated the distance between *Do Bigha Zameen* (a realist rendition of rural-urban poverty circulating in Indian A-circuits and international film festivals) and *Baghdad* (an *Arabian Nights* fantasy hybrid popular in subaltern circuits), a distance that could only be reconciled by Kumar.

Made a year later, *Boot Polish* picked up on the potential of the story of the urban street children Kanhaiya encountered in *Do Bigha Zameen*. The film also carried a more obvious echo of the narrative premise of another De Sica film, *Shoeshine* (1946). Moving the narrative to life in Bombay slums, *Boot Polish* was the story of the orphan siblings Bhola (Kumar) and his berry-loving sister Belu (Baby Naaz) and their quest to earn a dignified living in the city. Sharing the lot of millions in independent India, Bhola stands apart in his uncompromising honesty and his refusal to steal or beg. The tribulations of Bhola and Belu come to an end when they are adopted by a childless and good-hearted bourgeois couple and sent to school, as befitting the future citizens of the country.

As in the post-war European cinema, children have likewise been pivotal to postcolonial modes of representation where the trope of child development lends itself persuasively to narratives of nation-building and cultural transformation (Barker 2011). Examining the consolidation of state authority in Nehruvian India, Srirupa Roy points out that the ideal citizen was imagined as a masculine subject, iconically represented as a young boy. This frequently invoked figure of the 'infantile citizen' needed 'state tutelage and protection in order to realize the potential of citizenship' (2007: 7). As a consequence of the neorealist films, the ideal yet infantile citizen became the overarching element of Kumar's persona. While himself embodying national futurity on screen, the blueprint for Kumar's projected adult stardom was Dilip Kumar (1922–), 'Nehru's hero' and the king of tragedy, whose monumental stardom exerted an inspirational hold on Rattan Kumar's miniature.[2]

---

[2] Both in India and Pakistan film magazines suggest comparison with Dilip Kumar, as does the extract cited at the beginning of the piece.

Thus, carrying the Nehruvian hallmark, Kumar was a frequent presence in the film reviews and news reports of the 1950s, especially the *Filmfare* magazine, which included him in special columns, centre spreads and dedicated star features. In magazine photographs, Kumar was almost always well turned out, immaculately dressed, westernized – dressed more like a colonial *sahib* than a poor, Indian orphan on the street. Apart from acting, cricket and tennis were listed as his key interests. A 'Star Profile' article from 1955 carried three colour photographs of Kumar in different outfits and poses: as a rifle-wielding hunter with a *sola topi* and flamboyant red silken scarf against blurred woods; as a school boy next to his bicycle (Figure 8.1); and lastly in white cricket gear complete with a red cap holding a bat (Anon. 1955b: 12–13). Calling him and his *Boot Polish* co-star Naaz accomplished 'veterans' and 'old hands', the article detailed Kumar's off-screen life as Syed Nazir Ali. When not shooting, he attended the *Anjuman-i-Islam* (Islamic Association) school in Bombay and loved sports. Cricket had a special place as he led star teams from the industry for 'filmland cricket matches', which involved popular actors and actresses playing fundraising cricket matches. An important plan Kumar was working towards involved organizing a team of boys to play cricket in England in mid-1956. Of course, no plans of working in Pakistan or contemplating a move to the country are ever mentioned in these articles.

These reports, where Kumar is revealed to be different in real life than his on-screen roles, contributed to what Dyer identifies as the crucial marker of the 'authenticity of a star image' (1991b: 136). As a Muslim carrying a Hindu name, Kumar also signified a qualified national presence. Highlighting his Muslim identity through his real name and community school, the *Filmfare* article took care to effectively offset this 'fundamental anxiety of Indian nationalism' by emphasizing his birthplace Ajmer, an iconic place of Sufi devotion for both Hindus and Muslims (Devji 1992: 1). A further example of Rattan fitting perfectly well into the fraternal unity of post-Independence India was his image as an orphan of unknown origins and a brother. It was not only the dancing Travancore sisters, who 'treated Rattan like a brother' (Anon. 1955b: 13). Even for his fans, he held a similar appeal of a lost brother and a brother to the lost.

> I wanted to write to you ever since I saw you in *Boot Polish*. You resemble my younger and only brother whose death when he was just in his teens caused our family an irreparable loss … please send us your photograph … We have no photograph of our brother who is no more with us. (Anon. 1955a: 55)

Successfully incarnating the Indian national orphan for eight years, Kumar left for Pakistan in 1956; once there, his film image became implicated in an impossible situation of disavowal and entanglement, characteristic of the long-winded partition.

The arrival of the doppelgänger

In early 1956, *Filmfare* discreetly conveyed Kumar's migration by shifting its coverage of the star from the regular (national) pages to the 'news from other centres' section within the periodical. In the monthly column 'Film Letter from Pakistan' it was reported that Kumar was working in *Kafristan*, directed by another migrant from Bombay, Sibtain Fazli (Anon. 1956a: 51). In contrast, *Nigar Weekly*, the Pakistani magazine published from Karachi, carried a full article on Kumar's arrival and, unlike the Indian coverage of the child star in previous years, the article was strongly mediated by his father Abbas Ajmeri (Anon. 1956b). While the idea of choice remains

Figure 8.1 'Star Profile', *Filmfare*, 16 September 1954. Courtesy of the National Film Archives of India, Pune.

contentious and complicated when looking at partition migration, the case of Kumar as a young boy following his father to Pakistan underlines the complex phenomenon of the child star, who '[blurs] the lines of distinction between childhood and adulthood, naivety and experience, and vulnerability and power' (O'Connor 2008: xii). Having nurtured acting ambitions himself, Ajmeri came to cast a large paternal shadow on his son's orphan persona.

Kumar's arrival in Pakistan was announced in the twin-release of the star-vehicles *Bedari* and *Masoom* (Innocent, Shareef Nayyar, 1957). Released on 6 December 1957, *Bedari* and *Masoom* were *charbas* of Hindi films *Jagriti* and *Toofan aur Diya* (Oil Lamp in the Wind, Prabhat Kumar, 1956) respectively. Careful not to impact each other's business, *Masoom* was released in Karachi, inaugurated by the first 'first lady' of Pakistan, Begum Iskandar Mirza, at the newly built Odeon cinema, while *Bedari* was promised a 'grand gala opening' at Regent Cinema Lahore. The business figures of the two films are not available but film compendiums list *Bedari* as a 'superhit' and *Masoom* was among the nine films selected for export to Britain for the diaspora in 1960 (Anon. 1960: 4).

The 'primrose path of plagiarism' (Pakistan Film Fact Finding Committee Report [PFFFCR] 1960: 88) signified by the fair sprinkling of *charbas* in Pakistan's film output has remained a consistent concern in periodic evaluations of the industry. In elite and institutional commentaries, plagiarism was seen as antithetical to national aspirations and a source of collective embarrassment. 'One of the most disgraceful instances of plagiarism', as the *Pakistan Times* unambiguously chose to call it, was *Bedari*, starring Kumar in a double role. It was the year 1957, when remakes constituted nearly 20 per cent of local production, while together with official Indian imports these comprised almost 45 per cent of the total releases (PFFFCR 1960). The overall threat of Indian imports for local production appeared exacerbated by local imitations. Any breach of copyright rules did not bother the emboldened *charba* producer, as the copied film was probably not shown outside Pakistan, most certainly not in India. Often frame-by-frame 'carbons' of Indian films, with different sets of actors and poorer production values, these films were indeed meant only for the Pakistani markets.

As critical scholarship on film remakes as well as copyright regimes have argued, duplicates are not only standard production and distribution strategies, but 'harbour a positive power, which denies the original and the copy' (Sundaram 2009: 105). In her fascinating study of the 'too many copies' of *L'Arroseur arrosé* (The Sprinkler Sprinkled, Louis Lumière, 1895), Jane Gaines argues for a positive spin on the business practice, which provided 'a solution to the problem of too little product to meet the demand for "moving pictures"' (2004: 228). However, 'equally vital is the fun of subterfuge', as Gaines acutely observes in such duplicates the beauty of the business solution: speed, economy and most strikingly, retaliation (236).

It is befitting that the 'free for all' and 'property-less' moment of early cinema should provide production parallels in early Pakistan where a combination of factors such as low output, exhibition demands and absent copyright controls created a similar situation. The retaliatory stance of duplicates is further evident in the narrative stances of Pakistani *charbas* making them doppelgängers materialized by partition, existing in a competitive and antagonistic relationship with the Indian originals. That these were never released in India, and therefore went 'unheard' on the other side, does not diminish their significance. In their limited markets, these *charbas* were not a simple veneration of Indian films. Instead they were complexly motivated with respect to Indian films still seducing Pakistani spectators, and were as much about controlling images as controlling the market. Owing their existence and immunity to the segmented markets and separate sovereign authorities in the subcontinent put in place by partition, these *charbas* were a strategy to stand up to the 'bullying' of the Indian films.

Underlining the competitive impulse, Thomas Leitch points out that a film remake operates on the paradoxical premise that the remake is just like the original only better (1990). Since these remakes are also star vehicles, the competitive exertions are evident in Kumar's performance as well. Imbued with disavowal and confrontation, the retaliatory *charbas* were the rite of passage that Kumar went through in order to 'remake' his stardom in Pakistan. The first among these was *Bedari*, now inventoried as a patriotic film of Pakistan but at the time of its release a 'national shame'.[3]

> When one learns that this theme has not been conceived by any of our writers but the producer has lifted it – incidents, dialogues and music, all – from the Indian prestige picture *Jagriti*, the feeling of satisfaction is at once supplanted by shame … Minor changes in scenes, substitution of Pakistan for Hindustan, *mulk* for *desh*, Quaid-i-Azam for Gandhiji, Pakistan Zindabad for Bande Matram, and Aye Qaid-i-Azam for Raghupati Raghav Raja Ram, do not in any sense give the theme a new treatment … Already Bombay is jeering at the Pakistan film industry.
> (Anon. 1957b: 6)

'The bad name for Pakistan' travelled over airwaves as the Hindi service station of Radio Ceylon made pointed references to the Pakistani copy. Caustically remarking that 'even copying is difficult sometimes', the review called the Pakistani version 'a primitive film' and Kumar's performance was seen as a repetition of his work in *Jagriti*. A close comparison of *Bedari* with *Jagriti* reveals the pointed departures of the former, which are not 'minor', at least not when the remake mobilized a political, religious and cultural difference that just a decade earlier made Pakistan possible.

The remake as a rite of passage

A remake of Satyen Bose's earlier Bengali film *Paribartan* (Transformation, Satyen Bose, 1949), *Jagriti* was illustrative of 'Bombay's Bengali life made possible through Bengal's infiltration of Bombay cinema in the forties and fifties' (Gooptu 2011: 97). Bose, whose early films are 'contextualised by post-Partition Bengal' (Rajadhyaksha and Willemen [1994] 1999: 70), retained the region as the crucial reference point in *Jagriti*. Bengal was evoked through character names and attires, spatial features of the native village, and actors such as Abhi Bhattacharya (1921–) and Pronoti Ghosh, who were a 'feature of the Bengali-Hindi combination of the 1950s Bombay film' (Gooptu 2011: 97). Yet it was Kumar, whose star appeal was greatest for the Hindi film audience, who occupied the most prominent billing on the publicity poster, presenting a close-up of his contorted face as the disproportionately large centrepiece of the triad (Figure 8.2).

In its visual codes and narrative elements, *Jagriti* is intimately connected to the affect-laden popular print and calendar art of late-colonial India. In particular, it reproduces through the film medium the popular cartographic imagination of Mother India. Sumathi Ramaswamy's

---

[3] A comprehensive and popular film website Mazhar.dk lists *Bedari* earliest among the '24 Patriotic Movies from Pakistan'. Online at: http://mazhar.dk/film/db/Patriotic.php (accessed 10 December 2014).

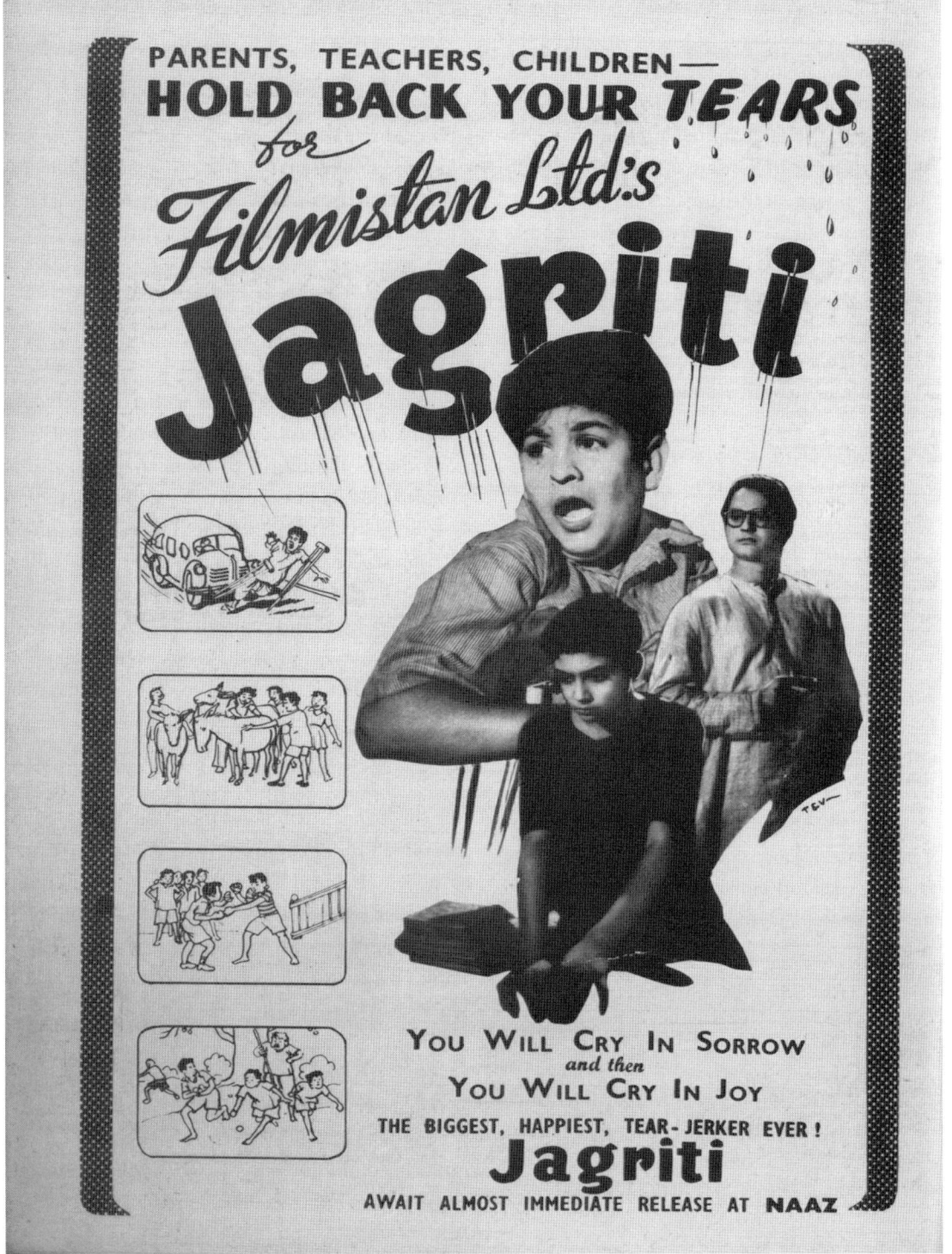

Figure 8.2 Poster of *Jagriti* (1954), *Filmfare*, 4 February 1955. Courtesy of the National Film Archives of India, Pune.

examination of the patriotic association of India with the sensuous, sacred imagery of the Mother Goddess and her hallowed sons, the 'pictorial big men', locates the primal tension of a nation striving to be plural, secular and modern yet resorting to the time-worn figure of a Hindu goddess (Ramaswamy 2010). She concludes that the undertow of a modernized Hinduism propels the imagination of India as Mother India, irrespective of the medium of imagination.

In *Jagriti* a mischievous village boy Ajay Mukherjee (Raj Kumar Gupta) is packed off, in a disciplinary measure, to a boys' residential school. There he meets the incapacitated Shakti Chowdhary (Kumar), son of a poor housemaid (Ghosh) and hence the target of derision among his other classmates. The boys, who both have exceptional capabilities, form a deep friendship. Soon enough, under Ajay's leadership, the students manage to oust the authoritarian warden of the school who is replaced by Bhattacharya, an equanimous teacher with new ideas. However, resistant to discipline and defiant of any authority, Ajay threatens to dismantle the enlightened regime. Ultimately, it takes Shakti's violent death to transform a remorseful Ajay.

Themed around the pedagogical preparation of the young 'sons' of India as its future guardians, *Jagriti* emphasizes a motivated vigilance regarding India's past and present to secure the freedom hard-earned by their fighting 'fathers'. The 'pictorial big men' of India's national movement, consisting of Mahatma Gandhi, Jawaharlal Nehru, Subhash Chandra Bose and Rabindranath Tagore, ubiquitous in popular calendar art, are plastered on the classroom walls in *Jagriti*. These images provide charged close-ups and cut-ins during the film. Abhi Bhattacharya's broad-shouldered and draped body, and his straightforward stare and cross-armed postures, recalls popular representations of the 'indispensable Vivekanand', the philosopher-patriot of the late nineteenth century who of all the 'neo-Hindu figures of Bengal … acquired and retained, over time, a pan-India and pan-Hindu resonance' (Sen 2006: 5). This influence, not limited to the teacher's physical appearance, is also evident in the pedagogical approach that the film upholds, with its roots in the modernist (educational) initiatives of the Bengal region, which also recalled the *Gurukula* system at Shantiniketan.

The suffering and wronged 'Mother India', a favoured representation in the late-colonial period, is embodied in Shakti's mother. In the song 'Chalo Chalein Maa' ('Let us go then Mother'), Ghosh, with long flowing hair and sari, sits under a large tree with the incapacitated Shakti resting in her lap while Ajay lurks nearby. This sequence is evocative of a painting *Bande Matarang* (I worship the mother) that appeared in *Balak*, a Bengali children's magazine, where mother (India) 'appears seated in a densely planted grove with a naked infant in her lap and other babies at play around her' (Ramaswamy 2010: 24). This illustration is among the rare but extremely charged depictions of maternal acts, which in other instances also work through Mother India's relationship with her sons of different religious communities.[4] Mother India's inclusive but equivocal maternity is central to *Jagriti*. The divided territories (Indian and Pakistan) of the subcontinent are anthropomorphized and individualized as Ajay and Shakti respectively. Played by Kumar, Shakti's incapacitated existence echoes the famous words of M. A. Jinnah on a 'maimed, mutilated and moth-eaten' Pakistan and the accompanying doubts over its

---

[4]One such particular illustration that appeared in *Intiya (1906)* shows the deity suckling four infants, suggesting the four religious communities of India (Ramaswamy 2010: 24).

survival (Jalal 1999: 21). Thus, Shakti's handicap, accident and death, as a violent loss affecting transformation, could well reference the partition of the subcontinent – especially of Bengal in the east.

Enacting the imperfection and death of the nation to which Kumar eventually migrated required a disavowal performed in the same affective currency as the one cobbled together by *Jagriti*. While Kumar's performance in the mythologizing *Jagriti* may have bolstered the patriotic credentials of his star image in India, in Pakistan it boded a political anathema. *Bedari* was therefore the child star's declaration of allegiance to Pakistan, which could only be constituted through a blow-by-blow dismantling of all that he had done in *Jagriti* and all that *Jagriti* had done to him. Retaliation was a way of managing the contradiction that was threatening to burst at the seams of Kumar's charisma. Thus, came about *Bedari*, the first film produced by his family production company Film Hayat and directed by Rafiq Rizvi, another recent film migrant from Bombay.

In a renegade fashion, *Bedari* transforms a patriotic Indian film into a 'gift to the (Pakistani) nation' (Anon. 1957a: 206). In its corrections, *Bedari* reveals the excisions and selections of the original and appropriates the narrative of *Jagriti* in order to 'better' it. Grafted onto a new context and repurposed for a new political situation, the remake fulfilled particularistic needs. The new context of Pakistan where *Bedari* was set and meant to be disseminated required obvious changes in markers of identity such as names, clothes and language. Ajay became Zafar and Shakti became Sabir. Instead of wearing a high-caste Bengali *dhoti* and eating on a low-rise wooden platform, the archetypal Anglo-Mohammaden paternal figure was dressed in a *sherwani* and ate on a dining table.

While a recalcitrant Ajay scribbled his decision to go to school in Devnagri, Zafar did so in the Urdu alphabet. While *Bedari* covers nearly all the action of the three-hour *Jagriti*, it does so in an abridged form of 130 minutes and is faster paced; as a copy, it does away with the setting up of a scene and sequence segues as the retaliatory impulse privileges the crudity of an unconcealed ideology over an aestheticized politicking. An hour shorter than the original, *Bedari* unfolds in an episodic manner, linked by title inserts at regular intervals emphasizing its Pakistani provenance. However, the most significant changes of *Bedari* are evident in the pointed corrections of counteractive histories, the song lyrics and the double role of Kumar.

The modern national icons of *Jagriti* – Gandhi, Nehru, Bose and Tagore – are replaced in *Bedari* with Quaid-i-Azam Jinnah, Liaquat Ali and Mohammad Iqbal. The medieval heroes are duly replaced by Central Asian invader figures such as Bin-Qasim, Saladdin and Mahmud Ghazni. In the open-air history lessons, *Jagriti* rejects the Aryan invasion theory whereas *Bedari* reinforces the iconoclasm of Mahmud Ghazni.[5] The play performed by students in *Jagriti* celebrates (Hindu) militaristic figures Maharana Pratap and Shivaji, known for their opposition to the Mughal state. In response, the play in *Bedaari* features Akbar, Birbal, Jahangir and Anarkali – the charismatic quartet of the Mughal franchise. While unclaimed by *Jagriti*, the Muslim figures associated with the subcontinent, medieval or modern, are at *Bedari*'s uncontested disposal as forerunners of the modern Muslim political state.

Retaining the tune and overall lyrics of the original songs of *Jagriti*, *Bedari* repurposes them for the different context. The first song 'Chalo Chalein Maa' in *Bedari* transforms the forlorn yet calm,

---

[5] The interpretation of Mahmud Gahzni's raid of the Somanth temple in 1026 has been projected as central to Hindu–Muslim relations (see Thapar 2005).

disabled boy from *Jagriti* into an anguished and embittered disabled adolescent, who lip-syncs the changed lines with a pointed grimace. The mother in the remake is discernibly Punjabi in her attire and physical build, and is played by the actress Ragini, who debuted in pre-partition Lahore's Punjabi sensation *Dulla Bhatti* (Roop Shorey, 1938). Changing the somewhat ambiguous and lyrical references of the original, which often come at the expense of the metre, both poetic and melodic, the remake imposes a strong mood of indignation, severance and self-realization.

> Chalo chalein maa sapnon ke gaon mein
> Kaaton se dur kahin phoolon ki chhaon mein
>
> (Let us go then Mother to the idyllic dreamland
> Away from thorns, in the gentle shade of flowers)
>
> Ho rahe ishaare reshmi ghataon mein
> (The gathering silken clouds signal [*Jagriti*])
>
> Kaise koi jee sake dukh bhari fizaaon mein
> (How can one live in oppressive surroundings
>   [*Bedari*])
>
> Rehna mere sang ma har dum
> **Aisa na ho ki bichad jaen hum**
>
> (Stay with me forever mother
> Else we may get separated)
>
> Ghoomna hai humko door ki dishaon mein
> (Leisurely we will wander in directions afar
>   [*Jagriti*])
>
> **Mere sach ki duniya hai tumhare paon mein**
> (My true world lies beneath your feet [*Bedari*])[6]

Appearing after the tragic death of Shakti, the last song in *Jagriti*, 'Hum Laye Hain Toofan Se' (We ferried through a storm), is a post-trauma articulation. It mobilizes primordial obligations by linking past sacrifices to future compliance through a status quo. Endorsing a Nehruvian commitment to the non-aligned movement and anti-nuclear position in the international diplomatic realm, the stance of restraint and caution is unceremoniously dropped towards the end and raised instead is the teacher's first calling forth the tricolour Indian flag to be fixed on the peaks. A decisive shift in lyrics, crescendo and gestures, *Jagriti* closes with the song and its veiled reference to Kashmir, 'the unfinished business of partition'. It is certainly interpreted as such by the homologous song in *Bedari*, when, cruising past the Quran and portraits of Muslim medieval warriors, the teacher reaches the map of Pakistan with ambiguous territorial limits. Not mincing any words, he reminds the students that Kashmir remains to be conquered and calls forth for fixing the star and crescent flag of Pakistan on the Himalayan peaks.

However, the cherry on *Jagriti*'s patriotic cake was the most popular eulogy to Gandhi, '*Sabarmati ke Sant*' (Oh Saint of Sabarmati). Cast in the favourite song genre of the Mahatma, the *bhajan*, or devotional song, it extolled the virtues of Gandhi's pacifist nationalist movement.

> De di humein azaadi bina khadag bina dhaal
> Sabarmati ke sant tune kar diya kamaal
>
> (You made us free without a sabre or a shield
> Oh Saint of Sabarmati you performed a miracle.)

Visually, the scene consists of a decorated hall in the school, filled with students facing Gandhi's smiling bust on a raised platform surrounded by flowers, ceremonial lamps and garlands. Propped by his crutches, Shakti 'sang' the ode standing a little ahead of the rest and closer to Gandhi. The crowd of students behind Shakti stood with their

---

[6]The last replacement is a reference to a Hadith, making the mother of Bedari an Islamic one, with paradise at her feet.

heads lowered, hands folded and, appropriate to their station, joined in the choral refrain. The song establishes a special relationship by predominantly cutting between close-ups of Kumar/Shakti and panning-shots of Gandhi's statue, imbuing Kumar with a Gandhian charisma. The song irrevocably linked a teary-eyed Kumar with the Father of the Indian nation and nearly all songs in *Jagriti* were a staple for repeated TV telecast and radio transmission each year on 'national days' including Gandhi's birth and death anniversary, Independence Day and Republic Day.

The hold of the Gandhian charisma on Kumar could only be countered, remade and, in the process, broken by invoking the man with the most compelling charm in Pakistan: Mohammad Ali Jinnah. Logically enough, 'Ae Quaid-i-Aazam' (Oh Supreme Leader) replaced the Saint of Sabarmati in the *Bedari* eulogy:

> Yun Di humein azaadi ki duniya hui hairaan
> Ae Qaid-i-azam tera ehsaan hai ehsaan
>
> (The world stood astonished at how you made us free
> Oh Supreme leader we are deeply indebted.)

Marked by a *darshanic* mode, the paean in *Jagriti* was restricted to the indoor space of a prayer meeting, fixed on the beheld object and charged by the beholder's devotion. There were no diversions in this visually sealed space. In contrast, in *Bedari* there is a clear discomfort with the idolatrous aesthetics of the original eulogy. A visually guarded adulation of Jinnah involved replacing the bust with a portrait and bleached-out stock-shots of his tomb, then still under construction, in Karachi. It was no longer the relationship of the beholder/beheld, but a more distant and unfixed perspective. More striking is the generous use of newsreel stock footage in the song, breaking away from the indoor space and combining historical footage of Lord Wavell's radio addresses, a reference perhaps to the Shimla Conference in June 1945; Jinnah inspecting army formations; celebrations of 14 August 1947, Pakistan's Independence Day; and military operations of the Pakistani army, suggesting perhaps the 1948 war with India over Kashmir. More significantly, *Bedari* challenged *Jagriti* (and Indian nationalism) where it truly hurt by making partition paramount. *Jagriti*'s celebration of Gandhi's non-violent leadership of India's independence had been made possible only by a careful avoidance of partition. In contrast, *Bedari* filled the visual space of its song with newsreel footage of refugee camps and the migrating populace, turning a representational constraint on its head by synchronizing a colonial documentary form with an Islamist idiom where leaving one's homeland for the sake of faith has a strong traditional precedent. While the eulogy to Gandhi identifies colonialism as the enemy and extols the virtues of non-violence, its counterpart in *Bedari* identifies Gandhi as the enemy by using the Indian News Parade film footage of the Gandhi–Jinnah Bombay negotiations of 1944 and unidentified military operations appearing *ad nauseam*, thus subverting the original ode on several registers.[7] *Bedari*'s eulogy ultimately posed the question of what was more exceptional: the independence of India or the attainment of Pakistan? While the partition footage besmirched any claims of a non-violent independence, *Bedari*'s celebration of Jinnah's miracle further dented *Jagriti*'s arrogant comportment of exceptionality.

---

[7]Indian News Parade short 'Gandhi and Jinnah negotiate for Communal Unity' (1944), online at: www.youtube.com/watch?v=e-Z-dSJE94.

The ultimate difference between *Jagriti* and *Bedari* is Kumar's double role in *Bedari*, playing both his original counterpart of the disabled boy Shakti/Sabir, as well as that of the lead protagonist Ajay/ Zafar. This fantastical premise of likeness, though acknowledged in the film, was hardly of any consequence to the plot. They are not twins separated at birth but friends who look the same. Ironically, some elements of the films, such as the exchanging of photographs between friends and the coping with the tragic death, work better with this 'identical friends' premise. With roots in magic and occult, the ultimate power of the doppelgänger is expressive of both death and immortality. Otto Rank's psychoanalytical explanation of the double motif finds it posing a question of identity: 'the confrontation of man with himself':

> The most prominent symptom of the forms which the double takes is a powerful consciousness of guilt which forces the hero no longer to accept the responsibility for certain actions of his ego, but to place it upon another ego, a double. (1989: 76)

The conundrum of Kumar's star image following his migration to Pakistan, like the case of contrasting identities within a (wo)man's mind, generates the double as a mechanism of self-preservation. Through the double role, *Bedari* simultaneously punishes 'Rattan Kumar' for his Indian act by killing off the homologous disabled character and redeems him as the able-bodied Pakistani. Intensifying his star appeal, the double role in *Bedari* offers the pleasure of a migrant star working through his changed nationality as well as a more ingenious denouement. In *Jagriti*, Shakti's death leaves the mother grief-stricken and nearly mad. While Ajay resolves to take responsibility of her, she continues searching for her dead son. After a brief interlude of reflection, the narrative moves to focus on Ajay's achievements, leaving the strand of the inconsolable 'mother' unresolved. However, in *Bedari*, because of their identical looks, Zafar could convincingly dress up like Sabir and 'become' him to reassure the mother. As the film ends with the duo walking into the horizon, the surviving 'son' of *Bedari* appears to be doing a better job of looking after the 'mother'. Despite a much inferior technical quality, the fantastical premise of unrelated yet identical friends affords *Bedari* a more comforting finish and the projection of a more effective nationalism.

One is tempted to pose a few 'what ifs?' regarding the circulatory context of the songs and the film. What if cinema-going Indians had seen the corrections of *Bedari*, especially the particular form of disavowal of a national hero by a child star? The replacement of Gandhi by Jinnah would be considered incendiary in India, and an added act of treason by a star wishing to rework his national stardom. What if the announcer on Radio Ceylon who shamed Pakistan had also mentioned Kumar's transgression? What if the silence maintained in India was not merely for an already precarious image of the Muslim minority but more importantly to conceal the artifice that all nationalisms necessarily entail? After all, the songs of *Jagriti*, including Kumar's ode to Gandhi, continued as patriotic songs par excellence long after Kumar had left India. In Pakistan, there was greater likelihood of familiarity with the Indian version, through illegal screenings of smuggled prints, maybe even a formal release, together with the movement of people across borders, Indian film magazines and radio transmissions. Yet *Bedari* was among the eight commercial successes of local production in Pakistan that year. Arguably its pleasure and later status as a patriotic film lies in elaborating a severance and embodying an antithesis, the overriding cultural logic of remakes of Indian films in Pakistan.

The paradox of nationalism's postcolonial modality in the Indian subcontinent is starkly evident in the divided stardom of Rattan Kumar. Owing his child-star image and popularity to Indian films made in Bombay, the replication of his charisma in Pakistan involved self-inflicted blows to the original image. While Kumar's intensified star presence in *Bedari* was arguably a showcase of the Lahore film industry's one-upping acquisition on Bombay, it also elaborated his reworked nationality through the trope of the double. As an extension of the qualities that the original lacks, the doubles (roles and films) are ultimately confrontations with self-identity and its entanglements with the ineradicable past, which in the case of India and Pakistan remain interminable national dilemmas.

Works Cited

Anon. (1954), 'Candidates for Stardom No. 37', *Filmfare*, 3 (3): 31.

Anon. (1955a), *Filmfare*, 4 (6): 55.

Anon. (1955b), 'Star Profile', *Filmfare*, 4 (19): 12–13.

Anon. (1956a), *Filmfare*, 5 (6): 51.

Anon. (1956b), 'Inse Miliye Kamsin Adaakar: Rattan Kumar', *Nigar Weekly*, 14 October.

Anon. (1957a), 'Once in a Decade Comes a Motion Picture Which is Remembered Forever: A Gift to the Nation: Film Exchange presents *Bedari*', *Pakistan Screen Annual*, p. 206.

Anon. (1957b), '*Bedari* - Another Plagiarised Version', *Pakistan Times*, 13 December, p. 6.

Anon. (1960), 'Pakistan Films and Trainees in Britain', *Pakistan Times*, 25 March, p. 4.

Anon. (1963), 'Readers Write to the Editor', *Eastern Film Magazine*, 4 (11): 41.

Barker, Clare (2011), *Postcolonial Fiction and Disability: Exceptional Children, Metaphor and Materiality*, Basingstoke: Palgrave Macmillan.

Chakravarty, Sumitra S. (1993), *National Identity in Popular Indian Cinema 1947–1987*, Austin: University of Texas Press.

Devji, Faisal (1992), 'Hindu/Muslim/Indian', *Public Culture*, 5 (1): 1–18.

Dyer, Richard (1991a), 'Charisma', in Christine Gledhill (ed.), *Stardom: The Industry of Desire* (London: Routledge), pp. 58–61.

Dyer, Richard (1991b), 'A Star is Born and the Construction of Authenticity', in Christine Gledhill (ed.), *Stardom: The Industry of Desire* (London: Routledge), pp. 136–44.

Fischer, Jaimey (2007), 'On the Ruins of Masculinity: The Figure of the Child in Italian Neorealism and the German Rubble Film', in Laura E. Ruberto and Kristi M. Wilson (eds), *Italian Neorealism and Global Cinema*, 25–53, Detroit, MI: Wayne State University Press.

Gaines, Jane (2004), 'Early Cinema's Heyday of Copying', *Cultural Studies*, 20 (2–3): 227–244.

Gooptu, Sharmishta (2011), *Bengali Cinema: An Other Nation*, London: Routledge.

Jalal, Ayesha (1999), *The Sole Spokesman*, Lahore: Sang-i-Meel Publications.

Leitch, Thomas (1990), 'Twice-Told Tales: Disavowal and The Rhetoric of the Remake', in Jennifer Forest and Leonard R. Koos (eds), *Dead Ringers: The Remake in Theory and Practice*, 37–62, Albany: State University of New York Press.

Majumdar, Neepa (2012), 'Importing Neorealism, Exporting Cinema: Indian Cinema and Film Festivals in the 1950s', in Saverio Giovacchini and Robert Sklar (eds), *Global Neorealism: The Transnational History of a Film Style*, 178–93, Jackson: University Press of Mississippi.

O'Connor, Jane (2008), *The Cultural Significance of the Child Star*, New York: Routledge.

Pakistan Film Fact Finding Committee Report [PFFFCR] (1960), Government of Pakistan, Lahore.

Rajyadhaksha, Ashish and Paul Willemen, ([1994] 1999), *Encyclopaedia of Indian Cinema*, Rev. edn, London: British Film Institute.

Ramaswamy, Sumathi (2010), *The Goddess and the Nation: Mapping Mother India*, Durham, NC: Duke University Press.

Rank, Otto (1989), *The Double: A Psychoanalytic Study*, trans. and ed. Harry Tucker Jr., Chapel Hill: University of North Carolina Press.

Roy, Srirupa (2007), *Beyond Belief: India and the Politics of Postcolonial Nationalism*, Durham, NC: Duke University Press.

Sen, Amiya P. (2006), *The Indispensable Vivekanand*, Delhi: Permanent Black.

Sundaram, Ravi (2009), *Pirate Modernity: Delhi's Media Urbanism*, New York: Routledge.

Thapar, Romila (2005), *Somanatha The Many Voices of History*, London: Verso.

Vasudevan, Ravi (1997), 'Voice, Space, Form: *Roja* (Maniratnam, 1992), Indian Film and National Identity', in Stuart Murray (ed.), *Not on Any Map: Essays on Postcoloniality and Cultural Nationalism*, 153–69, Exeter: University of Exeter Press.

Zamindar, Vazira (2007), *The Long Partition and the Making of Modern South Asia*, New York: Columbia University Press.

Chapter 9

From *Son of India* to teen king: Sajid Khan and transnational stardom

Meenasarani Linde Murugan

In his 1969 autobiography Sajid Khan, at age eighteen, tells the story of his life: 'I was born on the night of December 28, 1951, precisely at the moment the first star appeared in the sky over Bombay. If so, that star was a good omen, because many wonderful, surprising and unexpected things have happened to me' (Khan 1969: vii). Mysticism and magic abound in the book's section on 'the ancient land of India', 'where it all began'. By contrast, where the story ends Khan is 'becoming more and more Americanized with each day that passes. I hardly ever go out of the house without stopping to have a hamburger or a hotdog and a cold soda or a tall glass of milk. It's the American way, I guess, and I've adopted it' (Khan 1969: 81).

Khan began his career at a very young age when he played the part of young Birju in *Mother India* (Mehboob Khan, 1957). Khan's autobiography claims he 'wasn't quite four years old at the time' (1969: 4). After working in the Hindi film industry, he starred in his first US film, *Maya* (John Berry, 1966) (Figure 9.1). Attempting to bolster his popularity, Khan moved to the United States in 1967 and became a TV teen heart-throb and pop singer. The relative ease of his incorporation into a white, middle-class milieu, and in turn a white heteronormative structure of desire, demonstrates US youth culture's affinity for India in the late 1960s. I argue that while Khan's transnational stardom is predicated on a rehashing of Orientalism, his performance of Indian-ness engages a cosmopolitan modernity, wherein India is framed as hip, and he becomes an arbiter of cultural exchange.

Key to this ascendance to an elite cosmopolitan mobility is the discursive construction of a modest beginning. As Richard Dyer has argued, stars work through ideological contradictions (1979; 1986). They are presented as a unified individual who is not only just like everyday people but also more talented, beautiful and stylish than everyday people. One of the main ways that stars' everydayness was constructed was via an emphasis on their humble beginnings. Khan's autobiography emphasizes his obscurity and poverty: 'My parents were very poor, as are a great number of people in India. Sometimes there was nothing to eat but rice … and not very much of that either' (1969: 4). Such background detail would be given to further celebrate the star's hard work and independence in emerging out of this environment. Dyer refers to magazine reports of '[Joan] Crawford's struggle to the top from a background of poverty', which complemented the narratives of her 1930s films, such as *Laughing Sinners* (Harry Beaumont, 1931) and *Dancing Lady* (Robert Z. Leonard, 1933), in which she played struggling working girls (1979: 64).

Similarly, Khan's life experience is mirrored in the films *Mother India* and *Son of India* (Mehboob Khan, 1962). Khan notes that when landing the role of Birju 'I'd never seen a movie, so I didn't

Figure 9.1 Sajid Khan as Raji in *Maya* (John Berry, 1966). Lora & Sue, www.sajidkhan.com.

know what they were talking about. But they thought I'd be right for the part of the street urchin. I suppose I was. I practically lived on the streets' (1969: 3–4). In *Mother India*, Birju is a mixture of willful and adorable. Throughout the first portion of the film he is shown throwing tantrums and being mischievous as he distrustingly eyes authority figures. Despite his being a temperamental son, the film foregrounds his mother Radha's unconditional love and affection for him. Gayatri Chatterjee notes, 'Not only is Radha partial to Birju, [the film director] Mehboob was as well – as is clear from the amount of narrative and visual attention Birju receives … Sajid as Birju proved very popular with audiences and critics; and he captured Mehboob's heart' (2002: 45). Mehboob was so taken with Sajid that he 'conceived his next film *Son of India* [1962] exclusively for Sajid' (84 n.20).

In *Son of India*, his character does not live in rural poverty but in bustling contemporary Bombay. Vijay Mishra notes: 'As the title of the film indicates it is the "son of India," the young child Gopal, who becomes the figure around whom Mehboob Khan creates his new narrative of Indian modernity: the child carries the consciousness of the new nation in the interface of tradition and modernity' (2006: 21). This child version of nationalism and citizenship is made most evident in the musical sequence for 'Nanha Munna Rahi Hoon'. In it, Gopal (Sajid Khan) sings with his dog across different landscapes of India, from the mountains to fields to desert-like settings. At one point he even sings on an elephant. In the last minute he is back in modern Bombay and his song is heard over a parade of children marching and saluting while tanks accompany them. Khan's performance is simultaneously angelic and spritely. His kind eyes hold a close-up and his enthusiasm carries the continuity of patriotism among the various Indian landscapes.

Despite his portrayal of spunky independent children, once he became an actor he no longer lived a life of poverty. From 1955 on he benefitted from being adopted by Mehboob Khan, who directed Sajid in his first two films. Sajid recalls:

> So I moved into 'Shalimar', the Khans' big white mansion in Bombay. To me it looked like a palace … all ivory and clean, with a lovely garden in the back. But the biggest thrill of all was having my own room. It was painted a soft blue and filled with beautiful furniture. And I moved into the Khan family, too. The five children, all older than me, accepted me as their little brother right from the beginning. And Mr. and Mrs. Khan treated me just like one of their own children. (1969: 6)

It is noteworthy that what is emphasized for the presumed US teen fan and reader of his autobiography are the comforts of furniture and having one's own room. These material aspects of domesticity transcend the differences between nationality, ethnicity, race and class between Khan and his fans. While being adopted allowed Khan a life of comfort, wealth and opportunity, it also entangled his personal life and star labour from a very young age. His disconnection from his biological parents made him an interloper, a role he would go on to play in different families and across different cultures.

Coming to America

Maya marked Sajid Khan's transition into US culture. The film focuses on the adventures of Terry, a white American boy, Raji, a poor Indian boy and Maya, Raji's elephant. While Khan played Raji, Jay North, who was familiar to US audiences as the lead in the television show *Dennis the Menace* (CBS, 1959–1963), played Terry. A majority of the film was shot on location in India, and was produced by the King Brothers for MGM. In the film, Terry runs away from his father, who is a hunter in the jungle. Terry teams up with Raji to take the elephant Maya to a temple. In the film Raji is mostly shirtless, and when he wears clothes he is in rags.

While the film is set in modern-day India, the setting evokes a colonial past that could be found in Rudyard Kipling's stories or in Sabu's films such as *Elephant Boy* (Robert Flaherty and Zoltan Korda, 1937), *The Drum* (Zoltan Korda, 1938) and *Jungle Book* (Zoltan Korda, 1942). Despite the similarities between the roles offered to Sabu and Khan, Khan's talent and modernity is emphasized in press discourse. In a 1966 interview in the *Boston Globe*, Khan states, 'I am not like Sabu' (Davidson 1966: 14). He goes on: 'My father was not an elephant tamer, he was a director, producer and studio owner. He put me in *Mother India* when I was 3 years old. Someone gave him a bright idea—why don't you take your own son in the cast—so he did' (14). Khan completely elides his own poverty and adoption in this interview. Instead he confidently proclaims himself as already a star, and the child of Indian entertainment royalty. Throughout the interview, Davidson remarks on his confidence, describing Khan as having 'the style of a Beatle and the spirit of Cassius Clay' (14). This comparison to hip contemporary celebrities that are British and American as well as white and black demonstrates how, despite Raji's similarity to Sabu's characters, Khan is hip, self-assured and more than a bit entitled.

This interview appeared as part of the film's 1966 promotional tour of fifteen US cities. In the *Chicago Defender*, a photograph from Khan's visit to the Lincoln Park Zoo depicts Indu, the new baby elephant, meeting Khan (Anon. 1966: 14). Khan wears a sleek Nehru suit with beaded trim at the cuffs and collar. He crouches down to pet the cute baby elephant on its trunk. A group of eight boys, both black and white, on the other side of a chain-link fence, peek over to witness the scene. While Khan proclaimed his strong difference from the datedness and obscure beginnings of Sabu, promotional photographs such as these demonstrate the inextricability of colonial imagery from his marketing. This image echoes Sabu's visits to zoos when promoting his 1930s films. Michael Lawrence notes how the press 'described Sabu's appearances at public zoos in order to emphasise his peculiar affinity with animals' (2014: 29). 'When he was promoting *The Drum* in the United States in Autumn of 1938, Sabu visited Prospect Park Zoo in New York, and was photographed by the press feeding the elephants surrounded by crowds of fans and onlookers' (29). A similar scene is captured in Khan's appearance at the Lincoln Park Zoo, though Khan looks more trepidatious with the baby elephant than Sabu had done before him. Khan's later promotional material was more explicitly geared towards young, white teen girls, who were the desired readership for fan magazines such as *16*. Accordingly, the imagery of the elephant gives way to different markers of exoticism. However, this photograph and its publication in a widely circulated newspaper by and for black people demonstrates Khan's reception in a racially differentiated US market.

India on Cold War US television

After the release of *Maya*, the King Brothers spun-off the film into a television series with the same title that would be broadcast on NBC (1967–1968). Like the film, the series was shot on location in India, which was unprecedented at the time, and is extremely rare even today (Anon. 1967a: D22). The television programme's narrative and portrayal of Indians and India, like the original film, kept with the imagery of Kipling's texts and Sabu's films. Though these earlier products arrive out of a British colonial relationship with India, the US relationship to South Asia must be contextualized in relation to the Cold War.

Following Independence and partition, the United States became increasingly invested in fostering a democratic ally against the rise of communism in other Asian nations (McCarthy 2010: 130–1). Anna McCarthy discusses how US organizations such as the Ford Foundation led the way by 'awarding India more grants than any other "less-developed" country in the 1950s' (131, 293 n.39; see also Ford Foundation 1955, and Hertz 1961). This financial investment in India was complemented by the Foundation's attempts to breed a 'global civic awareness' among US citizens, via television programmes such as *Omnibus* (CBS, 1952–1956; ABC, 1956–1957; NBC, 1957–1961) (McCarthy 2010: 141).

Episodes that featured segments such as 'Music and Dance from India' (CBS, 10 April 1955) and 'Village Incident: India' (CBS, 1 March 1954), emphasized traditional, religious and rural aspects of Indian culture. Similarly, they complemented the post-war circulation of Indian cinema in the United States. One of the first Indian films to be exhibited in the United States was *Shakuntala* (V. Shantaram, 1943, 1947), based on a story from the *Mahabharata* (Armes 1987: 113). Though generally reviewed in *The New York Times*, the film is considered a charming attempt to mimic US commercial cinema: 'It's obvious too, judging by the direction, that an unflinching Indian eye has been fixed on Hollywood' (H.T. 1947: 22). By contrast, 1950s Indian films that received international acclaim reverberated the subject matter, style and ethos of Italian neorealist cinema. While Satyajit Ray is the filmmaker most closely associated with neorealism in India, Neepa Majumdar notes how neorealism's emphasis on scenes of poverty and the use of lesser-known or untrained actors impacted mainstream commercials films such as *Boot Polish* (Prakash Arora, 1954), released in the United States in 1958 (2011: 178–93).[1] Ray's *Pather Panchali*, scored by Ravi Shankar, premiered on 3 May 1955, as part of the Museum of Modern Art's (MoMA) *Living Arts of India* series, the performing arts companion to the *Textiles and Ornamental Arts of India* exhibition (Robinson 2010). Indian Classical dancer Shanta Rao and Indian classical

---

[1] Ray's relationship to commercial Indian cinema, Italian neorealism and the international art house market is more thoroughly discussed in Majumdar 2005. I do not claim that there were no other examples of Indian cinema circulating in the post-war USA. However, Ray's films were widely remarked on in the contemporary popular press; the circulation of his films discursively constructs India as rural and provincial. For a more capacious study of the post-war reception Indian cinema in the USA, see Majumdar 2008.

musicians Ali Akbar Khan (sarod) and Chatur Lal (tabla) also performed in MoMA's *Living Arts* series following their taping of the *Omnibus* segment 'Music and Dance from India'.

These various media forged a connection between India and the United States that was intended to be more enlightened than the colonial one with the British. Yet, with its emphasis on provincial settings, poverty and Hinduism, it did not stray far from British colonial imaginaries of India. While Indians were valued for their spiritual ideals and traditional arts, the post-war press still discursively constructed the nation as poor and provincial (Anon. 1955: 57–80). Additionally, this more 'enlightened' assessment of India by the United States coexisted with many post-war Hollywood films, such as *Bhowani Junction* (George Cukor, 1956), *King of Khyber Rifles* (Henry King, 1953) and *The Rains of Ranchipur* (Jean Negulesco, 1955) as well as the television programme *The 77th Bengal Lancers* (NBC, 1956–1957), which all celebrated British colonial rule of India. McCarthy describes the conventions of these post-war Hollywood films as 'a lush filmic world of bodice-ripping bandits and British soldiers', which 'are remarkably uniform across the minor subgenre that might be called "Hollywood Raj"' (2010: 132–3, 294 n.44).

However, while *Maya* (NBC, 1967–1968) defaulted to many British colonial tropes in its representation of India, certain episodes offered a glimpse of a bustling Bombay, more akin to contemporary Hindi films such as *Jaali Note* (Shakti Samanta, 1960), *Naughty Boy* (Shakti Samanta, 1962), *Teesri Manzil* (Vijay Anand, 1966) and *Jewel Thief* (Vijay Anand, 1967). In 'The Caper of the Golden Roe' (NBC, 14 October 1967) Terry and Raji are on the hunt for a temple idol. They begin at Chaupati Beach in Bombay. Dressed in sleek Nehru suits and wearing Gandhi caps they put on their sunglasses and hop in the back of a black Mercedes-Benz sedan. They drive down Charney Road and we see a crane shot of the wide highways along the beach. We then cut back into the interior of the car, as we see the boys observe the bustling city. We see people going in and out of storefront with bright yellow and orange painted signs. We see skyscrapers in the distance as well as fancier four-storey residential buildings with Islamic architectural embellishments. In this one sequence, we are presented with an India that is not only urban and growing but also a mix of cultures. The sheer scale of the city is emphasized and matches how Mehboob Khan shoots Bombay in *Son of India*. The seriality of the television programme allows Terry and Raji to have different kinds of adventures beyond rehashing colonial tropes. Here, as the 'Caper' title of the episode suggests, they are outfitted as spies in hip fashions, sunglasses and cars as opposed to rags.

The Americanization of Sajid

After shooting the television series in India, Khan, his family and the King Brothers determined it would be better for him to further his career in the United States. In addition to doing another promotional tour for the television show, Khan was adopted by a new family in Beverly Hills. Khan notes, 'I moved into my new home in Beverly Hills with Alan Courtney and his family. It's a big Spanish style house, with lots of grounds around it and a swimming pool in back' (1969: 36). Rather than being awed by the American splendor, Khan notes the parallels in his second adoption: 'Mrs. Courtney furnished a room for me that's as beautiful as the one I have at home in India' (1969: 36). A photo of him in the luxurious marble foyer of the Courtney house accompanies this part of Khan's narrative. He states 'I love this entrance hall of the Courtneys' home because it reminds me of Shalimar, our home in India' (37). Khan highlights the modernity and luxuries of

India, and specifically the Indian film industry. However, the similarities between the Khans and the Courtneys do not end with interior design.

Alan D. Courtney was not simply a generous soul but also a TV executive. He was the vice-president of MGM Television, which along with the King Brothers produced *Maya*. Additionally, he was the executive 'in charge of the studio's franchise programs' (Reifsteck 2000). Courtney not only eased Khan's transition into US teen life by opening up his home but also marketed the everyday practices involved in Khan's Americanization. In the February 1968 issue of the teen fan magazine *16*, a photo-spread invites you to 'meet my "American Family"' (Khan 1968). While Khan is credited as the author of the piece, he is also the subject of the story as he is in every photograph. We see him around the house doing mundane things such as playing the piano, talking on the phone and petting the family dogs. He is shown to be just like any other white, middle-upper-class American child; this is made explicitly clear in a photo of him in a cowboy costume surrounded by his affectionate 'siblings', the biological children of Courtney. The only representation of his 'Indian family', however, is a portrait of him and his mother, Nehboob Khan. Sajid concludes his story: 'We both love your country very much—thank you for having us here!' (61).

Khan is not only an adopted US teenager but also an exceptional Indian foreigner, as he has cultural pride while also seamlessly assimilating into white US society. Khan's is a star text that manages not only the contradictions between otherworldliness and everydayness (as Dyer has suggested) but also, in a transnational vein, the differences between a white American teenager and an Indian immigrant. Similarly, in the 1910s, silent cinema star Sessue Hayakawa managed transnational contradictions: Daisuke Miyao notes that despite Hayakawa playing characters that promoted Orientalism, '[the] most prominent image of Hayakawa in magazine articles was his Americanized family life with his wife' (2007: 136). Because he was Asian, this promotional material served to complement his 'screen persona as a heroic and moralistic defender of white American families' (136). Likewise, Khan is framed as someone who does not threaten the order of the white American family but merely enhances it. Here then, Khan's shift from child actor in India to US television star and eventual pop singer, demonstrates a parlaying of his national and cultural background into less of an exotic spectacle and more of a close libidinally invested encounter befitting any actor trying to be a teen heart-throb.

Teen king

Khan enrolled in Beverly Hills High School in 1967. However, his ambitions of furthering his career were met with obstacles as *Maya* was cancelled after its first season of eighteen episodes, ending its broadcast early in 1968. Still, Khan was intent on being a performer and in 1968 he released a record featuring his cover of 'Getting to Know You', from the 1951 Broadway musical and film *The King and I* (Walter Lang, 1956). Aside from updating the show tune with a bubblegum pop sound, the middle of his version features him singing in Hindi. This Hindi lesson is further complemented by the B-side's track, 'Hay Ram', a song in Hindi and English about peace and love. In the October 1968 issue of *16*, a full page is devoted to the lyrics to 'Hay Ram', which is described as 'An Ancient Hindu Love & Peace Song' (Anon. 1968e: 28). The lyrics – a mix of Hindi and English – are accompanied by a large photo of Khan giving a smoldering look as he poses with his arm above his head while reclining in a lawn chair. Musically and in the photographs his address is to a presumably young girl who is seduced by him while also feeling safe. Here, then, the emphasis on learning a new language or about a new culture mollifies the explicitly sexual address that is also present.

To promote his music, he appeared on seventeen episodes of the ABC weekend variety programme *Happening '68* between February 1968 and June 1969. He also performed on *American Bandstand* (ABC, 27 July 1968) (Figure 9.2) and was a contestant on *The Dating Game* (ABC, 1968) (Figure 9.2).² His promotion on these shows as a likable teen heart-throb was further supported by the large amount of fan publications about him. Cover photos, pin-ups and photo-features of Sajid on dates and with friends were constantly a part of magazines such as *16, Teen Screen, Tiger Beat, Outasite!* and *Fave* from 1968 to 1970 (see, for example, Anon. 1968a, b, d, 1969, 1970; Cartwright 1968).

These close encounters, such as his 1969 autobiography, *Sajid Khan: This Is My Story*, foregrounded Khan's sensitivity and everydayness. Unlike his earlier interview with Davidson where he was described as having 'the spirit of Cassius Clay', fan magazines emphasized his emotional vulnerability (Davidson 1966: 14). Khan was often shown as a wounded puppy or being fun and fancy-free in order to incorporate him into a white, middle-class milieu as opposed to having any kind of contestatory attitude or disruptive politics. Photos of him not only valourized the white American family but also featured him pursuing the typical leisure activities of the US teenager. Of course, like any other star, this 'everydayness' was largely manufactured.

Magazine features included staged photos of Khan playing with young fans at Surfer's Beach

Figure 9.2 Sajid Khan performing 'Getting to Know You' on *American Bandstand* (ABC, 27 July 1968). Lora & Sue, www.sajidkhan.com.

in Malibu (Anon. 1968a: 15). Photographs of Khan with other teen and child TV stars, who already connoted white American domesticity, underscored Khan's everydayness. Khan's association with his first co-star North, already familiar to US TV audiences as the leading mischievous boy-next-door in *Dennis the Menace,* helped to incorporate him into a

---

²I have not been able to recover the date in 1968 when *The Dating Game* episode with Sajid Khan was broadcast.

white, middle-class milieu. Fan magazines also played up this co-star relationship as a friendship by running features in which 'Sajid & Jay Tell All on Each Other!' (Anon. 1968c: 44–5). North introduces us to Khan, as if we were at a party; the feature presumes the reader's familiarity, via television, with North.

Actors such as Angela Cartwright made Khan not only seem friendly but date-able and desirable, as seen in the 1968 *Tiger Beat* feature 'A Dreamy Day with Sajid' (Cartwright 1968: 8). Amidst photos of the cute couple on Khan's motorcycle or sharing a milkshake, Cartwright exclaims: 'Every girl should have a date with Sajid once in her life! Every girl should be able to feel the way I did on this beautiful day we spent at the beach' (8). Cartwright advertises all the perks of Khan. Despite his Americanization, Khan is Indian and therefore not white. Here, then, Cartwright makes him safe, appropriate and palatable for the assumed white teen-girl fan. Notably, Cartwright is not framed here as romantic competition for the young reader, rather she is the reader's best friend, confidante and sister. Casting Cartwright in this role presumes the reader's long familiarity with Cartwright on television as the spunky daughter and teen in popular family sitcoms such as *Make Room for Daddy* (CBS, 1957–1964) and *Lost in Space* (CBS, 1965–1968).

Similarly, photographs of Khan with Desi Arnaz Jr. hanging out in the Beverly Hills High School cafeteria create a seemingly everyday scene of teenage life (Khan 1969: 58–9). In the late 1960s, Arnaz Jr. was familiar to youth audiences because of his pop-rock band, Dino, Desi & Billy, which also featured the son of Dean Martin. In 1968, Arnaz Jr. and his sister Lucie Désirée Arnaz played opposite their mother, comedy legend Lucille Ball, in the sitcom *Here's Lucy* (CBS, 1968–1974). But even before this, Khan's 'friend' was intensely familiar to readers and TV viewers, because of the success of his parents Ball and Desi Arnaz on *I Love Lucy* (CBS, 1951–1957), and subsequent comedy and variety specials. In fact, Ball's pregnancy with Arnaz Jr. was written into *I Love Lucy*, so that Arnaz Jr. came into this world at the same time as the character 'Little Ricky' did. Here, then, photographs with actors such as North, Cartwright and Arnaz Jr. not only dramatized Khan's everydayness but also incorporated him into an already and intensely TV-mediated form of white American domesticity and teenage life.

Despite this staging of everydayness, fan magazines did not completely withhold from playing up the exoticism of India or 'the Orient', writ large. In their popular history of *16*, Randi Reisfeld and Danny Fields note, 'The magazine played the foreign card to the max [...] There were photos of him "praying," or meditating, and lots of articles, while always bearing the romantic *16* stamp, in which he articulated the cultural differences between India and America' (1997: 85). In a two-page colour pin-up of him from the February 1968 issue of *16*, Khan is pronounced the magazine's 'Teen King' as a crown stamp appears over a dashing headshot of him in a glorious maroon turban (Anon. 1968b: 34–5). Casting a similar look to a smoldering Rudolph Valentino, Khan's exoticism is heightened here. The comparison to Valentino is made explicit on the back cover of his autobiography, which proclaims Khan as 'the handsome young actor whose phenomenal popularity is beginning to rival that of the legendary Rudolph Valentino'.

The comparison to Valentino not only works because they are both popular stars with beautiful faces but also because of Valentino's association with Orientalism through films such as *The Sheik* (George Melford, 1921). Strikingly, Valentino's association with 'the East' and his feminized beauty became integral to producing a large fan base of women (see Hansen 1986). However, because Khan is already from 'the East', he does not need to put on brownface makeup or rim his eyes with kohl. Rather, he needs to simply represent it by changing out his American clothes for Indian ones and casting a pose that rehashes Orientalist tropes. While this performance of an exoticized Indian-ness may detract from the Americanization pursued in other parts of the magazine, it further serves to incorporate Khan into a white structure of desire that has long-been invested – as seen in the case of Valentino – in the beauty and style of 'exotic' men.

'They're living in a dream world in America'

Khan's easy incorporation into white American culture was aided by a larger interest in India by US youth culture in the late 1960s. The relationship between India and the USA became even more imbricated as aspects of Indian culture, such as the Nehru jacket, were being appreciated and appropriated in the USA. Popular media aided in this cultural appropriation of India as evidenced in the February 1968 issue of *16* magazine, where Monkees member Davy Jones shows us his favourite achkans, a garment more widely known as the Nehru jacket (Stavers 1968a, b). Another Monkee, Peter Tork, tells editor Gloria Stavers, who often stands in for the young reader, that 'the *Upanishads* are simply but beautifully written, I mean, they are quite easy to understand. You can buy the Mentor pocket edition for about 50 cents' (Stavers 1968a: 10). From clothing attached to India's Independence movement to sacred Hindu texts, whatever political and cultural alterity the late 60s counterculture earnestly appreciated and appropriated became quickly commodified within the pages of many teen fan magazines.

Garments like the *achkan* or Nehru jacket could quickly signal hipness even if the artists who wore them and the music they performed had no other associations with India. The hipness of India and its fashions became so ubiquitous that in 1968 a New Good-Lookin Talking Ken doll was released in a red Nehru jacket and red shorts (Rubin and Melnick 2006: 154).

Despite India's popularity in youth culture, not all stars were as eager to adopt the hippie lifestyle. In an interview with *The Baltimore Sun* in November 1967 North states: 'Life in India is still primitive. If the Hippies in America really want to get back in time they should go to India. They'll scream in five minutes. They're living in a dream world in America' (Anon. 1967b: 227). Khan also notes the similarities between hippies and his homeland, as he states in his autobiography, 'American clothes strike me very funny, mainly because Nehru jackets, beads and things like that aren't American at all, but Indian! I have a whole collection of Nehru jackets and caftan-type shirts, so I don't really know whether I'm being very American or very Indian' (Khan 1969: 83).

Though Khan continued to make variety show appearances, by 1969 he lacked much of an acting career to warrant his marketing. However, he maintained his teen fan magazine presence by foregrounding the importance of cosmopolitan cultural exchange. He was constantly in the process of Americanization as the youth he surrounded himself with aspired towards Indianization. As his single 'Getting to Know You' suggests, this international translation and exchange happens between individuals, but more specifically, friends, girlfriends, boyfriends, brothers and sisters.

In both the musical and film versions of *The King and I*, Christina Klein argues, the 'Getting to Know You' number demonstrates how 'sentiment works … as the medium of education' (2003: 201). Though Klein discusses this musical at length and its Orientalist ramifications, in emphasizing the role of sentiment, she also complements the work done by Lauren Berlant on both *The King and I* and Harriet Beecher Stowe's novel *Uncle Tom's Cabin* (1852). Berlant notes that these products and productions are made supposedly on behalf of sentimental 'subjects' and 'link the overwhelming pressures to survive everyday life and overwhelming desires to inhabit an imaginary space of transcendent identity whose mirror of the quotidian allows the utopian and the practical to meet intimately, and in a text you can buy that will give you an experience you cannot, at this time, have elsewhere' (1998: 648). A similar dynamic is at work in these teen fan magazines and bubblegum pop records, where the address to the young girl allows her to imagine herself as the one special sweetheart and ultimate soul mate of her favourite Monkee or Sajid Khan. Yet this exchange is only made possible by watching the show, buying the text or, in this case, purchasing the magazine or record.

Intercultural exchange, then, occurs as a 'commoditized relation between subjects who are defined not as actors in history but as persons who shop and feel' (637). Yet, rather than completely disavow this kind of intercultural exchange, I think it is productive to see the marketing of Khan and his various records and television programmes as well as Indian commodities such as Nehru jackets or *achkans* as participating in what Mica Nava has characterized as a 'visceral cosmopolitanism' (2007). Nava explores how everyday practices of fashion consumption, nightclub dancing and cinema going produce 'a loosening of national identification and a positive engagement with difference' (2007: 5). Being a fan of Khan or dressing in a Nehru jacket could have opened up many, presumably young, white Americans to have a positive engagement with India and perhaps challenge their racism and xenophobia. Yet, as this investigation of his transnational star text has shown, the process by which Khan enacts a 'visceral cosmopolitanism' for his fans involves amplifying exoticism and, more importantly, valourizing white American society and culture.

Khan returned to India in 1970 after not being able to secure a new consistent television gig. Despite the waning of Khan's career in the USA, his trajectory can be seen as setting a precedent of Indian-ness, and significantly Indian entertainment, as transnationally mobile. For many people in the history of South Asian diaspora, mobility has been tied to forced displacement and hard precarious labour (see Prashad 2000 and Bald 2012). However, the elite cosmopolitan mobility of Khan demonstrates how certain Indians in the post-war climate were able to move from society's margins to the centres of culture. Post-war Indian writer Santha Rama Rau performed the role of cultural translator for the US audience of her paperback novels and magazine essays (see Burton 2007). Yet for Rau and Khan, much of their visibility involved a transference in which the USA was framed as the new promised land of opportunity, as opposed to the old colonial power of Britain. It is through an investment in American-ness, then, that cosmopolitan mobility is achieved. By historically recovering Khan's narrative, we see how the success of South Asians in US popular media is often predicated on a celebration of the nation-state. Ironically, then, Khan's transnational stardom vividly dramatizes how that 'first star which appeared in the sky over Bombay', in all his celestial glory, has to become domestically grounded within the confines of the white US nation and family in order to be recognized.

Works Cited

Anon. (1955), 'The World's Greatest Religions: Part I: Hinduism,' *Life*, 7 February, pp. 57–80.

Anon. (1966), 'While Admirers Of,' *Chicago Defender*, 16 July, p. 14.

Anon. (1967a), 'Location Filming of Maya Series Half Completed,' *Los Angeles Times*, 31 July, D22.

Anon. (1967b), 'Great to Ride an Elephant Except You Have Farther to Fall,' *Baltimore Sun*, 19 November, p. 227.

Anon. (1968a), 'Sajid's Real Luvs,' *Fave*, February, pp. 14–15.

Anon. (1968b) '*16*'s Teen King,' *16*, February, pp. 34–5.

Anon. (1968c), 'Sajid & Jay Tell All on Each Other!,' *16*, February, pp. 44–5.

Anon. (1968d), 'Sajid – Kiss His Tears Away,' *16*, April, pp. 18–19.

Anon. (1968e), 'Sing-Along with Sajid on His Very First Recording,' *16*, October, p. 28.

Anon. (1969), 'Sajid And His Friends,' *16*, December, pp. 24–5.

Anon. (1970), 'The Sighs of Sajid,' *Tiger Beat*, May, p. 65.

Armes, Roy (1987), *Third World Film Making and the West*, Berkeley: University of California Press.

Bald, Vivek (2012), *Bengali Harlem and the Lost Histories of South Asian America*, Cambridge, MA: Harvard University Press.

Berlant, Lauren (1998), 'Poor Eliza,' *American Literature*, 70 (3) (September): 635–68.

Burton, Antoinette (2007), *The Postcolonial Careers of Santha Rama Rau*, Durham, NC: Duke University Press.

Cartwright, Angela (1968), 'A Dreamy Day with Sajid,' *Tiger Beat*, August, pp. 8–9.

Chatterjee, Gayatri (2002), *Mother India*, London: British Film Institute.

Davidson, Sara (1966), 'Sajid—The Star of the Show,' *Boston Globe*, 1 July, p. 14.

Dyer, Richard (1979), *Stars*, London: British Film Institute.

Dyer, Richard (1986), *Heavenly Bodies: Film Stars and Society*, Basingstoke: Macmillan; London: British Film Institute.

Ford Foundation, Office of the Representative in India (1955), *The Ford Foundation and Foundation Supported Activities*, New Delhi: Ford Foundation.

Hansen, Miriam (1986), 'Pleasure, Ambivalence, Identification: Valentino and Female Spectatorship,' *Cinema Journal*, 25 (4) (Summer): 6–32.

Hertz, Willard S. (1961), *Roots of Change: The Ford Foundation in India*, New York: Ford Foundation.

H. T. (1947), 'At the Art,' *The New York Times*, 26 December, p. 22.

Khan, Sajid (1968), 'Meet my "American Family",' *16* (February), pp. 60–1.

Khan, Sajid (1969), *Sajid Khan: This Is My Story*, ed. Floyd Ackerman, New York: Grosset & Dunlap.

Klein, Christina (2003), *Cold War Orientalism: Asia in the Middlebrow Imagination, 1945–1961*, Berkeley: University of California Press.

Lawrence, Michael (2014), *Sabu*, London: British Film Institute.

Majumdar, Neepa (2005), '*Pather Panchali* (1955), Satyajit Ray', in Jeffrey Geiger and R. L. Rutsky (eds), *Film Analysis: A Norton Reader*, 510–27, New York: W. W. Norton Company.

Majumdar, Neepa (2008), 'Immortal Tale or Nightmare? *Dr. Kotnis* between Art and Exploitation', *South Asian Popular Culture*, 6 (2) (October): 141–59.

Majumdar, Neepa (2011), 'Importing Neorealism, Exporting Cinema: Indian Cinema and Film Festivals in the 1950s', in Saverio Giovacchini and Robert Sklar (eds), *Global Neorealism: The Transnational History of a Film Style*, 178–93, Jackson: University Press of Mississippi.

McCarthy, Anna (2010), *The Citizen Machine: Governing by Television in 1950s America*, New York: The New Press.

Mishra, Vijay (2006), *Bollywood Cinema: A Critical Genealogy*, Wellington: Victoria University.

Miyao, Daisuke (2007), *Sessue Hayakawa: Silent Cinema and Transnational Stardom*, Durham, NC: Duke University Press.

Nava, Mica (2007), *Visceral Cosmopolitanism: Gender, Culture and the Normalization of Difference*, Oxford: Berg.

Prashad, Vijay (2000), *The Karma of Brown Folk*, Minneapolis: University of Minnesota Press.

Reifsteck, Greg (2000), 'Alan D. Courtney,' *Variety*, 12 May, online at: http://variety.com/2000/scene/people-news/alan-d-courtney-1117781559/ (accessed 22 February 2015).

Reisfeld, Randi and Danny Fields (1997), *Who's Your Fave Rave?* New York: Boulevard Books.

Robinson, Andrew (2010), *The Apu Trilogy: Satyajit Ray and the Making of an Epic*, London and New York: I.B. Tauris.

Rubin, Rachel and Jeffrey Melnick (2006), *Immigration and American Popular Culture*, New York: New York University Press.

Stavers, Gloria (1968a), 'Monkees & You,' *16*, February, pp. 3, 8–10, 12, 14.

Stavers, Gloria (1968b), 'Come to Davy's Grand Opening of Zilch I!', *16*, February, pp. 22–5.

Chapter 10

Harbhajan Maan: The transnational migrant success story of Punjabi cinema

Harjant S. Gill

From airplane to 'roadplane'

The advertisement for the Indo-Canadian Bus Company opens with an Air Canada airliner, prominently displaying the red maple leaf across its tail, touching down on the runway. The arrival of the airliner is followed by time-lapse of passengers exiting the gates at New Delhi's Indira Gandhi International airport. A long queue of cars stretches into the distance, presumably waiting to receive the arriving passengers. Dressed in a pink polo shirt and denim jeans, with a blue cardigan draped over his shoulders and dark aviator sunglasses covering his eyes, Harbhajan Maan, one of the most celebrated actors of Punjabi cinema, breezes past the awaiting cars making his way towards the camera. 'Landing at the Delhi airport just to wait for delayed trains or relatives? Leaving an airplane's comfort to endure the hustle and bustle of public transportation stuck in India's notorious traffic jams?' laments Maan (in Punjabi). 'For every Punjabi settled abroad, wasn't this the primary impediment keeping them from returning home?' Maan retorts as he approaches a luxury bus with the words 'Indo-Canadian' sprawled across its side. 'You no longer need to suffer in vain … Indo-Canadian bus is here to change the game,' Maan continues, shifting from the frustrated traveller persona into his characteristically paternalistic tone of voice. 'This world-class luxury bus will pick you up directly from the airport arrival gate,' he informs the audience. 'As you leave the comfort of your airplane, experience the comfort of this roadplane!'

Indo-Canadian is a privately owned bus company operating across India's northern state of Punjab that has, over the last decade, successfully capitalized on the rapidly growing demand for transportation between major cities across Punjab to the nearest international airport, which lies 275–300 kilometres south in the nation's capital city of Delhi. Maan, one of the most successful singers and actors in Punjabi cinema, also rose to prominence over the last decade for his portrayals of diasporic and transnational Punjabi migrants. For Indo-Canadian to feature Maan as its spokesperson is no mere coincidence. This assemblage of the private bus service that specializes in servicing the route that transnational Punjabi migrants take on their journeys to and from the airport, with images of Maan, the poster boy of Punjabi cinema seen peddling services related to transnational mobility, speaks directly to the aspirations of middle-class Punjabi families across the region. For young men growing up in the Punjabi countryside, many of whom regard transnational migration as their only path to class mobility and economic success, Maan represents the embodiment of contemporary notions of successful Punjabi masculinity; a transnational migrant who can effortlessly travel across national boundaries, undergoing the various embodied transformations such movement requires, and claiming citizenship and belonging in diaspora as well as at home in Punjab.

Harbhajan Maan and Punjab cinema

Born in 1965, Harbhajan Maan started his career as a playback-singer in the early 1980s, performing Punjabi folk songs and Bhangra music. He gained mainstream recognition with his 1992 song 'Chithiye, Ne Chithiye' (Letter, Oh Letter), a pain-filled lament of a lonely Punjabi mother writing a letter to her migrant son. Maan went on to star in nine prominent Punjabi films, most of which feature narratives centred on transnational migration and diasporic communities living across North America, Europe and Australia. Compared to his peers, Maan's tenure as the poster boy of Punjabi cinema has lasted the longest, from 2002 to 2009. Maan's most notable films released in these eight years include: *Jee Aayan Nu* (Welcome, Manmohan Singh, 2002); *Asa Nu Maan Watna Da* (We Are Proud of Our Nation, Manmohan Singh, 2004); *Dil Apna Punjabi* (Our Heart is Punjabi, Manmohan Singh, 2006); *Mitti Wajaan Maardi* (The Soil Beckons, Manmohan Singh 2007); *Mera Pind* (My Village, Manmohan Singh, 2008); *Jag Jeondeyan De Mele* (To Meet and Celebrate While Alive, Baljit Singh Deo, 2009); and *Heer Ranjha* (Harjit Singh, 2009) (Figures 10.1 and 10.2).

Maan's career also remained one of the most illustrious as his films ushered a revival within a fledgling cinematic industry at the turn of the century. This revival followed nearly a decade of steady decline in the number and quality of films being produced in the Punjabi language, resulting partly from the political and economic turmoil and religious insurgency the region experienced in the late 1980s and early 1990s (Dhillon 2006; Gill 2012; Singh 2006). During this time period Punjab also witnessed a steady increase in emigration from the region as many landed families, fearing the political instability, sent their sons abroad (Chopra 2010). While the insurgency has since ended and the region has stabilized, the trend towards transnational migration continues among Punjabi Sikh families. Even though the inherent distrust among most Punjabi Sikhs of the

Figure 10.1 Harbhajan Maan with his wife Harminder Kaur Maan at a publicity event for his 2009 film *Heer Ranjha*. Courtesy of Harjant Gill.

Figure 10.2 Maan being interviewed on PTC Punjabi News Channel at a publicity event for his 2009 film *Heer Ranjha*. Courtesy of Harjant Gill.

Indian government makes the decision to leave their homeland easier, current migration trends are largely economically driven. It is motivated by the desire among landed Punjabi families across the state to be part of the growing middle class and participate in the kind of consumerism only made possible by remittances and investments of transnational capital sent back home (Chopra 2010; Mooney 2011; Walton-Roberts 2004).

The cultural, economic and political shifts enabled by globalization in the late twentieth and early twenty-first centuries has resulted in an accelerated mobility of images, capital and people across national boundaries, providing increasingly greater prominence to diasporic citizens within nations' political and cultural apparatuses, the terms of these movements and participation vary from region to region (Appadurai 1996; Benhabib and Resnik 2009; Clifford 1997; Schiller, Basch and Blanc 1995; Singh and Thandi 1999). Given the linguistic diversity of Indian popular culture, the overarching narrative of migration from India that encapsulates varying experiences of transnational migrants and diasporic citizens is often translated and articulated within regional histories to gain a deeper sense of ethnic loyalties, regional affinities and diasporic communities' relationship with the nation (Benei 2008; Singh 2012). I examine the performances and popularity of Maan as a Punjabi film hero, his rise to stardom in conjunction with the global circulation of Indian films (regional as well as Hindi films) and the growth of a new genre of 'NRI [Non Resident Indian] films' that celebrates the experiences of transnational migrants and member of the diasporic communities. In doing so, I explore the ways in which such circulations differ on regional levels, producing varying terms of engagement and meanings around notions of class, gender, citizenship and belonging.

Maan's on-screen persona and representations of heroic masculinity diverge from prior more traditional archetypes of Punjabi and Sikh manhood popularized by the veteran actors of Punjabi cinema. Films released in the 1980s and the early 1990s celebrate the rural, landowning upper-caste 'Jat' farmer, his hyper-masculine physique cultivated through manual work, and his unwavering commitment to his land and the agrarian landscape of the region, as the pinnacles of his achievements (Gill 2012). Contrasting Maan's popularity and performances against his predecessors', his arrival signals a shift in the notions of nationhood, belonging and the politics of representation within Punjabi cinema and popular culture to prioritize the experiences of transnational migrants over the rural farmer, and privileging diaspora over homeland as the site for cultivating cultural authenticity and influence. The settings and plotlines of Maan's films echo this change as focus shifts from regionally situated narratives set exclusively in Punjabi villages to an increasing move into more urban, transnational and diasporic landscapes. Above all, through discursive practices around the concepts of cultural authenticity and traditions encapsulated within the notions of 'Punjabiyat' (the sense of being Punjabi)[1] and 'Punjabi *Sabhyachar* [culture and traditions]', Maan's film regards the inclusion of Non Resident Indians (NRIs) and diasporic Punjabi Sikh communities as given, providing transnational citizens with a renewed sense of prominence and participation within regional and national imaginaries.

Drawing on Inderpal Grewal and Caren Kaplan's use of the term 'transnationalism' to, 'problematize a purely locational politics of global-local or center-periphery in favor of ... the lines cutting across them' (1994: 13), this chapter also unpacks Maan's performances and cinematic persona to think about how the circulations of Punjabi films challenge the centrality of Bollywood and the Indian nation-state in representations of and processes related to transnational migration, while simultaneously reproducing regional gendered and caste hierarchies within the diasporic milieu. As Purnima Mankekar notes, 'mass media are among the most crucial channels of socialization among diasporic communities, and they play a crucial role in the creating of imaginary homelands for diasporic subjects' (1999: 732). Drawing on familiar tropes of nostalgia and overt paternalism directed at diasporic viewers, Maan's films equate the consumption of Punjabi cinema with servitude to regional culture, privileging the region over the nation as a space to anchor belonging.

Maan's popularity within Punjab can also be credited to his role as the de facto cultural ambassador between regional and diasporic audiences of Punjabi cinema. Maan's films serve as a window into audience interests and experiences, emblematic of greater shifts taking place in gender roles and social life of Punjab as the region's economy and landscape is gradually transformed through processes related to transnationalism, globalization and the neoliberal restructuring of the Indian economy (Brosius 2010; Chopra 2010; Mooney 2011). Maan's on-screen migrant persona solidifies a new archetype of Punjabi transnational manhood that serves as a source of encouragement and affirmation for the growing desire and willingness among Punjabis, especially young unmarried Punjabi men, to leave their homes in search of a better, more financially prosperous future abroad.

Farmer, soldier, migrant

Prior to Maan's arrival on the cinematic screen, Punjabi film heroes largely occupied one of two of the following archetypes: the hardworking Punjabi farmer committed to caring for his family, his village and most importantly his land; and

---

[1] Srijana Mitra Das provides a useful definition of *Punjabiyat*. 'It refers to a commonly held, all-encompassing view of Punjabi culture, society and being Punjabi as an individual. The term thus refers to larger structures of social or community organizations (such as kinship networks, caste identities, religious beliefs and practices, understanding of gender roles, etc.) as well as to individual Punjabi values (such as bravery, resilience, honor, heartiness)' (2006: 468–9). Also see Pritam Singh for a detailed discussion on the notion of *Punjabiyat* in a global context (2010).

the loyal Punjabi/Sikh solider or revolutionary committed to defending his nation and his faith. Cultivated through hours of manual work in his fields, as Radhika Chopra notes, practices related to learning masculinity and being a man in rural Punjab have historically been shaped above all through the relationship of a man to his land and are transcribed on to the body itself (Chopra 2004: 44). A Punjabi farmer's sculpted physique, his strength, his posture, his adornment in traditional attire such as a *paag* (a turban), a *kurta* (a long cotton tunic) and Punjabi *jutti* (pointed leather slippers), continue to define these historical representations of hegemonic Punjabi manhood.

In addition to borrowing from Hindi cinematic traditions, as regional films often do, popular Punjabi films released in the 1980s and the 1990s often took their aesthetic and stylistic cues from Pakistani and Urdu cinematic traditions (commonly referred to as Lollywood) as well as Urdu stage plays. Produced with low budgets and poor production values, Punjabi films released in the 1980s and the 1990s often relied on crude jokes and featured overtly exaggerated theatrical performances, as Ali Khan and Ali Nobil Ahmed note 'catering largely to a male audience from the poor and illiterate sections of society' (2010: 154). In Punjabi films from the 1980s and the 1990s, the hero's masculine identity was equally shaped through landownership, his patrilineal descent and his caste status as belonging to a *Jat* (land-owning) family, a group that has historically enjoyed economic and political hegemony in the region (Gill 2012; Mooney 2011). The popularity of the 1981 film *Putt Jattan De* (Son's of Jat Farmers, Jagjit Gill), and the perennial circulation of the title song and references to the film, serve as testaments to the salience of the landed-farmer status as the idealized embodiment of heroic masculinity in Punjabi cinema and popular culture.

Putt Jattan De popularized a whole genre of what are colloquially referred to as *Jat*-themed films or *badla* (revenge) films (Figure 10.3). Most of these films deploy fairly formulaic cinematic tropes where the annexation of familial land and/or the loss of familial honour resulting from the violation of women's *izzat* (sexual propriety), serve as the inciting incidents that challenge the hero's manhood and his position within his community.

Figure 10.3 Guggu Gill (left) and Yograj Singh (right) faceoff in a revenge-themed Punjabi film *Anakh Jattan Di* (Ego of Jats) from 1990.

The circumstances of his life compel introspection, ultimately leading him towards realizing his agency. He is duty-bound to rectify the injustice by exacting revenge on the perpetrators, resulting in an action-packed climax and ending where he emerges as victorious with his masculinity unblemished. Popular *Jat*-themed and *badla* films featuring veteran actors including Guggu Gill, Yograj Singh, Dara Singh and Veerendra personified familiar tropes in regards to masculinity, borrowing liberally from films being produced in neighbouring regions in places such as Lahore (Ahmed 1992: 317), as well as Bombay, where films such as *Sholay* (Embers, Ramesh Sippy, 1975) defined the dominant style and aesthetic popular among Indian audiences in the 1970s and the early 1980s

A slightly less common, yet equally salient archetype of heroic masculinity in Punjabi cinema remains that of a Sikh *fauji* (soldier) a turban-wearing soldier fighting on the frontlines of a battlefield along with his comrades to defend his nation's honour. Narrated in the form of historical reconstructions, these cinematic representations also privilege the physical achievements and emotional resolve of the film's hero. Confronted with a series of moral ambiguities and challenges, the hero demonstrates his masculine resilience through unwavering devotion to his nation and faith. His willingness to sacrifice individual comforts and desires by engaging in the religious tradition of *shaheedi* (martyrdom) serves as a testament to his heroic masculinity. Another equally prolific Punjabi singer-turned-actor, Gurdas Maan, has frequently portrayed these characters on screen.

Both archetypes of the landed-farmer and the Sikh-solider glorify and celebrate the male body, its physical characteristics and association of masculinity with steadfast doggedness, as the idealization of Punjabi and Sikh masculinities. They attempt to embody the concept of *soorma* (brave-hearted warrior), a heroic stature rooted in Sikh history, and later in colonial-era practices and policies that strategically privileged Punjabi and Sikh soldiers over their Hindu and Muslim counterparts within the British Army (Cohn [1987] 2004; Kalra 2005). Given the hegemony of Punjabi masculinity within the broader landscape of South Asian masculinities (Chopra, Osella and Osella 2004; Kalra 2009), it is no coincidence that until the 1980s, in addition to farming, joining the Indian armed forces or law enforcement remained the preferred occupation for most men across Punjab. However, the early twenty-first century, following the effects of globalization on the region, birthed new desires for neoliberal consumption and transnational travel. And as the costs associated with agriculture continue to rise, making farming increasingly unsustainable, Nicola Mooney notes, 'migration is now the singular stuff of Punjabi dreams of family progress' (2011: 170).

While transnational migration from Punjab, especially of Punjabi Sikh men, has been an ongoing phenomenon that dates back to the colonial period (Axel 2001; Bhachu 1986; Brah 1996; Leonard 1992; Shah 2011), the archetype of the Punjabi migrant remained largely absent from the cinematic screen and popular imagination until Maan's arrival. Only a handful of Punjabi films made in the 1980s and the 1990s feature transnational migrants as the central characters. Most notable of these include a film titled *Long Da Lishkara* (Reflection of the Nose Ring, Harpal Tiwana, 1986), about a returning migrant named Raja (starring Raj Babbar). Whereas within Maan's films the process of migration is presented as an opportunity and actively sought after, in *Long Da Lishkara* the act of leaving home is equated with voluntary exile necessitated by familial circumstances. Serving as the inciting incident that propels the plot forward, Raja's return from Canada is also prefaced by the familiar shot of an airliner touching down on a runway, followed by a celebratory homecoming sequence where Raja steps out of a taxi dressed in a silver jacket, denim jeans, and riding boots as he crosses the threshold of his ancestral home where the entire village has gathered to greet him.

Yet unlike Maan's seamless arrival at the airport, Raja's return is fraught with tensions and contradictions. His return to his village in adulthood where his mother resides is presented as an eventuality. Even after studying abroad in Canadian universities, he is expected to take up farming and devote himself to managing his family's property. The film ends without offering any indication that Raja would leave again. On the contrary, his gradual physical transformation from looking like a transnational migrant to looking like a landed-farmer, which forms one of the narrative arcs of the film, is accented with a sense of absolution. Tension arises within this process of reincorporation as Raja struggles to negotiate his progressive outlook on caste and class with the customs of his homeland that remain fixed in the region's social history. Raja's attempt to challenge existing caste and gender hierarchies mark him as an outsider. His presence is met with suspicion and mistrust, as villagers increasingly see him as a threat to the social fabric of village life. When he falls in love with a woman of lower social status, the quest that ensues is equally about Raja's attempts to challenge the norms of village life as well as trying to reincorporate himself into the social space of his ancestral home. While Raja emerges triumphant in carving out a space for himself and his desires, audiences are left with the sense that his acceptance into the landscape surrounding him is far from complete.

Contrasting *Long Da Lishkara* with more recent films featuring migrant narratives, Maan's characters are rarely seen transgressing caste and class boundaries, especially in their selection of prospective lovers and partners. Far from challenging or abandoning traditional identity categories and caste hierarchies, the popularity and success of the transnational migrant characters Maan portrays rely on the recuperation and reinforcement of these social boundaries, both at home and in the diaspora. Unlike Raja, Maan's characters rarely struggle to reincorporate themselves into the social space of their homeland. Instead of resisting regional class and caste privileges and hierarchies, Maan's characters often draw on his patriarchal descent and his status as a son of a landed *Jat* farmer to serve as a source of inspiration and celebration to claim what he perceives as his rightful space within the village's social structure. The transformations from being a transnational migrant to being a *Jat* famer and back to transnational migrant are seamlessly achieved with minimal effort.

The ideal migrant

Maan's films are not the only ones to satiate desires for a glimpse into diasporic life and the experiences of transnational migrants. In fact, as regional filmmakers across India have often done in the past, Punjabi filmmakers follow the contemporary trends within the larger and more resourceful Hindi film industry (also referred to as Bollywood), creating localized representations of narratives and themes popular on a national level. Indian cinemas, led by the Hindi film industry, 'went global' in the early 1990s, following the neoliberal restructuring of the Indian economy that gave birth to the category of the NRI, an economic and cultural strategy endorsed by the national government to increase diasporic investment, involvement and commitment to the homeland (Brosius 2005; Jolly, Wadhwani and Barretto 2007; Kavoori and Punathambekar 2008). Maan's films borrow heavily from the aesthetics of Hindi films released in the mid- to late 1990s, particularly the 1995 blockbuster hit *Dilwale Dulhania Le Jayenge*

(The Brave Hearted Will Take Away the Bride, Aditya Chopra, *DDLJ* hereafter), a film that is widely credited for having established the 'NRI genre'. Though in Hindi and featuring Bollywood actors and Hindi cinematic sensibilities, *DDLJ* too chronicles the lives of a Punjabi family living in London and their return to their homeland and village set within the agrarian landscape of Punjab. While their journey across national boundaries is the central feature of most NRI films produced in Hindi as well as Punjabi, the nuances within these migrant experiences and how the diaspora is represented differ significantly.

Carefully crafted within NRI films (in Hindi and Punjabi), the journey across national boundaries and the practices related to transnational travel, represent important sites of transition and transformations as a way of reincorporating diasporic subjects within the social milieu of the homeland (Gill 2012; Mankekar 1999; Sharpe 2007). Building on James Clifford's classification of travel as a, 'range of material, spatial practices that produce knowledges, stories, traditions, comportments, musics, books, diaries, and other cultural expressions' (Clifford 1997:35), Mankekar notes that 'diasporic subjects do not just travel, they also forge identities and communities shaped by particular forms of longing and dwelling' (1999: 749). The popularity of NRI films featuring diasporic narratives underscores the significance of popular cultural forms, including cinema, in reproducing particular types of diasporic subjects for audiences back home.

The emergence of what Jenny Sharpe refers to as the 'respectable NRI' in Indian cinemas coincides with the growing urban middle class in India at the turn of the century, financed partially though the transnational circulation of capital, remittances and increased investment in the homeland (2007: 77). In keeping with the formation of the ideal NRI and second-generation diasporic citizen, within Hindi films such as *DDLJ*, migrant women often represent the embodiment of traditional South Asian womanhood, what Gayatri Gopinath refers to as the 'emblems of national traditions and morality' (2005: 18; Sharpe 2007: 77). As we see in *DDLJ*, women's mobility is carefully surveilled and policed by the family's patriarchs, and often their only access to transnational migration is mediated by the men in their lives, as daughters and brides of NRI husbands (Mankekar 1999; Mehta 2007; Sharpe 2007). Whereas in Hindi films such as *DDLJ*, it is often the female protagonist who represents the site of transformation, as we see Simran (*DDLJ's* leading character) abandoning her Western clothing and sensibilities in favour of traditional Punjabi attire and obedience to regional customs and rituals (Sharpe 2007: 78), in Punjabi films starring Maan the focus of these transitions and transformations remains fixed entirely on the male body.

Maan's debut film *Jee Ayaan Nu* also narrates the story of a successful Canada-based Punjabi family with a marriage-aged daughter (named Simar), who during a visit to Punjab falls in love with Inder, a college-aged son of a landed family played by Maan. Despite the two families' shared caste and class status, Simar's family calls off the engagement upon Inder's refusal to emigrate to Canada as a *gharjamai* (live-in-son-in-law or house-husband). In the aftermath of their breakup, Inder resolves to move to Canada on his own merits, proving to Simar's family that he is capable of accessing transnational migration and being a successful diasporic citizen without his in-laws' support, and thereby worthy of claiming Simar as his bride without having to endure the humiliation associated with being a *gharjamai*, a status often imbued with a sense of desperation and failure within a culture where matrilocal residence patterns are rare.

Unlike Hindi films such as *DDLJ*, where diasporic women are seen actively choosing to submit to the institution of patriarchal Indian family, these choices for Punjabi women are rendered further invisible in Maan's film where the focus remains squarely on the men within their families and their ability (or inability) to access transnational migration. Far from being monitored or surveilled, Maan's mobility and ability to migrate is depicted as the ultimate exercise of his patriarchal privilege and an affirmation of his upper-caste *Jat* manhood. As Maan's characters repeatedly reinforce, in the early twenty-first century, migration from Punjab is no longer a one-way journey out of the country but a 'circular process' where visiting and remitting money home is just as important a feature in the narrative of being a successful migrant as the initial act of leaving to seek and secure a more prosperous future elsewhere (Chopra 2010: 113).

Maan's cinematic personas mark the emergence of a new model of idealized masculinity that is able to claim citizenship and belonging through the types of 'flexible' practices necessitate by transnational mobility (Gill 2016; Ong 1999). In doing so, Maan's characters also repudiate the prior stereotypes of Punjabi migrants as either Sikh refugees in exile who have tumultuous relationship with the nation, or disaffected second-generation youth who have lost their *sanskar* (moral values) and forgotten their *sabhyachar* (culture), whose return might be fraught with the types of tensions and contradictions confronted by Raja in *Long Da Lishkara*. Maan, on the other hand, is shown as navigating the unfamiliar terrain of transnational mobility with the ease of a seasoned globetrotter, effortlessly shifting from his white-collar occupation (as a doctor or engineer) in the USA or Canada to performing manual labour and tilling his own land back in Punjab. In *Mitti Wajaan Maardi*, we witness Maan go from wearing a sports jacket and driving in a convertible through the streets of San Francisco to wearing a white *kurta* (cotton tunic), a colourful turban and cultivating his fields with his tractor upon arriving in Punjab without any significant obstacles. Unlike Raja in *Long the Lishkara,* Maan's characters remain vested in their caste hierarchies. Being a *Jat* is part of their inheritance that remains dormant until their return to Punjab, where its recovery allows them to fully realize the process of reincorporation.

Punjabi films starring Maan also differ significantly from Hindi films such as *DDLJ* featuring transnational migrants largely in the way in which the diaspora is conceived and depicted. Where as in *DDLJ* London is shown to be a place fraught with physical dangers and moral depravity that only intensifies the longing for the comforts and nurturance of the homeland, Maan's films depict the diaspora as a safe and familiar place; a mere extension of Punjab. Instead of arriving in a cold, unfamiliar, foreign land where newly arriving migrants are usually confronted with different languages and customs, Maan's films feature idyllic images of diasporic communities residing in the comfort of suburban ethnic enclaves such as Surry, Brampton and Yuba City, located in safe proximity from crime-ridden cities such as Vancouver, Toronto and San Francisco, viewed as repositories of immorality and corruption.

Even though *Mitti Wajaan Maardi* (The Soil Beckons) opens with the iconic images of San Francisco's skyline and landmarks such as the Golden Gate Bridge and Lombard Street, the camera quickly shifts to lengthy montages of the lush green fields of Yuba City, a predominantly Punjabi suburb in central California. We see shots of Punjabi families enjoying the midday sun in their neighbourhood parks while elderly men and women wearing turbans and *shalwar kameez* (a traditional outfit worn by Punjabi women) shuffle in and out of a Sikh temple. Through this careful reproduction of the landscape of home within the diaspora, Maan's films promote the sense that the diaspora is merely an extension of the homeland, minimizing the kinds of linguistic and cultural barriers that Hindi films such as *DDLJ* often highlight. The inner-city fears of violence, discrimination, exploitation and even moral corruption are replaced with less threatening suburban concerns of being overworked, longing for home and the perennial worries related to the loss of *sabhyachar* (culture, traditions, language).

Representations of the diaspora and homeland within Hindi and Punjabi films also differ in a key manner that is significant. In Punjabi films featuring Maan, the references to *watan* (nation) are often ambiguous defined, the expression 'mera watan' (my nation) referring interchangeably from my *pind* (village), to my Punjab, to my India. Despite its refusal to explicitly endorse the separatist Khalistani project following the Sikh struggle for an independent homeland that lasted through the mid-1980s and 1990s (Axel 2001; Mahmood 1996), Maan's films reinforce regionalist notions of a Punjabi Sikh nation as an imagined spaced that extends beyond the national boundaries to incorporate diasporic communities in the USA, Canada and England. This discursive ambiguity is deliberate, as Maan's film attempt to simultaneously cater to audiences in Punjab as well as audiences in the diaspora, many of whom remain critical of India's role as their nation-state, if not still vested in the possibility of a separate Sikh homeland. In doing so, Maan's films promote what Rajanpreet Nagra notes as, 'Punjabi nationalism' over 'Indian nationalism', legitimizing 'diasporic identity as Punjabi identity' (2011: 167).

The concern with the loss of *sabhyachar* (culture) and the preservation of *Punjabiyat* are central themes in most of Maan's films. Moral corruption in the diaspora and greed back in the village where the absence of family members makes illegal seizures of land and property more likely, often operate as the central devices for producing conflict in almost all of Maan's films. The responsibility and privilege of recovering *sabhyachar* and modelling for the diasporic community how to be a 'respectful NRI', rest squarely on Maan's shoulders. Imbued with overtly paternalistic rhetoric, Maan's cinematic personas and the characters he portrays narrate the script for successful masculinity that most young Punjabi men, especially unmarried ones, eagerly embrace and aspire to follow, defining to a large extent what it means to be an ideal transnational migrant and diasporic citizen.

Touring abroad

The cinema-going audiences in Punjab, largely young men and women across the region, approach Punjabi films such as *Jee Aayan Nu* and *Mitti Wajaan Maardi* very differently from Hindi films featuring narratives about Punjabi migrants such as *DDLJ,* and more recently *Singh is Kinng* (Anees Bazmee, 2008), an over the top slapstick comedy about a Sikh migrant who finds himself caught up in the criminal underworld of Sydney. While most of the young men and women I spoke to while conducting fieldwork across Punjab consume Hindi films with the expected sense of scepticism, knowing that these portrayals are exaggerated, fantastical and unrealistic, the same audience members regard Punjabi films, especially Maan's films, as a far more authentic and believable representation of their own and their community's experiences.[2] As an audience

---

[2] Based on interviews and ethnographic research conducted across Punjab between January and December 2009.

member once instructed me, 'Singh is Kinng is just another Hindi film cloaked in Punjabi *tardka* [flavoring],' he continued, 'If you want to see the *asli* [authentic] Punjab and Punjabi *sabhyachar* you have to watch Maan's films.'

As we exited the movie theatre in Chandigarh, the capital city of Punjab, after having seen one of Maan's most recent films, *Jag Jeondeyan De Mele*, with a young man named Jassi who was just getting ready to move to Canada on a student visa, I asked him about his impressions of the film and Maan's acting. Jassi replied, 'theek he si! AC di hava kha li, Canada di ser kari li, hor kee phaldan hai?' (the film was average, but you got to sit in an air-conditioned room for three hours, and he took you on a scenic tour of Canada, what more do you want?) Jassi's reply was instructive in the sense that it made me realize that, above all other qualities, Maan's on-screen representations are popular among young Punjabi men because they offer an idealized glimpse into a life in a community they themselves aspire to one day join.

While Maan's films are instilled with a sense of authenticity and realism rarely afforded to Bollywood or even Hollywood films, Punjabi audience members also realize that for many who cannot afford to finance the kind of travel Maan undertakes (a one-way ticket on Indo-Canadian costs 2200 rupees, around 35 US dollars) the possibility of similar mobility remains a distant dream. For many young Punjabi men, Maan's films allow them to indulge in a fantasy of being transnationally mobile and living in the diaspora, which, unlike the popular Bollywood representations, holds some promise, however bleak, of turning into their reality someday.

The characters that Maan portrays on screen are considered successful for their ability to circumvent the limitations of everyday life at home and in the diaspora while remaining firmly rooted in traditional patriarchal values and caste and gender hierarchies. These unthreatening, idealized and inviting depictions of life in the diaspora further reassure men such as Jassi about their decision to emigrate, subduing their fear about the foreign land they will soon arrive in, legally or illegally. Whether he is helping young men such as Jassi to navigate the unfamiliar terrain of transnational migration or helping relieve the travel-related anxieties of migrants returning home, undoubtedly Harbhajan Maan has acquired a unique status in Punjabi cinema and popular culture: that of a tour guide, or a cultural ambassador of sorts, bridging the gulf between diaspora and home.

Works Cited

Ahmed, Akbar S. (1992), 'Bombay Cinema: The Cinema of Metaphor for Indian Society and Politics', *Modern Asian Studies*, 26 (2): 289–320.

Appadurai, Arjun (1996), *Modernity at Large: Cultural Dimensions of Globalization*, Minneapolis: University of Minnesota Press.

Axel, Brian Keith (2001), *The Nation's Tortured Body: Violence, Representation, and the Formation of Sikh "Diaspora"*, Durham, NC: Duke University Press.

Benei, Veronique (2008), '"Globalization" and Regional(ist) Cinema in Western India: Public Culture, Private Media, and the Reproduction of Hindu National(ist) Hero, 1930s–2000s', *South Asian Popular Culture*, 6 (2): 83–108.

Benhabib, Seyla and Judith Resnik, eds. (2009), *Migrations and Mobilities: Citizenship, Borders and Gender*, New York: New York University Press.

Bhachu, Parminder (1986), *Twice Migrants: East African Sikh Settlers in Britain*, London: Routledge.

Brah, Avtar (1996), *Cartographies of Diaspora: Contesting Identities*, London: Routledge.

Brosius, Christiane (2005), 'The Scattered Homelands of the Migrant: Bollywood Through the Diasporic Lens', in Raminder Kaur and Ajay J. Sinha (eds), *Bollyworld: Popular Indian Cinema Through a Transnational Lens*, 207–38, New Delhi: Sage Publications.

Brosius, Christiane (2010), *India's Middle Class: New Forms of Urban Leisure, Consumption and Prosperity*, New Delhi: Routledge.

Chopra, Radhika (2004), 'Encountering Masculinity: An Ethnographer's Dilemma', in Osella, Osella and Chopra (eds), *South Asian Masculinities: Context of Change, Sites of Continuity*, 36–59, New Delhi: Women Unlimited.

Chopra, Radhika (2010), *Militant and Migrant: The Politics and Social History of Punjab*, London: Routledge.

Chopra, Radhika, Caroline Osella and Filippo Osella (eds) (2004), *South Asian Masculinities: Context of Change, Sites of Continuity*, New Delhi: Women Unlimited.

Clifford, James (1997), *Routes: Travel and Translation in the Late Twentieth Century*, Cambridge, MA: Harvard University Press.

Cohn, Bernard ([1987] 2004), *Bernard Cohn Omnibus*, New Delhi: Oxford University Press.

Das, Srijana Mitra (2006), 'Partition and Punjabiyat in Bombay Cinema: The Cinematic Perspectives of Yash Chopra and Others', *Contemporary South Asia*, 15 (4): 453–71.

Dhillon, Kirpal (2006), *Identity and Survival: Sikh Militancy in India 1978-1993*, New Delhi: Penguin Books.

Gill, Harjant (2012), 'Masculinity, Mobility and Transformation in Punjabi Cinema: From *Putt Jattan De* (Sons of Jat Farmers) to *Munde UK De* (Boys of UK)', *South Asian Popular Culture*, 10 (2): 109–22.

Gill, Harjant (2016), 'What the Sikh Turban Means to Masculinity in These Transnational Times', in *Plainspeak*, online at: www.tarshi.net/inplainspeak/voices-sikh-turban-masculinity-transnational/ (accessed 7 February 2017).

Gopinath, Gayatri (2005), *Impossible Desires: Queer Diasporas and South Asian Public Cultures*, Durham, NC: Duke University Press.

Grewal, Inderpal and Caren Kaplan (1994), 'Introduction: Transnational Feminist Practices and Questions of Postmodernity', in Inderpal Grewal and Caren Kaplan (eds), *Scattered Hegemonies: Postmodernity and Transnational Feminist Practices*, 1–33, Minneapolis: University of Minnesota Press.

Jolly, Gurbir, Zenia Wadhwani and Deborah Barretto, eds (2007), *Once Upon a Time in Bollywood: The Global Swing in Hindi Cinema*, Toronto: TSAR Publications.

Kalra, Virinder S. (2005), 'Locating the Sikh Pagh', *Sikh Formations*, 1 (1): 75–92.

Kalra, Virinder S. (2009), 'Between Emasculation and Hypermasculiniy: Theorizing British South Asian Masculinities', *South Asian Popular Culture*, 7 (2): 113–25.

Kavoori, Anandam P. and Aswin Punathambekar, eds (2008), *Global Bollywood*, New York: New York University Press.

Khan, Ali and Ali Nobil Ahmad (2010), 'From *Zinda Laash* to *Zibahkhana*: Violence and Horror in Pakistani Cinema', *Third Text*, 24 (1): 149–61.

Leonard, Karen Isaksen (1992), *Making Ethnic Choices: California's Punjabi Mexican Americans*, Philadelphia: Temple University Press.

Mahmood, Cynthia Keppley (1996), *Fighting for Faith and Nation: Dialogues with Sikh Militants*, Philadelphia: University of Pennsylvania Press.

Mankekar, Purnima (1999), 'Brides Who Travel: Gender, Transnationalism, and Nationalism in Hindi Film', *Positions*, 7 (3): 731–61.

Mehta, Monika (2007), 'Globalizing Bombay Cinema: Reproducing the Indian State and Family', in Gurbir Jolly, Zenia Wadhwani and Deborah Barretto (eds), *Once Upon a Time in Bollywood: The Global Swing in Hindi Cinema*, 20–42, Toronto: TSAR Publications.

Mooney, Nicola (2011), *Rural Nostalgias and Transnational Dreams: Identity and Modernity Among Jat Sikhs*, Toronto: University of Toronto Press.

Nagra, Ranjanpreet Kaur (2011), 'British by Right, Punjabi by Heart: Diaspora Portrayals in Punjabi Films', *Sikh Formations*, 7 (2): 161–75.

Ong, Aihwa (1999), *Flexible Citizenship: The Cultural Logics of Transnationality*, Durham, NC: Duke University Press.

Schiller, Nina Glick, Linda Basch and Cristina Szanton Blanc (1995), 'From Immigrant to Transmigrant: Theorizing Transnational Migration', *Anthropological Quarterly*, 68 (1): 48–63.

Shah, Nayan (2011), *Stranger Intimacy: Contesting Race, Sexuality, and the Law in the North American West*, Berkeley, Los Angeles and London: University of California Press.

Sharpe, Jenny (2007), 'Gender, Nation, and Globalization in *Monsoon Wedding* and *Dilwale Dulhania Le Jayenge*', in Gurbir Jolly, Zenia Wadhwani and Deborah Barretto (eds), *Once Upon a Time in Bollywood: The Global Swing in Hindi Cinema*, 70–91, Toronto: TSAR Publications.

Singh, Harleen (2006), 'Tur(banned) Masculinities: Terrorists, Sikhs, and Trauma in Indian Cinema', *Sikh Formations*, 2 (2): 115–124.

Singh, Pritam (2010), 'Punjab, Punjabi and Punjabiyat', *South Asian Ensemble*, 2 (3): 100–12.

Singh, Pritam (2012), 'Globalisation and Punjabi Identity: Resistance, Relocation and Reinvention (Yet Again!)', *Journal of Punjab Studies*, 19 (2): 153–72.

Singh, Pritam and Shinder S. Thandi, eds (1999), *Punjabi Identity in Global Context*, New Delhi: Oxford University Press.

Walton-Roberts, Margaret (2004), 'Returning, Remitting, Reshaping: Non-Resident Indians and the Transformation of Society and Space in Punjab, India', *Transnational Spaces*, 78–103, London: Routledge.

Chapter 11

Helen: The Chin Chin Chu girl
Sudesh Mishra

The other's delayed disavowal

It is possible to argue that what differentiates the golden era cinema of the 1950s from the heady dancehall or courtship dramas of the 1960s and beyond is a notable shift in the dynamic of avowal and disavowal with regard to the structure of conjuration involving the self and other. Hindi cinema of the golden era, which might be labelled the cinema of social criticism, imagines the self in relation to socialist modernity with its stress on the social contract, duty of care, *satitva* (spousal devotion as conveyed in sacrificial acts of virtue, service and chastity), labour-sensitive technological advancement, *vishwas* (bonds of trust that hold together individuals, families and communities), ethical poverty, *izzat* (communally sanctioned forms of honour) and self-sacrifice for the national good. The espousal of these values and virtues is, however, predicated on conjuring up the scandalous other (capitalist modernity and Western cultural norms and sexual practices), which is constitutive of – and yet poses an ever-present danger to – the dynamic of avowal within the context of the national imaginary. This dynamic contributes to the logic of not-becoming other in films that concentrate predominantly on the protracted miseries of self-avowal. The other is summoned from the crypt of the national imaginary so as to enable painful and repetitive acts of resistance that constitute the self in a manner consistent with a Nehruvian understanding of identity, sexuality, culture and political modernity. The dancehall dramas of the sixties, drawing on the global explosion in popular Western music and the associated culture of social rebellion and sexual permissiveness, do not simply give up on the dynamic of disavowing the other. Rather, they take delight in impersonating the other for long periods, strategically postponing the inevitable moment of disavowal. Miseries of avowal are replaced by the extended pleasures of disavowal. The upshot is that dancehall dramas are concerned with the protracted enjoyment involved in the eventual disavowal of the other. Consequently, song-and-dance sequences begin to displace plot progression. This, in turn, leads to the decline of the cinema of social criticism and the rise of the petit bourgeois romance where the spectacle, and spectacular *jouissance*, triumphs over sociopolitical commentary and commitment (Mishra 2012: 819–23). The heroes and heroines of dancehall dramas readily masquerade as the Western other for long periods and disavowal occurs usually at the point of denouement. But what happens when the masquerade fails or when the self becomes other to the degree that the dynamic of disavowal fails? Or, indeed, when the other's otherness is so threatening and overwhelming, so amorphous and alluring, so dissolute and irredeemable, that it must be fatally or repressively returned to the crypt of the national imaginary? Heroes and heroines are alert to the provisional and ludic nature of the masquerade (and so rarely cross the line of no return), but dancehall dramas also throw up liminal, inveterate and expendable types who either do not conform to hegemonic notions of the self or are fatally predisposed to the lure of the other. The most riveting figure of this type in popular Hindi cinema goes by the name of Helen Jairag Richardson. For much of the late 1950s, and the years spanning the 1960s and the 1970s, Helen was the figure of an unassimilable otherness: she was regularly cast as the radical other who attracted, imperiled and repelled the self in a multitude of ways. A shape-shifting signifier of an incurable otherness (Chinese prostitute and Malay village belle, Anglo-Indian mistress and rape-worthy Christian, belly-dancing Arab and alcoholic European) she exemplifies the pitfalls of a failed masquerade, the risk of *being* rather than *playing* the other. She arrogates to herself, as Anustup Basu notes, the customary patriarchal monopoly on sexual pleasure, endangering the normative account of women as 'pure ethical theorems, or as reproductive machines' (2013: 145). Helen's unassimilable otherness permitted the dancehall drama to indulge voyeuristically in life-worlds it imagined as belonging to the other, albeit as part of a broader exhortatory logic that allowed the hero and heroine to take dubious enjoyment on the long road to avowing a dominant Hindu worldview. In this worldview, which is an integral part of the national imaginary where the self-other dynamic gets played out, the self is rendered as patriotically postcolonial, ethically conservative, economically middle class and sexually hetero-patriarchal. Without Helen as the sacrificial foil, as the non-masquerading other to ephemeral masqueraders, there would be no *jouissance* in the dynamic of avowal and disavowal that lies at the heart of Hindi cinema.

As the exemplary figure of otherness, of manifold otherness, Helen has been the subject of a couple of thought-provoking studies by Jerry Pinto and Anustup Basu. Pinto's sharp-witted biography of the screen star (as opposed to the real-life woman) affords a detailed account of how she came to assume multiple avatars of otherness (courtesan, gypsy, moll, senorita, vamp, nightclub dancer, *femme fatale*, fisherwoman, foreign spy and the like) over the course of her long career. In his account she is an abstract figure of otherness never reducible to any one of her myriad incarnations (2006: 63–101). Basu's article also concerns multiple forms of otherness. He draws on Helen to shed light on the public, and therefore profanely unsanctioned, manifestations of femininity. Basu makes the startling point that Helen's predecessors, represented by Nadia, Sulochna, Aruna Devi, Durga Khote and Maya Banerjee, all of whom starred in colonial-era films of the 1930s, were not constrained in their otherness by the dictates of the dominant ethos. He calls this ethos the 'Brahminical culturalism of the nationalist middle class' (Basu 2013: 141). By contrast, Helen's screen femininity cannot evade the interpellations of the Hindu nationalist ethos as symptomatically captured in the cinema of the post-Independence period. The actress begins to feature sporadically in the films of the golden era but comes into her own in the 1960s, when dancehall dramas supplant the more realistic cinema of social criticism. The crucial point here is that the emergence of the dancehall drama alters the diegesis without undermining the plot, which continues to revolve around the invocation and exorcism of scandalous others. At the level of the diegesis, however, the protracted miseries of self-avowal vis-à-vis the other is replaced by the pleasures of the masquerade in delaying the disavowal of the other. The abject social spaces of the cart-driver, the vagabond, the homeless poet and the impecunious peasant are replaced by the romantic hill station, the plush nightclub, the psychedelic smuggler's den, the flamboyant botanical garden, the posh private party, the insinuating hotel room and assorted bourgeois interiors. The dancehall drama devotes an increasing number of chronotopes (measurable in reels of celluloid) to the recreational masquerade and, consequently, to manifestations of otherness. A chronotope, according to James Clifford, consists of any 'setting or scene organizing time and space in representable whole form' and includes the *mise en scène* (1992: 101). It is here, in these chronotopes of *jouissance*, that otherness assumes two distinct forms and attributes. The first consists of the eradicable otherness of transitory masqueraders while the second concerns the incorrigible otherness of characters who are not masquerading or who are unable to distinguish the authentic self from the masquerading other. Consequently, the ambivalence that pervades the self's interaction with the other, and which is constitutively necessary to the national imaginary, has to be, in the final instance, renounced by heroes and heroines. Vijay Mishra makes a kindred point when he alerts us to Hindi cinema's 'capacity to carry deconstructive or transgressive moments,' but only insofar as these are regulated by the general *dharmic* injunctions that govern it (2002: 33). When the principal masqueraders shed their masks, as they must in compliance with the infinitely transportable plot, the incurable otherness of the other is revealed in the clear light of day. Thereafter, it is didactically returned to the crypt only to be re-invoked in the next dancehall flick. Little wonder, then, that Helen's manifold otherness is predicated on her manifold deaths and resurrections.

Chronotopes of otherness

Still, it would be wrong to assert that this otherness is simply an affair of the body, the protean and imprecise phenotype of the hybrid offspring of a Burmese-Spanish mother and a French father. Nor is it merely a case of the staggering breadth of Helen's cross-cultural wardrobe or the deliberate cultivation of a norm-defying gait or the penchant for wayward habits and appetites and the failure to decipher the law of the masquerade built on the logic of delayed disavowal. Moreover, we cannot limit her otherness to the lyrical impropriety of her songs, to the objectification implicit in sexually charged proper nouns (Kitty, Ruby, Lily and the like) or to the auto-erotic tactility evident in the thrusting of hips and the stroking of assorted erogenous parts of the body. Doubtless these contribute substantially to our sense of her irredeemable otherness, but this would be swiftly neutralized if she were cast much in the same manner in the tradition of Western cinema. The point is that her characters are placed in chronotopes that accrue value negatively and differentially by the image-signs surrounding them. Ferdinand de Saussure's insight into language systems is germane in this respect. Declaring that all 'values emanate from the system', de Saussure notes:

> When they are said to correspond to concepts, it is understood that concepts are purely differential and defined not by their positive content but negatively by their relations with the other terms of the system. Their most precise characteristic is in being what the others are not. (2004: 67)

Analogously, Helen's otherness is expressed by her being what the others are not within the system of the national imaginary. The negative logic of value attribution (she is not this, not that – not chaste, not respectable, not clothed, not abashed, not abstinent, not private, not *desi*, not trustworthy, not domesticated) lacks positive terms precisely because her screen characters are, more often than not, consigned to scandalous chronotopes – bathtubs, nightclubs, pools, fast cars, dancehalls, barrooms, beaches, cages, *kothas*, bedrooms, brothels, seedy dens and the like. These chronotopes of disrepute are sharply distinguished from the socially sanctioned chronotopes of the mother's hearth, the *mandir*, the wife's kitchen, the extended family home, the horse-driven cart, the sociable tea party, the legitimate office, the conjugal bed, the pristine mountains and so on. If the virtuous chronotopes associated with socially sanctioned figures account for all that Helen is not, the same dynamic applies to the disreputable chronotopes of her habitation. When the self's masquerade comes to an end, as it must at the point of denouement, the sanctioned heroine or hero is revealed to be the sum of all the attributes relationally differentiated from the other's chronotopes. The crucial point here is that the various strands comprising Helen's otherness (such as her exotic phenotype, unhampered sensuality, outlandish costumes, unspeakable appetites, objectifying proper nouns, lyrical come-ons and auto-erotic tactility) are image-signs of sundry scandalous chronotopes that are negatively and relationally constituted by any number of virtuous chronotopes identified with image-signs sanctioned by the national imaginary.

Helen in cameo

This dynamic shows itself from the very outset and is reiterated and reinforced over the course of the next twenty years. In *Howrah Bridge* (Shakti Samanta, 1958), for instance, Helen introduces herself as Chin Chin Chu in a song-and-dance number staged inside a hotel owned by a homicidal villain who also happens to be ethnically Chinese. The displaced political anxieties concerning India's tensions with China aside (which, incidentally, led to a brief border war in 1962), the hotel-as-chronotope is relationally distinct from the chronotope associated with the masquerading hero, Prem (Ashok Kumar), who checks into the establishment under a *nom de guerre*. Prem's motives are pure: he is in pursuit of his brother's killers. He bears along with him the absent chronotope of the family home, suggestive of fraternal affection, honour and the rule of law. In contrast, Helen is invoked as an image-sign to underscore the scandalous character of the hotel. She is other in name, in fashion (she sports a silken gown and an exotic fan), in mien (her face is heavily powdered and her eyes are artfully slanted) and in the lyrical impropriety of the song she sings. She makes it plain that she is on the prowl for clients: 'My name is Chin Chin Chu / A moonlit night, me and you / Hello, mister, how do you do?' Halfway through the number Chin Chin Chu turns to Prem: 'Hey mister, you and I / It's good that we have met / Seeing you I am all aflutter, / I am Alladin's girl / Cast my spell, chu, chu, / and you're to Sinbad turned.' Suddenly, as if under the spell of the song, Chin Chin Chu is sartorially metamorphosed. Courted by sailors in starched navy whites, she whirls about in a skirt and blouse, flitting insouciantly from one suitor to the next. This scene frames an axiom that is played out in countless scenes featuring Helen: to wit, the scandal of the other is precisely the sorcery of mutability that allows it to multiply, to spawn multiple others, without expropriating values coextensive with chronotopes of the self.

Chin Chin Chu's part is exhausted after the 'item number' in *Howrah Bridge*. Given that her reputation was built on her prowess and versatility as a dancer (a poisoned chalice at best from the perspective of the national imaginary), Helen's cameo roles became something of an obligatory article in the genre of the dancehall flick. In the period spanning the early 1960s and the late 1970s she reigned as the queen of the item number, affording viewers extravagant, if gratuitously inserted, relief from the tedium of the plot.

Whenever her otherness did not serve an edifying purpose culminating in the delayed disavowal of the other by masquerading protagonists, she was called upon to inaugurate one or another chronotope with scant reference to the plot. Her sudden appearances in clubs, dens, parties and village fetes certainly engendered chronotopes of otherness; if, however, the role failed to drive the dynamic of delayed disavowal, she would vanish abruptly and inexplicably. In *Singapore* (Shakti Samanta, 1960), for example, as she bursts into the folksy 'Rasa Sayang' with her Malay compatriots, a disguised Shyam (Shammi Kapoor) joins them so as to shake off his pursuers. The hero's mimicry is purely expedient and ends with the song. When he exits this scene provisionally, Helen, who is not masquerading and who is there to provide local context and colour, exits the screen terminally. In *Anari* (The Simpleton, Hrishikesh Mukherjee, 1959) she plays a beauty queen whose sole function is to illuminate the hero's sexual naivety vis-à-vis her own worldly ways. This achieved over a song, she, too, departs. In *Junglee* (Savage, Subodh Mukerji, 1960) she is the glamorous adversary with whom the heroine competes for her beau's affections. Here the rivalry is presented as innocuous play, but it grows, as we shall see, much darker in films where her characters are driven by love, lust or lucre. In *Ganga Jumna* (Nitin Bose, 1961) she is cast as a *kotha-bai* or courtesan and performs the *mujra* for the legless villain, Hariram. The song accompanying the *mujra* dwells slyly on self-interest and wicked hearts, suggesting that this chronotope, at least, is devoid of sanctioned masqueraders. Hariram has no qualms about purchasing sex and the courtesan, paid handsomely in jewellery, is happy to sell it to him. Both are irredeemable others in the moral economy of the national imaginary.

The rationale behind the cameo changed little in the 1970s. Helen is still found pirouetting and cavorting inside the villain's den. In *Bikhre Moti* (Scattered Pearls, Chanakya, 1971) the den is a factory for stuffing handmade dolls with contraband gems. Before Helen comes into view, fez-clad male dancers hurl knives at the sculpture of a female nude. They proceed to slit the nude down the middle from head to toe until a real woman – what one might call the gem of a contraband woman with medusa locks – lies revealed. Helen is, of course, smuggled into the scene to reinforce the den's notorious chronotope where organized crime, illegal labour, murderous violence, sexual exotica and national betrayal form complementary values. The price for my heart, she sings provocatively, is no more than a superficial glance. It is the price one might be expected to pay for a contraband doll in the bazaar. If she is an alluring artefact indistinguishable from a contraband commodity in *Bikhre Moti,* in the finely crafted thriller, *Inkaar* (The Refusal, R. N. Sippy, 1971), she is a scythe-wielding barmaid, unequivocally of fisher stock, who both arouses and keeps in check a crowd of drunken revelers at a seedy bar. The song commences with the montage of the actress immuring an ant inside a glass. The lyrics imply that the male revelers are no different from the ant. She, on the other hand, is a sweet temptation, and, if they are not drawn to her sugary fluids, she promises to bow out of the scene. She then invites them to give up alcohol for some of her, infinitely stronger, brew. This chronotope is meant to add another layer to the hard-boiled character of the arch-villain (Amjad Khan) who ends up in a brawl because of the attention Helen lavishes on him. Once he has decked the rival and departed, Helen's role becomes instantly redundant. Eventual acts of disavowal, in the cameos cited above, concern villainous others (murderers, smugglers, debauchees and kidnappers) who are integral to the plot. Helen might set up the scandalous chronotope and delight in the stigma, but her evanescence indicates that she is brought in simply to frame the chronotope of sexual indecorum. This chronotope is merely one of several chronotopes forming a signifying chain of otherness invoked from the crypt of the national imaginary in order to be disavowed. Not being the principal other in the dynamic of disavowal, Helen appears fleetingly.

The exceptional Helen

For the rest of the chapter, I want to focus on precisely those films where Helen appears as an integral element in the plot, thereby prolonging the enjoyment of the masquerade of otherness by various protagonists. First, however, it is critical to point out that she is not cast perpetually in the role of the scandalous other to normative values and virtues. Basu points to films such as *Kabli Khan* (K. Amarnath, 1963) and *Aaya Toofan* (Came the Typhoon, Mohammed Hussain, 1964), where she plays the leading lady, but observes that these films comprise 'a subliminal underbelly of Islamic and worldly attractions' and thus strictly fall outside the dynamic of the Hindu national imaginary (2013: 144). Then there are films such as *Hum Hindustani* (We are Indians, Ram Mukherji, 1960), *Woh Kaun Thi* (Who Was She? Raj Khosla, 1964) and *Dil Daulat Duniya* (Heart, Wealth, World; P. N. Arora, 1972) where she is presented agreeably and even grudgingly assimilated into the national imaginary. The trouble is that such instances are so few that they comprise exceptions validating the general rule. Moreover, even when she plays characters not radically divergent from the normative self as enjoined by the national imaginary, she bears telltale traces of otherness. In *Hum Hindustani,* she is cast as Kalpana, born in a well-to-do Hindu family and betrothed to the hero's brother, Satyen. Unlike Suken (Sunil Dutt) who is inflexible on ethical matters, and upholds the ways of god, work and truth, Satyen (Joy Mukherjee) is willing to vacillate on all three fronts to safeguard the family's fortune and its privileged place in the world. Kalpana weds Satyen once he has disavowed values that render him other and returned to the fold of the extended family, but she is never quite the ideal fiancée sponsored by the national imaginary. Apart from being, in one smouldering scene, improperly alone in a bourgeois interior with her half-naked beau, she is unconvinced that he is not a thief even when appealed to directly. The authentic *satitva* would have no such misgivings about her future husband. In the ghost story, *Woh Kaun Thi*, Helen plays Seema, the hero's intended, until she is killed off to make way for Sadhana. Seema lives alone in a modern apartment lined with wallpaper and accessed by an elevator. The interior of this chronotope (plainly a psychocultural giveaway) is tastefully decorated with porcelain horses and dogs, framed scenes and there are flowers arranged in vases. Chinaware is used during the dinner Seema hosts for Anand (Manoj Kumar). At the song-and-dance party for doctors and nurses, Seema swings and twists in a tasseled frock, and, later, appears in a knee-length skirt and blouse for the romantic duet with Anand. She sings that she might die of happiness, not knowing that, despite not putting an ethical foot wrong, she will be terminated in the next scene because of her strange taste in furniture and attire. The absence of family and genealogy does not help matters. In *Dil Daulat Duniya*, Rita (Helen) fails to shed attributes of otherness until the very end when she appears in full Hindu bridal gear and cheerfully weds her second-string beau, Puppu (Jagdish). Up until the moment she disclaims her interest in the hero, Vijay (Rajesh Khanna), to an anxious Rupa (Sadhana), she never fits – or, rather, fits too well given that the house is a mansion – into the household run by the big-hearted squatter, Udharchand Shikarpuri (Om Prakash). Rita is sister to Vijay's friend, Raju, but every scene reveals her to be more 'other' than Hindu. In the mansion's garden, she wears a low-necked blouse and red flared-trousers, in sharp contrast to the sari-clad Rupa and her sister-in-law, Kiran, who sports a *mangal sutra*. Next, we find her lounging in a bathtub, stark naked except for the foam-clouds of a dubious modesty, singing a song about love. From their separate rooms, Vijay and Rupa join in, but the three-way split screen indicates that Rita's state of undress is culturally at odds with their clothed bodies. Vijay is buttoned up to the neck in *kurta pyjama* while Rupa dons a *shalwaar kameez*. Subsequent scenes show Rita to be, if not quite the other, certainly a cultural misfit. She turns up in Vijay's room late at night (and then, too, in boyish shorts with cross-stitched braces), luxuriates by the pool in a swimsuit, fails to read a letter written in Hindi and is derided for her culinary skills whereas Rupa's are praised. There are no prizes for guessing who bags Vijay.

Dying for the hero's arms

Helen truly comes into her own in those films where her character is notoriously other but also sufficiently evolved to become a core element in the plot. In these films, and there are some memorable ones, she is pivotal to the dynamic of the other's delayed disavowal that defines the cinema of the 1960s and the 1970s. In the whodunit, *Gumnaam* (Unnamed, Raja Nawathe, 1965), she plays a private secretary, Kitty Kelly. Kitty is one among several lottery winners set down on a deserted island by an unknown killer who picks them off one by one. It turns out that Kitty is implicated, along with others, in the murder of her employer, Sohanlal. Unbeknownst to his niece, Asha (Nanda), Sohanlal is part of a criminal triumvirate consisting of Sohanlal, Madanlal and Khanna. Betrayed by his villainous partners, Madanlal escapes from prison, kills Khanna, who, in the meantime, has done away with Sohanlal, and, disguised as Madhusudan Sharma, stages the harrowing drama on the island. It is chiefly through Helen's character, revealed in her interactions with sundry others, that we come to grasp the attributes sanctioned by the national imaginary. Kitty's otherness is deliciously overdetermined. She is Anglo-Indian; intersperses her Hindi with phrases from English; connives in the murder of her boss; entertains the inebriated and sleazy Rakesh in her room (and cheekily nicknames him Rake); informs Rake that she has experienced vice as well as virtue; wears a skimpy skirt that distracts the butler (Mehmood) and induces a lustful daydream; bids Dharamdas to 'try his luck'; delights in the skirmish she provokes between Rake and Dr Achari; resorts to sexual innuendo while lauding Sharma's muscularity; succumbs to Rake's entreaty and so contradicts her earlier view that she likes drunks but not drinks; bursts into a superficial carpe diem song (with a distinctly Celtic beat) while others are being brutally cut down; and, lastly, throws a glass of whisky down Asha's throat when she runs to her for comfort (Figure 11.1). This last violation of the sanctity of the heroine, along with her own sexually fallen state, immediately seals her fate. She is found hanging from a tree in her skimpy lavender swimsuit. The chronotopes most prominently associated with Kitty are the bedroom, the daydream and the beach – all sites of an intolerable *jouissance*. Kitty's overdetermined otherness impacts on the way the dynamic of delayed disavowal works in relation to Asha. Prior to the drinking scene with Kitty, which leads to a song, Asha has run away from Anand (Manoj Kumar). She imagines that he has behaved menacingly while he is irked by her inability to trust him implicitly. 'Do not,' remonstrates Anand,

Figure 11.1 *Gumnaam* (Raja Nawathe, 1965).

'ask why or wherefore, but keep faith in me and all shall be revealed.' Anand is, of course, importuning Asha to adopt *satitva* values as sanctioned by the national imaginary. Consequently, Asha's recourse to the whisky supplied by the irredeemable other flouts *dharma* itself. Normally, this would be tantamount to an unforgiveable contravention, but the hero comes by in the nick of time to enforce the injunction. He slaps her around a few times and reminds her that she is not Kitty. This reminder, which comes late in film, returns us to the first song-and-dance number where a masked Asha – not Kitty – rocks and rolls to Rafi's 'Jaan Pahachan Ho' (Know the other). In short, Asha's masquerade of the other is fraught with risks. It requires the intervention of the sanctioned patriarch who is charged with restoring the heroine to her rightful place in the national imaginary. For this to occur, Asha has to disavow the values represented by the doomed Kitty. Anand's masquerade as the potential serial killer contains no such ethical risk: he turns out to be an undercover cop in pursuit of the real villain. Once the dynamic of disavowal runs its course, the protagonists are restored, alive, to the national imaginary.

Helen is on top of her game in the superb thriller, *Teesri Manzil* (The Third Storey, Vijay Anand, 1966), where she plays Ruby, a professional dancer based in Mussoorie who is in love with a drummer named Rocky (Shammi Kapoor). Whatever else she might be, Ruby is not Hindu. The film begins with a woman falling to her death from the third storey of a hotel, followed by Ruby's enigmatic warning to Rocky not to venture out because of his rumoured attachment to the dead person. Ruby is cast as a worldly, scheming and spiteful beauty as well as the ill-fated other woman in the relationship between Sunita (Asha Parekh) and Rocky. Sunita arrives at the hill station to avenge her sister's death (which is due to homicide not suicide), and holds the innocent Rocky responsible for her seduction, so he adopts the *nom de guerre* of Anil Sona. The purpose of his masquerade is to win Sunita's heart and to defer the moment of disclosure as he needs time to demonstrate that he is not the callous libertine, the imaginary other, she takes him to be. Since most of the action takes place inside the hotel's scandalous chronotope, there are multiple others as well as multiple forms of masquerade, all intimately bound up with the dynamic of delayed disavowal. Rocky is, of course, a degenerate other in the eyes of Sunita. Even as Anil he stands accused of base motives when they are stranded in the wilderness overnight. At every turn he has to rebut the attributes and appetites associated with this fantasized other. Rocky's constancy, and his espousal of the real virtues of sincerity, restraint and honour, shows through in the way he conducts himself with Ruby. In the magnificent duet, 'Oh haseena zulfo wali' (Hey, you with the lovely hair), Rocky grasps the theatricality of his onstage character whereas Ruby views it as coextensive with her real feelings for him. This is not uncommon with Helen's characters. Suzie in *China Town* (Shakti Samanta, 1962), Jameela in *Night in London* (Brij, 1967) and Lovelina in *Agent Vinod* (Deepak Bahry, 1977) remain qualitatively the same, whether they are on- or offstage. When enacting a song-and-dance number as part of the cinematic inset, Helen's onstage character tends to intersect with the character she plays in the diegesis. Her otherness, since it is intrinsic to her and therefore not strictly staged, spills over into the diegetic world. She is the scandal that makes public what should forever remain private, namely, unshackled libidinous drives. Within her reside monstrous appetites capable of causing havoc to the injunctions of the superego that make civilization, marriage, family and *dharma* possible. This is precisely the point made in *Sampoorna Ramayana* (Babubhai Mistry, 1961) where she plays the oversexed Surpanakha, transformed from a fair-skinned angel into a black monstrosity when rebuffed, first by Rama and then Laxmana. Consequently, she is different from those protagonists who grasp the distinction between the law of the masquerade, which underpins scenes in hotels and nightclubs, and the law of the national imaginary, which demands that the masquerade be brought to an end to reveal the 'essential' self. This distinction shows up in *Teesri Manzil* when the normally restrained Sunita masquerades as the other in the rock and roll club. The duet she sings with Anil, with its quavering orgasmic refrain of 'aaahahaja, aahahaaja' (come, come), is far more shocking than anything Ruby could have dreamed up, but we know that Sunita is putting it on for Anil in order to get to Rocky. Her impersonation of the other (she dons Western clothes, lets down her hair and sings lewd rock and roll) is both provisional and a ruse. We withhold our judgement because she has disavowed the other implicitly and will do so explicitly. Ruby, on the other hand, cannot make that distinction, and, at one point, refuses to perform without Rocky. Rocky's co-presence is the primary clause in her contract with the establishment. Not only does she blur the line between life and stage, appearance and essence, she also insinuates that she might have done away with the competition and means to do so again, thus smudging the line between death and desire. Moreover, it is because of her machinations that Anil's revelation of his real identity leads to his public denouncement by Sunita. Ruby's love, then, is demonstrably narcissistic, manipulative and self-interested. She poses a direct threat to the normative couple sanctioned by the national imaginary and so must die at the hands of the villain. For the other, as Ruby states so poignantly in her death throes, the price for being in the arms of the hero is death. It is the ultimate form of disavowal reserved for her by the national imaginary.

In *Pagla Kahin Ka* (Madman from Somewhere, Shakti Samanta, 1970), Jenny pays an even heavier price for her failure to adhere to the standards of the *satitva*. She is raped by the villain, marries him and plunges to her death when he shoves her off a cliff. The cinematic chronotopes are so sharply demarcated that we are left in no doubt that she is due to meet a sticky end. The opening scene places her in a nightclub as a cabaret dancer; she is shown romancing the hero, Sujit (Shammi Kapoor), on the beach in the early hours of the morning; she lives in an apartment with a chain-smoking Goan aunt and is deprived of genealogy; she disavows the hero when she lies in the courtroom (albeit at his behest); she admits Shyam (Prem Chopra) into her bedroom and is raped for this impropriety; and her wedding festivities take place inside the chronotope of a nightclub. Whereas Jenny inhabits one scandalous chronotope after another, the *satitva,* Shalini (Asha Parekh), who plays a caring psychiatrist, dwells largely in the virtuous chronotope of a hospital. She also appears in the bucolic chronotope idealized by Sujit and critical to the restoration of his sanity. Thus, in this film, a classist as well as a xenophobic logic underpins the choice of chronotopes. More crucially, however, normative selves and values are defined negatively insofar as they emerge as a consequence of the others' failure to measure up. Shyam's rape of and marriage to Jenny brings into relief Sujit's unwavering friendship, loyalty, restraint, code of honour and self-sacrifice – attributes sanctioned by the national imaginary. This is made plain in the wedding scene where he inserts himself between Jenny and Shyam, declaring caustically that one is a paragon of love and fidelity while the other is an example of great and enduring friendship. Likewise, Shalini's selfless care, which cures Sujit's insanity, takes on normative value in relation to its root cause in his betrayal by his friend and fiancée. Shalini's duty of care comprises the changeless love of the *satitva* and transcends love's masquerade captured during the song-and-dance numbers. Consequently, she is a central figure in the dynamic of the other's disavowal. When Jenny tells Shalini she was socially obliged to marry her rapist (for the sake of her *izzat*), she replies that Sujit would have forgiven *her* for the rape but not for the marriage. When pressed what Shalini's response would have been to the assault, the *satitva* replies that she would have committed suicide and/or killed Shyam. Curiously, Shalini's delineation of the traits of the *satitva* is prefigured by Jenny in her initial reaction to Sujit's overtures. She protests that a common dancer is not worthy of him, conveniently forgetting – for such is the power of hetero-patriarchy – that he is an orphan as well as a singer in the same nightclub. By espousing the virtues of the national imaginary, Sujit leaves behind the chronotope of the nightclub, gives an exemplary account of the self and is rewarded by being incorporated into the dominant ethos and class. He goes off with the sari-clad and salaried psychiatrist.

Jenny is resurrected in *Immaan Dharam* (Faith and Law, Desh Mukherjee, 1977). Reminiscent of Monica from *Caravan* (Nasir Hussain, 1971), we find her plonked at the bar, sloshed. It is midnight and the tavern has closed for business. Even so, she demands another peg of whisky and reacts with insolence and violence when refused. The intriguing aspect to this scene is that the preceding scene prepares us for it through an analogy that has the suggestive force of a montage. There is a party of villains at another bar where, drinks in hand, they are discussing the profits they make from adulterated goods (cement, grain, clothing and medicine), and the image of decency they need to project to society by undertaking charitable works. When the scene cuts from this scandalous chronotope to the next one, it has the effect of augmenting our sense of Jenny's notoriety. She is not spatially coextensive with the villains in that she is in a different bar, but she might as well be given the proximity of the two scenes, the similarity of the chronotopes and the values associated with the actress. Jenny's drunken shenanigans land her in court where she employs the services of the serial perjurer, Ahmed (Amitabh Bachchan), to evade justice. Drunk and violent in one scene, she cheats justice in the next and is party to a lie in the third when she hires Ahmed to pose as her daughter's prodigal father. Jenny exudes otherness: she is Catholic, a barfly, a perjurer and an unmarried single mother who appears not to know the identity of Pinky's father. This is equivalent to being a prostitute in the discourse of the national imaginary. Her saving grace is she wants a different life for Pinky, presumably a life free from chronotopes of notoriety, and so puts her in an educational hostel for Catholics. In the end, Pinky is incorporated into a sanctioned family, but Jenny – encumbered by the ghosts of Monica, Carmen, Lily, Ruby, Kamini, Kitty and Rita – cannot cheat her celluloid fate. The injunction against her redemption, which commences around 1957, has by 1977 become an inviolable law. Consequently, when Ahmed gives up his dishonest ways (which is always a form of masquerade with heroes, since concealed virtues eventually win out) and turns towards the path of faith and rectitude, he cannot put an end to the fatal dynamic of the other's disavowal. He makes a selfless attempt to do so by informally marrying Jenny, and so becoming Pinky's father, but this gesture is designed to save the child from the mother's destiny. The moment Ahmed wins the sanction of the national imaginary (which is always surreptitiously Hindu in its stress on the interchangeability of faiths), Jenny is doomed to breathe her last in his arms. She is the adulterated would-be wife instructively injected with a lethal dose of adulterated medication. It remains for Ahmed, now a sanctioned hero, to present a moving account of what the national imaginary has done to the other. In the mesmerizing 'post-mortem' scene, he informs the physician that Jenny's life was a struggle against the world (self) and herself (as other), and that death was its outcome. Then, in a marvelously ironic inversion, he points out that her soul was destroyed in the struggle and that her body should be spared the indignity of a post-mortem. When the physician explains that her death was unnatural and they have to cut her open to ascertain the cause, Ahmed counters with the grim retort that they would never find the real venom of scandal and loneliness that caused her death. Thus, in one unforgettable scene featuring Hindi cinema's greatest actor, the national imaginary is indicted for its remorseless pursuit and persecution of the other.

Even in the early 1970s, Helen was starting to be displaced as the exemplary figure of otherness. In *Caravan*, for instance, where she plays the villainous Monica, it is Aruna Irani who, as the shameless gypsy dancer, Nisha, poses the real threat to the sanctioned hero and his beloved. It is Nisha who is destined to take the proverbial bullet in the end while Monica, bound hand and foot, is left to mull over her dilemma in a bedroom. In *Hare Rama Hare Krishna* (Dev Anand, 1971), it is Zeenat Aman who plays the role of the drug-taking, sexually permissive Janice, destined to die in the end for violating the codes of the national imaginary. Increasingly, as Basu has argued, blue-blooded heroines, such as Zeenat Aman and Praveen Babi, start to incorporate into their characters elements of otherness associated with Helen, and so representations of femininity, especially from the 1980s onwards, begin to assume more ambivalent and composite forms. Basu points out that in the post-emergency years 'the profane "being public" of the woman becomes an imperative for middle class education, professional uplift, and

Figure 11.2 *Don* (Chandra Barot, 1978).

economic sustenance' (2013: 153). The injunctions of the national imaginary are no longer enforced because plots, in the aftermath of the collapse of the Licence Raj in the 1990s, become far less didactic and the protagonists far more ambiguous. The otherness associated with ephemeral cameos and item numbers is also disrupted. The figure-perfect heroines of the twenty-first century no longer shy away from cameos, since the notoriety of the item number has become an essential element in on-screen and off-screen marketability. In the recent reinterpretation of *Don* (Farhan Akhtar, 2006) it is Kareena Kapoor who plays the ill-fated Kamini and sings 'Ye mera dil pyar ka diwana', whereas the role was handed to Helen in the original version (Figure 11.2). Highly sexualized one-off item numbers are performed by Deepika Padukone in *Dum Maaro Dum* (Take a Shot, Rohan Sippy, 2011), Priyanka Chopra in *Goliyon Ki Raasleela: Ram-Leela* (A Play of Bullets: Ram-Leela, Sanjay Leela Bhansali, 2013), Katrina Kaif in *Agneepath* (The Path of Fire, Karan Malhotra, 2012) and Kareena Kapoor in *Dabangg 2* (Arbaaz Khan, 2012). Ahmed, it seems, was not exactly on the mark about Jenny's demise at the hands of the national imaginary. Far from being dead, she appears to have transformed it and lives on, desirably, dangerously and deliciously, inside the multifaceted cinematic self.

Works Cited

Basu, Anustup (2013), '"The Face that Launched a Thousand Ships": Helen and Public Femininity in Hindi Film', in Mirel Sen and Anustup Basu (eds), *Figurations in Indian Cinema*, 139–57, Basingstoke: Palgrave Macmillan.

Clifford, James (1992), 'Traveling Cultures', in Lawrence Grossberg, Cary Nelson and Paula Treicher (eds), *Cultural Studies*, 96–116, New York: Routledge.

Mishra, Sudesh (2012), 'Yahoo! Shammi Kapoor and the Corporeal Stylistics of Popular Hindi Cinema', *Continuum*, 26 (6): 15–32.

Mishra, Vijay (2002), *Bollywood Cinema: Temples of Desire*, New York: Routledge.

Pinto, Jerry (2006), *Helen: The Life and Times of a Bollywood H-Bomb*, New Delhi: Penguin.

de Saussure, Ferdinand (2004), 'Course in General Linguistics', in Julie Rivkin and Michael Ryan (eds), *Literary Theory: An Anthology*, 2nd edn, 59–71, Oxford: Blackwell.

Chapter 12

'She's everything that's unpardonable': Hema Malini, dream girl on a motorbike

Rosie Thomas

Hema Malini was launched as India's Dream Girl – and Raj Kapoor's co-star – in *Sapnon ka Saudager* (Seller of Dreams, Mahesh Kaul) in 1968. She has been selling dreams to Indian audiences ever since. In a career spanning almost five decades – and despite a highly controversial off-screen life – Malini has retained her Dream Girl crown, successfully reinventing herself in every era. Her most recent incarnation is @dreamgirlhema where, as Bharatiya Janata Party (BJP) MP for Mathura since 2014, she tweets her views on India today.

Malini was the undisputed queen of Bombay cinema in the 1970s and early 1980s. She co-starred with all the leading male actors of the day and commanded the highest fees of any female star.[1] In an era of relentlessly male-centred films, she often held top billing following the spectacular success of her dual role as *seedhi-saadhi* (innocent) Seeta and rebellious Geeta in Ramesh Sippy's *Seeta aur Geeta* (1972). Throughout the 1970s Malini's roles ranged from docile beauties to feisty firebrands; they also spanned comedy, melodrama and action, invariably showcasing her skills as a trained *Bharatanatyam* dancer.[2] When the romantic roles dried up after motherhood, Malini retained a popular career as an action heroine in the 'avenging woman' films of the 1980s and as both freedom-fighting warrior women and avatars of the goddess Amboo in television dramas of the 1990s. 'Can you think of a face other than Hema*ji*'s that would radiate *bhakti* and *shakti* simultaneously?' asked Punit Issar, director of her TV serial *Jai Mata Ki* (Hail, Holy Mother, 1999) (Mukherjee 2005: 196). *Bhakti* and *Shakti* – religious devotion and female power – lie at the heart of the Hema Malini conundrum.

The most intriguing feature of Malini's extraordinary longevity as a star and celebrity – she has outlasted all her female counterparts of the 1970s – is the enigma of the star persona that has developed over the years. Whilst considered the epitome of 'traditional Indian values' and chaperoned on film sets well into her thirties, she was scandalously involved in a number of romances with male co-stars in the 1970s, culminating in her secret – and illegal – 'marriage' to the

---

[1] In 1981 her earnings were estimated at between 15,000 and 20,000 rupees (then £1,000–£2,000) per day. Amitabh Bachchan was said to earn twice this. (Thomas 2013: 220).
[2] Bharatanatyam refers to a form of classical Indian dance that was promoted within the twentieth-century nationalist movements as an exemplarily 'respectable' tradition, deliberately purged of association with its origins in *devadasi* temple dancing – and hence prostitution.

already-married Dharmendra in 1980 and her two 'love children' with him in the early 1980s.³

This chapter suggests that the key to her successful persona was precisely its ability to encompass apparently contradictory ideals that resonated with key social concerns of the era: she appeared the perfect female star for post-Nehruvian India of the 1970s and early 1980s. Focussing on the moment in the early 1980s when this persona – and her stardom – were under greatest scrutiny and strain, this chapter explores how these apparently contradictory facets were negotiated, both within the gossip press of the day and across four big films of the era: *Naseeb* (Destiny, Manmohan Desai, 1981), *Kranti* (Revolution, Manoj Kumar, 1981), *Jyoti* (Light, Pramod Chakravarty, 1981) and *Razia Sultan* (Kamal Amrohi, 1983). I argue that Malini was a far more significant factor in the gradual acceptance of strong, independent women characters within Bombay cinema's ideal moral universe than has been acknowledged to date. I conclude by asking how and why she was able to convert this controversial star persona into political capital for the BJP in 2014.

Fieldwork

When I was carrying out my first fieldwork in Bombay in the early 1980s, Malini's luridly painted features stared down from enormous film poster hoardings throughout India's cities. Her face also adorned – and sold – everything from 'Dream Girl' fireworks, beauty creams, textiles and weighing machine cards to calendar art, gossip magazines and fan postcards. Two images of Malini particularly fascinated me. The first was a postcard that appeared ubiquitously amongst hawkers' wares on the footpaths of Bombay (Figure 12.1).

Figure 12.1 Postcard of Hema Malini bought on Bombay streets in 1980.

A beatific Malini, in sleeveless yellow dress, leans on a quasi-classical Indian sculpture of a headless female torso. While Malini's own breasts are discreetly hidden, the sculpture's naked breast is centre-bottom frame. Malini simultaneously smiles alluringly and hides unattainably behind the lump of stone that bars all advances. The image neatly condenses a key paradox. On one hand, Dream Girl Hema Malini, the paragon of Indian beauty and propriety, appears disarmingly unattainable and modestly covered; she wears bangles (traditional symbol of a Hindu wife and thus controlled sexuality) and, through a 'traditional,'

---

³Two biographies of Malini are available for readers wanting a more detailed account of her life-story: Mukherjee 2005 and Somaaya 2007. See also Mukherjee 2011.

Khajuraho-style sculpture of a Hindu goddess, is metonymically associated with Hindu India's artistic and cultural heritage. On the other hand, she and her sexuality are overtly on display for her viewers: she is posing for the camera (or artist) and returning its gaze; she wears westernized dress that bares her shoulders and upper arms (taboo according to 'traditional' mores); she wears a 'modern' watch; and she leans on a bare-breasted torso – objectified female body – that hazily summons up the erotic world of the Indian temple dancer.

The image brilliantly sums up her contradictory appeal through a familiar mechanism of display and denial: it offers us the queen of desirable femininity within Indian patriarchal fantasy whilst simultaneously denying that Hema offers herself thus.[4] Malini's sexuality is controlled – and fixed in stone – by the men who construct her image, and the Dream Girl remains both the perfectly asexual Indian woman and the one that infects men's wildest dreams.

The second image that caught my attention began to appear in the gossip press at least two years before the release of Manmohan Desai's *Naseeb* in May 1981. This apparently mildly shocking still from the film showed Malini, in crash helmet and jeans, proudly astride a motorbike. The gossip magazines repeated this image frequently, suggesting a special frisson, and the film industry seemed animated by it. Filmmakers repeatedly told me that Hema had 'class', and all were agreed on her *bharatiya nari* or 'traditional Indian woman' appeal. Such phrases also recurred in the gossip press. In 1980 a letter writer to *Star and Style* asserted that Hema stood as a representative of 'perfect Indian womanhood (no stripping)'.[5]

The surprise at seeing images of Malini on a motorbike had to be understood in the context of what was effectively a taboo at that time on women driving any two-wheeled motor vehicle. Not that the image itself was unfamiliar: paintings of women sitting or standing, proudly or coyly, beside scooters or lambrettas had been a mainstay of the popular calendar art for many years. Nevertheless, I was repeatedly told that Indian women could not ride scooters and keep their 'respect': to ride a motorized two-wheeler would brand a woman as 'fast' and, even in Indian cities, few would risk their reputations in that way.[6] Yet here was India's Dream Girl, unashamedly riding high astride two wheels.

In an earlier essay I outlined the 'ideal moral universe' of the Bombay cinema of that era as a central dynamic that defined paradigms of 'good' and 'bad' (or expected and unacceptable) forms of behaviour and required that the forces of good triumph over evil (Thomas 1995). In practice, 'good' was subtly conflated with the 'traditional', or that which is 'Indian', 'bad' with the 'non-traditional' and the 'non-Indian'. The narrative function of most heroes/heroines was not to embody good but to mediate between these two poles. Through such mediation certain elements of the non-traditional would become gradually legitimated and incorporated within the acceptable category of the 'modern' – that is, connotations of, for example, love marriage or women driving motorbikes could be shifted over time through careful

---

[4]Malini was the most exaggerated example of this disavowal mechanism ('I know but nevertheless'), although it was largely true of all heroines of that era. See Kasbekar 2001.
[5]Vijayalakshmi Ramamirthan in *Star & Style*, 22 February–6 March 1980, p. 54. Raakhee is also included in this accolade.
[6]The only exception was the city of Pune, where college girls and others could, apparently without censure, ride various kinds of light bike and scooter. Allegedly, the tradition of Maratha horse-riding women, who devised a unique way of wearing the sari, tied – as trousers – between the legs, was at the root of this anomaly.

negotiation of the contexts within which they appeared. Thus films – together with texts such as film star gossip – were an important locus for the ongoing negotiation and transformation of an 'Indian' identity, within which sexuality and modernity were two key discourses and men's control over women's sexuality, through the ideologies of chastity and *izzat*, was a recurrent motif.⁷

Whilst the Amitabh Bachchan persona was in the vanguard of negotiating a new model of masculinity in 1970s Bombay cinema, the Malini persona was at first sight not so obviously innovatory. Stars such as Rekha, Zeenat Aman and Parveen Babi did far more to disrupt conventions of female stardom in the 1970s, both on and off screen, making an explicit sexuality increasingly acceptable through their figure-hugging and revealing dresses, sexy dances, westernized lifestyles, independence from family and less zealously asserted 'chastity'. However, those stars were only ambivalently accepted as models of modern Indian womanhood: their negotiated distinction from the 'vamp' was always precarious. Filmmakers repeatedly told me that the reason none of them ever succeeded in usurping Malini's 'Number One' position, despite great fan popularity and successful films, was that they were 'too westernized'. Malini uniquely retained the public persona of 'traditional Indian womanhood' – and the respect and adulation of the Indian audience – while gradually encompassing almost all the 'non-traditional' behaviours and transgressive representations of her rivals. How did the good Tamil Brahmin girl from Madras manage this?

Dream Girl

Malini was catapulted into the film industry in 1965 by her mother, the formidable Jaya Chakravarty, who had instilled the work ethic from an early age. While other children played, young Hema was forced to practise her dancing and make the rounds of child talent competitions and patriotic dance performances (Mukherjee 2005: 17–27; Somaaya 2007: 4–11). *Amma* (mother) watched her prodigy like a hawk: although she naively bound Hema to a ten-year contract with her first producer B. Ananthaswami, she did secure her unprecedented launch publicity.⁸ Malini's face graced the front cover of *Indian Express* on New Year's Day 1966, and the marketing campaign for her first release *Sapnon ka Saudagar* as Raj Kapoor's Dream Girl saw a massive poster campaign across Indian cities, including life-sized cardboard cut-outs of Malini on walls and lampposts, promising India's citizens that 'The Dream Girl is Coming' (Mukherjee 2005: 40). Advertisements ran:⁹

> Beware, the dream girl is on the prowl, a gypsy come to steal your heart ... A gifted dancer takes you on a flight of fancy ... Dream Girl Hema Malini has a look that pierces through the heart ... A graceful dancer, Hema Malini contributes some sizzling dances for this dream movie.

Despite the hyperbole, the movie flopped. However, it established Malini as a rising star and adumbrated some of the later themes of her star persona: the alluringly innocent gypsy girl and the 'gifted' – and 'sizzling' – dancer. A number of roles

---

⁷*Izzat* and *laaj* both refer to controlled female sexuality. The connotations of *izzat* are broader, conveying a general sense of prestige, honour, respect, while *laaj* refers more specifically to female chastity/virginity. Both embody the idea that female 'honour' reflects on the honour of the whole kin/affine network. See Thomas 2013: 244–71; see also 174.
⁸During the first six years of this contract he paid her a pittance (3,000 rupees a month, plus 100 rupees per shooting day) whilst he charged other producers 300,000–400,000 rupees per film for her services. Only a court case released her from this, apparently on humane grounds (Somaaya 2007: 34–6; Mukherjee 2005).
⁹Author's fieldnotes, 1981.

opposite top male stars followed and she had at least one, and often two or more, superhits every year throughout the 1970s, starting with the 1970 blockbuster thriller *Johny Mera Naam* (Johny Is My Name, Vijay Anand) in which she starred with Dev Anand as a lively, trouser-suited, 'modern' girl who helps a benignly roguish playboy break an international smuggling ring.

Seeta aur Geeta (1972) clinched her super-stardom, earning her *Filmfare*'s Best Actress award and a reputation for comedy. The film negotiated the contours of an acceptably 'modern' Indian womanhood through using the doubling device, a long-standing motif of Indian cinema in which facets of femininity (or masculinity) are split between two (or more) characters played by the same star (see Majumdar 2009: 136–42). In this exuberant comedy, Hema played identical twin sisters split at birth and brought up in different households. Seeta is a paragon of docile purity, a pious, sari-clad, Cinderella figure and long-suffering slave of a wicked, overtly westernized and money-grabbing stepmother. Geeta is a boisterous gypsy-girl, who earns her own living as a roadside acrobat and dancer. The film is a comedy of mistaken identities in which each twin, by chance, ends up in the other's household and chooses to play along with the mistake, to the perplexed horror of the household members and of the girls' respective fiancés.

Whilst Seeta grossly epitomizes the *sati-savitri* (devoted wife) stereotype of 'ideal Indian womanhood' – her name refers to Rama's wife, the ideally self-sacrificing model woman of Indian mythology – Geeta encompasses a number of apparently transgressive images. She refuses the subservience to her stepmother that Seeta had accepted; she does not know how to wear a sari; she appears at a wedding in a slit skirt and (apparently) drunk; she roller-skates; she brandishes a whip; she taunts the police and she dances in public. However, while she challenges – and subverts – the Seeta model of ideal femininity, Geeta remains firmly within the traditional domain. She shows horrified disgust at a bikini-clad 'vamp' at a Bombay hotel swimming pool and she attacks the wicked stepmother and her vain, grotesquely coiffured and painted daughter. Geeta's status as a gypsy-girl outsider – outside the realm of strict Hindu (or Muslim) society – to some extent legitimates her earthy sensuality, drawing on romanticized notions of rural innocence as close to nature. The film's negotiation of morality around the Geeta character is, at points, precarious – wherein lies much of the film's pleasure and humour – but is ultimately firmly resolved by both twins being reincorporated within the social order through marriage.

The device of the gypsy persona recurred a number of times in Malini's career, from *Raja Jani* (Mohan Segal, 1972), in which the gypsy street-singer turns out to have been an orphaned princess, to one of her most famous and iconic roles as the tough, high-spirited, golden-hearted Basanti in Ramesh Sippy's *Sholay* (Flames, 1975).[10] Basanti, like Geeta, is a rural outsider, who earns her living driving a tonga (horse and cart), who chatters amusingly, who is naively simple but takes no nonsense from the heroes and who proves her loyalty to her true love, played by Dharmendra, by dancing on broken glass to appease the sadistic villain who has threatened her life.[11] Basanti is sensual and independent but, being an unsophisticated rural belle, can be read as chaste and

---

[10]On the election trail, even today, crowds are said to chant 'Basanti zindabad' (Long Live Basanti) when she appears.
[11]This is a reference to an iconic scene in *Pakeezah*. In turn, the scene in *Naseeb* in which Asha drives John home on the back of her motorbike and grimaces at his nervous chattering, is an amusing reference to, and direct reversal of, one in *Sholay*.

therefore fundamentally within the domain of the 'traditional' moral order.

Although Malini played a spectrum of roles in the first decade of her reign, including a stream of glamorous semi-westernized roles, invariably love stories, usually with co-star Dharmendra, sometimes with Jeetendra – and at least once with both – her star image was fairly well defined.[12] She was known for her 'glamour girl image' but simultaneously for her propriety, despite the fact that she had throughout the decade been wearing increasingly revealing dresses. A *Star and Style* competition in 1980 asked its readers, 'For a good woman-oriented film whom would you choose, Hema or Raakhee?' The winning letter read:

> So, if the subject is about a calm-looking innocent girl, or a chatter-box with an accent on comedy, or a classical dancer, Hema is a better choice. But if the subject needs a mature woman (even slightly vampish) or the script has scope for melodrama, Raakhee will fit in perfectly. Mod outfits are better on Hema than on Raakhee.[13]

But alongside these images, another theme was emerging. Throughout the 1970s and early 1980s, Malini's screen persona became increasingly associated with images of female strength and power, a theme that would accelerate in the 1980s with the rash of 'avenging woman' films across Indian cinema and television as a whole (see Gopalan 2000).

Transition

By 1980, Malini's screen persona was noticeably in transition. Four films on the sets in 1980–1981 suggest two key mechanisms by which apparently bold transgressions of the moral code were being negotiated: the use of the *viraangana* (warrior woman) prototype to legitimize the figure of the strong fighting woman, and increasing use of fragmentation to frame and contain the excesses of aberrant femininity.

In Kamal Amrohi's *Razia Sultan*, Hema plays an historical warrior queen, the eponymous thirteenth-century Sultan of Delhi, whose controversial romance with an Abyssinian slave led to her downfall. The *viraangana* had been a key trope of Indian silent cinema and the Parsi stage, as well as a favourite image of the nationalist movement, and this had underpinned the Fearless Nadia phenomenon of the 1930s and 1940s (see Thomas 2007: 294–308, esp. 300–1; Thomas 2005: 35–69). In what Kathryn Hansen describes as 'this startling counterparadigm of Indian womanhood', warrior queens were not constrained by *sati-savitri* morality but could choose their own lovers, dress as men, display physical strength and command and fight alongside men – all in the cause of championing good against evil and protecting their country (Hansen 1992: 188–98). *Razia Sultan* revels in scenes of Malini on horseback, in male-warrior attire, fighting with sword and dagger and asserting her right to choose her own lover, played by Dharmendra. Although not released until 1983, stills from the film and anticipatory discussion filled the movie press in 1979 to 1981, especially as the storyline was deliciously inflected by Malini's real life 'scandalous' romance with Dharmendra.

In *Kranti*, a 1981 superhit set in India's mid-nineteenth-century Freedom Struggle, Malini was again shown fighting for her country. In a complicated plot, she plays a spoiled princess who

---

[12] *Samraat* (Storm, Mohan Segal, 1982), a story based on a love triangle that had startling echoes of a 'real life' triangle between the stars concerned. See Mukherjee 2011.
[13] Vijayalakshmi Ramamirthan in *Star & Style*, 22 February–6 March 1980, p. 54.

gives up her comforts, joins a group of freedom-fighters, marries Bharat (Manoj Kumar), a brave, patriotic peasant farmer, and fights for freedom. Although in no sense a true *viraangana* – for most of the film she plays a devoted if plucky wife and village belle danseuse – the first and last scenes of the film (between which the film unfolds as flashback) include the memorable image of Malini as mother and avenging widow on horseback proudly brandishing her rifle. *Kranti*'s immense popular success helped to establish the fighting woman motif as an additional element of Malini's star persona, as well as linking her to the populist patriotism of Hindutva ideology, which would become an increasingly important element of her persona as her political career developed.

The fighting image also inflected Malini's roles in the 'family socials' of the day. In spring 1981, Bombay streets were flooded with posters for *Jyoti*, a melodramatic family drama about a *bahu's* (daughter-in-law's) problems with her wicked brother-in-law and avaricious stepmother-in-law. The posters showed Malini in a demure white sari, brandishing a whip, as she champions the underdog and, Fearless Nadia-style, returns order to the moral universe by turning the whip on her villainous brother-in-law. Malini later acknowledged: 'For the first time I was playing a fiery housewife and I enjoyed beating up the villain with a whip. So did the audience' (Somaaya 2007: 106). For Malini, it would be only a short transition from these films to her successful stream of avenging women films and television serials of the 1980s, from the gun-toting khaki-clad cop of *Andha Kanoon* (Blind Law, T. Rama Rao, 1983) to *Aandhi Toofan* (Hurricane, B. Subhash, 1985), a B-movie hit that consciously remodelled Malini in the Fearless Nadia mould. According to director Babbar Subhash, 'She was brilliant in all the action sequences. From bullet fight to sword fight, she did everything with elan. We worked on her costume and gave her [the] "Fearless Nadia look", prompting the media to dub her "*Hunterwali* Hema"' (Mukherjee 2005: 81, 143).[14]

As discussed above, Malini's early career had been marked by the range of her star persona, either through double roles (e.g. *Seeta aur Geeta*) or through playing malleable Pygmalian figures (e.g. *Hum Tere Aashiq Hain*, I am your lover, Prem Sagar, 1979). In *Dream Girl* (Pramod Chakravorty, 1977), she played five roles – Sapna, Padma, Champabai, Dream Girl and Rajkumari – alter egos through which she stole money to build an orphanage.[15] With multiple roles Malini could, in a single film, be comfortingly homely and also exceptionally glamorous and precariously transgressive. *Naseeb*, Malini's second major superhit of 1981, took the fragmented nature of the ideal Indian woman even further, not through multiple roles but through a multifaceted 'character' whose persona encompassed an unfeasibly broad span of the moral universe, even according to the fantastical, comic-book illogicality of a Manmohan Desai film.

Naseeb was, at the time, the most expensive film ever made in India and the last significant success of the 'multi-starrer' vogue.[16] Malini, one of its three female stars, played Amitabh Bachchan's

---

[14] *Hunterwali* (woman with the whip) was Fearless Nadia's nickname (referring to her first hit film). The 'Hunterwali Hema' trend extended to Malini's own ventures as a television producer in the late 1980s and 1990s, when she made a number of series starring strong, fighting women.
[15] The film's Robin Hood theme harked back to the silent-era hit, *Wildcat of Bombay* (Mohan Bhavnani, 1927), in which India's first female superstar, Sulochana, played eight roles.
[16] Multi-starrers were films that crammed as many top stars into key roles as the producer's budget allowed. By the early 1980s, when it became clear this was not an infallible recipe for box office success, the trend petered out.

love interest, Asha, a glamorous singer.[17] The film's convoluted storyline is remarkable for the variety of images of Asha that erupt in the course of the film. The various facets can be broadly grouped into four clusters:

(i) Traditional Indian woman: this persona wears saris and decorously-sleeved blouses, lives with her mother and younger sister and is patently domesticated: she is seen chopping onions in her kitchen, preparing a meal for her fiancé John (Bachchan)'s first visit to her home. Unambiguously Hindu, this Asha is a dutiful daughter who seeks her mother's approval of her choice of husband, a poor waiter whom she loves because of his *dil* (big-heartedness). She rebuffs all improper male advances (even her beloved's early attempt to kiss her hand) and she condemns drink: 'Mr Vicky, you are a respectable man, and in the hands of a respectable man alcohol does not look good.'[18] She never smokes and, throughout, she disapproves of westernized values, telling her fiancé, who is apparently reneging on a vow to marry his childhood sweetheart: 'This isn't *vilayat* (the West), where they get engaged to one person and marry another.'[19] She later appears as a coy bride, dressed in white (John's foster mother is Christian), and smiles demurely as Vicky (Shatrughan Sinha) hands her as *amaanat* (something given in trust) to his best friend John following the film's *dostana* subplot.[20]

(ii) Independent career woman: this persona is a wealthy and famous singer-cum-model, who roams the streets and waterways of England unchaperoned, is capable and self-sufficient, can fend for herself, engages in witty repartee with men and avoids being fooled by them. She supports her mother and sister financially, defies her mother to support her sister's marriage plans, and chooses her own (non-Hindu) husband.

(iii) Glamorous cabaret singer: this persona wears a low-cut, black-sequin sheath dress and pink boa in one scene, a tight red Spanish flamenco costume in another. In the first, a performance in a five-star hotel, she emerges from a basket of flowers and gyrates seductively with her mic; in the second, she steps out of a giant Campari bottle and performs a sensual Spanish dance routine. She is both actively flirtatious with her male audience and also on display for it: shots of her gliding into camera, posed provocatively atop a piano or draped over a double-bass, suggestively place her as an instrument that can be 'played'.

(iv) Dare-devil super-woman: Asha/Malini wears masculinized (and westernized) clothing – crash helmet, trousers and black motor-bike jacket in one scene, denim jeans, jacket and cap in another – and she rides a powerful motorbike. She snaps her fingers at the hero and gives him a lift home on the back of her bike. She has superhuman strength and fights fearlessly to defend her virtue and, later, as ringleader of the heroines, actively protects the heroes, organizing their high-wire rope escape. However, the first time we see this persona her *izzat* is threatened by villainous men: she is cornered and defending herself with a shard of broken glass in a boat on the Thames in the first instance, caught in a net in a Bombay

---

[17] The key romantic stars were Hema Malini, Reena Roy, Kim, Amitabh Bachchan, Shatrughan Sinha and Rishi Kapoor.
[18] *Mr Vicky, aap ek achche aadmi hain aur ek achche aadmi ke haath main sharaab ki botal achchi nahin lagti.*
[19] *Yeh koi vilayat nahin hai, jahan mangni se kissi ki aur shaadi kissi se*! There is an ironic double-entendre here, which depends for its effect on familiarity with gossip about Malini's personal life and her own broken engagements with Jeetendra and Sanjeev Kumar (and, according to Mukherjee, also Girish Karnad).
[20] In the popular *dostana* theme, two male friends fall in love with the same woman and the one who discovers this sacrifices his love – and often his life – for the male friendship (*dostana*).

underground car-park in the second, and in each case needs a hero to save her.

These facets are not directly contradictory (i.e. she is not condemning drink in one scene and swigging whisky in the next), but they are an uncomfortable combination according to the logic of Bombay cinema's ideal moral universe. Conventional signifiers of 'non-tradition' (and hence immorality) – women riding motorbikes, wearing revealing clothes or defying their mothers – are incorporated within an overall Asha 'character' that is acceptably a heroine and hence fundamentally morally sound. The film negotiates this through three key devices: framing, fragmentation and positioning.

Malini's first appearance within the film is a calculated framing that neatly, if schematically, sets up the parameters of the Asha persona. She is singing for an advertising shoot in London when the NRI director, in bowler-hat and pinstripe suit, asks her to wear a bikini.[21] She sanctimoniously refuses: 'I signed this contract only to promote the good things of my country, not these vulgar things.'[22] Although Asha is alone, independent, the object of spectacle and in *vilayat* (the West), she has been emphatically distanced from westernized Indians: her refusal to wear a bikini (and to date a stranger, Vicky) marks a fundamentally controlled sexuality and places her as patriotic and 'traditional'. The star-struck Vicky reinforces this by referring to Asha as the 'naaz aur laaj' (pride and honour) of India and reprimanding the director as a *vilayati cauve* (foreign crow).[23] 'In leaving India have you left behind your Indian sense of respect? In our country, women look beautiful when they put on clothes, not when they take them off.'[24] Although this introductory scene is self-parodically schematic and not easily reconciled with many later scenes, it will inflect their meanings.

Secondly, the fragmentation of the Asha character allows her sexuality to be both overtly on display and, simultaneously, denied and firmly controlled. As discussed earlier, Malini's star persona embodied this opposition directly through an ongoing process of display and denial, which depended upon a fetishistic disavowal mechanism and upon exploitation of the ambiguities of the variety of 'traditional' models of femininity, such as Hindu goddesses, legends and classical art forms. Fragmentation also featured more broadly in Bombay cinema of that era: aspects of 'womanhood' were often divided between a number of characters in the fiction. Notably, extremes of 'uncontrolled sexuality' were split off into vamp characters. Even in *Naseeb*, Asha's heroism and propriety are reasserted with the appearance, in the underground carpark, of Miss Sweetie, the villain's mini-skirted moll, with whom Asha gets into a fistfight – and wins. Moreover, Asha's different personae relate primarily to the different registers of the film: linear narrative, song and dance, and action.

Despite its fragmentation, the Asha character retains overall coherence, primarily through its positioning in relation to the male heroes and the

---

[21] 'NRI' refers to Non-Resident Indian. In the codes of Hindi cinema, bikinis were a central signifier of (potentially) uncontrolled sexuality and 'non-traditionalism', closely associated with ideas (and fantasy) about Western sexual licence. For an interesting discussion of this scene as fundamentally about the power of the star, see also Majumdar 2009: 176–7.

[22] *Contract zaroor kiya hai, wo bhi sirf issliye ki meri desh ki achhi acchi cheezein yahan mashhoor hon, aisi behuda cheezein nahin.*

[23] See note 7 above.

[24] *Hindustan chor diya toh kya Hindustaniyon ki izzat karna bhi chor di? … apne desh main larkiyan kapre uthar kar nahin, balki pahen kar khubsoorat lagti hain.*

logic of male desire. We see Asha first through the eyes of a fascinated male hero, Vicky, and as object of spectacle for the fictional advertising film camera (and for us). From this scene onwards, various tensions are in play around two oppositions, one concerned with controlling and being controlled, the other with protecting and being protected. Asha is, in her early scenes, repeatedly rescued from villains – twice by Vicky in England, then by John in Bombay. She is next presented as threatening to ruin or control men because of her desirability: John's and Vicky's love for Asha threatens both their friendship and their lives and happiness – they each turn to drink when she is unattainable. All three heroines (and their potentially uncontrolled sexuality) are brought under control by the heroes through a scenario of men exchanging women: the three women and their boyfriends appear in a baroque glass mansion, vulnerable, pretty and ready for marriage, until a villain's machine gun prematurely shatters the idyll. Once the heroes have reconciled with their birth-father (in a quasi-Oedipal scene), the heroines reappear, positioned as their protectors: first in a supremely potent image of all three, led by crash-helmeted Asha, thrusting through a window astride a powerful motorbike; later perched high on a tower-block, with telescope and megaphone, organizing the heroes' rope escape from a burning tower.

Thus, while Asha may ride a motorbike, the image coexists either with her needing male protection or her acting as protector of men – once her sexuality has been safely controlled by the male order. This, of course, reflects a familiar theme in ideas about femininity in Indian society: controlled female sexuality (equated characteristically with the mother figure) is idealized as a fount of traditional values and source of power for men.[25] While the *Naseeb* heroines are overtly non-traditional – astride a motorbike – they are structurally placed in the film in ways that fit a very familiar and traditional model of femininity, thereby setting up a potential ambiguity around the overtly transgressive image of women motorbike-riders that allows it to be redefined as acceptably 'modern' rather than unacceptably immoral.

Gossip star persona

If the paradoxes involved in negotiating an acceptable 'modern' Indian womanhood, whilst retaining elements of the 'traditional', led to uncomfortable resolution in the films, this negotiation was infinitely more precarious in the gossip press – the other major arena in which film stars are constructed. Publications peddling film star gossip had existed in India since the 1930s but in the 1970s, with the arrival of Shobha De[26] as editor of *Stardust*, the focus of the English-language magazines turned to 'scandals' and salacious gossip about stars' indiscretions, narrated in a supercilious tone that was at once prurient and moralistic.[27] The least event became the pretext for melodrama and a barrage of comment, opinion and questions, allowing for obsessional recirculation of familiar material from the world of Bombay film gossip mythology.

Gossip press writing on Malini in the late 1970s and early 1980s detailed with relish her rows with her family, particularly her mother; it avidly followed her notorious affairs, from the dramatic last-minute broken engagement to Jeetendra to her long-standing and tempestuous romance with

---

[25] For discussion of the 'fierce power of chastity', see Thomas 2013: 252.
[26] Née Rajadhyaksha.
[27] For more on gossip magazines see Dwyer 2008.

Dharmendra, a very securely married man; it slyly uncovered and triumphantly revealed her secret bigamous 'marriage' with Dharmendra; and it had a field day when it could announce the arrival of her 'love child'. However, this press also repeatedly referred to this god-fearing, pure vegetarian, Iyengar Brahmin as an 'ideal Indian woman', a 'traditional woman' and, of course, the 'dream girl', and the thrust of much of the writing about her was concerned with this paradox, invariably constructed around 'controversies'.

'She's Everything That's Unpardonable' ran the title caption of a 1979 *Cine Blitz* article investigating, as usual, the mystery of the 'real' Hema Malini and illustrating this with one of the controversial *Naseeb* motorbike skills discussed above.[28] The article ran the gamut of accusations by Malini's 'detractors' and defence from her admirers. The (female) journalist ended by restating the paradox:

> A confirmed roue in the industry told me, 'When I look at all the other women in the industry – the Zeenats, the Parveens, the Shabanas, I wonder what they must be like in bed. I don't think that of Hema. Every instinct rebels. I want to worship her from afar.'[29]

Between 1979 and 1982, gossip press stories about Hema wove these themes across four key areas of 'controversy': Hema's social manner, her professional life, her family life and her romances, marriage and motherhood. The writing style was largely speculative and questioning, asking specifically 'How does Hema get away with it?' but also setting in motion a wider worrying of the limits of acceptable female behaviour in modern India.[30]

Manner

The 'mystery' of Hema's reserved manner was a central preoccupation. On one hand it was celebrated as the key to her 'dignity' and 'respect': 'Hema can do anything and get away with it. Her dignity is her armour against cheapness … She expects the other person to keep to his place. Like Amitabh she is very reserved and very aloof.'[31] On the other hand, her 'hoity-toity'[32] manner was castigated as cold and snobbish: 'They said … that she was a snob and quite insufferable. That she was too high 'n' mighty. That she was above sitting around on the sets between shots and disappeared into her make-up room with her gaunt aunt.'[33]

At issue was the paradox of the female film star: whilst according to the norms of ideal Indian behaviour it was unacceptable to be 'cold' (without *dil*), a dignified reserve was an essential signal of a woman's respectability and modesty. In fact Hema's reputation as 'Thandi Malini',[34] or 'the Ice Queen who Dharam once thought would never thaw',[35] undoubtedly did much to legitimate her later 'scandalous' relationship with him, although

---

[28] *Cine Blitz*, February 1979, p. 18.
[29] Ibid., p. 23.
[30] I am concerned here with examining how this portrait of a 'modern' female star is constructed and where the tension points appear to lie (i.e. what is most insistently spoken – or denied). While the question of the 'truth' of what is written in these magazines plays a crucial part in their fascination (i.e. they are overtly preoccupied with discovering whether stars are 'telling the truth,' and implicitly always provoking the question of whether the journalist is 'telling the truth'), such questions are irrelevant here. I am not concerned with what Malini 'really' does or thinks, only in how the magazines present this.
[31] *Cine Blitz*, February 1979, p. 23.
[32] *Stardust*, August 1982, p. 20.
[33] *Cine Blitz*, February 1979, p. 18
[34] *Stardust*, October 1981, p. 31. (*Thandi* = cold)
[35] *Super*, May 1981, p. 45.

her 'detractors' portrayed her 'pretended modesty' as hypocrisy. Nevertheless, Malini was allowed her say, however patently a half-truth. 'Right from my first film I've set the limit – if the role needed it, I'd expose my back and my legs up to my knees, that's about all, never my cleavage. Till today, I don't wear sleeveless dresses or blouses.'[36]

Professional life

The second area of manufactured controversy revolved around questions of how hard Malini worked, how deserving she was of her exceptional success, how ambitious – or even ruthless – she was. Frequent references were made to her work ethic, professionalism and concern for her producers. Thus, she was 'working round the clock again'[37] and always got up early: 'Somehow my eyes open at sharp 6 … and then I'm in a mad rush.'[38] Whatever the state of her emotional life, she did her *pooja* (prayers) and diligently practised her *Bharatanatyam* every day. Moreover, 'Unlike other heroines she's a very reliable artist. She'll never let you down.'[39] Whilst there were niggles from 'detractors' who claimed her 'non-cooperation' had lost them money or grumbled that 'the mighty Malini, despite her millions, demands half a dozen coconuts and a basket of fruits from the producer with whom she is shooting at lunchtime', this was generally just a pretext for another so-called controversy. According to *Stardust*, 'behind the brave front, Hema is a bit perturbed by the talk—especially since people also accuse her of harassing her producers and dishonouring her contracts. Hema denied it angrily.'[40]

With her marriage and subsequent pregnancy came scope for stories about the conflicting ties of home and family: 'Will Pregnancy Ruin What's Left of Hema's career?' headlined *Star & Style*, who public-spiritedly 'decided to take the pulse of the industry on this vital question', long before Malini was actually pregnant.[41] When, despite journalists' stories about 'her desire to retire to full-time housewifery and motherhood',[42] she eventually returned to the studios after her daughter's birth, speculation was rife. Had Dharmendra failed her? Or was she a 'modern' woman combining work and motherhood?

There was a distinct tension around her working-life, for film stardom was dangerously 'non-traditional' work, acknowledged in Malini's own insistence that 'my daughter will never be a film star'.[43] *Bharatanatyam* dancing was infinitely more respectable for a patriotic, middle-class, 'traditional' woman and consequently often emphasized as a key element of Malini's star persona and special aura.[44] Answering a question in *Super* about the peace and tranquility in her face in *Meera* (Gulzar, 1979), she replied, 'I think my being a dancer helped. Dancers are known to

---

[36]*Super*, February 1980, p. 25.
[37]*Stardust*, August 1982, p. 21
[38]*Super*, May 1981, p. 41.
[39]*Cine Blitz*, February 1979, p. 22.
[40]*Stardust*, October 1981, p.33.
[41]*Star & Style*, 8–21 August 1980, p. 39.
[42]*Stardust*, August 1982, p.21.
[43]Ibid. Her daughter, Esha Deol, did become a successful film star in the 2000s. Female stardom in India was, especially in the 1980s, an intrinsically delicate matter: the very fact of being on display and available to the male gaze (and desire) and of being associated with, what was often referred to as, a 'dirty' film industry, meant that adulation was problematic: she could hardly be straightforwardly 'traditional' and her persona had therefore to be carefully managed.
[44]See note 2. Malini's *Bharatanatyam* dancing is said to give her 'class'.

be devoted to God. Also, I am a very religious and Godfearing person.'[45]

Nevertheless, the mere presence of a 'respectable' Indian woman in the 'dirty' film industry remained problematic and was dealt with on at least one occasion by absolving Malini of direct responsibility. Not only was she said not to socialize at *filmi* parties and to find the *filmi* crowd 'boring' and 'uneducated',[46] but also she had famously been forced into films by her mother.

> I remember I was reluctantly waiting on the lawn wearing a pink sari. I had not been ambitious even then. Only my mother was keen that I give a screen test. But I've been lucky. I did not have to struggle ... Several times I'd decided to leave films, but I didn't. This phase just doesn't seem to end. It's in my destiny, I suppose. I'm looking forward to the time I'll be happy and free.[47]

Malini was thereby constructed as the model *dharmic* film star: it was in her destiny to be a top film star; she accepted her lot and performed the duty conscientiously but apparently without involvement.

Family

Stars' fraught relationships with their families were an important theme in gossip stories, especially as most Bombay stars of that era lived with their parents and siblings. Female stars often financially supported large extended families, thereby setting the stage for questions about how far a daughter's duty to her family should go. Mostly, these families – and particularly female stars' mothers – were presented in the gossip as avaricious leeches; Malini's was no exception. A *Stardust* article entitled 'Exploitation Begins At Home! Real Life Incidents of How Star Families Loot the Heroines!' thundered:

> Almost all the heroines of the industry were hens who laid the golden eggs for their families ... our actresses are made to stay alive, slog and earn to satisfy the greed and ambition of their good-for-nothing relatives! ... After satisfying her *amma*'s ambition of becoming a producer and her brother's wish to become an industrialist, Hema was heartbroken when none of them came to her rescue when the income-tax raided her house recently.[48]

Gossip stories regularly decried Mrs Chakravarty's habit of taking large sums of money by signing chits on her daughter's name and setting up reckless production ventures. Although Malini nobly denied being 'the Cinderella who is put to work while the rest of the family lives off her money', she simultaneously lashed out against her mother:

> I don't like my mother producing films at all ... My mother has become so busy that she has no time even to accompany me for outdoor shootings. Probably she feels I've become old enough to look after myself. [49]

---

[45] *Super,* February 1980, p. 27.
[46] *Super,* May 1981, p. 45.
[47] *Super,* February 1980, p. 25.
[48] *Stardust,* January 1983, p. 35.
[49] *Super,* February 1980, p. 23. In fact, Malini's mother had accompanied her on film sets over many years, and when she became too busy her 'gaunt aunt' took over as chaperone, despite the fact that Hema was in her thirties and known to be having an affair with a married man. The accompanying family member was an important signifier of 'traditional' decency and respectability. Malini's 'upbringing' was often quoted (somewhat paradoxically) to underline her decency ('a solid conservative Iyengar family in the South', *Star & Style,* 7–20 March, 1980, p. 17).

However, sympathies were often on Mrs Chakravarty's side, especially regarding Hema's romantic transgressions. 'Who'll Marry Hema Now?' ran headlines in the late 1970s when *amma* was attempting, unsuccessfully, to arrange a marriage for her daughter, forcing her to meet eager aspirants to the role of Dream Girl's husband.[50] Malini remained adamant over her love for Dharmendra, despite gossip allegations of hypocrisy: 'she tries to make out as if she's really the *seedhi-saadhi* ideal daughter people think her to be'.[51] A picture of constant family rows was painted, 'Mrs Chakravarty has thrown endless tantrums',[52] with *amma* complaining about having a daughter as obstinate and amoral as Hema, while Malini complained of her family's interference when she, anyway, was the major breadwinner.

If her own mother proved something of a tyrant, other mothers saw in Malini the ideal *bahu*. Co-star Sanjeev Kumar described how:

> The bride my mother had chosen, Hema Malini, and her aunt came over for dinner … [My mother] told me she admired [Hema's] simple charm and asked me why I didn't propose to her … She also sensed Hema's good nature, which obliterated all fears of my being dominated or pushed around … Seeing her keenness, I … approached [Hema] with a straightforward, direct, honest proposal, besides which there was a growing fondness on my part too.[53]

Many men apparently agreed. According to *Super*:

> In every man's private dream of his own slippers and his own hearth, hers was the face—now laughing, now scolding, ever homely—that fitted the dream … Those imbroglios with Jeetendra and Sanjeev Kumar were glossed over by her millions of adoring dreamers, as mere gossip. Hema, like Caesar's wife, was above reproach.[54]

Romance/marriage/motherhood

The gossip press enthusiastically peddled stories of Malini's affairs with Sanjeev and Jeetendra, both of whom believed she would marry them and were 'devastated' when she dropped them. However, Malini's long-standing romance with Dharmendra was the central focus of controversy, offering scope for endless fascination and speculation over the nature of 'pure love', what place bigamy and second wives should have in the modern world, and the morality of their expedient – temporary – conversion to Islam to make this marriage possible.[55] On one hand, Hema was branded a 'home-breaker', 'adulteress', unfeeling schemer and 'ostracised from her community'; on the other, she was characterized as the ideal wife, mother and lover, living in well-deserved bliss. According to *Stardust*, 'The Dharmendra–Hema Malini love affair has been a national issue for the

---

[50] After 1974 and the Jeetendra debacle, Malini's father ran Sunday teas for prospective grooms: 'Chakravarti sought a practical answer by lining up prospective Iyengar grooms for his daughter. Every Sunday, he invited qualified professionals, engineers and IAS officers for tea at home. "When it was time, I was summoned from my room to join the conversation. Most of these prospective grooms were so nervous in my presence that their tea cups and saucers rattled in their hands," she recalls with wry amusement today.' Somaaya 2007: 42, 52.
[51] *Super*, February 1980, p. 23.
[52] *Super*, July 1980, p. 14.
[53] *Star & Style*, 14–27 December 1979, p. 17.
[54] *Super*, February 1980, p. 20.
[55] Articles were spun around questions such as: Can this tempestuous relationship last? Should a woman continue an affair with a married man who has no intention of leaving his wife? How should a second wife behave? What can she expect? How might a traditional vegetarian Iyengar woman live with an alcoholic meat-eating Punjabi Jat?

last four years. Discussed in Parliament as well as in households, the couple has been alternately ridiculed and glorified.'[56] Questions abounded:

> In the past decade, the Hema-Dharam *affaire* [*sic*] … has been at the buttend of kitty-party jokes, journalistic sly humour and millions of 'romance'-fed fans' guileless wonder. There is a slight change today. Some time back, the burning question was: Where will it all end? Now it is: *How could they have got married*? Isn't there a law against *bigamy*?[57]

There was a range of final opinions on the matter, although columnists mostly concluded that 'Dharam and Hema are still India's greatest love couple … the fact that [they] decided to shed all hypocrisy … and assume full public responsibility for their actions is not only gutsy but admirable.'[58]

Malini's ecstasy in the role of Dharmendra's wife became the theme of 1980: 'Hema's face is effulgent again'[59] or 'Sparkling eyes, glowing face, Hema looked a picture of total bliss.'[60] With her baby's arrival in November 1981, descriptions of the idyll moved into hyperbole. When she wasn't bathing, feeding or massaging her daughter, she was apparently playing dutiful wife:

> Hema seemed so perfectly content with both her new roles … 'Dharam is at my house very often. Of course I get a chance to do small wifely chores for him. I don't feel deprived of any such opportunities.'[61]

Nevertheless, the muckraking continued with constant insinuations that the relationship was cracking: Dharmendra was having flings, was over-possessive, was turning to drink under the strain or was neglecting his duties to Malini and his daughter. Moreover, the magazines worried away at the fact that the marriage was illegal and the child technically illegitimate, even proposing that Dharmendra 'knew that Hema would have to bear the brunt of being the first "unwed mother" in the industry'.[62] Malini resolutely continued to insist: 'I don't care what people have to say about me: I am a Godfearing person and I know that I haven't harmed anybody.'[63] At issue was the role of individualism in a modernizing society. How far should love come before duty to family or society? How far should people disregard social convention and the disapproval of others to seek individual personal happiness? Whilst the affair was championed as a 'defiance of the accepted norms and rules of society – the ultimate triumph of love over all man-made barriers',[64] Hema's own justification was in terms of personal happiness.

> Unrelenting, getting through the chill, cutting across the snowstorm of ugly rumours and uglier controversies, she decides to live for herself: … 'Every individual is entitled to seek his or her source of happiness … All the time I'm working, and my time belongs to others. If a few moments, which I can call my own, give me happiness, I'll take them at all costs.'[65]

---

[56]*Stardust*, October 1981, p. 30.
[57]*Super*, July 1980, p. 13.
[58]*Stardust Annual*, 1981.
[59]*Super*, July 1980, p. 14
[60]*Stardust*, October 1981, p. 31.
[61]*Stardust*, August 1982, p. 22.
[62]*Stardust*, October 1981, p. 30.
[63]Ibid., p. 33.
[64]Ibid., p. 30.
[65]*Super*, February 1980, p. 25.

To sum up, in each of these four domains the Malini persona was constructed as both a paragon and 'unpardonable', as both 'good' and 'bad'. Echoing the fragmentation of the Asha character in *Naseeb*, as well as the disavowal that marks the postcard image with which we began, Malini's off-screen gossip persona presented at least one facet in each domain that was fundamentally 'traditional', alongside flagrant defiance of other aspects of this tradition. The comparatively open-ended gossip text ran parallel to, and in tension with, the films themselves, producing a complex star persona that walked the tightrope between tradition and modernity and offered rich pickings for ongoing exploration of the burning social questions of the day.

Conclusion

If Nargis Dutt was the perfect Mother India for India's 1950s, Hema Malini was the sacred cow of its 1970s and 1980s. I have suggested that Malini's ability to embody a range of contradictions and to provoke controversy placed her as the ideal female star for India in the decades that followed the Nehruvian nationalist consensus. Her multi-faceted star persona enabled negotiation of how womanhood might be lived in a new era in which 'traditional values' were accommodating to a globalizing, modernizing world. Her perfectly sculpted features, large compassionate eyes and ability to radiate calm contentment provided a blank slate onto which perfect Indian womanhood in the Hindu *sati-savitri* tradition could be projected. Alongside this, she had a grace and agility of movement, together with a flair for sparky comedy and tough talking – not to mention a fascinatingly colourful private life – which made her a credible rebel. Over time, especially after marriage and motherhood, her persona became increasingly identified with female power in the *shakti* and *viraangana* modes, whilst never quite losing the *bhakti* or quiet devotion.

How did she convert this glittering star capital into political and social power? After endorsing her male co-stars as BJP parliamentary candidates – Vinod Khanna in 1999, Dharmendra in 2004 – she won a Rajya Sabha nomination in 2003 and her own parliamentary seat in 2014. She rose energetically to the challenge of national office. However, as MP for Mathura and Vrindaban, Malini has continued to court controversy, nowadays through her twitter handle. In July 2015, she caused a media storm by blaming the driver of a car hit by her Mercedes for his own daughter's death (Singh 2015). Earlier, as a newly elected MP, she not only tweeted for local schoolchildren to clean up their city but also campaigned to purge Vrindaban's temples of elderly widows from other states (Ghosh 2014). Brand Hema seems perfect for a politics that looks back to a romanticized Hindu tradition yet idealizes individualism and cannot tolerate matter out of place – or widows out of Bengal or Bihar. Malini's star persona, embracing both Hindutva and the struggle to define an Indian modernity for the global age, embodies and lays bare the contradictions of this political ideology. Today Hema Malini is still 'everything that's unpardonable', whilst remaining a role model for many older Indian women, and an ongoing focus for controversy. The Dream Girl continues to peddle dreams to the Indian public.

Works Cited

Dwyer, Rachel (2008), 'The Indian Film Magazine, *Stardust*', in Aswin Punanthambekar and Anandam P. Kavoori (eds), *Global Bollywood*, 240–67, New York: New York University Press.

Ghosh, Deepshikha (2014), '"Widows From Bengal, Bihar, Stay There. Why Crowd Vrindavan?": Hema Malini',

NDTV, 17 September, online at: www.ndtv.com/india-news/widows-from-bengal-bihar-stay-there-why-crowd-vrindavan-hema-malini-667204 (accessed 24 February 2017).

Gopalan, Lalitha (2000), 'Avenging Women in Indian Cinema', in Ravi Vasudevan (ed.), *Making Meaning in Indian Cinema*, 215–37, New Delhi: Oxford University Press.

Hansen, Kathryn (1992), *Grounds for Play: The Nautanki Theatre of North India*, Berkeley: University of California Press.

Kasbekar, Asha (2001), 'Hidden Pleasures: Negotiating the Myth of the Female Ideal in Popular Hindi Cinema', in Rachel Dwyer and Christopher Pinney (eds), *Pleasure and the Nation: The History, Politics and Consumption of Public Culture in India*, 286–308, New Delhi: Oxford University Press.

Majumdar, Neepa (2009), *Wanted Cultured Ladies Only! Female Stardom and Cinema in India, 1930s–1950s*, Urbana: University of Illinois Press.

Mukherjee, Ram Kamal (2005), *Hema Malini: Diva Unveiled*, Mumbai: Magna Books.

Mukherjee, Ram Kamal (2011), 'Marrying Hema', in Jerry Pinto (ed.), *The Greatest Show on Earth*, 307–12, New Delhi: Penguin India.

Singh, Mahim Pratap (2015), 'BJP MP Hema Malini Blames Father of Girl Who Dies in Accident', *Indian Express*, 9 July, online at: http://indianexpress.com/article/india/india-others/girls-father-should-have-followed-traffic-rules-says-hema-malini-after-accident/ (accessed 24 February 2017).

Somaaya, Bhawana (2007), *Hema Malini: The Authorised Biography*, New Delhi: Lotus Collection.

Thomas, Rosie (1995), 'Melodrama and the Negotiation of Morality in Mainstream Hindi Film', in Carol Breckenridge (ed.), *Consuming Modernity: Public Culture in a South Asian World*, 157–82, Minneapolis: University of Minnesota Press.

Thomas, Rosie (2005), 'Not Quite Pearl White', in Raminder Kaur and Ajay Sinha (eds), *Bollyworld: Indian Cinema Through a Transnational Lens*, 35–69, New Delhi: Sage.

Thomas, Rosie (2007), '*Miss Frontier Mail*: The Film That Mistook its Star for a Train', in Monica Narula, Shuddhabrata Sengupta, Jeebesh Bagchi and Ravi Sundaram (eds), *Sarai Reader 07: Frontiers*, 294–308, Delhi: CSDS.

Thomas, Rosie (2013), 'Sanctity and Scandal: The Mythologisation of Mother India', in *Bombay Before Bollywood: Film City Fantasies*, 244–71, New Delhi: Orient Blackswan.

Chapter 13

Sridevi, queen of farce: Comedy, performance and star persona in popular Hindi cinema

Nandana Bose

The chapter examines the polysemic stardom of Sridevi in 1980s to early 1990s commercial Hindi cinema, and argues that her unique persona was significantly shaped by her natural talent and flair for farce and slapstick comedy, at a time when there were few substantial roles for women in the typical 1980s testosterone-driven, action-adventure *masala* films. A versatile comedienne, Sridevi's uncanny knack for making audiences laugh depended on her spontaneous comic timing and her unique ability to shed her inhibitions in front of the camera. Known as Hindi cinema's 'queen of comedy', she unleashed an array of exaggerated facial expressions and contortions; dynamic (and often sexualized) body movements; a boisterous physicality and charismatic on-screen presence, with the energy of a naturally gifted dancer; which were perfectly complemented by a giggly, pitchy, childlike voice that spoke with a 'funny' accent, thus contributing to the overall hilarity of her comic acts and antics. Her comic repertoire included slapstick and anarchic gags; impersonations, masquerades and disguises; double roles; riotous comic song and dance routines and unconventional on-screen behaviour that distinguished her as a unique female star in mainstream Hindi cinema. I also argue that she was infantilized through various pretextual (star physiognomy and body) and textual elements of *mise en scène* (costume, hairstyle and performance), and sound (voice, accent and speech); and extra-textually by the popular print media that undermined her transgressive physical comedy, thereby appealing to paternalistic Hindi film audiences who would (mis)perceive her as a mischievous yet entertaining child-woman.

Despite Sridevi's superstar status in the 1980s and 1990s, this chapter represents one of the first academic studies on her, thus seeking to redress a surprising lacuna within the subfield of Indian star studies. It is based on archival research involving popular film magazines and trade journals, and is informed by *mise en scène* analyses, particularly of star performance, extra-textual materials (publicity and promotional ephemera), discursive print media practices and sound studies. It also represents another case study of contemporary female stardom in keeping with my past and current research agenda of conscientiously writing women into the historiography of Indian cinema; to record and recognize women's creative work, their talent and labour; and to treat them as fascinating and valuable texts worthy of critical thought, enquiry and analysis. In this sense, my work is indebted to, and inspired by, the groundbreaking scholarship of Neepa

Majumdar (2009) on 1930s and 1940s female stars and playback singers Lata Mangeshkar and Asha Bhosle; Rosie Thomas (2005) on 1930s and 1940s stunt queen 'Fearless' Nadia; Jyotika Virdi (2003) on Meena Kumari and Dimple Kapadia; by the pioneering interventions of Behroze Gandhy and Rosie Thomas (1991) on 1950s superstar Nargis and 'modern feminist' Smita Patil; and more recently, by Anustup Basu (2013) on the Anglo-Indian dancer/*femme fatale*, Helen.

Sridevi was often famously referred to as 'the female Amitabh Bachchan' (Anon. 1992: 35; Rajadhyaksha 1987: 40); her inclusion 'add[ed] to the market value of a film … Films [were] made for her and around her' (Anon. 1992: 35); the central roles of big-budget films were often written exclusively for her, a rare occurrence that was an acknowledgment of her star power (Jahagirdar-Saxena 1989: 37); and the marketing campaign for the 1989 hit film *Chandni* (Yash Chopra) 'revolve[d] entirely around … Sridevi, confirming her as India's top female star' (Rajadhyaksha and Willemen [1994] 1999: 488). The all-important distributors of the 1980s Hindi film industry agreed that 'a Sridevi starrer, like an Amitabh Bachchan starrer, [managed] to break even in the long run. Which, they say, [was] the hallmark of a Number One star' (Ahmed 1989: 19). She had an 'initial draw. Her name … guarantee[ing] queues on the opening day. As importantly, distributors [were] willing to buy a Sridevi movie as soon as it [was] announced' (Anon. 1987b). She was 'the one actress who can make a difference to the price of a film' (Rajadhyaksha 1987: 40). At the height of her stardom, Sridevi was the 'highest paid actress in India (until she was displaced by Madhuri Dixit) and the main sales asset of one of India's most expensive films at the time, *Roop Ki Rani Choron Ka Raja*' (Queen of Beauty King of Thieves, Satish Kaushik, 1993) (Rajadhyaksha and Willemen [1994] 1999: 219). For the popular commercial director Manmohan Desai, Sridevi was 'the actress for the masses. She [exuded] sensuality … and [seduced] the audience' (Anon. 1988: 53). Director Yash Chopra, in a 1989 interview with the popular, English-language film magazine, *Filmfare*, made the following observation on her stardom:

> In the star hierarchy, there are at least six vacant rungs after Sridevi. Her position is the same as Amitabh Bachchan's was at his peak. She's the only heroine who commands a sustained fan-following. People come to see *her* even if the film is not up to the mark. (Ahmed 1989: 24)

Hindi film comediennes: Sridevi as the queen of farce

Comedy has rarely been a popular, stand-alone genre in mainstream Hindi cinema. It is usually one of the many genres subsumed within the all-encompassing *masala* film; a subplot providing comic relief, a distraction temporarily interrupting the main narrative thread, and humour of a kind that appeals to the lowest common denominator, largely dependent on farce and slapstick. One of commercial Hindi cinema's favourite, lowbrow, comic devices is to poke fun at 'people suffering from physical drawbacks and speech impairments', and ridicule 'their linguistic peculiarities that are inevitable in a country that has great cultural and social diversity' (Chatterjee 2003: 341).

> Fat people (singer-turned-actress Tuntun is an example), short men (like the four-foot nothing Mukri) and characters that speak Hindi with a pronounced drawl (Asit Sen in numerous films), stammer, or have a heavy regional accent have been … [ridiculed]. As a result, moviegoers in India, more often than not, laugh at, rather than laugh with, the comedians. (341)

Major Indian film comedians focus on making 'people laugh, and they strive to do that with the help of whatever professional tools are available to them: sight gags, madcap escapades, slapstick routines, double entendres, or just plain buffoonery' (343). Farce, as a genre of comedy, uses buffoonery and horseplay and typically includes crude characterization and ludicrously improbable situations that involve boisterous gags and slapstick comedy. It aims at entertaining audiences through situations that are highly exaggerated, extravagant and thus improbable, and the plot depends upon a skillfully exploited situation rather than upon the development of character.

Its emphasis on chaos, anarchy, thrills, and gags is often considered too rough and aggressive, and hence, unsuitable for the 'fairer sex'. But certainly not so for Sridevi, whose spontaneous instinct for the absurd and the farcical, and her comic timing, remain unmatched in the history of commercial Hindi cinema. To quote her: 'I enjoy doing comedy. It's the challenge of going against my nature that goads me to do them. In real life I am not at all the bubbly, effervescent kind, though I *am* fun loving. But, in front of the camera, I seem to acquire this strange power to do just about anything without inhibition' (Ahmed 1990: 25). The comedienne-as-star in mainstream Hindi cinema is unusual, Sridevi being a welcome exception, due to:

> Longstanding and deep-rooted cultural bias against women performing comedy. The idea that femininity is incompatible with humor dates back to before the nineteenth century and lingers to the present day. Traditionally, women are thought to be too emotional, too passive, and too morally pure to engage in, or even enjoy, comedy, which has the potential to be raucous, rebellious, and antagonistic. (Wagner 2013: 40)

Hindi film comediennes have historically been cast in minor roles, typecast and caricatured in terms of their 'abnormal', unattractive physical appearances (such as the obese Tuntun and Kumkum), or laughed at for their high-pitched, tinny voices and heavy regional accents. Any chance of presenting truly transgressive comedy is thus immediately undermined by making these female comics pathetic and laughable in a patriarchal film industry for 'women who engage in comic performances have the potential to subvert the social structures that keep them oppressed; by poking fun at those in power, especially men, women have the ability to expose their weaknesses and challenge their authority' (40).

It is also unusual for a Hindi film comedienne to be both attractive and the star of a film, Madhubala being an exception, which Sridevi clearly was in the late 1980s and early 1990s. A disjuncture is created for viewers: whilst she embodies conventional notions of beauty and femininity vis-à-vis her physical appearance, she sharply deviates from that image in terms of her on-screen behaviour and body language. Her screen persona thus offers 'a heterodox merging of elements typically perceived as incompatible: at once "classical" (in her beauty) and "grotesque" (in her slapstick)' (46).

Star vehicles: Physical comedy, double roles and disguises

K. Raghavendra Rao's *Himmatwala* (Brave Man, 1983) was Sridevi's first breakthrough Hindi film, and 'a vehicle for the successful entry of South Indian production capital into Hindi cinema and the best known of the several Jeetendra-Sridevi films usually referred to as "South" pictures in the Bombay media' (Rajadhyaksha and Willemen [1994] 1999: 460). Much like her screen father played by Amjad Khan – who is best remembered for his iconic role as the villain, Gabbar Singh, a whip-cracking leader of a gang of bandits in the landmark curry western *Sholay* (Flames, Ramesh Sippy, 1975) – Sridevi is the leader of a girl gang, first glimpsed in a tight leather pant suit, cracking a whip; a voluptuous, role-playing dominatrix, over-sexualized through close-ups of her (in)famous 'thunder thighs' (Anon. 1992).[1] She engages in vigorous and violent physical comedy – exercising, jumping into ponds, climbing trees; teasing, mocking, threatening to bite men; kicking, clawing, fighting, dueling with a stick. Her untamed, free-spirited, wild, energetic on-screen presence is reiterated by the telling lyrics of the song 'Ladki Nahi Hai Tu' – 'she's not a girl, but an animal.' Such anarchic buffoonery and horseplay performed with utter confidence and aplomb by a female star in Hindi cinema is undoubtedly rare, and threatens conventional notions of femininity and cultural expectations of women.[2] The transgressive physical comedy of Sridevi,

> Provides audiences with an alternative to the ubiquitous stereotype of women as demure, passive, well-behaved, and above all, humorless. Slapstick comedienne transgressed gender boundaries by performing the type of rough physical comedy that many contemporaneous observers felt should be reserved for men. (Wagner 2013: 41–2)

The recurring narrative device of the doppelgänger, or the double role, is a key star vehicle. Doubling is the ultimate recognition of superstar status for a Hindi film actor.[3]

> A double role in a Hindi film serves a purpose that goes well beyond the mere requirements of the narrative: it has a commercial motive …. [giving] a big, saleable star more footage and that ensures the film a better popular response. As in *Ram aur Shyam* (Dilip Kumar), *Judwa* (Salman Khan), *Seeta aur Geeta* (Hema Malini), … the lead actor or actress played two siblings, one meek, the other a go-getter. (Chatterjee 2003: 407)

It allowed Sridevi the freedom to fully explore diverse character roles such as the contrary twin sisters Anju and Manju in *Chaalbaaz* (Trickster, Pankaj Parashar, 1989), Pallavi and Pooja in *Lamhe* (Moments, Yash Chopra, 1991) and Sonia and Priya in *Gurudev* (Godman, Vinod Mehra, 1993). As Meheli Sen observes, 'it's so important to have her be a goofball *and* a sex-kitten within

---

[1] Sridevi's hyper-sexualized yet infantilized persona is one of the intriguing dualities that emerge in any close scrutiny of her star text. Commenting on another song in *Mr. India*, Ravi Vasudevan writes: 'In the most sexual of her performances, [she] is sensualized by the lovemaking of an invisible man. It could be argued that this empty space invites the insertion of the male spectator, [but] it is somehow still consistent with the *narcissistic, auto-erotic regime of sexuality implied in the persona of this female star*' (Rajadhyaksha and Willemen [1994] 1999: 219; emphasis added). A possible explanation (which demands further examination) may be found in such films as *Nashilee Jawani* (Intoxicating Youthfulness, I. V. Sasi, 1986), which was promoted as her first 'sex' film (219).

[2] Her comic persona is highlighted in promotional materials of her breakthrough Hindi film *Himmatwala*. In a full-page poster printed in *Filmfare*, 16 March 1983, vol. 32, no. 6, Sridevi is precariously balanced sideways on the hero's back in the foreground while making a funny face at the reader. *Filmfare* described her role as 'the spoilt hussy … that excited the public imagination. Here was a young woman oozing the sort of sex appeal that can never fail to titillate. Shiny lipstick, naughty eyes, a figure that refuses to shed its baby fat, that's how the audience loves them' (Anon. 1987b). The contradictory duality imbricated in the star text, of hyper-sexuality and infantilism, is evident in this media report that refers to her 'sex appeal' on the one hand, and 'baby fat' on the other.

[3] For more on the imbrication of doubling and female stardom in Hindi cinema, see Majumdar 2003.

Figure 13.1 Sridevi's memorable impersonation of Charlie Chaplin's *The Tramp* in Shekhar Kapur's *Mr. India* (1987).

the same films—almost as if these are two halves of the star-body.'⁴ In the words of Sridevi: 'I love the challenge of playing two contrasting characters in the same film. In most Hindi films, the heroine's role is limited. A double role makes up for it … it makes it more substantial' (Ahmed 1989: 22). As the aggressive Manju in her first double role in *Chaalbaaz*, Sridevi kicks, punches and beats up men, and purchases liquor. In a fight sequence with one of Hindi cinema's iconic villains, Shakti Kapoor, she transforms into a female action figure. Although such behaviour is certainly at odds with perceived notions of how proper women should behave in Indian society, it draws laughter from viewers as,

> Rebellious humour mocks the social rules, and, in its turn, can be seen to challenge, or rebel against, the rules (202) … If the social world is full of codes that restrict what can be said and done, then delight can be taken in breaking the rules that constrain social actors. (Billig 2005: 207)

Masquerade, impersonation, cross-dressing and disguise are essential components of the Sridevi star text. Her tramp impersonation of Charlie Chaplin in Shekhar Kapur's classic film *Mr. India* (1987) is arguably her most acclaimed comedic act (Figure 13.1). Slightly speeded up for comic effect, she performed one gag after another with such ease that it astonished Kapur, who kept lengthening the scene, and heralded her natural, yet hitherto unrecognized, latent comic talent to Hindi film audiences. For her,

> *Mr. India* only emphasized my flair for comedy. If you see some of my Telugu and Tamil films you'll find that I have always been doing the funny bit, even in my song sequences … [*Mr. India*] gave me a lot of freedom in front of the camera, to explore myself. And I really let myself go. (Ahmed 1990: 25–7)

According to the popular English-language print media, one can 'trace her flair for the absurd to her abiding fancy for the Chaplinesque brand of comedy' (25). Her impersonation can be interpreted as a fan's homage to a comedic legend whose films she would repeatedly watch (25).

For Sridevi, 'the challenge is in making crazy situations entertaining' (Ahmed 1989: 23), which she accomplishes with ease when she jumps out

---

⁴Meheli Sen, personal communication, 13 March 2015.

of a cake, and when four funny faces of the star magically appear, in successive order, at every corner of a blackened frame during one of the renditions of *Roop Ki Rani Choron Ka Raja*'s titular song sequence, 'Main hoon roop ki rani' (I am the queen of beauty) (Figure 13.2). Such framing composition that spotlights her fourfold dramatic variants is an emphatic testament of Sridevi's inimitable star power. Masquerading as a Japanese princess in the same film, her doll-like appearance in a kimono is complemented aurally by a pitchy, giggly, child's voice. Disguises can be liberating since one's ethnic, religious and gender identities are temporarily hidden from scrutiny and judgement. As a Tamilian speaking in heavily accented Hindi, disguise is an effective strategy for Sridevi to transcend linguistic, ethnic and regional divisiveness, and appeal to a wider demographic of North Indian viewers. Disguises also provide more opportunities to engage in socially inappropriate behaviour without the fear of being identified and punished.

In *Gair Kanooni* (Illegal, Prayag Raj, 1989), paired opposite the popular star-comedian Govinda, she assumes numerous masquerades whilst indulging in a range of morally questionable, transgressive acts – as a con artiste, a fraudster and a pickpocket, who cheats vulnerable people of their money. Sridevi's character impersonates the goddess Lakshmi while tricking poor devotees into parting with their money, which, if it wasn't for the comedic performance of a superstar with mass appeal, could, in all likelihood, be perceived as offensive to a Hindu majoritarian society. She masquerades as a blind woman eliciting both sympathy and money, and as a schoolgirl in uniform she fakes a fainting spell on a car bonnet so that she can eventually steal money and an expensive watch. In due course, she also gets drunk and rides a motorbike. As Andrea Greenbaum points out, 'female comics must eschew conventional notions of social behavior' (1997: 118–19). It is also worth pointing out that 'comedy … can be bold, assertive, and above all transgressive. It can

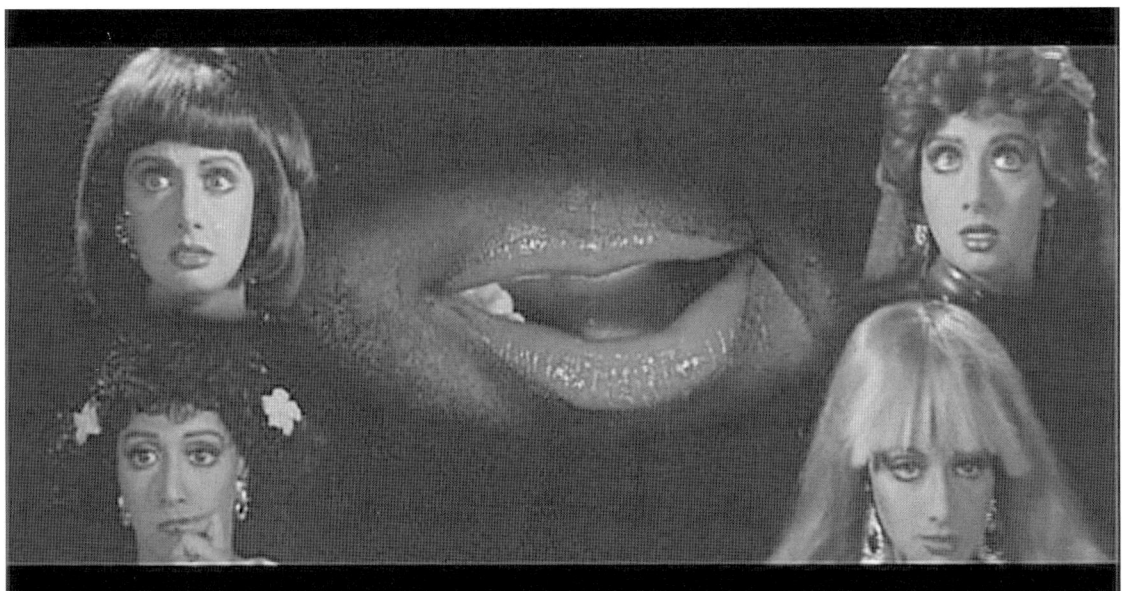

Figure 13.2 Unusual, decentred edge-of-frame composition of a female star that showcases her expressive range in a song picturization from *Roop Ki Rani Choron Ka Raja* (Satish Kaushik, 1993).

be used to question authority, to upset the status quo, to deflate the powerful, and to challenge the social order' (Wagner 2013: 40).

The aforementioned comic routines are presented as set pieces, typical of the 'cinema of interruptions' that abruptly halt the narrative flow (Gopalan 2002). 'In conventional Hindi films ... comic situations are usually treated ... in the manner in which song-and-dance routines or stunt sequences generally are: as set pieces designed for a specific purpose and nothing more' (Chatterjee 2003: 339). Steve Seidman stresses the 'extrafictional' nature of comedian-centred films, calling attention to 'anything that interrupts the smooth exposition of a fictional universe' (1981: 15). Sridevi's uproarious performances disrupt and interrupt the narrative flow, monopolizing on-screen space, filling the frame with her various avatars and upstaging her male co-stars.

Infantilized star persona

I posit that there is an infantilized (yet hyper-sexualized) dimension to Sridevi's star persona, which may explain the incompatible tensions between mainstream popularity and unconventional (even transgressive) femininity inherent in her polysemic star text. Numerous and consistent iterations of the infantile aspects of her star persona (even in dramatic roles as Pooja Bhatnagar, the child-woman in love with a much older man in *Lamhe,* or as Nehalata Malhotra, who regresses to a childlike existence due a traumatic head injury, in the critically acclaimed 1983 film *Sadma* [Trauma, Balu Mahendra]) may offer an explanation for her 'mass appeal' and superstar status despite her outrageous comedic antics and shenanigans that entertain, challenge conventional notions of femininity and momentarily liberate the spectator from paternalistic cultural restrictions.

Infantile costume and hairstyle: Costume and hairstyle play an important role in accentuating the naturally youthful star physiognomy. Although Sridevi's character, Seema, is a crime reporter in *Mr. India*, her infantile hairstyle of two bow-tied long braids undermines the seriousness of her profession and her credibility. This child's hairstyle of pig-tails, or bangs and a blunt cut, emphasizing her round face and large expressive eyes, who occasionally sticks her finger into her mouth, is repeated in most of her films from this period. For instance, in *Chaalbaaz*, Sridevi, as vivacious Manju, is costumed in the colourful clothes of 1980s designer Leena Daru, and appears doll-like, sporting a vibrant, yellow-orange headband and bow that accentuates her cherubic face and round eyes. 'With her "sequined dress and feather look" (as described by choreographer Chinni Prakash) ... inch-long false eyelashes' (Rajadhyaksha and Willemen [1994] 1999: 219), and heavy make up, Sridevi appeared in such flamboyant, burlesque costumes, blingy accessories and audacious headdresses (in true slapstick tradition) that her on-screen fashion style was perceived as distinctly camp, gesturing towards her star appeal as a gay icon.

Infantile body language and mannerisms: In arguably her most acclaimed carnivalesque, comic song and dance routine, 'Hawa Hawaii', from *Mr. India*, she indulges in rebellious, transgressive behaviour that follows in the rich tradition of slapstick comedy by shaking her bottom at the camera/audience, sticking her tongue out, pulling faces, rolling her large round eyes and fluttering her eyelashes. There is the momentary enjoyment of social disruption for the spectator. As Billig observes:

> The notion of rebellious humour conveys an image of momentary freedom from the restraints of social convention. It constitutes a brief escape, or ... a moment of transcendence ... As James Sully wrote in his *Essay on Laughter*, 'the laughter

at what is lawless, and still more at the indecent and the profane, certainly derives a part of its gusto from a sense of relief from restraint, which is a main ingredient in the enjoyment of all license' (1902: 118). Freud developed this idea with his claim that tendentious humour provides a means of temporarily escaping from a prohibition. (2005: 208)

Carnivalesque comic song and dance routines, unique to Sridevi's star persona, present a 'festive terrain that breaks down boundaries between performers and audience, celebrates transgression, and simultaneously mocks and affirms' (Bakhtin 1984: 31).

In the comic song picturization featured in *Chaalbaaz*, 'Na jane kahan se aayi hai' (Don't know where she's come from), an appropriation of Gene Kelly's 'Singin' in the Rain' performance, a raincoat-clad Sridevi pulls funny faces, shakes her bottom at the camera, rolls her eyes and drapes herself across a taxi with a beer bottle in hand. She also displays her penchant and natural flair for comic dancing as she prances around the psychedelic set in easy, fluid, uninhibited body movements, dancing atop carts, taxis and other vehicles, captured in fast motion for heightened comedic effect. The star body is dynamic, and constantly in motion:

> Her energy on screen is electrifying … The implication that she is controlled by her body rather than by her mind or heart adds to her erotic appeal and makes her performances all the more transgressive, as a woman who was comic as well as unapologetically sexual could be especially threatening to those who were already uncomfortable with women who didn't adhere to traditional gender roles. (Wagner 2013: 56)

Sridevi's character whistles, wiggles her bottom and publicly consumes alcohol in the company of men who egg her on to win a drinking bet with the hero (played by the star Anil Kapoor who was often her co-star) in *Gurudev*'s 'Mere kaha mano' (Listen to me) song sequence; however, the shock of witnessing this seemingly subversive act by an Indian woman is quickly undermined when she is found out to be a fraudster who has actually been drinking black tea. Nonetheless, Sridevi, in the tradition of 'slapstick comediennes could be seen as exhibiting an especially deviant image of femininity … as they rejected traditional feminine qualities such as passivity and diffidence and instead took part in wild brawls alongside their male co-stars' (44).

Infantile voice, 'funny' accent and mispronunciations: Sridevi's voice plays a significant role in consolidating her infantilized persona. Her speaking voice has a certain 'childlike' quality, much like the singing voice of the legendary playback singer Lata Mangeshkar, possibly indicative of the persistent traces of her past career as a successful child star in the regional cinemas of Tamil, Telugu and Malayalam, predating her career in Hindi cinema. A giggly, high-pitched, thin, quivering, childlike voice, suggestive of vulnerability and innocence – the cinematic voice perfectly complements, and even accentuates, the visual persona of the infantilized star comedienne. As Mary Ann Doane observes, 'the voice is not detachable from the body which is quite specific – that of the star … [The] voice serves as a support for the spectator's recognition and his/her identification of, as well as with, the star' (1980: 36). Michel Chion terms the tendency for the human voice to attract attention over all other sounds as 'vococentrism' (1999: 6). In the case of the infantilized star, the voice may be even more important than the visual persona, since 'space, for the child, is defined initially in terms of the audible, not the visible', and because 'for the child the voice, even before language, is the instrument of demand' (Doane 1980: 44). As the amnesiac woman who behaves like a twelve-year-old in *Sadma*, she screeches, screams and yelps, modulating her voice to suit her character by bringing about a higher pitch to the dialogue delivery. Even the youthful, high-pitched, playback singing voice of Kavita Krishnamurthy (who sings many of the popular songs picturized on Sridevi) solidifies the childlike aspects of the star persona. The innocent, chaste, infantile quality to her voice, firstly, intensifies her comic, often slapstick, performances; and secondly, beguiles and endears her to audiences as a mischievous child would. This thereby allows her to 'get away' with rambunctious, and often anarchic, comic acts that challenge patriarchal social and gender norms regulating women's behaviour in the public sphere and underpin traditional notions of femininity, middle-class morality and respectability.

Another crucial aspect of the star voice is the use of dubbing, due to her initial difficulty with Hindi, which was occasionally reported in print media (Anon. 1986), trade papers and even acknowledged by herself ('I didn't know much Hindi, so my dialogue had to be dubbed, but now I speak my own lines.' [Ahmed 1989: 19]). One prominent trade journal, *Film Information*, goes into great details about her imperfect Hindi pronunciation and diction:

> The star who hails from South had difficulty speaking the language, as do most of them from the South. It was for this reason that her voice used to be dubbed by ghost voices in the beginning. For a couple of years now, however, Sridevi has herself been dubbing her dialogue. But, the No. 1 perfect heroine has yet to perfect her Hindi ... Next time you watch a Sridevi film, mark at least this defect: She speaks 'ai' as 'a' (as 'ese' instead of 'aise'; 'jese' instead of 'jaise'. (Anon. 1989b)

Ethnic jokes about accented Hindi speakers have been a long established, problematic and perennial source of lowbrow humour and comic stereotypes in a country as linguistically diverse as India. Her heavy 'south Indian' accented Hindi is another source of hilarity for mainstream Hindi film audiences, imparting a distinctively humorous inflection to her voice that differentiated her from other female stars, such as Madhuri Dixit, whom she was often pitted against by the media. Arguably her imperfect Hindi diction and mispronunciation further consolidate her childlike persona as her mistakes are suggestive of an inarticulate child who hasn't learnt how to speak properly.

Another possible explanation for her infantilized persona could be the persistence of the child star in Sridevi's adult roles in popular Hindi cinema, in terms of character, voice and performance. She began her career as a child actress at the age of five in the Tamil film industry, co-starring with the Tamil superstar Sivaji Ganeshan in her debut, *Kandhan Karunai* (Merciful Kandhan, A. P. Nagarajan, 1967) as the child, Muruga (Rajadhyaksha and Willemen [1994] 1999: 392). According to popular film press,

> Sridevi, in fact, [was] a rare product of the cinema – a successful child star-turned-successful heroine. She never had to sit at home getting over that awkward period between adolescence and adulthood. As a child woman, Sridevi was being cast in films like 'Moonru Maduchu,' in which she played a girl in her early teens. (Rajendran 1983: 22)

Sridevi would also be accompanied by her mother on set during film shoots in order to protect her from any possible harassment that she could experience in a predominantly male work space, and it was widely reported in the media that her mother was in charge of her career until her untimely death. Thus, even off screen, she was treated like a child who needed protection from the adult world. To further consolidate my argument, I would like to emphasize how, much like an infant, Sridevi shows little signs of embarrassment on screen; instead she is an uninhibited presence, utterly unselfconscious and carefree. In her words, 'once I go in front of the camera, God knows how, my inhibitions vanish and I feel that I am in a different world' (Ahmed 1989: 23). Billig makes the following observation that:

> Infants do not even show the physiological characteristics of embarrassment, such as blushing … The infant is regularly placed in situations that would be embarrassing to an older child … If embarrassment is a social reaction, then it has to be learnt. Unsocialized infants cannot display appropriate signs of being flustered when behaving in a socially inappropriate manner, because they do not know how to behave in socially appropriate ways. (2005: 221–2)

Her clownish persona reduces her to a joke, and as an infantilized comedienne, her immense potential for subversion is undercut by projecting her as non-threatening to the status quo. If she had not been infantilized by her costume, hairstyle, voice and behaviour, she would have been too provocative, threatening and even off-putting for mainstream Hindi film audiences as her riotous comic routines, song and dance sequences and masquerades would violate the imposed boundaries of social acceptability. As Seideman reminds us, 'the comedian … a modern, secularized variant on the clown, defined as much through personality as through desires–is someone who refuses to or is unable to conform to social expectations and thus becomes a disruptive force in the story world' (Jenkins 2013: 157). Sridevi's infantilized persona contains and sanitizes her boisterous, anarchic gags and uninhibited on-screen behaviour, and makes it acceptable to conservative 1980s Indian audiences who perceive her as a rebellious, mischievous, wild child, bent on breaking social mores and conventions whilst unaware that she is actually transgressing predetermined patriarchal gender norms and expectations. The child behaves inappropriately and indulgent Indian audiences laugh. As Billig observes,

> Children are likely to butt in when they should not, use inappropriate forms of address, speak too loudly, too softly, too directly, mumble too much, and so on … Sometimes … what is forbidden becomes an object of temptation and desire. The child will take delight in breaking the rules. (2005: 205)

Print media discourse

The popular English-language, nationally circulated print media reinforces, as it simultaneously perpetuates, Sridevi's infantilized child-woman persona. A close examination of *Filmfare* (1986 to 1992 issues) and other popular film magazines of the 1980s and 1990s, *Movie* and *Star & Style*, reveal a consistent tendency to emphasize her youthful physiognomy and voice: 'her sex appeal coupled with an innocent face' (Chowdhury 1986: 20); her 'bubbly girlish quality … Sri looks very girlish, no matter what she wears' (the star, Rekha quoted in Anon. 1988: 53); and her 'main advantage […] her baby face' (Taran Adarsh quoted in Anon. 1988: 54). Film critic-turned-director, Khalid Mohamed observes how 'she still has that baby face … [and an] Alice-in-Wonderland vulnerability. She can be a wide-eyed ingénue' (Ahmed 1990: 18). The now-defunct popular film magazine, *Movie*, declares, 'Sridevi, the current No. 1 can be a child, with those saucy, saucer-eyes … The child-adult blend is an "innocent bomb," a combustible combination,' whilst describing her as 'the baby-faced cutie-pie' (Anon. 1989a: 71–2).

In fact, the words 'baby face' and 'child-woman' are the two most repeated epithets in the press discourse on her during the time period under consideration, consolidating the infantilization of Sridevi's public image.[5] This is further reiterated by the star's acknowledgment of such public discourse in a 1992 *Filmfare* interview: 'I know it's said that I have a baby face and a baby voice' (Mohamed 1992: 12). Consider the following *Filmfare* write-up:

> What she has going for her is a *cherubic, bubbling presence* on screen. Plus, there's that uncanny *doll-like ability* to do whatever the director tells. Ask her to shed a tear and she'll deliver a bucket. Ask her to laugh and there'll be *peals of child-like giggles*. Ask her to look angry and those *mesmeric saucer eyes* will drip venom. *Ask her to look vulnerable and she'll crouch her shoulders till you want to run up to the screen and protect her.*
> (Anon. 1987b: 20, emphasis added)

Media discourse on Sridevi's 'naughty roles' (Anon. 1988; Ahmed 1990: 25) repeatedly foreground her infantile star persona and unique performative style, often comparing her to famous Hollywood child stars and comic book characters. She is described as 'rolling her round eyes, pulling a tongue, bouncing around like a happy child …, becoming the Indian version of Lois Lane' (Rajadhyaksha 1987: 39). She is what 'the audience always wants to see a … *chulbuli ladki* [bubbly girl] on the screen' (Mohamed 1992: 11). Sridevi's infantile physiognomy is even compared to the famous American child star, Shirley Temple:

> From a child wonder and girl-woman of the 1970s to the queen of the matinees in the '90s, her career has been unusually long and substantial … Hers may be an angelic, cherubic face that recalls America's precocious scene stealer Shirley Temple. Hers may be a voice with a child's fluting, sing-song rhythm. (10)

Projecting an anarchic yet lovable half-child, half-woman persona who transgresses conventional behavioural norms and expectations of Indian women with her uproarious comic acts, Sridevi was accepted by indulgent mainstream audiences owing to her uncanny ability to unleash the child within her through her infantilized persona, which was shaped by her physiognomy, costume and hairstyle, facial expressions, gestures and body movements, childlike antics and voice.

Sridevi's untimely death on 24 February 2018 elicited a collective outpouring of national grief and mourning on a scale rarely witnessed for an ageing female star in contemporary India, and a prolonged media frenzy that whipped up a maelstrom of salacious gossip and rumour-mongering, and conspiracy theories surrounding the seemingly mysterious circumstances leading to her death by drowning. The astounding and wide-ranging reactions to her tragic demise, particularly from the LGBTQIA community in India, underscored both the uniqueness of her star persona and the fact that crucial dimensions of her stardom, which are beyond the focus and scope of this chapter, remain unexplored in Indian star studies. These are namely the queer, homoerotic affect and auto-eroticism Sridevi expressed through the spaces of her iconic song picturizations and fantasy sequences, which subvert heteronormative, patriarchal regimes; her contributions as a prolific child star in the Tamil and

---

[5] Certain other tropes in the English language film press that coalesce to construct her star image are her superstar status and constant comparison with Amitabh Bachchan; her hyper-sexualized image; her versatility as an actress; her imperfect Hindi and need for dubbing; and her flair for comedy, which is surprisingly a mere subtext in press coverage of her polysemic stardom.

Telugu film industries; and considerations on how posthumous fame prompts a revisionist appraisal of a career that spanned, over five decades, the many linguistic cinemas of India.

Works Cited

Ahmed, R. (1989), *Filmfare*, 38 (4): 18–25.

Ahmed, R. (1990), 'The Greatest', *Filmfare*, 39 (8): 17–27.

Anon. (1986), 'Sridevi often has her voice dubbed', *Filmfare*.

Anon. (1987a), 'Rekha: My Favourite', *Filmfare,* 36 (14), 16 July.

Anon. (1987b), 'Sridevi: Devastating', *Filmfare*, 36 (5): 17–21.

Anon. (1988), 'Impressions …', *Filmfare*, 37 (10), 16 May.

Anon. (1989a), 'The Stuff Women Are Made of: Steel, Scandal, Sex Appeal', *Movie*, 1 September, pp. 71–2.

Anon. (1989b), 'Sridevi's Hindi', *Film Information*, 17 (2).

Anon. (1992), 'Sridevi: The Last Empress?', *Filmfare*, 41 (2): 31–6.

Bakhtin, Mikhail (1984), *Rabelais and His World*, trans. Hélène Iswolsky, Bloomington: Indiana University Press.

Basu, Anustup (2013), 'The Face that Launched a Thousand Ships: Helen and Public Femininity in Hindi Film', in Meheli Sen and Anustup Basu (eds), *Figurations in Indian Film*, 139–57, Basingstoke: Palgrave Macmillan.

Billig, Michael (2005), 'Embarrassment, Humour and the Social Order', *Laughter and Ridicule: Towards a Social Critique of Humor*, 200–35, London: Sage.

Chatterjee, Saibal (2003), 'Comedy: Laughter and Comic Relief', in Gulzar, Govind Nihalani and Saibal Chatterjee (eds), *Encyclopaedia of Hindi CinemaI*, 339–53, New Delhi: Encyclopaedia Britannica (India) and Mumbai: Popular Prakashan.

Chion, Michel (1999), *The Voice in Cinema*, trans. Claudia Gorbman, New York: Columbia University Press.

Chowdhury, A. (1986), 'Is the Best Good Enough?', *Filmfare*, 35 (4): 20.

Doane, Mary Ann (1980), 'The Voice in the Cinema: The Articulation of Body and Space', *Yale French Studies*, 60: 33–50.

Gandhy, Behroze and Rosie Thomas (1991), 'Three Indian Film Stars', in Christine Gledhill (ed.) *Stardom: Industry of Desire*, 107–31, London: Routledge.

Gopalan, Lalitha (2002), *Cinema of Interruptions: Action Genres in Contemporary Indian Cinema*, London: British Film Institute.

Greenbaum, A. (1997), 'Women's Comic Voices: The Art and Craft of Female Humor', *American Studies*, 38 (1): 117–38.

Jahagirdar-Saxena, S. (1989), 'Pankaj Parasher: "The Press Doesn't Matter!"', *Filmfare*, 38 (6): 37.

Jenkins, Henry (2013), 'Mel Brooks, Vulgar Modernism, and Comic Remediation', in Andrew Horton and Joanna E. Rapf (eds), *A Companion to Film Comedy*, 151–71, Malden, MA: Wiley-Blackwell Publishing.

Majumdar, Neepa (2003), 'Doubling, Stardom, and Melodrama in Indian Cinema: The "Impossible" Role of Nargis', *Postscript*, 22 (3): 89–103.

Majumdar, Neepa (2009), *Wanted Cultured Ladies Only! Female Stardom and Cinema in India, 1930s–1950s*, Urbana: University of Illinois Press.

Mohamed, K. (1992), 'Sridevi: Dangerous', *Filmfare*, 41 (12): 9–13.

Rajadhyaksha, Ashish and Paul Willemen, eds ([1994] 1999), *Encyclopaedia of Indian Cinema*, Rev. edn, London: British Film Institute; New Delhi: Oxford University Press.

Rajendran, G. (1983), 'Two Girls in a Photo-finish', *Filmfare*, 32 (16): 22.

Seidman, Steve (1981), *Comedian Comedy: A Tradition in Hollywood Film*, Ann Arbor, MI: UMI Research.

Rajadhyaksha, G. (1987), 'Sridevi: Out of Reach?' *Filmfare*, 36 (2): 39–45.

Thomas, Rosie (2005), 'Not Quite (Pearl) White: Fearless Nadia, Queen of the Stunts', in Raminder Kaur and Ajay J. Sinha (eds), *Bollyworld: Popular Indian Cinema Through a Transnational Lens*, 35–69, New Delhi: Sage.

Virdi, Jyotika (2003), *The Cinematic ImagiNation: Indian Popular Films as Social History*, New Brunswick, NJ: Rutgers University Press.

Wagner, Kristen Anderson (2013), 'Pie Queens and Virtuous Vamps: The Funny Women of the Silent Screen', in Andrew Horton and Joanna. E. Rapf (eds), *A Companion to Film Comedy*, 39–60, Malden, MA: Wiley-Blackwell Publishing.

Chapter 14

The irresistible badness of Salman Khan

Shohini Ghosh

On 10 September 2010, my friend and I, as was our practice, went to see the new Salman Khan film on its first day of release. The film was *Dabanng* and it had been released on a Friday that was expected to be Eid but turned out to be Jamat-ul-vida (the last Friday before Eid). The theatre was packed. Several rows looked more prominent than others because they had been occupied by boys in white caps and kurtas who had come straight from the Friday prayers. When Salman Khan made his entry, the theatre exploded with thunderous applause. The crowd whistled and clapped and the boys with white caps danced in the aisles. The exhilaration of the moment reminded me of a friend's description of watching a Salman Khan film in the old city of Hyderabad during Moharram: 'You should have seen the way they cheered when he came on the screen,' he had said. 'You would think a Messiah had arrived.'

The fame and notoriety of Salman Khan

Salman Khan is arguably Bollywood's most controversial star. To admit to being a fan of Salman – especially if one is a feminist and to all appearances reasonable – is to elicit astonishment and disbelief. While the star, along with Aamir and Shah Rukh Khan, has been part of Bollywood's ruling triumvirate exerting tremendous command over the box office and their expansive fan bases, it is commonly assumed that Salman-starrers cater primarily to the 'substratum of the urban lumpen and working-class male audiences', pejoratively described as the 'lowest common denominator' (Sen 2013: 12). The ripped, muscular body of Salman – an object of much veneration by his fans – is confirmation for many that his star appeal has more to do with brawn than brain. 'The ridicule directed at bodybuilding,' observes Yvonne Tasker, 'stems in part from the ambiguous status of the musculature in question'; for some critics, muscles are merely 'non-functional decoration' (1993: 78, citing Louvre and Walsh 1988: 96). The locus of deep ambiguities, the star text of Salman Khan is created as much by his on-screen performances as his off-screen reputation. This chapter is an attempt to understand the possible reasons why, among his legion of fans, Salman Khan has a special affiliation to the subaltern Muslim.

On 6 May 2015, a Bombay Sessions Court found Salman Khan guilty of culpable homicide and sentenced him to five years' rigorous imprisonment for a drunken driving incident in 2002, in which his Land Cruiser ran over sleeping pavement dwellers, killing one and injuring others.¹ On the same day, the High Court granted him a suspension of sentence (interim bail) pending appeal.² The verdict provoked an impassioned and polarized debate. Industry professionals expressed their sympathy for Salman while most commentators in the mainstream media criticized the star for using his privileged status to get speedy bail. Regardless of their opinion of the star, almost all TV channels devoted the day to the unfolding events. 'TV news kept its promise to give viewers carpet coverage of the verdict relegating all else,' wrote media critic Shailaja Bajpai, who criticized the 'excessive coverage' as being characterized by 'incoherence, sensationalism, melodrama, creative journalism and questionable new priorities' (2015: 14). The media event around Salman Khan was no less notable for the fan frenzy on display. Thousands gathered at his house and on the premises of the court, and lined the stretch of road that lay between the two. Hundreds had travelled from various parts of India to be with 'Bhaijaan' when the courts delivered their judgement. As the news of the interim bail spread, the crowds whose spirits had been dampened by the verdict went into a frenzy of celebration.

Despite his popularity, Salman Khan has remained throughout his two-and-a-half-decade long career, the enfant terrible of Bombay cinema. Reporting on the car accident in 2002, *Outlook* magazine wrote:

> It's very easy to hate Salman Khan. Even within the industry, the 37-year old compulsive chest-barer isn't too popular. Former girlfriend Somy Ali had to suffer the indignity of having a drink poured over her head at a restaurant. His most recent ex, actress Aishwarya Rai, has even gone public about his abusive behaviour … In the past Salman has even tried to barge into her apartment, rammed into her car on a film set and even abused her co-stars. (Kakodkar 2002)

The annals of cyberspace are replete with stories about his fits of violence, unpredictable mood swings and criminal cases for drunken driving and poaching endangered animals. Notwithstanding the dark side of Salman Khan, the star's box office saleability and devoted fan base is unshakeable. In 2006, *Filmfare* wrote:

> What's more, the personal controversies just don't seem to stick on screen or off it. In fact, his bad boy image imbues him with a recklessness that both sexes seem to find attractive. And his many friends in the industry swear allegiance to him as fervently as his fans do.³

---

¹On 28 September 2002, a car allegedly driven by the actor rammed into the American Express Bakery in Bandra killing one person and injuring four others. Salman reportedly fled the scene. His lawyers have argued that the car was not being driven by him and nor did he flee the scene. In 2002, he was charged under Section 304 (I) of the IPC for 'causing death through rash and negligent driving'. In 2013 the Mumbai court ordered a retrial under the non-bailable section 304 of the IPC for 'culpable homicide not amounting to murder'. He also faces criminal charges for allegedly poaching a blackbuck, an endangered animal, during the shooting of *Hum Saath Saath Hain* in 1998. Khan's lawyers maintain a website providing information about the cases: www.salmankhanfiles.com/files/ (accessed 24 March 2015).

²Khan was sentenced to five years' rigorous imprisonment under IPC 304 (II) for culpable homicide not amounting to murder, one year's simple imprisonment (SI) for causing grievous hurt, three months' SI for minor injuries, two months' SI for failing to give data about his driving license, six months' SI for drunk driving and two months' SI for not carrying his license. The sentences are to run concurrently. Salman Khan appealed to the Mumbai High Court, which, on 10 December 2015, acquitted him of all charges. An emotional Salman Khan broke down as the verdict was announced. In response to a petition filed by the Maharashtra government, the Supreme Court directed the actor to respond to the appeal and issued notice that the final decision on the matter would be delivered by the Supreme Court.

³*Filmfare*, February 2006, p. 66.

Salman Khan began his career as the romantic lead in the smash-hit *Maine Pyar Kiya* (Sooraj Barjatya, 1989) and, over the next two-and-a-half decades, consolidated his superstardom with eighty-nine films (excluding guest appearances) out of which sixteen are 'all time blockbusters', and thirteen are classified as 'hits' or 'semi-hits'. After *Maine Pyar Kiya,* Salman acted in a series of flops but managed to maintain, through the decade, an average of three or four releases every year. By the mid-to-late 1990s, the star was ruling the box office, especially in the B and C centres.[4]

The premier Bollywood film magazine *Filmfare*, whose covers through the 1990s were dominated by Shah Rukh Khan, was slow to acknowledge Salman's success. The December 2003 issue of *Filmfare* listed the ten most powerful people in the industry, with Amitabh Bachchan and Shah Rukh jointly occupying the first position and Aamir the second. Salman was absent from the list (Anon. 2003). In 2004, he made his entry on to the power list and occupied the seventh position. In 2005 he moved up to the fifth slot and *Filmfare* wrote:

> Sometimes numbers don't tell the whole story. They don't tell you for instance that Salman Khan has more mass appeal than the other two Khans. Not only does he have a huge audience overseas and in the multiplexes, he is a much larger draw at the B and C centres as well. That's what makes any Salman Khan film a decent bet. Even better, he needs no big banners or hotshot directors, he can manage his own. Thank you. (Anon. 2005: 66)

The same issue ranked him fourth in the list of the industry's top ten actors after Shah Rukh Khan, Amitabh Bachchan and Aamir Khan. Even though Salman had starred in more flops than Shah Rukh or Aamir, he maintained an overall success of 56.06 per cent.

In 2009, Salman Khan's career took a sharp upward swing with the blockbuster *Wanted* (Prabhu Deva), followed by the stupendous success of *Dabanng* (The Fearless, Abhinav Kashyap, 2010), a film that converted a large section of the more elite multiplex audience into Salman fans. *Outlook* reported:

> Despite his unquestionable star appeal, box office clout and exclusive membership of the Khan trinity, Salman has been largely sidelined as the B and C centre hero, the one loved by the masses and inconsequential for the classes. But the resounding success of *Dabanng* changed everything. An action-comedy set in the rural badlands, *Dabanng* was not only a sensation in Salman Khan's traditional fan base but also captured the imagination of the urban middle classes who were prone to deride Salman-starrers as lacking 'class' and 'taste'. (Joshi 2010)

In an interview with *Tehelka Magazine*, Salman described *Dabanng* as a 'sten-gun assault on the polite multiplex crowd' who he hoped would 'whistle and dance on the chairs', which is precisely what they did (Chaudhary 2010). Reeling under the shock of *Dabanng*'s success, national weeklies such as *Outlook, India Today, Tehelka* and *Brunch*

---

[4]The industry categorizes exhibition centres as A, B and C class centres on the basis of market size, often measured in terms of the population of the place and its purchasing power. Geographically, B and C refer to non-metropolitan centres that are characterized by poor infrastructure, lower pricing of tickets and low levels of investment. The profile of B and C centres are rapidly changing. Since the multiplex economy is reaching a point of saturation in the A centres, the next phase of growth is expected to come from tier 2 and tier 3 cities. The box office income is expected to accrue from multiplexes in mall properties. See FICCI-KMG report 2015, online at: www.kpmg.com/IN/en/IssuesAndInsights/ArticlesPublications/Documents/FICCI-KPMG_2015.pdf.

carried, for the first time, cover stories on the star. The success of these two films were followed by *Bodyguard* (Siddique, 2011), *Dabanng 2* (The Fearless Returns, Arbaaz Khan, 2012), *Ek Tha Tiger* (Once There Was a Tiger, Kabir Khan, 2013), each of which crossed the 100 crore mark.[5] Made with a budget of 80 crore and shot over several international locations, *Ek Tha Tiger* swept both Salman-strongholds and multiplex audiences. At the time of its release, it was Salman's most expensive and profitable film. The following year, *Kick* (Sajid Nadiadwala, 2014) earned 165 crores in the first week and over 300 crores by the end of the fourth week. With an estimated annual income of 244 crore rupees, Salman Khan is today Bollywood's most saleable star and the undisputed hero of both the 'masses' and the 'classes' (Lall 2015) (Figure 14.1).

How is Salman Khan's stardom distinct from that of Shah Rukh Khan and Aamir Khan? Unlike the other two, Salman, until very recently, seldom worked with top directors or big banners and has been as willing to work with unknown heroines as with known ones. Shah Rukh Khan started his career playing dark and unconventional roles in films such as *Baazigar* (The Risk-taker, Abbas-Mastaan, 1993) and *Darr* (Yash Chopra, 1993) – parts that were originally turned down by Salman Khan and Aamir Khan, respectively – and *Anjaam* (Consequences, Rahul Rawail, 1994) but, after the meteoric success of *Dilwale Dulhaniya Le Jayenge* (The Brave Hearted Will Win the Bride, Aditya Chopra, 1995) and *Kuch Kuch Hota Hai* (Something Happens, Karan Johar, 1998), has largely worked around his romantic image (the exceptions being Farhan Akhtar's *Don* [2006] and

Figure 14.1 Salman Khan. Getty Images.

Don 2 [2011]). Through his films and countless endorsements for high-end products, Shah Rukh Khan has been a lifestyle icon for upward mobility and self-made success. His biographer, Anupama Chopra writes:

> A leading monitoring firm called the Agency Source (TAS) tabulated that between 1994 and 2006, Shah Rukh appeared in 281 print ads and 172 television commercials. In 2005 alone, he endorsed approximately 34 different products. Shah Rukh was the ubiquitous symbol and conduit for the new consumerist society. (2007:160)

---

[5] At the time of its release, *Ek Tha Tiger* held the record for the highest single day collection (32.92 crore) and the highest opening day collection (32.92 crore). The worldwide gross for the films has crossed 330 crores. In India net collections are about 198 crores rupees and the distributor share from the Indian box office stood at 105 crores rupees (Figures provided by Kabir Khan on 12 September 2012).

After Shah Rukh Khan it was Aamir Khan who was paid handsomely for endorsing brand names. An exceptionally talented performer and innovator, Aamir Khan has been a steady favourite of the urban multiplex audiences. His successful TV show *Satyamev Jayate* (Truth Alone Prevails, Star, 2012–) consolidated his position as an inspirational brand ambassador for corporate social responsibility. Both Aamir Khan and Shah Rukh Khan are commendable icons for an aspirational, post-liberalization generation spread across India and the diaspora. They belong, in the words of Ranjani Mazumdar to the 'experience of a new delirium of urban life' that is related to the new frenzy of urban consumption (2007: xxii, xxi). Salman has walked a different route. As his success in the B and C centres demonstrate, a very large slice of his traditional fan base comprises non-metropolitan subalterns for whom the changes unleashed by the forces of globalization did not accrue immediate benefits and who matter little to the multiplex economy. Provincial towns, suburban areas, urban slums and *mohallas* are spaces where Salman reigns. Called 'the king of single screens', Salman's stardom is located along the underbelly of the very landscape over which Shah Rukh Khan and Aamir Khan reign (Anon. 2012).

Salman Khan's superstardom has relied on his versatility with romance, comedy and action and the large majority of his early successes are romantic comedies that served to display the star's gym-toned body and excellent comic timing. Yet, paradoxically, were we to consider the actor's most popular images in circulation – whether in cyberspace or sold as posters on the streets – the star text is inextricable from the aura of the action hero. If numbers were any indication, then out of the eighty-nine films that he has acted in his action films would amount to only a handful and would include *Baaghi: A Rebel for Love* (Deepak Shivdasani, 1990), *Jaagruti* (The Awakening, Suresh Krishna, 1992), *Veergati* (Martyrdom, K. K. Singh, 1995*), Karan Arjun* (Rakesh Roshan, 1995), *Jeet* (The Victory, Raj Kanwar, 1996), *Auzaar* (The Weapon, Sohail Khan, *1997), Tumko Na Bhool Payenge* (Never Will I Forget You, Pankaj Parashar, 2002), *Garv: Pride and Honour* (Puneet Issar, 2004), *Tere Naam* (In Your Name, Satish Kaushik, 2003), *Lucky: No Time for Love* (2005), *Wanted* (Prabhu Deva, 2009), *Dabanng* (2010), *Bodyguard* (2011), *Ek Tha Tiger* (2012), *Dabanng 2* (2012), *Jai Ho* (Long Live, Sohail Khan, 2014) and *Kick* (Sajid Nadiadwala, 2014). The diegetic universe of Salman Khan action films are affiliated to the films of crime and action, the majority of which are gangster films. The violence and terror of the worlds of these films invoke a sense of dystopic exile and entrapment within the city that stands in contrast to the utopic worlds inaugurated by the urban romance and family films.[6] Delineating exhaustively the cinematic city of the gangster films, Ranjani Mazumdar contends that these films present us 'with an alternative topography, an alternative community, and an alternative urban consciousness' (Mazumdar 2007:151). This 'informal city' of the gangster films, where 'chase sequences are deployed to navigate the density of the city' public spaces, comprise of 'alleys, claustrophobic hutments, docks', 'abandoned factory sites' and 'half-constructed buildings' (160). Prior to *Ek Tha Tiger*, the protagonist played by Salman in his action films is most frequently a

---

[6]Bollywood action films are unique in their deep entrenchment within a melodramatic mode where action and emotions are inextricable. Consequently, action films are frequently propelled by narratives of attachment – to friends, lovers, parents, siblings or a cause. Because of his consecutive successes with action films, fans often ask Salman why he has stopped acting in 'romantic films', to which his reply is that all his action films are also romance films. The inextricability of action and romance are often signalled by titles such as *Baaghi: A Rebel in Love* and *Lucky: No Time for Love*.

subaltern from the urban underclass, who inhabits this 'informal city' and whose 'basic resource of survival' and most potent arsenal is his personal body (Biswas 2013: 237).

The master trope of Salman Khan's stardom is his ripped and six-packed muscular body. Both action and romantic melodramas starring Salman are designed to display the body of the star, in particular his famous torso. The much-awaited moment in a Salman Khan film is when his shirt comes off for a fight or song sequence. A recurrent trope fashioned over many films, this moment has acquired a cultic popularity. The aesthetic contemplation, as it were, of Salman Khan's torso, travels across different films creating a rhizomatic, intertextual relay where romantic melodramas merge with action films to create an archive of the spectacular star body.

Salman Khan and the Muslim

The cusp of the new millennium witnessed heightened communalization as Hindu Right forces consolidated political power following the demolition of Babri Masjid. Muslims were cast as unreliable citizens whose loyalties were perpetually in doubt. The anxiety suffered by the ordinary Muslim – randomly targeted for interrogation, torture and incarceration merely on the basis of suspicion – found reflection, as it were, in the unpredictable vicissitudes that beset Salman Khan. Like Sanjay Dutt before him, Salman was sent to jail, brought to trial and never declared innocent. Despite urban legends about his generosity and philanthropic work, Salman, even at the best of times, walks a risky tightrope. The shadow of crime and the possibility of punishment persist like shadows. There is no telling when he will slip and fall from the Olympian heights of superstardom into the dark crevasse of notoriety. In an interview, he confessed

to admiring heroes who are able to come back from the edge, after being vanquished, to reclaim their respect and dignity (Chopra 2015: 80). This could well be an analogy for the star himself who, after every crisis, manages to rise from the ashes. Salman's ability to survive in adversity may explain why among his legion of fans, the underprivileged Muslims form a devoted constituency. It was this very constituency that more recently was angry and disappointed when Salman Khan made peace with Narendra Modi (now prime minister of India), widely believed to have been responsible for the genocide of Muslims in Gujarat, 2002. In February 2014, journalist Syed Firdaus Ashraf wrote that Salman's new film *Jai Ho* (Sohail Khan, 2014) failed at the box office because disappointed Muslim fans had boycotted the film in protest against his softened stance in favour of Modi. Ashraf writes:

> Not only did Salman Khan call on Modi in Gandhinagar on the eve of the release of his *Jai Ho*, but also dined with him, apart from flying kites, during Makar Sankranti. He also described Modi as a 'good man,' and followed it up with an interview where he said that since the judiciary had given Modi a clean chit why should he apologise for the Gujarat riots? (2014)

Ashraf writes that that the Urdu press, which rarely reports on Bollywood news, commented extensively on this. Majlis-e-Ittehadul Muslimeen leader Asaduddin Owaisi appealed to Muslims to boycott *Jai Ho*. The community's disillusionment with the star seemed to have impacted the box office. According to Ashraf it was clear that '*Jai Ho*'s opening weekend collections did not reflect the usual fan frenzy of a Salman Khan film'.

> The collections say it all. More than a week after its release *Jai Ho* has huffed and puffed its way past Rs 100 crore collections, while *Dabangg 2* (December 2012) did a business of Rs 158.5

crores; *Ek Tha Tiger* (August 2012) earned Rs 198 crores. Even the middling *Ready* (June 2011) did Rs 125 crores. (Ashraf 2014)

Urdu newspapers happily declared that Salman had paid the price for supporting Modi. While obviously not all his fans are Muslims, Ashraf believes that, among the Khan triumvirate, Salman is closest to the community. A barbershop in a Muslim neighbourhood, he says, is bound to have Salman posters on display. While Shah Rukh's posters are occasionally present, Aamir is largely absent despite his unquestionable box office status. 'But Salman', writes Ashraf, 'will reign over the dingy space in the splendour of his hairstyles and clothes' (2014).

Ashraf further argues that Muslims constituted a critical mass for single-screen theatres and therefore no big film would be released during Ramzan, the month of abstinence for Muslims (ibid.). Yet, writes Ashraf, the Eid that follows Ramzan has almost entirely been claimed by Salman Khan.

During Eid, when most of his films are released, there is a heightened circulation of Salman Khan's photographs. A prominently displayed photo-shopped poster in Old Delhi shows Salman Khan wearing a white prayer cap and keffiyeh holding a *tasbi* (prayer beads) in his hands. The star's special affiliation to multiple constituencies of Muslim viewers has evolved through chance, accident and intuition as well as the off-screen circumstances through which his on-screen persona began to be understood. And since no fan base is ever homogeneous, Salman Khan's films address a diversity of spectatorial positions within this constituency. Consider, for instance the invocation of multiple subject positions in *Dabanng*. By simultaneously splitting and merging the star/Salman Khan with his on-screen character/Chulbul Pandey, the pious festivities of Eid are inoffensively reconciled with on-screen celebrations where the hero rouses the small-town police force with the twin intoxication of what is prohibited in orthodox Islam: music and alcohol. 'The lyrics do not specify what is being drunk', laugh music directors Sajid-Wajid in the 'The Making of *Dabanng*', 'but those who like their drink, will greatly enjoy the song'. In other sequences, 'Muslimness' is mapped onto the *mise en scène* through locations, property, architecture and the aesthetics of clothing; for example, the song-sequence for 'Sach, sachi tere nazrein', which was shot in Dubai and Abu Dhabi. Such cultural signifiers are recognized easily by Salman Khan's huge following in South Asia and the Middle East.

To suggest that Salman Khan has a special appeal to Muslims is not to argue that his success is confined only to Muslims. The documentary *Being Bhaijaan* (Shabani Hassanwala and Samreen Farooqui, 2014) is about three Hindu boys and their followers who have dedicated their lives to the worship of Salman Khan. Despite his strong personal identification with Islam, his star persona seamlessly reconciles a number of religious and cultural identities both on and off screen. His deep attachment to his multireligious family, known for celebrating Eid and Ganesh Chaturthi with equal gusto, is an integral part of his star discourse. *Hindustan Times* reported: 'In this modern Muslim home, Hinduism, Islam and Christianity co-exist happily, thanks to the efforts of the Marathi Brahmin Salma Khan (originally Sushila Charak) her husband Salim Khan and his second wife Helen who is a Catholic' (Ahmed 2012). 'I feel blessed to be born and brought up in a house that respects every religion', says Salman, 'In *Galaxy* [the building where he and his family live] God is one, though our paths to reach the almighty are different' (Ahmed 2012). On *Aap ki Adaalat*, 6 September 2006, Salman tells show-host Rajat Sharma 'My mother is Hindu, my father is Muslim, my second mother is Catholic, so *hum*

Hindustan hai (we are India)'. In Bollywood, a cosmopolitan appeal is common to all superstars, but for Muslims, the lure of Salman Khan could well be enmeshed with the many conundrums of living in a culturally diverse society where real and imagined erotic desires frequently exceed the limits of social prescriptions.

It may be of interest to the cinephile to note that in an industry where the normative male protagonist has usually been Hindu, Salman was the first among the three Khans to play the role of an on-screen Muslim in *Sanam Bewafa* (Treacherous Lover, Saawan Kumar Tak, 1991) followed, more significantly, by *Tumko Na Bhool Payenge*. In *Saawariyan* (The Beloved, Sanjay Leela Bhansali, 2007), the character of Iman (played by Salman Khan) is introduced in silhouette offering *namaz* in pouring rain, framed against the contours of a mosque. The image is chromatically striking and painterly. In *Sultan* (2016), Salman Khan plays the eponymous Muslim hero, a beloved and unbeatable wrestling champion. At a time when Islamic cultural markers were considered suspect, the characters played by Salman Khan in films such as *Tumko Na Bhool Payenge* and *Garv: Pride and Honour* were creating a space for the expression of dissent.

In *Garv: Pride and Honour* Salman Khan plays Arjun Ranawat, an honest cop who believes that 'traitors have no religion' and who strongly endorses 'encounter killings' as the best way to eliminate criminality. For Arjun, criminality and corruption are not endemic to outliers but embedded within the state and legal system. The ostensible enemy is Pakistan but, as Ranawat repeatedly shows, the enemies of the country are everywhere and occupy the highest echelons of power. When his conscientious colleague Haider Ali (played by Salman's brother Arbaaz Khan) is transferred on the grounds that Muslims cannot be trusted to fight their brethren, Arjun takes his protest to the highest authorities. In a scene that dramatically mobilizes the cinematic conventions of Bombay cinema, Arjun condemns as 'unconstitutional' the reprehensible 'communal' mindset that had effectively alienated thousands of young Muslims.

A more allegorical dissension plays out in *Tumko Na Bhool Payenge*, a 'puzzle film' with an intricate emplotment (of which certain elements are clearly inspired by *The Long Kiss Goodnight* [Renny Harlin, 1996]). Veer Pratap Singh (Salman Khan) is the only son of Thakur Pratap Singh, a feudal landowner, engaged to marry his fiancée, Muskaan (Diya Mirza). Veer's happy and idyllic life starts getting disrupted when unexplained hallucinatory visions keep appearing from another life. In one of his visions, he is attacked by a huge wolf-like dog while in another he sees himself, or a phantom double, being chased. As these visions keep intruding into his life, he begins to suspect that there is more to his past then he can remember. He asks those around him to help him fill the gaps. His parents, lover and friends provide explanations but each version is different. His body, so lovingly nurtured by his parents, carries scars of injuries whose history of infliction seems lost. One day a crisis precipitates a series of incidents during which Veer is seen to possess lethal fighting skills for which he has no memory of ever being trained. Finally, Pratap Singh is compelled to tell Veer the truth about his arrival into their family. Veer, he says, is not their biological son but had come to them, three years back, wounded and unconscious. When he revived, he could not remember his past. Having just lost their own son, the couple eagerly embraced him as their own. An unsettled Veer takes permission from his parents to set out in search of his lost history.

When Veer gets off the train in Bombay, he is gripped by a sense of déjà vu and uncanny familiarity. He runs into people who recognize him but he cannot remember them. The police seem to be hunting for him but he has no idea why. As he unsurely navigates the unknown landscape of the city he hears the *azaan*. What follows is perhaps one of the most striking sequences in the film. As Veer follows the *azaan* into the Masjid, he finds his body enacting a sequence of rehearsed and familiar gestures; washing his hands and feet as part of the ritual ablutions and, as the camera moves around him in a circular track, covering his head with a handkerchief. The dynamism of the camera comes to a halt as he kneels down to pray. The camera, now still and contemplative, observes him in close-up as he rediscovers each bodily ritual gesture. In a sequence comprising mid-shots and close-ups that separate Veer from the other supplicants, a routine collective ritual becomes an introspective personal journey into the lost labyrinth of the past. The practised enactments of the body become the first step to accessing the hidden recesses of a forgotten history. Veer sends up a prayer: 'You have told me what I am, now tell me who I am'.

The puzzle is yet unsolved. As he steps out of the mosque a young boy calls him 'Ali Bhaijaan' and embraces him affectionately when suddenly he is shot dead by an unidentified assassin. As his past starts unravelling in fragments we learn that Veer is Ali, a hired hitman whose closest friends and comrades were his girlfriend Mahek (Sushmita Sen) and his friend Inder (Inder Kumar). The young teenager who dies in front of him is his beloved younger brother Azaan. They had been orphaned in childhood and Ali had brought him up like a son. Now he was dead and Ali had not even recognized him. But the police are still after him. As they give him chase, Ali runs along a rail track and jumps onto a moving train. As he enters the compartment, the visitations return, first as flashes, then more coherently and finally play out in front of him like a seamless film leading up to the final moment of remembrance: the betrayal by Inder, his trusted friend and business partner. Selling out to a political coterie for a large sum of money, Inder frames Ali on a false assassination charge. When Ali tries to flee in order to escape the police, Inder traps him on a train, shoots five bullets into him and lets him fall into the river. Inder goes back and marries Ali's girlfriend, Mehak. The past unfolds like a film. As one Ali watches, Inder pushes the other out of the door. As the train hurtles across a high bridge over a river, we watch Ali's body in freefall. The affective charge of the 'betrayal' sequence is intensified through rendering the images dreamlike and painterly. Ali, who watches the images unfold in the dark compartment, is framed by noiresque lighting while the betrayal of his phantom double unfolds through a grainy sepia-tone, rendered unreal through canted close-ups.

Inder's treachery is not only the pivot around which the narrative unfolds but also the locus of the film's affective charge. For this unexpected and terrible betrayal, Ali avenges himself. Deploying his muscular body as resistive shield and retaliatory weapon, he destroys all those who were complicit with Inder's treachery. Having avenged himself, he returns, to live with his adoptive family. Embracing Pratap Singh he says, 'My name is Ali and I am a Muslim'. Pratap Singh pushes him away angrily: 'How dare you bring religion between a father and son? Is this what I have taught you?' Overcome with emotion, Ali embraces his father who says, 'You are my son. That's all'. The father–son embrace at the end of the film is a moment of utopic reconciliation in dystopic times. By allowing the cinematic reconciliation to be made on the terms laid down by the Muslim protagonist, the film allows an exilic community to wrest back its desires and aspirations from the debris of majoritarian prejudice. A parable of intimate betrayal and retaliation *Tumko Na Bhool Payenge* is an allegorical assertion that there can be no peace without justice.

The accessibility of films on the internet has altered the chronology of watching films. Notwithstanding their dates of release, all films are now available for streaming at all times. *Tumko Na Bhool Payenge* did average business when it was released but is, over the years, gaining currency among Salman cinephiles who keep revisiting the actor's older films. Yet, the significance of the film is intimately tied to the moment of its release. Elaborating on how Deleuze understood history, Richard Rushton argues that 'films can express certain things during certain historical periods that they cannot during other historical periods' (2012: 7). *Tumko Na Bhool Payenge* was released on 22 February 2002, just five days before the Godhra train incident that became the trigger for the state-wide carnage that killed several hundred Muslims. The pogrom rode on the back of an aggressive campaign by Hindutva groups to build a Ram temple in Ayodhya, in the very place where the Babri Masjid once stood (see Varadarajan 2002). It was during this dark and foreboding lead-up to the Gujarat Genocide that posters of the film started appearing across the city. Pegged heavily as an Eid release and featuring a celebratory Eid Mubarak song, the pre-publicity itself became, in that moment, a mark of resistive cultural assertion.

Conclusion

What is the lure of the star text? Through her research on the modelling industry, Elizabeth Wissinger effectively demonstrates that affective responses are hard to articulate coherently or even at all. Thus 'an image can have an effect that does not necessarily correspond to its meaning or without meaning anything in particular to the viewing subject that it affects' (2007: 236–7).

The body of Salman Khan, where desire and apprehension collide in equal measure, affects his detractors and fans differently and in ways that are frequently conflicted and ideologically inconsistent. For his detractors, the body of Salman Khan is always on the brink of violence, leaving in its reckless trail the death of sleeping pavement dwellers and endangered animals. For his fans, the body of the star is a protean object of aesthetic delight and, more affectively, an embodiment of impossible dreams.

The eponymous 'Tiger' (Salman Khan) of *Ek Tha Tiger*, is an Indian spy who, during an international mission, falls in love with his Pakistani counterpart (Katrina Kaif). For the entire length of the film, Tiger's religious identity is left ambivalent. When, at the end of the film, the associations of a 'traitor' and an 'anti-national' begin to coalesce around the figure of Tiger, he is revealed to be a Hindu, thereby throwing into disarray commonplace assumptions about religions and nationalisms. Moreover, the denouement of the film liberates narratives of Indo-Pak romance from privileging one country over another. Breaking the established convention of the lovers heading for the home and country of the male protagonist as in *Tere Pyar Mein* (For Your Love, Hassan Askari, 2000), *Gadar Ek Prem Katha* (The Turbulence: A Love Story, Anil Sharma, 2001) and the more gentle *Veer-Zaara* (Yash Chopra, 2004), the lovers in *Ek Tha Tiger* turn their backs on both countries and make the world their home. In the Eid blockbuster *Bajrangi Bhaijaan* (Brother Bajrangi, Kabir Khan, 2015), Salman plays the role of 'Bajrangi', an acolyte of the monkey god Hanuman, who undertakes the arduous mission of escorting a lost six-year-old Muslim girl back to her parents in Pakistan.[7] The journey transforms

---

[7] For a discussion of Bajrangi Bhaijaan read http://thewire.in/2015/07/24/in-bajrangi-bhaijaan-hindutva-meets-its-nemesis-right-at-home-7159/.

Bajrangi, whose growing attachment to the child leads him to enter spaces that would be anathema to a devout Hindu. The film is a utopian fable about Hindu–Muslim/Indo–Pak friendship unravelling through the crossing of forbidden bodies. One more time, the body of Salman Khan becomes the affective landscape across which utopian reconciliations unravel.

Works Cited

Ahmed, Afsana (2012), 'In Sallu's house, God is One', 20 September, online at: www.hindustantimes.com/chandigarh/in-sallu-s-home-god-is-one/article1-932829.aspx (accessed 16 June 2015).

Anon. (2003), 'The Power List: Who Rules the Dream Factory?', *Filmfare*, 52 (12), December: 32–50.

Anon. (2005), 'The Filmfare Power List 2005', *Filmfare*, 55 (2), February: 55–82.

Anon. (2012), 'Salman's gift to all single-screen theatre staff', 12 July, online at: www.indiatvnews.com/entertainment/bollywood/salman-khan-gift-to-all-single-screen-theatre-staff-4609.html (accessed 16 June 2015).

Ashraf, Syed Firdaus (2014), 'Why Salman Khan's Muslim Fans Are Angry', 3 February, online at: www.rediff.com/movies/column/why-salman-khans-muslim-fans-are-angry/20140203.htm (accessed 16 June 2015).

Bajpai, Shailaja (2015), 'Telescope: Breathless over Salman', *India Express*, 7 May, online at: http://indianexpress.com/article/opinion/columns/telescope-breathless-over-salman/ (accessed 16 June 2015).

Biswas, Moinak (2013), 'Bodies in Syncopation', in Meheli Sen and Anustup Basu (eds), *Figurations in Indian Film*, 236–52, Basingstoke: Palgrave Macmillan.

Chaudhary, Shoma (2010), 'Is the Measure of this Man just a Moustache?' *Tehelka Magazine* 7 (37) September 18: 38–45.

Chopra, Anupama (2007), *King of Bollywood: Shah Rukh Khan and the Seductive World of Indian Cinema*, New York: Warner Books.

Chopra, Anupama (2015), *The Front Row: Conversations on Cinema*, New Delhi: Harper Collins Publishers India.

Joshi, Namrata (2010), 'Sallu Boti, Anyone?', *Outlook*, 20 September, online at: www.outlookindia.com/article/sallu-boti-anyone-/267041 (accessed 16 June 2015).

Kakodkar, Priyanka (2002), 'You Khan't Do That: Public Uproar Apart, Salman Could Still Drive Away Free', *Outlook*, 14 October, online at: www.outlookindia.com/article/you-khant-do-that/217552 (accessed 16 June 2015).

Lall, Pavan (2015), 'The Cash Machine Demigod', *Fortune*, May, pp. 95–104.

Louvre, Alf and Jeffrey Walsh (1988), *Tell Me Lies about Vietnam: Cultural Battles for the Meaning of the War*, Milton Keynes: Open University Press.

Mazumdar, Ranjani (2007), *Bombay Cinema: An Archive of the City*, New Delhi: Permanent Black.

Rushton, Richard (2012), *Cinema After Deleuze*, London: Continuum.

Sen, Meheli (2013), 'Introduction', in Meheli Sen and Anustup Basu (eds), *Figurations in Indian Film*, 1–20, Basingstoke: Palgrave Macmillan.

Tasker, Yvonne (1993), *Spectacular Bodies: Gender, Genre and the Action Cinema*, London: Routledge.

Varadarajan, Siddhartha, ed. (2002), *Gujarat: The Making of a Tragedy*, New Delhi: Penguin Books India.

Wissinger, Elizabeth (2007), 'Always on Display: Affective Production in the Modeling Industry', in Patricia Ticineto Clough and Jean Halley (eds), *The Affective Turn: Theorizing the Social*, 231–60, Durham, NC: Duke University Press.

Chapter 15

Shah Rukh Khan starring as Shah Rukh Khan: Performance style, audience expectation and self-parody

Charlie Henniker

Shah Rukh Khan is arguably the biggest film star in India and is recognized globally, with a strong fanbase in the global Indian diaspora as well as having ardent, non-diasporic European fan groups (most notably in Germany), a phenomenon that reflects the international footprint of Hindi cinema. This chapter will examine how Khan has built a commercial empire alongside a catalogue of blockbuster films by establishing himself as both brand and commodity, and in so doing assert that his acting and performance style is intrinsic to this activity. It will show that in addition to being in the right place at the right time, Khan has manipulated circumstances in order to maximize financial and marketing returns on the use of his own image. Such an investigation into Khan's acting, commerciality and the role played by his audience is overdue, and as a cultural icon with global reach he is deserving of further scholarship that assesses more than just his star power and cultural resonance. Using *Devdas* (Sanjay Leela Bhansali, 2002) and *Billu* (Priyadarshan, 2009) as case studies to analyse Khan's performance style in order to support the wider argument (supplemented with reference to several of Khan's films post-1995), the chapter will also demonstrate that this branding and commercial success depends on a symbiotic relationship between Khan and his audiences.

In 2014 Khan was the second richest actor in the world. He has starred in eleven of the top twenty-five highest grossing Indian films outside India (Dwyer 2014: 68; Sinha 2014). When he appeared on BBC One's prime-time TV chat show *Friday Night with Jonathan Ross* in the UK in 2010, despite being the only guest not regularly seen on UK television, his was the image selected to promote the show on iPlayer (the BBC's online catch-up service) to its 1.4 million daily users. Hollywood film producer and mogul Harvey Weinstein has reportedly referred to Khan as 'the most famous person you've never heard of', as well as 'the biggest star in the world' (Nixey 2013).

Born on 2 November 1965 into a modest Muslim family in Rajinder Nagar in west Delhi, Khan did not have the wealthy and privileged start in life that many of his industry peers enjoyed. He dabbled in theatre during his time at college (studying mass communications at New Delhi's Jamia Millia Islamia University) and appeared in TV series as well as a TV movie before relocating to Bombay to pursue a romantic interest (to whom he is still married) and a career in film. Khan appeared in his first few releases by 1992 but *Deewana* (The Crazed Lover, Raj Kanwar,

1992) was his official debut in film and also the award-winning, audience-pleasing appearance of that year. Three years later he would take the lead in an era-defining film and barely look back – he appeared to come from nowhere, overnight, and take the nation by storm.

In India images of Khan are ubiquitous, above all in urban areas. He appears on billboards, magazine covers, product packaging and TV. Although Khan is just as likely to be promoting a multinational brand as one of his films whenever he appears in these media, this does not make him any less prolific as an actor: he has appeared in well over eighty films. Khan was the star of one of the most successful releases in the history of Indian cinema, *Dilwale Dulhania Le Jayenge*, hereafter referred to by its popular acronym *DDLJ* (The Brave-Hearted Will Take Away the Bride, Aditya Chopra, 1995), a film that can be said to have established the 'Bollywood' genre and which continues to run in a cinema in Mumbai to this day, passing its 1,000th successive week late in 2014 (Dwyer 2014: 22). Khan exemplifies one of Richard Dyer's assertions about stars, that 'performers get to be stars when what they act out matters to enough people' (1986: 19).

Lastly, in the field of film studies, critics and academics have frequently taken Khan as their subject or departure point: this chapter contains references from this substantial and vibrant body of scholarship. In 2010, a three-day international conference entitled *Shah Rukh Khan and Global Bollywood* was held at the University of Vienna and attended by dozens of the authors and scholars, in addition of course to Khan's most committed fans. This led to an edited volume of academic articles and essays from the event being published by the conference organizers in 2015 (Dudrah, Mader and Fuchs 2015). In one chapter Elke Mader discusses Khan's 'participatory audience' and points to the global immediacy of his image and any content concerning him, but also the 'prosumer' audience that is able to adapt and appropriate Khan's image by remixing and recutting to generate new content; this concept is distorted to a disturbing extent in *FAN* (Maneesh Sharma, 2016) where an obsessed – and later crazed – fan of Khan's film star character Aryan Khanna (who shares the same name as Khan's son in real life) performs sequences inspired by Khan's films and manages to impersonate him, effectively reversioning his life in the second half of the film (Mader 2015). Mader refers to fan art and fan fiction in a study that points to the global eagerness to depict, construct and consume the image of Khan, something that makes *FAN* seem less far-fetched than a typical thriller movie.

Shah Rukh Khan's popularity and brand

Film stardom is a quality attributed to individuals as much for their role outside the films they appear in as within them. The media landscape in India and beyond dictates that the films themselves are 'often relegated to the periphery' and that 'the contemporary Hindi film star is a multidimensional, transmedia personality' (Mitra 2013: 196).

Many of the sources cited in this article circle around the question of why Khan is so endearingly popular among his audiences. Khan himself puts the phenomenon down to fate, not generally crediting his endeavour and planning, and in a statement perhaps designed to seem humble says 'I am a great, fantastic accident of being the right person at the right place at the right time. That is the description of my success' (Gahlot 2007: 35).

The Hindi film star community is famously dynastic and nepotistic, with large *filmi* families dominating the landscape in league with established actor-producer partnerships, making it difficult for an actor with no connections to break into the industry above a certain level. To have been successful as a film star and in particular as an outsider who 'gatecrashed into Bollywood' (Gahlot 2007), Khan must have distinctive, appealing looks and a charismatic on-screen presence – though the former attribute is not necessarily a prerequisite in Indian cinema if we ascribe to the view that the 'rule in Hindi cinema in particular and Indian cinema in general [is] that the heroine will be both good-looking and sexy but the hero will be neither' (Kesavan 2008: 15). Khan's looks are generally thought of as unusual or unconventional, and the fact that he – in common with many other Indian film stars – doesn't look especially Indian is partly explained by his Pathan heritage. In addition, the physical resemblance between Khan and Dilip Kumar, a star of an earlier era in Hindi cinema, may have played a role in the younger actor's early acceptance with mainstream audiences.

Another unusual factor in Khan's success is his emergence on the film scene as the villain, playing possessive, murderously jealous or ambitious characters (referred to as 'negative roles' in the Indian film industry) in two hit films shortly after making his debut: *Darr: A Violent Love Story* (Fear, Yash Chopra, 1993 – hereafter reffered to as *Darr*) and *Baazigar* (Gambler, Abbas-Mustan, 1993). Perhaps these roles reflect the very reasons Khan is so popular with audiences considering his story as an actor: he didn't stand a chance in the first place as an actor with no connections, he is said to have arrived in Bombay (Mumbai since 1996) to pursue and marry the love of his life in a story that echoes the plotline of *DDLJ*, and as such he represents the outsider in his early films. Even in his more recent films he riffs on this notion of being an outsider or struggling underdog, whether it's the aspiring junior artist Om Prakash in *Om Shanti Om* (Farah Khan, 2007) or Gaurav the die-hard fan in *Fan* – both

films structured around double roles in which these characters are set against a more realistic depiction of the star as, put simply, a star. Khan is somebody audiences can identify with on a large scale. He represents the notion that anything is possible, even for a person with the odds stacked against them or seen as 'other', a myth with real resonance in a country with several barriers to entry for those not born into an elite caste or social background – but by being everywhere at all times he simultaneously appears as 'the quintessential pan-Indian male' (Cayla 2008: 1). In *Chennai Express* (Rohit Shetty, 2013) Khan's character Rahul repeatedly utters the phrase 'Do not underestimate the power of a common man!', emphasizing his role as a regular guy who works in a sweet shop (albeit a highly profitable one judging by the scenes depicting his home and workplace) and who simply happens to get caught up in an escapade that will test the power of love over parochial force. Rahul ends up saving the day, naturally, and on the way his character makes passing references to other films Khan has starred in: *DDLJ* in particular is lampooned, from Deepika Padukone's heroine boarding the moving train with Rahul's assistance in the same style as the 1995 film, to the signature theme tune being sung by Rahul.

Jokes like this depend on the audience knowing Khan and his body of work – even his character's name is a reference to its recurrence in various of his previous films (e.g. *Dil To Pagal Hai* [The Heart is Crazy, Yash Chopra, 1997], *Kuch Kuch Hota Hai* [Something is Happening, Karan Johar, 1998] and *Kabhi Khushi Khabhie Gham* [Sometimes Happiness, Sometimes Sadness, Karan Johar, 2001]) including his incarnation in *Darr*. Such playful intertextuality is of course nothing new in Hindi cinema, nor in cinema as a medium. Kishore Valicha says of the relationship between film texts: 'cinema cannot be pure … the film image cannot carry only self-referring messages; film cannot help but carry information that is ideological, social, cultural, etc.' (1988: 20). The cultural inevitability of intertextuality in a media landscape overflowing with images of Hindi film stars is what induces Khan's comedic references. In a film industry where actors are so prolific (certainly compared to Hollywood – Tom Cruise, a useful comparison when it comes to star power, age and years active as an actor, has appeared in around fifty films while Khan, who has been called 'India's answer to Tom Cruise' has appeared in eighty-plus [Ciecko 2001: 5]) and their presence so unavoidable thanks to their sponsored appearance across virtually all media, film audiences in India have a strong shared knowledge of any major film star's work. Dyer's assertion that star images are always 'extensive, multimedia, intertextual' could not be more appropriate than when applied to Khan and his work (1986: 3). India is a place where '[the] characters that build up the star text may amount to something greater than the films' (Dwyer 2014: 35), all thanks to this media overflow.

Intertextuality 'functions in terms of the unavoidability, the apparent naturalness, of literary and cultural codes, the only defence against them appearing to be employing them ironically' (Allen 2011: 87). For a star such as Khan this is true, and the 'naturalness' of his image appearing everywhere can only be enhanced through a concerted response to it – the most fruitful approach being to perpetuate and remind audiences of his prevalence, to consistently and playfully reassert his dominance by riffing on his existing popularity. This in turn contributes to his own mythology and creates a kind of feedback loop: the more commercially successful films Khan appears in, the more powerful he is as a star; and the more he repeats the winning formula but with a knowing, self-parodying wink back to the audience within those films, the more accustomed the audience becomes to associating Khan in any film, no matter the subject, with the body of his work in others. In short, Khan's audiences pay to see him do what he has taught them he should be doing. Thus, they expect him to behave in a certain way, and he does so by presenting different versions of his star persona – this being for many stars 'an idiosyncratic set of gestures, movements, poses and expressions that become a major part of their trademark' (Shingler 2012: 37).

Anupama Chopra points out that celebrity endorsements were relatively uncommon when Khan first began accepting sponsorship deals from brands, in a move that quickly cemented his ubiquitous status:

> The constantly running commercials made Shah Rukh an omnipresent celebrity. He usually had two to three film releases every year, but the Shah Rukh Khan persona was ceaselessly available for consumption on television and in print ads. (2007: 160–1)

His producers and directors were of the same age and attitude as him: 'educated, city bred, technology savvy, and bottom-line smart … all in their twenties when they made the decade's biggest blockbusters' (162). Since these early days a typical Khan film now 'virtually guarantees the spectacle of Pepsi cans in hand' due to his long-standing partnership with the soft-drinks brand (Ciecko 2001: 126), to give just one example. Such is the normalcy of this brand-star relationship now that in more recent films Khan has exhibited both aspects simultaneously – such as the startlingly flagrant confluence of interests in *Om Shanti Om* where Khan, playing a movie star within the film, stands beneath a giant billboard of himself advertising Tag Heuer watches (Figure 15.1). The poster is from a campaign the brand had run in India before the film's release and is at the very least 'a wry comment on SRK's ubiquitous iconicity as the pusher of umpteen consumer brands' (Sarkar 2013: 216). In early 2015, the lead photograph of Khan on Tag Heuer's website was of him behind an old-fashioned movie camera – an image that reflects much of the discussion above. Similarly, in *Happy New Year* (Farah Khan, 2014) the majority of the action takes place in the Atlantis hotel at The Palm resort in Dubai, a popular destination for Indian holidaymakers and economic migrants, so much so that in late 2016 Visit Dubai launched a tourism campaign fronted by Khan entitled 'Shah Rukh Khan's personal invitation to Dubai #BeMyGuest'. Khan's production would have benefitted financially from the partnership with Atlantis, while audiences worldwide made the association between Khan's image and the Dubai lifestyle: a connection this powerful justifies a 'personal' invitation as part of a promotional campaign that leads with the name of the star, then discloses the location.

Shah Rukh Khan's stardom is, I propose, a result of a skilful blend of his natural performance skills and his willingness to spot commercial opportunities, beginning at a time when India was ready for new consumerist fantasies as the older Hindi film aesthetic, 'glamorous realism' championed by Yash Chopra from the late 1960s onwards (lush scenes in Kashmir, designer houses, intensely Indian or Punjabi values) gave way to a new set of ideals (branded sweaters, lavish weddings, international skylines) with India's economic liberalization in 1991.

Khan's opportunism and timing makes him entrepreneurial, but his manipulation of his image on screen and off makes him a talented brand manager: it is one thing to lend his face and voice to products, quite another to ensure that this presence is reflected in his films wherein he effectively cites his existing work as the standard audiences should expect before replicating it, letting

Figure 15.1 A genuine Tag Heuer advertisement featuring Shah Rukh Khan is used as a backdrop for a fictional character, played by Shah Rukh Khan, in *Om Shanti Om* (Farah Khan, 2007). Screengrab from *Om Shanti Om* (Red Chillies Entertainment, 2007).

everyone in on the joke in the process. Khan has successfully positioned himself as someone who can do anything, without any qualification beyond his fame, and positioned his audiences as people who will pay to see him do whatever this is. As a result, he himself becomes a commodity: a versatile star able to carry his charisma and style over to a variety of characters and genres. This process can also apply more broadly to male film stars in India:

> The male star (or 'hero' in Bollywood parlance) is now at once a consumer agent and commodity, a producer and a projection, a singing (lip-syncing) and dancing sex symbol with an excess of charisma and effect, a fashion victim and a huckster. (Ciecko 2001: 121)

Acting, performance and Shah Rukh Khan

'Acting' and 'performance' are slippery terms, with different applications and nuances according to media, cultural and regional contexts. Constantin Stanislavski's central text on the subject, *An Actor Prepares*, acknowledges this: 'it must be admitted that we cannot reduce this study of the inner life of other human beings to a scientific technique' ([1936] 2013: 31). In Hollywood, major stars are often considered to be fine actors and a heavy emphasis is placed on the dedication to interpreting a particular role, with this process often mythologized and as much discussed as the film. While the development of Khan's six-pack provided substantial tabloid fodder, firstly for *Om Shanti Om* and latterly for *Happy New Year* (Farah Khan, 2014), this signals more of a move towards pin-up status than a commitment to something vital to the success of a particular role, but is reminiscent of the transformations undergone by Brad Pitt for *Troy* (Wolfgang Petersen, 2004) and Jake Gyllenhaal for *Prince of Persia: The Sands of Time* (Mike Newell, 2010). For Khan, a change in body shape is simply an updated look, helping to ensure he remains relevant and worthy of discussion outside his films and endorsements. It is not something intrinsic to a character he is portraying. This is a development of the observation in general that:

> The male at the end of the twentieth century is groomed, maintained, exercised and dressed in the clothes of consumer society, an object of his own narcissistic gaze while inviting the gaze of the audience on his often fragmented body in a way traditionally associated with women. (Dwyer and Patel 2002: 84)

Indian film stars can come to represent a global, franchise-centric emblem for the nation in the same way that Hollywood stars of a certain era could embody the 'American Dream' or portray 'all-American' heroic characters. Khan is not alone in this space. Shilpa Shetty has grown from Indian film star to international icon as a result of her timely appearance on UK reality television show *Big Brother*. At a time when a new India was being discussed in international media and touted by tourism ministers and economics commentators alike, Shetty's steadfastly virtuous behaviour on the show coupled with her showbiz glamour made her 'emblematic' of 'India Shining' despite having been 'never regarded as a critically acclaimed actress' (Mitra 2013: 194, 189). While Shetty has since chosen to focus her efforts on building a brand outside (but stemming from) the film industry by becoming a 'corporate diva' and investing in luxury businesses, she nonetheless demonstrates the power of a film star with international exposure yet few acting credentials. Hollywood stars navigate similar territory, as documented by Pam Cook in her book on Nicole Kidman. Kidman has attained a level of stardom that simply doesn't reflect her skill as an actor nor her choice of roles over the years, and quickly became a 'commodity' star who, like Khan, was able to fit into many different archetypes. A commodity star 'is market-driven and is the incarnation of the commercial imperatives of the global media industries' (Cook 2012: 21). Khan, Shetty, Kidman and many other stars fit this definition, though Khan seems able to be market-driven but also to corner the market.

A distinct skillset is required of actors in commercial Indian cinema, and unlike most of their Hollywood counterparts they should be able to dance, lip-sync and cry just as effortlessly as they should be able to carry melodramatic story arcs and transition between comedy, drama and action genres within one film with ease – 'Acting is exaggerated … Stereotypes related to character and situation are common' (Gokulsing and Dissanayake 2004: 99) in commercial forms of Indian cinema. To that end, placing 'acting' in Indian cinema by means of the canonical and mostly Western texts on the subject is problematic. Moreover, the criteria outlined above indicate that an accomplished performer is perhaps a more appropriate requirement of the mainstream film industry in India (as opposed to a talented actor). This is changing with the emergence of the *hatke* ('different') cinema and independent films in India, which sometimes run to the same length (around three hours) as a Bollywood film but dispense with song and dance, replacing spectacle with challenging plot lines and a call for sustained and quality acting (see Dywer 2011). *Ship of Theseus* (Anand Gandhi, 2013) is a good example of a modern, independent film made in India that uses storytelling techniques, production methods and design sensibilities that have much more in common with cinema from Europe and North America, and relies in the main on talented actors who are not stars.

In film, acting is one of the key components of storytelling but is usually in concert with a variety of other emotive and narrative devices such as music, visual effects, locations, costume, make-up and so on. Additionally, a star's performance is of importance to the financial success of a film: it's an established director or a star name that can help financiers envision the level of success the film will have. Khan has positioned himself as being a bankable star by repeating the successful aspects of his performance in films over and over, but by off-setting his ubiquitous brand presence with film and character roles that rely on an audience's awareness of his body of work. Broadly, this leads to either common-man-doing-good roles where the audience suspend disbelief, or to parody roles that riff on Khan's (over)exposure. This doesn't work for all film stars, however. Al Pacino is a Hollywood star known for being a tremendous actor but who has fallen victim to scripts that put his films 'into two loose categories: shouters and sleepwalkers'. Like Khan, Pacino began his acting career in theatre and then arrived in the film industry 'cocky … virtually unknown' before becoming an overnight sensation.' (Prospect Team 2014). Sustaining such initial success is a challenge for any film star, but some minor setbacks aside Khan's trajectory has been steady and exponential.

Khan began studying acting under Barry John, a UK-born theatre practitioner who established the Theater Action Group in New Delhi. When he joined the group Khan quickly became known as a flamboyant and gestural actor, raised on a diet of Hindi films and encouraged by the free, workshopping method favoured by John. Khan quickly secured TV and low-budget film work. There is an indication in some accounts that while he had a certain style and presence, he wasn't prepared to take a different approach or deviate by adhering to the lessons of others.

This is backed up by the star's perspective later on in life: 'I always play a role as Shah Rukh Khan playing a role. It's never the role being essayed by Shah Rukh Khan' (Chopra 2007: 60). In short, it seems unlikely that Khan has spent much time 'searching for the Stanislavskian super-objective' (Brook [1968] 2008: 34) or pursuing any other classical methods, focusing instead on building a star text and brand using his 'natural' performative charm and presence. At present, Khan has more or less eschewed acting for performance in stating that he does not wish to please critics, who are 'a niche audience of five to seven people', instead he likes to make films for a 'larger spectrum of people' (Chhabra 2014). This approach seems efficacious in the case of *Happy New Year*, for example, for which he (re)gained a six-pack and received almost unanimously poor reviews – offending minority groups along the way – but for which he also saw the biggest opening ever for a Bollywood film in India at the time, grossing fifty million US dollars at the box office. By now this is typical Khan fare, with slight deviations into films such as *Swades: We, the People* (Ashutosh Gowariker, 2004) and *Chak De! India* (Go For It! India, Shimit Amin, 2007) showing a more naturalistic and understated persona but still one that brings life-changing leadership to communities in need – that is, still 'hero' roles.

The larger-than-life presence that Khan brings to so many of his roles is fuelled by parody, and sometimes pastiche, as 'a pastiche is very like that which it pastiches' (Dyer 2007: 54). Comedy is a genre Khan can execute well, and his films usually feature a comedy strand (among the many other genres that might appear in the film) cashing in on a misunderstanding, awkwardness when encountering a love interest or other challenge, or simply exuberant physical comedy. Just as the art of clowning depends on close attention to the audience and its responses, as casting director Michael Shurtleff has it 'A heightened sense of humor means a heightened awareness of other people, therefore a greater ability to communicate and ability to do so' (2009: 154). Khan's sense of humour is well documented and feeds into his playful retorts to the media, his ability to make grand statements about being the best actor in the world and his willingness to participate in joking, lighthearted conversations with the media. One educational book, aimed at children and all about Khan, claims with some authority that the star 'says and does things to shock people' (Holt and Phalke 1996: 4). This lighthearted sensibility is carried over into Khan's willingness to play himself (or a version of himself) in films such as *Om Shanti Om*, *Billu* and *Luck By Chance* (Zoya Akhtar, 2009). In this last example he is credited as 'himself' in the film, and tells an aspiring young actor that 'An actor's work – apart from acting – is really to choose the right kind of roles'. In doing so Khan proves himself an actor who is acutely aware of his audience and its place in his success.

On the subject of people performing as themselves, James Naremore states that 'people in a film can be regarded in at least three different senses: as actors playing theatrical personages, as public figures playing theatrical versions of themselves, and as documentary evidence' (Naremore 1990: 15). Khan seems to inhabit the first two of these spaces at different times. He certainly emphasizes the 'theatrical' aspect: Khan's groping, stuttering and histrionic style is one of his most established performance types, and can be witnessed in most scenes in which he portrays heightened emotion, usually crying freely. In *Darr* his stammering over the name 'Kiran' became an iconic aspect of both the film and his career. Khan himself says that 'We act also a little louder than, er, regular western films' (Ross 2010). Speaking specifically about *DDLJ* and *Kal Ho Naa Ho* (Tomorrow

May Never Come, Nikil Advani, 2003), Ravi Vasudevan describes the star's performative style:

> In both of these films, Khan's performance style markedly lacks any of the conventional signs of interiority, and plays on a hyperbolic surface histrionics that, along with the attributes of the tease who is forever taking people for a ride, suggests an indeterminacy of character viewpoint. (2010: 369)

This consistent and familiar style of acting leads him further into the practice of 'performing', as he routinely delivers the same set of techniques to an established fanbase. In addition to being an accomplished performer, Khan is a professional entertainer – somebody who knows which buttons to press and how to deliver what an audience wants, or expects, time after time. This makes his performance less relevant in terms of acting and more so in terms of what he is presenting under a type of contract with the audience, when 'it is not so much what the performer is doing that renders the performance highly ostensive (hence presentational) as much as the audience's recognition that what they are doing is what they always do' (Shingler 2012: 45).

Devdas

Devdas is effectively a masterclass in Khan's performance tropes. The film updates the classical narrative and is bold and star-driven (opposite Khan as Devdas was Aishwarya Rai as Paro, a favourite among international beauty brands) from a director known foremost for his visual splendour. This modern version is 'meant for the post-MTV generation; it is loud, melodramatic, ornate and laced with elaborate musical set-pieces' (Gokulsing and Dissanayake 2004: 115).

In playing a London-returned, wealthy young man whose adherence to traditional Indian values is still strong after several formative years apart from his family, Khan is able to dominate the film from the outset as an anticipated novelty and curiosity, and as a character that the community in the film have been missing (and lacking) until his return. Devdas's cajoling and teasing of Paro after years of silence, which switches drastically into a fiery declaration of love combined with outrage that Paro should ever think he felt otherwise, is reminiscent of the scene of Raj's cruel teasing of Simran after a night of too much drinking (in which she initially believes they have had sex) in *DDLJ*, immediately after which he chastises her for believing he could be anything other than virtuous and Indian in values: 'Mai Hindustani hu'. In both cases, Khan gets to be cheeky but also chastely Indian and virtuous – and as in many of his films, Indian also means Hindu: '*Chak De India* is SRK's first significant appearance as a Muslim protagonist in a Hindi film', representing a 'mistrusted ethnic minority' (Bhattacharya 2013: 110, 115) with *My Name Is Khan* (Karan Johar, 2010), a few years later, pursuing a more international political angle.

Devdas moves from the initial lightfooted presence in a relatively happy home to a man betrayed by his family and separated from his childhood sweetheart, unable to wed Paro and resorting to alcohol to drown his sorrows. Entertained by a courtesan, the majority of the film shows Khan on the verge of tears, and later on the brink of death, overtaken by whisky, emotions or both – cue much of the stammering delivery that characterizes Khan's speech, emotions manifested by uncontrollable shaking, and tears that flow readily but seemingly in spite of Devdas's efforts to control and suppress them.

Khan deploys extremes here to great effect. They convincingly pass as 'acting' – audiences can read all the signs easily – and serve to isolate his character: nobody else is behaving at such extremes, which makes his pain seem louder and more significant than the suffering of Paro, for instance. It invites pity and empathy on the part of the audience, as it compounds his sorry state and he is seen as being almost irrecoverably lonely. Devdas does very little to improve his lot and seems to sink into this state of despair very rapidly, which is almost anti-heroic (especially considering the conquesting in most of Khan's other films).

The responses to Khan's character within the film reflect the sentiment of the film-going public. He is the one everyone is excited to see, much like a film star is an attraction when appearing in public life. He has had a rarefied experience that nobody else he encounters seems to understand, just like a celebrity. He picks up vices that would be considered unsavoury in most, yet is still loved – people seem to look over this, as they would in real life with a film star in India, preferring to idolize than to ridicule or judge. Khan then fulfils the emotional requirements of each scene to an almost ludicrously full extent, before dying tragically (perhaps killing himself) and permanently disrupting the lives of those around him.

Devdas is introduced to the audience in a way that reflects this parallel and reinforces Khan's star entrance. First the audience is told Devdas is on his way, and the excitement that surrounds this signals his arrival as a major event. Then characters in the film see him, describe him or report his arrival – while the audience do not. Then Khan's voice is heard, his hands are seen opening a door, before finally he is revealed to the audience: such an entrance depends entirely on the star power of Khan (and in fact Paro is introduced in fragments too, before her face is revealed in the double illumination of a lightning flash and a *diya* held before her) and its reception depends on the audience's willingness to build anticipation. Glimpses and teasing shots hint at the magnitude of Khan's screen presence, just as with the introductions to his characters in *Kal Ho Naa Ho, Main Hoon Na* (I'm Here Now, Farah Khan, 2004) and *Kabhi Kushie Kabhie Gham*, before the audience is granted a type of *darshan* – the experience of beholding Khan.

Billu

Billu opens with the cinematically familiar disclaimer that 'All characters in this film are fictitious and bear no resemblance to any person living or dead'. This is ironic in the overall context of the film, once Khan's character is established as a hugely successful film star named Sahir Khan. Sahir is set to complete filming for his upcoming blockbuster in the same village that his estranged childhood friend now lives in, unbeknownst to either party. Billu is by now a barber with a wife and two children, struggling to support his family and the butt of his neighbours' jokes as his shop suffers a decline in trade thanks to a rival: a new, modern salon. Much of the film centres around Billu's unlikely connection to Sahir and the way the villagers respond to this: either disbelievingly or with jealousy, and almost always by clamouring for a chance to meet the star personally, a compulsion many cinemagoers would identify with.

The film is intertextually playful from the outset. The credit sequence features close shots of items from a barber shop alongside cast and crew names: the editor credit appears next to a pair of scissors, the producer alongside a box containing rupee notes and coins inside, and so on. This is a film that means to reference film. The village itself is an idealized version of a simple, largely rural community – yet all its inhabitants are obsessed with Sahir Khan and know his films. Key details show that *Billu*'s audience is being presented with more than just a version of Khan: his actual film posters cover the walls of the village, and within the film's narrative Sahir adopts Khan's entire oeuvre. The audience are to believe that Sahir Khan has the same cultural context as Shah Rukh Khan, and there is no better shorthand than to selectively suggest that Sahir is Shah Rukh, or vice versa (Figure 15.2).

The first time Khan appears in *Billu* it is in a film-within-a-film, a song sequence that seems intended to satirize the actor's normal style but sits somewhere between parody, pastiche and accuracy. As with the visual introduction examples listed above he is first seen from behind; after a few shots from this angle he turns to camera and looks directly into the lens, just as he shoots into the lens. Shortly afterwards a montage of Khan's most dramatic and iconic moments from films spanning his entire career is intercut with crowd shots of adoring fans waving (real) posters and chanting his name. Crowds gather at every shoot and are at times uncontrollable, in a nod to the real production challenges posed when an Indian film unit shoots in a public space.

The overall effect here is to confuse the boundaries between Khan's public persona, his archetypal performance style and the character of Sahir. This makes it acceptable for Khan to play himself. The audience have a shorthand through which they can understand the context of the film, which presents a world in which everyone is a fan of Shah Rukh/Sahir Khan. The effect is replicated and developed in *FAN* where not just the star but the fan is portrayed by Khan. The opening credits spell out, for an audience ready to suspend disbelief, that Shah Rukh Khan is 'IN and AS FAN'.

It's not just Khan's film appearances that are covered off in *Billu*, as his business interests and commercial work are referenced too. The clapper board used during a fairground scene clearly displays the insignia for Kahn's own production

Figure 15.2 A film star arrives for a film shoot surrounded by fans and security: Shah Rukh Khan plays Sahir Khan, whose background is communicated through other movie posters and scenes from Shah Rukh Khan's career in *Billu* (Priyadarshan, 2009). Screengrab from Billu (Red Chillies Entertainment, 2009).

company, in a joke that seems indulgent but also designed to reward the audience members that recognize it. And Billu's children avidly discuss an advertisement in which the star appears in a bath full of petals, surrounded by models – a direct reference to 'his most feminine incarnation' in a Lux advertisement, a brand hitherto exclusively advertised by female stars (Cayla 2008: 7).

Throughout *Billu* the most striking aspect of Khan's performance is that he doesn't actually say very much until the end. Irrfan Khan, who plays Billu, carries the film as an actor but Sahir Khan only really appears in montages and brief bouts of exposition, save for the final emotional speech at a school event in which Khan unleashes the familiar set of performative flourishes, with voice shaking and eyes about to brim with tears. He tells a heart-warming story that he unwittingly converts into a reality for the audience he is addressing, before making an appearance in the humble home of his old friend. The messaging here is clear and supported by an earlier scene: behind all the crowds and media frenzy, film stars are real people too, and in some cases know what it's like to grow up with very little and work towards stardom. This reflects Khan's own story, which, while not rags-to-riches, is closer to that than the story of many of his contemporaries. Khan's most compelling performance in a film about a version of himself (in which he plays a version of himself) is when recounting a supposedly fictional version of his own story.

Conclusion

Khan is charismatic and attractive as an on-screen personality, most likely hired by film producers in order to perform as the star Shah Rukh Khan. On some occasions, Khan is that producer (he owns a film production and distribution company – Red Chillies Entertainment – which mostly produces films Khan stars in); on some others, his wife is. Acting is a subset of his skills and attributes, which include a strong sense of humour, enough charisma to ensure an audience backs him against the odds or if at any point his character seems morally dubious, and advanced business acumen that dictate his film choices in order to sustain and strengthen his brand. It's of note that Khan has stated that he sees advertising as his 'alternate profession' (Cayla 2008: 2).

Audiences pay to go and see a Shah Rukh Khan film, not a new, high-concept thriller or a character-driven drama that happens to have Khan starring in it. This is a result of the combined forces of the high stakes in Indian film industry financing in general (a film can close and sink without trace after just a few days) requiring a lead name; established cast and crew teams working on films to repeat the success of previous projects; and the hand that film stars can have in the production of the films they appear in. If entertainment is 'basically decided by those people responsible (paid) for providing it in concrete form' (Dyer [1992] 2002: 20) and stars 'are involved in making themselves into commodities' (Dyer 1986: 5) then Khan is truly a world-class entertainer and film star. In *FAN*, Khan plays the superstar but also his obsessed and murderous fan: in representing his brand and its most extreme consumer he pushes the self-referential envelope even further, all the while recalling shades of *Darr*, one of his earliest successes, and reminding audiences of the unique and particular challenges of his own stardom.

It may be that towards the end of his career Khan will turn back to his early theatre days and his appearances in experimental films and unconventional roles, and alter the positioning he has held for over twenty years. But as the lines between his commercial enterprises and his film work as a star continue to blur, it is more likely he will pursue an entrepreneurial and capitalist route as a global entertainment brand. Having come from virtually nothing to becoming an international film star, or the (often self-professed) King of Bollywood, it will be hard for Khan to turn back or deviate from the particular performance style he has crafted, one which reliably rakes in the rupees. Shah Rukh Khan can act, but he won't unless it makes good business sense.

Works Cited

Allen, Graham (2011), *Intertextuality*, 2nd edn, Oxford: Routledge.

Bhattacharya, Nandini (2013), 'The Man Formerly Known as the Actor: When Shah Rukh Khan Reappeared as Himself', in *Hindi Cinema: Repeating the Subject*, 110–25, London: Routledge.

Brook, Peter ([1968] 2008), *The Empty Space*, St Ives: Penguin.

Cayla, Julien (2008), 'Following the Endorser's Shadow: Shah Rukh Khan and the Creation of the Cosmopolitan Indian Male', *Advertising and Society Review*, 9 (2).

Chhabra, Aseem (2014), 'The Only Way Shah Rukh Khan Can Redeem Himself Now', *Quartz*, 28 October, online at: http://qz.com/287948/is-it-too-much-to-now-expect-shahrukh-khan-to-do-a-good-film/ (accessed 30 January 2015).

Chopra, Anupama (2007), *King of Bollywood: Shah Rukh Khan and the Seductive World of Indian Cinema*, New York: Warner Books.

Ciecko, Anne (2001), 'Superhit Hunk Heroes for Sale: Globalization and Bollywood's Gender Politics', *Asian Journal of Communication*, 11 (2): 121–43.

Cook, Pam (2012), *Nicole Kidman*, London: British Film Institute.

Dudrah, Rajinder, Elke Mader and Bernhard Fuchs (2015), *SRK and Global Bollywood*, New Delhi: Oxford University Press.

Dwyer, Rachel (2002), *Yash Chopra*, London: British Film Institute.

Dwyer, Rachel (2011), 'Zara Hatke!: The New Middle Classes and the Segmentation of Hindi Cinema', in Henriek Donner (ed.), *Being Middle-Class in Contemporary India: A Way of Life*, 184–208, London: Routldge.

Dwyer, Rachel (2014), *Picture Abhi Baaki Hai: Bollywood as a Guide to Modern India*, Gurgaon: Hachette.

Dwyer, Rachel and Divia Patel (2002), *Cinema India: The Visual Culture of Hindi Film*, London: Reaktion Books.

Dyer, Richard (1986), *Heavenly Bodies: Film Stars and Society*, Hong Kong: St. Martin's Press.

Dyer, Richard ([1992] 2002), *Only Entertainment*, 2nd edn, London: Routledge.

Dyer, Richard (2007), *Pastiche*, London: Routledge.

Gahlot, Deepa (2007), *King Khan*, New Delhi: Roli Books.

Gokulsing, K. Moti and Wimal Dissanayake (2004), *Indian Popular Cinema: A Narrative of Cultural Change*, Stoke-on-Trent: Trentham Books.

Holt, Julia and Shubhra Phalke (1996), *Shah Rukh Khan*, London: Basic Skills Agency.

Kesavan, Mukul (2008), *The Ugliness of the Indian Male and Other Propositions*, Raniket: Black Kite.

Mader, Elke (2015), 'Shah Rukh Khan, Participatory Audiences, and the Internet', in Rajinder Dudrah, Elke Mader and Bernhard Fuchs (eds), *SRK and Global Bollywood*, 200–20, New Delhi: Oxford University Press.

Mitra, Sreya (2013), 'From Heroine to "Brand Shilpa": Reality Television, Transnational Cultural Economics, and the Remaking of the Bollywood Star', in Russell Meeuf and Raphael Raphael (eds), *Transnational Stardom*, 187–206, New York: Palgrave Macmillan.

Naremore, James (1990), *Acting in the Cinema*, Berkeley: University of California Press.

Nixey, Catherine (2013), 'Bigger than Tom Cruise, but have you heard of him?', *Times*, 2 August, p. 4 (Arts Supplement).

Prospect Team (2014), 'The Full Pacino: Why Has One of Cinema's Greatest Actors Descended Into Self-Parody?', *Prospect*, February, online at: www.prospectmagazine.co.uk/arts-and-books/al-pacino-decline-shouting-bfi (accessed 30 January 2015).

Ross, Jonathan (2010), *Friday Night with Jonathan Ross*, BBC One, TX 22:35 GMT 5 February, Episode 4/25.

Sarkar, Bhaskar (2013), 'Metafiguring Bollywood: Brecht after *Om Shanti Om*', in Meheli Sen and Anustup Basu (eds), *Figurations in Indian Film*, 179–201, Basingstoke: Palgrave Macmillan.

Shingler, Martin (2012), *Star Studies: A Critical Guide*, Basingstoke: Palgrave Macmillan.

Shurtleff, Michael (2009), *Audition: Everything an Actor Needs to Know to Get the Part*, New York: Bloomsbury.

Sinha, Kounteya (2014), 'Shah Rukh Khan Second Richest Actor in the World', *Times of India*, 21 May, online at: http://timesofindia.indiatimes.com/entertainment/hindi/bollywood/news-interviews/Shah-Rukh-Khan-second-richest-actor-in-the-world/articleshow/35431720.cms? (accessed 8 April 2015).

Stanislavski, Constantin ([1936] 2013), *An Actor Prepares*, London: Bloomsbury.

Valicha, Kishore (1988), *The Moving Image: A Study of Indian Cinema*, London: Sangam Books.

Vasudevan, Ravi (2010), *The Melodramatic Public: Film Form and Spectatorship in Indian Cinema*, Ranikhet: Permanent Black.

Chapter 16

The curious case of Katrina Kaif: NRI stardom and ethnicity in Bollywood

Midath Hayder

The continued popularity and success of Katrina Kaif is a curiosity in itself. A mixed-race star, Kaif has succeeded in the post-liberalization Bollywood era despite originally having no acting experience, being unable to speak Hindi and lacking any connections in the industry. Though there have been mixed-race stars before, none have been as successful in the contemporary era: Kaif has appeared in popular films such as *Ek Tha Tiger* (Once There Was a Tiger, Kabir Khan, 2010), *Jab Tak Hai Jaan* (As Long As I Live, Yash Chopra, 2012) and *Bang Bang!* (Siddharth Anand, 2014). Starring many times as a non-resident Indian (NRI), she has also been regarded as a sex symbol as evidenced by her winning fan vote polls such as 'Sexiest pin up girl' and 'Hottest figure' in Hindi cinema (Anon. 2008c: 62). By discussing Katrina Kaif's stardom, this chapter seeks to analyse the shifting discourses of female ethnicity in post-liberalization popular culture. I will do this by reviewing a few key films in Kaif's career as well as closely reading magazine articles and analysing the discourses surrounding her. I have focused on *Filmfare* magazine from 2007, Kaif's breakthrough year, up to the most current issues available at the time of writing. I will highlight some of the ways that filmmakers have used Kaif's ethnic femininity for novel film roles/campaigns (namely genre roles, item songs, NRI films and endorsements) and will be speculating on some of the possible reasons for her success.

Kaif was born on 16 July 1983. Her father is Indian (from Kashmir) and her mother is Irish. In the British press Kaif is often positioned as representing the British Asian diaspora (Manzoor 2007; Meo 2003; Waheed 2010), despite the fact that she lived in many parts of the world as a child. Though she is half-Indian, it appears that she has lost contact with her father (Anon. 2009c: 74), but it is unclear at what age this happened. She speaks Hindi with a Western accent (as a result of her upbringing around the world, but definitely not solely British-influenced as is often assumed). The following is a typical comment from an interview feature describing Kaif in 2008:

> The odds were heavily against her. For starters, she's a foreigner, she didn't know Hindi. As if that wasn't enough she had a very British accent and looked like one too. The general opinion was that Indians brought up on the *desi* diet of Madhuris and Sridevis would find her unpalatable. (Anon. 2008a: 50)

In these remarks, Kaif is assumed to be 'unpalatable' because of her outsider status, and this is further compounded by the comparison to Madhuri Dixit (1967–) and Sridevi (1963–2018), who are both deemed comfortably local. But Kaif's success comes directly from this 'unpalatable' quality, which has been an endless source of intrigue and fascination for audiences. The assumptions made in the above quote fail to acknowledge that the '*desi* diet' is constantly changing and evolving and thus is always contextual. Kaif's entry into the industry comes at a time when India's relationship to the rest of the world is more receptive, taking full advantage of the globalized Bollywood audience's diverse taste as well as their fascination with fair skin (which has always been palatable).

After her breakthrough, Kaif appeared in less glamorous roles in 'credible' films such as *Yuvraaj* (Subhash Ghai, 2008) and *Raajneeti* (*Politics*, Prakash Jha, 2010), which, however, were less successful. In a 2009 interview Kaif stated:

> I do not believe that you have to take off your make-up and look simple to prove you're an actress ... I'm not going to make a morose film, which no one will watch just so people take me seriously as an actress. (Anon. 2009a: 45)

Apparent here is the tension between appearing in less commercial roles to gain credibility or in more glamorous roles for financial reward. The agenda set by the commercial imperatives of the industry means that Kaif is increasingly pressured into capitalizing on her looks (which as a foreigner are a point of intrigue for audiences), over starring in less successful but more substantial or 'credible' roles.

Mary Beltrán (discussing stars in Hollywood) argues '[mixed] race is increasingly an identity category available to stars, but one that is unstable when it comes to its impact on their careers' (2009: 166). Kaif is an especially unstable star, as her foreignness is part of her intrigue but also part of the reason why she is derided and a crucial defining factor in her stardom/casting/endorsements. Her inability to speak fluent Hindi is mentioned frequently in articles about her, and in negative criticism of her performances. For example, in December 2007 *Filmfare* advised her thus: 'How about adding a little zing to your performances? And while you're at it, get a diction coach' (Anon. 2007b). What can be considered here is the fact that part of her appeal is due to her being foreign; her Western-accented Hindi may appeal to some of her fans. In recent years the the appearance of stars such as Sunny Leone, Amy Jackson, Jacqueline Fernandes, Nargis Fakhri and Giselli Monteiro suggests that the practice of hiring foreigners means that diction coaches are more common (it is also important to remember that diction coaches have also been hired for native stars before to help with accents/dialects).

Performance has been an issue in the star discourse of Katrina Kaif. She has been widely derided for her acting abilities, partially attributed to her accent but also to a lack of formal training. For example, a fan letter in *Filmfare*, one reader writes (in 2008): 'I always thought that to be the No.1 actress, you should at least know how to act!' (Anon. 2008b: 12). Yet the situation is maybe more complex if the fact that many of her roles are dubbed is taken into account. In Kaif's breakthrough film *Namastey London* (Vipul Amrutlal Shah, 2007) the actress is not dubbed, which is logical, since she plays an NRI. However, shortly after this breakthrough, Kaif was dubbed in many films, such as *Apne* (Anil Sharma, 2007), *Partner* (David Dhawan, 2007), *Welcome* (Anees Bazmee, 2007), *Race* (Abbas-Mustan, 2008) and *Yuvraaj*, which would have severely hindered her performance. That Kaif was dubbed in these films, which were either flops or less successful than her later hits, may again suggest that her accent (which affects her performance) is a part of her appeal and was critical in establishing her as a star. Furthermore, the fact that some filmmakers chose to dub her, while others did not, suggests the industry's uncertainty about what a 'NRI star' should actually sound like and which aspects of her foreignness they wanted to play up more: her looks or her accent.

'Believe in your dreams and make them happen'

Stars exist outside of films; TV adverts and magazines are one place they have a continued presence. Female stars are paid considerably less than their male counterparts. One way to offset some of this is through adverts and endorsements. Bollywood is one place that light-skinned stars have been validated (Osuri 2008: 115), which means that Kaif is much sought after for adverts and endorsements. If white femininity is marketed as desirable and associated with success (116) its associations with Kaif through skin creams, and discourses of her fame and fortune, are perfectly apt for demonstrating this. She is often reduced to a commodity, allowing her light skin to be a canvas for different products to be marketed on, including fairness creams. One way to read these endorsements is as a contradiction. For example, Kaif has featured in adverts for the skin cream, Olay 'Natural White'. Contrarily, her fair skin is from her ethnic background and not due to the use of said product, demonstrating the fallibility/futileness of these products that encourage European standards of beauty.

One campaign that strategically exploits the fluidity of her image is in her jewellery endorsements. For example, in an advert for Nakshatra in *Filmfare* (6 November 2013) Kaif is adorned in a white lace dress, wearing a silver necklace and earrings. The tag line reads 'Divine Luck'. Kaif's whiteness allows her to be dressed as a Western bride in order to advertise jewellery, representing an affinity with the West. This image is especially of note as it exaggerates and plays with her whiteness. The tag line references popular discourses about Kaif (she is sometimes referred to as Bollywood's lucky mascot). Her 'luck' can be read as code for her ethnicity, as being fair skinned brings her many opportunities as does her proximity to whiteness. However, she is able to also appear in more traditional Indian clothes. For example, she is pictured wearing a black sari with a short blouse (Anon. 2009b), demonstrating her ability to be pictured in different looks. Both are costumes in which she is able to display her various cultural affiliations, as it is the product (in this case the jewellery) that is the main object of the advert. In this way advertisers are demonstrating a willingness to keep Kaif's image flexible, for wider appeal to consumers and to commodify her ethnic ambiguity.

Kaif's appeal has been well noted by investors as she is heavily sought after for endorsements (anything from jewellery to chocolate). This is most evident in her being the first Bollywood star to have her own Barbie doll. In many ways the Barbie advert provides some of the most interesting comment on the contradiction of Kaif's star text. That a mixed-race star was chosen as the first Bollywood star to have a Barbie doll modelled on her indicates that her selection was most likely a way of using the appeal of her foreignness to target the Indian market. Barbie is a major global brand, and there have been many suitable stars who could have led the campaign before.

The advert is where many of the contradictions are most apparent. Kaif is pictured up close and in a soft focus, emphasizing her beauty, while a finger-picked guitar plays gently over the soundtrack. A little girl is shown playing with a doll, while the voiceover says, 'Nearly every girl in the world grew up playing with Barbie. I was no different'. However, the voiceover is dubbed (despite being in English, the voiceover is much lower than her actual voice). This demonstrates a disavowal of Kaif as a performer, as she is reduced simply to her image and features and appears more as an avatar than a star. It is her beauty that the producers want to exploit, not her performance, which in itself demonstrates an attitude towards female stars.

There are more obscure meanings that can be inferred from the doll itself, as there is little resemblance between the doll and Kaif. There are no distinguishing characteristics that the doll has (for example, a costume from one of Kaif's films). The costume itself is ambiguous, appearing similar to both a Western formal dress and a sari (the asymmetric neckline suggesting the drape of a sari). The doll has similarities with Kaif in that it is neither quite Western/Indian. The dress strategically appropriates from both cultures, creating an avatar that is dubious (as it does not quite assign itself to either culture). Instead, the doll has a generic feature that is as ambiguous as Kaif's star text. The voiceover suggests that anyone could be a star and asks if they will have their own Barbie. Thus, the advert plays on Kaif's success story and her proximity to whiteness is used to validate such representations of femininity. The commercial appears to place both Kaif and the doll as aspirational icons but also plays on discourses of fate and luck (code for her ethnicity), which have been a large part of Kaif's star text.

Namaste Katrina! The breakthrough years

The NRI subgenre was initiated by the success of *Diwale Dulhania Le Jayenge* (The Brave-Hearted Will Win the Bride, Aditya Chopra, 1995; hereafter *DDLJ*), which had a significant impact upon how the cinematic NRI has been portrayed. While the NRI character was once a villain (Sharpe 2005), in *DDLJ*, the NRI is the hero. However, the same gender politics apply, as '[the] men decide the course of action, and the women, the repository of Hindustani culture and values, toe the line' (Chopra 2002: 81).

Kaif's breakthrough film was the NRI romantic comedy *Namastey London*, of which the above is also true, although the film does vary in the exact formula, namely being heroine led. Though the film focuses on a NRI heroine, the film still positions Indian culture as the superior one. Kaif's character, Jazz, must choose between two life partners, an Englishman (Charlie Brown) or an Indian (Arjun). While Jazz is an active agent in pursuing her own desires (her father is ineffectual in deciding her husband) she still chooses the Indian as her husband. Jazz may have seen the difficulties of assimilation into Charlie Brown's family, hence the preference for the Indian suitor. In this case, the brave bride takes the groom.

The cinematic NRI/diaspora has often become associated with certain specific stars. The depiction of this struggle makes a break away from *DDLJ* and *Kal Ho Naa Ho* (Tomorrow May Never Come, Nikhil Advani, 2004), in offering the white foreigner as a potential legitimate partner (which played out in a sub-story, in which a white woman converts to Islam to marry her boyfriend). However, in keeping with the NRI genre, the film asserts that it is men who pass on culture and Indian heritage, hence Indian/Asian men can marry NRI and white women, but NRI women cannot marry white characters as to do so would break the patrilineal arrangement of family and culture.

One way that *Namastey London* is the counterpart to *DDLJ* is the different depictions of the NRI woman. For example, the 'Hindi movie heroines are nearly always virgins, and *DDLJ* is not the kind of film in which transgression of that rule is possible or even thinkable' (Chopra 2002: 70), but this is not the case in *Namastey London*, where Jazz openly speaks about sex (or at least to scare away a potential groom). Though the film counteracts this by not portraying any sex scenes, the heroine-NRI is at least uttering her desires, even if the form betrays the convictions of the characters. While Jazz boasts of her sexual exploits, this is perhaps undermined by the fact that she does end up marrying the Indian. Furthermore, drinking is another issue in NRI films. While NRI characters have been drunk on screen before, this was typically under certain conditions. In both *DDLJ* and *Kal Ho Naa Ho*, for example, the heroines, Simran (Kajol) and Naina (Preity Zinta), get drunk under the supervision of the hero played by Shah Rukh Khan. The casting of Kaif may have also been strategic for this role; as an unknown outsider/foreigner, the filmmakers had a licence to portray her more easily as promiscuous or 'wild', as her star text had yet to be rendered. This is further reiterated by the fact that there was very little promotional material about Kaif during the release of this film, despite her being a relative newcomer. A pull-out feature about the film (*Friday Fever*, March 2007), mentions her very little. It appears that, despite being a heroine-led film, there was little intention to launch Kaif as a star, and her casting was purely to enable the character to be more transgressive than the Simran/Naina types of earlier NRI films. Essentially, however, while Jazz is able to drink, undermine her parents and date whoever she wants, very little of what she does is transgressive. Instead, her character modernized the NRI girl slightly (in terms of having a career, relationships, fashion) but ultimately did not subvert the ideology of the NRI film.

One reason for the break away from the conventional depiction of NRI women is that Katrina Kaif's ethnic background grants her the ability to be more fluid, as it is difficult to identify her simply. She has a lack of film pedigree (not belonging to any film dynasties) nor has she the Miss World credentials of Aishwarya Rai or Priyanka Chopra. This outsider status means that she is able to appear as a sex icon. Despite this, her performance neither conforms to nor betrays traditional forms of Indian femininity. Essentially, there is very little to be offended about in her character, as taboos may be spoken about (connoting modernity) but never broken, and her characters always ultimately conform to the traditional.

So Kaif's casting in *Namastey London* may have been due to her ethnicity and outsider status, and the filmmakers capitalized on this. While *Namastey London* was a romantic comedy drama, *New York*'s (Kabir Khan, 2009) subject matter and themes were much more serious. The film tells the story of three Indians in New York after the 9/11 terrorist attacks. The character of Maya is more similar to the melodramatic types of an earlier period of Indian cinema (akin to the 1970s heroine, who would sacrifice herself for the hero). Maya sacrifices herself for her husband Samar, despite the fact that he is a terrorist and is planning an attack. The shift from the romantic comedy *Namastey London* to the identity melodrama *New York*, suggests a belief that audiences are comfortable viewing Kaif as an on-screen representation of the NRI across different genres.

The film's title, the reduced run time and the reduction of songs suggest an attempt to perhaps broaden its audience. For these reasons, it is worth noting the casting of Katrina Kaif and Neil Nitin Mukesh, whose looks are racially ambiguous as both have fair skin and Mukesh has brown hair. The casting in this film, then, may denote an attempt to soften the Indian features of some of the characters in order to globalize the image of the film. Additionally, Kaif's depiction of Maya as modern may also serve to broaden its appeal. For example, Kaif's femininity appears in two iterations. Firstly, she appears as a young wild student (signified by her bright-red-tinted hair), who is carefree and tomboyish (playing American football). These features make her appear as someone who has the ability to assimilate (shown by how popular she is). In the second half of the film, she appears as a devoted housewife who also works as a human rights lawyer. She wears suits and wears her hair up to demonstrate her suitability to work in the office. The student and professional versions of Maya represent the NRI as comfortable. Both are also Western, therefore demonstrating a modern Indian femininity (which would have more global appeal). Although the film aimed to appeal to a broader audience by depicting the NRI as young, modern and desirable, the potential of this film may have been hindered due to its presentation of the FBI as a cause of terrorism rather than a solution.

This era of Kaif's career (2007–2011) has her in varying roles, some glamorous and some serious. This demonstrates the struggle of many female actors to accept either 'credible' film roles or the more lucrative blockbuster films. *New York* is a serious film, since the aftermath of 9/11 for many Indians is a crucial issue. In *New York*, she uses her own voice (as opposed to the many dubbed roles she had earlier), and this enables her to give the performance more in terms of emotions, which is typically seen as a way to add credibility to performance. Her death at the climax of the film makes her a tragic figure, further adding to the melodramatic trope of sacrifice that the heroine in Indian cinema is applauded for making. Kaif is depicted here as a modern NRI (her job as a human rights worker has her clothed in business suits). Nonetheless, her death signifies that the fate of NRI women is still bound up with the actions of men, demonstrating her ability to still conform to the moral code and not challenge the power of men.

Katrina Kaif's beauty and sex appeal are major factors in the promotion of her films and, in this respect, *New York* is no different. Though the film is about the lives of three NRIs and the impact of 9/11, the promotional material at times confused the seriousness of the films. For example, the remixed version of 'Mere Sang' appears to have an MTV-like quality to it. Despite not lip-syncing in the song sequence in the film, she does so in the remixed version. Kaif is filmed alone, playfully gesturing, smiling in various locations. The utilization of Kaif here serves to exploit her image for promotional purposes. Her beauty and cuteness are being used to promote the film, betraying its serious content. Perhaps by advertising the film this way the film reduces its political message in order to appeal to audiences seeking entertainment. Either way, Kaif's fluidity allows filmmakers to exploit her Western-ness for different purposes, which is in this case is for a serious film about NRI politics, while also adding glamour for its promotion.

If Zeenat Aman (1951–) was able to deviate from traditional forms of cinematic heroines and demonstrates her own 'reformulations of the Indian heroine' (Gehlawat 2012: 59), then Kaif is an inheritor of this model of femininity and would star as her very own Sheela/Sheila (Sheela being the name for Zeenat Aman's character in the film *Qurbaani* [Khan, 1980], who has her own item song). For the most part, Kaif's film roles have been characters that are generally representative of the modern Hindi cinema heroine such as Aman but also contain some discrepancies. For instance, her characters are often depicted as having either uninhibited or tomboyish traits, such as in *Namastey London*, *New York*, *Mere Brother Ki Dulhan* (My Brother's Bride, Ali Abbas Zafar, 2011), *Jab Tak Hai Jaan* and *Dhoom 3* (Blast 3, Vijay Krishna Acharya, 2013). Her femininity is Western: she is usually depicted wearing skirts and dresses rather than saris, and she is often shown at rock concerts, bars, nightclubs and other 'Western' spaces, to which the 'vamp' traditionally belongs. Kaif's otherness is further suggested by the fact that she has been cast as a NRI on many occasions (sometimes even when the film is set in India). Despite this, her characters never transgress the moral boundaries usually placed around the heroine. Kaif has thus cultivated a harmless and sexually non-threatening persona, which gives her a broad appeal. By having done so, Kaif can appear both traditional and modern at the same time, quelling any anxieties about her otherness. The appeal and eroticism of Kaif's stardom partially stems from her ability to portray other forms of femininity – the wild side – but, ultimately, she submits to an Indian (patriarchal) moral code. Despite similarities to the vamp (smoking, drinking), Kaif is actually tame in comparison to the vamp (whose sexuality was seen to be uncontrolled). Essentially, her image is clean, which allows a disavowal of voyeurism of her on-screen vampishness (Kasbekar 2002: 296) allowing the audience to enjoy the sexual fantasies of mixed-race stars in a benign way. While reflecting on her appeal, Kaif described her own looks as 'inoffensive and slightly nondescript', adding that she is 'just pleasant' (Anon. 2009c: 74). By flirting with attributes of the vamp (which she counters with her 'inoffensive' looks) Kaif acknowledges her on-screen predecessors but engages with the modernity that stars such as Zeenat Aman signified. The lack of transgression allows Kaif to become a universal figure of modernity that does not threaten the status quo; thus, her ethnicity makes her very popular for advertisements and endorsements, despite being full of contradictory discourses.

Kaif's outsider/foreign status is also utilized later in her career in films such as *Zindagi Na Milegi Dobarra* (You Won't Get Another Life, Zoya Akhtar, 2011). The film is a coming of age/road movie that follows three friends, Kabir (Abhay Deol), writer Imran (Farhan Akhtar) and workaholic Arjun (Hritik Roshan) on a trip around Spain. Along the way they meet Laila (Katrina Kaif) who eventually falls in love with Arjun. Laila teaches him to enjoy life, and tensions amongst the friends are resolved. The film acknowledges Kaif's racial ambiguity, as when she is first approached she is asked if she is from Brazil and she replies, 'Half US, half India' and that she lives in London, demonstrating the diversity of Indians living abroad. Both character and casting highlight the complexities of the modern Indian identity (and the NRI). As a road movie set in Spain, the film exhibits all the privileges that Indians are now able to afford. Antique cars and designer villas are part of the cosmopolitan lifestyle that liberalization has brought (Kamble 2015). Laila's ambiguity and apparent availability means she appears as another consumable object of this very lifestyle. Kaif's ambiguous status supports this, and her casting here changes the significance of the meaning of her character.

Laila is not only an instructor but also an ambassador for the kinds of opportunities that liberalization has afforded them. These cosmopolitan experiences are now there for Indians to enjoy, and Kaif's casting as Laila (and their scuba-diving instructor) presents her as an agent in this process. The West (here, Spain) is not a place of corruptible influence and instead is a place to be explored and consumed, with the help of Kaif as a not-quite-foreign exotic spectacle that is obtainable. Kaif's film roles here also remark a difference in the attitude towards the outsider post-economic liberalization, namely one that is more open (though not entirely so). Much like in the Barbie campaign, Kaif is symbolic of the new-found consumerism of a modern India.

Ajay Gehlawat argues that Laila demonstrates all the character traits of the Anglo-Indian (drinking, premarital sex) and that the film portrays this in a positive manner (2015: 83). This demonstrates the shifting discourses of ethnicity in a post-liberalized economy. In the past Anglo-Indians have often been presented through the Gothic strategies and seen as 'an excess of British colonialism'. (MacDonald-D'Costa 2009: 347). Whereas the Anglo-Indian community is a group within the nation (which complicates the idea of a homogenized Indian identity), Kaif's outsider-ness poses less of a threat and is free of any colonial attachments; hence, she is able to be presented as young, modern and cosmopolitan rather than as a member of the aged, isolated Anglo-Indian community (MacDonald-D'Costa 2009).

Not quite Chin Chin Chu

Katrina Kaif has always been seen as desirable, even before she participated in item songs; of particular note is her sex appeal (shown by the types of polls she won such as 'Sexiest pin up girl' mentioned earlier), as it demonstrates a sexualization of her foreignness. She is not the first mixed-race star to become associated with the item song, as 'actresses that played the vamp character were more often than not "foreign" themselves … it was easier for audiences to view these characters as removed from the mainstream, further objectifying and marginalising the vamp character itself' (Rekhari 2014: 140). Though Kaif is not a vamp, her foreigner status may make her appear 'removed from the mainstream' and the sexualization of her and the item song demonstrates some similarities to the vamp, mainly the sexualization of a foreign body (as it was easier to accept these bodies outside of the Indian moral realm). Conversely, in his discussions of Helen, Anustup Basu discusses her arrival at a very significant point in Indian cinema. He states that 'Helen could thus emerge only as a vamp – the absolute counterpoint to the nation imagined a woman – in the new dispensation of the free republic' (2013: 144). Thus, modern film stars emerge in a different historical context, one of economic liberalization and globalization, from that of the vamps of the 1960s/1970s. Hence ethnic/foreign stars arrive at a point of consumption and modernity. Furthermore, Diane Negra states that 'the ethnic woman has often symbolized excess and exaggeration' (2001: 16). This 'excess' became prominent in such item songs as 'Sheila Ki Jawani' in *Tees Maar Khan* (Farah Khan, 2010), 'Chikni Chammeli' in *Agneepath* (Malhotra, 2012) and 'Kamli' in *Dhoom 3*. If Helen had to be the vamp because of an image of the new imagined nation, Kaif is associated with a post-feminist image of the modern Indian woman.

Kaif is also participating in a more recent trend whereby 'actresses rely on in item numbers to express their versatility, create media coverage and earn large amounts of money' (Rekhari 2014: 144), which is more common and not exclusive to mixed-race stars (and can even include male stars). Stars such as Kareena Kapoor, Aishwarya Rai-Bachchan and Priyanka Chopra may have performed item songs, but their participation in this trend materializes differently. Kareena Kapoor's familial connections are well known and represented, whereas for Rai-Bachchan and Chopra, their Miss World credentials subsume and soften the taboos over female sexuality – all three stars are sanctioned through patrilineal forms of attachment, through family or the male gaze of the beauty pageant. Another outsider who has also found fame in the item song is Candian-Indian and industry outsider, Sunny Leone. Hence although domestic stars may be performing item songs, Kaif's participatation circulates closer to the discourses of mixed-race/foreign stars. Kaif's mixed-race background harks back to taboos of the colonial era, when Anglo-Indian women were unavailable for Indian men (Gangoli 2005: 149).

This may explain why there is a fascination with Kaif, as in her films she appears more available and attainable for the hero (she will typically end up with the Indian hero even when faced with a choice, such as in *Namastey London* and *Jab Tak Hai Jaan*). Kaif's stardom may be an attempt to subsume anxieties about racial taboos by demonstrating the availability of NRI/foreign women.

The item song 'Sheila Ki Jawani' featured in the film *Tees Maar Khan* takes place on a film set, as opposed to the cabaret bar in which many of Helen's songs were set. In its modern iteration, this item song has to take place here, so as to associate it with an earlier era of Hindi cinema (as can be seen in 'Dard-e-Disco' in *Om Shanti Om* [Farah Khan, 2007] which also takes place on a film set). By doing so, it parodies this cinematic tradition but also partakes in the pleasures of its exhibition. This places the item song into an invention of the cinema, as it is being produced for a film. The association between item songs and sex is alluded to by a sign that appears in the opening, which says 'Blue films presents Sheila Ki Jawani' (blue films are another term for porn films). The film is about a thief who pretends to be a film producer in order to fool a village and to rob a train. The 'film within a film' parodies many film tropes, the item song being one of them. By reducing it to being set in a film studio, the item song is part of a nostalgic, but also seedy, view of Indian cinema (and one that can only be explored by an outsider/foreigner).

The male vocals in the song lament an unconditional love typically depicted by the hero for the heroine from a bygone era. Sheila rejects this cinematic love, instead insisting on 'money, cars, luxury villas' as a way to win her over. This neoliberal view disavows the humble hero, who typically insists on his love being the only need for a successful relationship. While Tabrez Mirza Khan's (Akshay Kumar) old cinematic style romantic love is being rejected; this can be read as a parody whereby this type of romantic intent is dated. Kaif's Sheila is modern (that is to say neoliberal) and wishes to consume goods that are afforded by her desirable body. In the song, lyrics such as 'I am too sexy for you' and 'I won't fall into your hands' demonstrate her desirability but also elusiveness. It is a commodity that is desired for, yearned for, but never really within the grasp of the audience. Her physical features are commodifiable and afford her the position to demand these capital items.

Though her body is presented to the audience, Kaif's sexuality appears non-threatening (demonstrated by the presentation of her body for the male gaze), and by appearing as a comedic song (signified by its excessiveness) any potential sexual agency is reduced. Furthermore, its appropriation as a song used on TV talent shows (broadcast to a family audience) demonstrates the use of Kaif as a non-offensive and safe vehicle for any form of erotic spectacle. The reception of Kaif is representative of globalization: whereas once the foreign item song girl was a vamp, now she can be the heroine.

The costume emphasizes Kaif's abdominal muscles, fetishizing her body, which is demonstrated by the belly-dance-type moves that she performs. Part of this sexualized image is offset by discourses that surround the production of such song sequences and her body. That Kaif had to undergo special training and weight-loss programmes demonstrates that for her this was unnatural and was only done for the sake of the role. This creates a clear demarcation between her and any overt sexualization, removing any threat of female sexual agency. By trying to appear as non-threatening, it counterbalances her status as sex symbol and eases the tension of consuming an overtly sexualized performance. Furthermore, by deconstructing the image of Sheila, it produces a counter image to earlier ethnic stars. Helen, for example, would not feature outside of the cinema as heavily. Her sexuality and dance moves would appear as a natural part of her persona rather than as part of a carefully constructed image produced by choreographers, nutritionists, fitness trainers and so on. In this instance, Kaif is not being represented as sexually promiscuous; instead the image enters into the globalized media market, as an image that is set to go viral on the internet (or as a ring tone or on TV promos) for bigger box office returns. While the assertativeness of recent item song girls may show some resistance to the male gaze (Gehlawat 2015: 60) in Kaif's item songs there remains a male arbitrar. For example, Tabrez is actively trying to stop Sheila from dancing because she is supposed to be for his gaze only. Furthermore in 'Kamli', the item song sequence takes place as an audition, in which if the hero takes his eyes off her, she fails the test. Thus, in both sequences the assertiveness is structured around the male gaze (literally), which limits its potential to be read as resistant. Furthermore, many of the close ups emphasize the beauty of the item song girls, and are more reminiscent of beauty product adverts; hence, the effect of liberalization on the item song girl is to present her as a billboard for more endorsements/products. The assertiveness of such stars then can be read as a willingness to sell more products and tie-ins.

After portraying the heroine, NRI, item girl and wild party girl, these personas would be consolidated in *Jab Tak Hai Jaan*. Her character Meera Thapur is an amalgamation of her earlier on-screen iterations, and can be seen as a consolidation of glamorous star image, NRI identity and traditional personas. Meera smokes (a habit that is now not limited to the vamp), goes clubbing and is intimate with men. Despite being cast in a romantic melodrama, her sex appeal is exploited, as can be seen in the club song sequence where Samar

(Shah Rukh Khan) actively encourages her to indulge in her wildness. These instances are possible, precisely because Kaif is able to transgress cultural borders. Kaif's outsider status renders her culturally and ethnically fluid and she is free to be cast in whichever way the filmmakers require of her, which also adds to her allure.

In addition, this ethnic fluidity is demonstrated in some of her more recent films. The move towards genre cinema in recent Bollywood demonstrates the potential for shifting representations of mixed-race/outsider stars. As a foreigner, she is able to portray more global/Hollywood types of characters. For example, in *Zindagi Na Milegi Dobarra* she portrays the carefree NRI who is able to promise wild adventure in the road movie genre, and in *Bang Bang* she is cast as the wide-eyed rom com figure as seen in Hollywood, such as Jennifer Garner in *13 going on 30* (Gary Winick, 2004) or Anne Hathaway in *The Devil Wears Prada* (David Frankel, 2006). The latter is further signified by her costume (of knitted cardigans and woolly hats, which serve to infantilize her, but also highlight her affiliation with the West). Kaif's foreignness allows her to play these roles that co-opt Hollywood genres such as the road movie and the romantic comedy. Both these films were successes, and the increased frequency of genre cinema in Bollywood may mean that Kaif's differences allow her to be cast in different roles, which other stars who lack the NRI/foreigner connection may be excluded from (or perform less convincingly).

Conclusion

Katrina Kaif's cameo in *Bombay Talkies* (Anurag Kashyap, Dibakar Banerjee, Karan Johar, Zoya Akhtar, 2013) demonstrates the fragmentation of her star image. For example, she appears on screen in an item song (sex symbol), on a poster (star), as a

Barbie doll (commodity) and as a fairy godmother (Figure 16.1). While these incarnations represent the multifaceted relationship that audiences have with film stars, they also demonstrate the ends to which film producers and advertisers exploit the image of stars. What is specific to Katrina Kaif is that they also demonstrate the commodification of her image – as either an item song girl or to endorse products – and suggest the different ways her stardom can be interpreted by the audience.

Kaif's professionalism is an important part of her star persona. By appearing in films such as *Jab Tak Hai Jaan* and working with the legendary Chopra family, Kaif could be attempting to be taken more seriously and solidify her place in the film industry. Other aspects of her professionalism are manifest in the preparation and training that she undertakes for item songs. For example, a 2013 feature in *Filmfare* shows her in the gym, with quotes about the different looks she achieved for her item songs (Anon. 2013b: 42). By doing so, she exposes the hard work involved in achieving the star image. However, this also counter balances her sexy image by showing how it takes many months to achieve and is thus highly constructed, which further demonstrates the power of disavowal in Hindi cinema (Kasbekar 2002). Overall, *Filmfare* magazine is keen to suggest that Kaif is hardworking and humble, and hence justly rewarded with fame akin to many success stories of immigrants globally (and the American dream).

While Kaif's racial background may bring her success in endorsements, it still remains problematic. In one article she is described as 'the perfect example of an outsider who dreams to make it large in the big bad world of movies' (Anon. 2013a: 22). Her career and success demonstrate that, as with the figure of the NRI, Indian identity has been extended to include even those not fully Indian (even though it was her Indian-ness that allowed her to become a star in Bollywood in the first place). As such, Kaif's construction as the 'other' has been rendered into something that is approachable and non-threatening. Her

Figure 16.1 *Bombay Talkies* (Karan Johar, Dibakar Banerjee, Zoya Akhtar, Anurag Kashyap 2013).

involvement with the 'big bad world of movies' constructs Kaif as the harmless, unadulterated outsider (which draws on the myth of the colonial white woman as pure/innocent). A big part of Kaif's allure is her inoffensiveness. Her looks have been exploited for stardom, but her figure embodies a muted and demure persona that does not threaten the Indian woman ideal. For many audiences, it is the myth of attainable whiteness (through products and consumption) that has the allure; hence, Kaif is reduced to her westernized features. Her proximity to whiteness, by contrast, does not guarantee her a prominent position in the cinema – in many of her more recent films she is reduced to playing the side role.

Kaif's mixed-race identity has created unique opportunities for filmmakers to explore new genres, ideas and representations of the traditional Indian heroine. Since her turn as item song girl, however, her appearance in the cinema has been reduced. For example, Kaif's contribution to *Dhoom 3* is reduced to the song sequence 'Kamli' and she is relegated to the supporting cast, despite appearing prominently in the promotion of this film. It appears then, that her sexualized image has led her to be more visible in adverts than in the cinema. This can be seen in the reduction of her prominence in *Filmfare* magazine from this period onwards (though this is also due to the rise of other stars). In the period 2008–2010 Kaif appeared in this magazine as a complex character, whereas post-Sheila her appearances tended to be reduced to adverts and the gossip sections. As a female star, the struggle to maintain more substantial roles is difficult; such is the way for commercial film acting. Her film career has been unique, as she was the first major NRI star, and comparisons with Helen demonstrate the problematic attitudes to not-quite-Indian woman that are still prevalent in modern Indian media today.

Works Cited

Anon. (2007a), 'Friday Fever', *Filmfare*, 56 (3), March.
Anon. (2007b), 'Who's Hot Who's Not', *Filmfare*, 56 (12), December: 82.
Anon. (2008a), *Filmfare*, 57 (11), 25 June: 50.
Anon. (2008b), *Filmfare*, 57 (15), 21 August–3 September: 12.
Anon. (2008c), *Filmfare*, 15 October.
Anon. (2009a), *Filmfare*, 58 (4), 4 March: 45.
Anon. (2009b), *Filmfare*, 58 (18), 14 October.
Anon. (2009c), *Filmfare*, 58 (24), 23 December.
Anon. (2013a), *Filmfare*, 62 (6), 10 April: 22.
Anon. (2013b), *Filmfare*, 62 (8), 8 May: 42.
Basu, Anustup (2013), '"The Face that Launched a Thousand Ships": Helen and Public Femininity in Hindi Film', in Meheli Sen and Anustup Basu (eds), *Figurations in Indian Film*, 139–57, Basingstoke: Palgrave Macmillan.
Beltrán, Mary C. (2009), *Latina/o Stars in U.S. Eyes: The Making and Meanings of Film and TV Stardom*, Urbana: University of Illinois Press.
Chopra, Anupama (2002), *Dilwale Dulhania Le Jayenge*, London: British Film Institute.
Gangoli, Geetanjali (2005), 'Sexuality, Sensuality and Belonging: Representations of the "Anglo-Indian" and the "Western" Woman in Hindi Cinema', in Raminder Kaur and Ajay J. Sinha (eds), *Bollyworld: Popular Indian Cinema through a Transnational Lens*, 143–62, London: Sage.
Gehlawat, Ajay (2012), 'The Construction of 1970s Femininity, or Why Zeenat Aman Sings the Same Song Twice', *South Asian Popular Culture*, 10 (1): 51–62.
Gehlawat, Ajay (2015), *Twenty-First Century Bollywood*, Abingdon: Routledge.
Kamble, Jayashree (2015), 'All Work or All Play? Consumption, Leisure and Ethics under Globalization in *Zindagi Na Milegi Dobara*', *South Asian Popular Culture*, 13 (1): 1–14.
Kasbekar, Asha (2002), 'Hidden Pleasures, Negotiating the Myth of the Female Ideal In Popular Hindi Cinema', in Rachel Dwyer and Christopher Pinney (eds), *Pleasure and Nation: The History, Politics and Consumption of Public Culture in India*, 286–308. New York: Oxford University Press.

MacDonald-D'Costa, Alzena (2009), 'India's Uncanny: Anglo-Indians as (post)Colonial Gothic', *Continuum: Journal of Media & Cultural Studies*, 23 (3): 335–49.

Manzoor, Sarfraz (2007), 'Cultural Exchange', *Guardian*, 23 March, online at: www.theguardian.com/film/2007/mar/23/2 (accessed 30 June 2016).

Meo, Nick (2003), 'Bollywood Confidential', *Guardian*, 29 September, online at: www.theguardian.com/film/2003/sep/29/india (accessed 30 June 2016).

Negra, Dianne (2001), *Off-White Hollywood: American Culture and Ethnic Female Stardom*, London: Routledge.

Osuri, Goldie (2008), 'Ash-coloured Whiteness: The Transfiguration of Aishwarya Rai', *South Asian Popular Culture*, 6 (2): 109–23.

Rekhari, S. (2014), 'Sugar and Spice: The Golden Age of Hindi Movie Vamps, 1960s–1970s', in Vikrant Kishore, Amit Sarwal and Parichay Patra (eds), *Bollywood and its Other(s): Towards New Configurations*, 133–45, Basingstoke: Palgrave Macmillan.

Sharpe, Jenny (2005), 'Gender, Nation, and Globalization in *Monsoon Wedding* and *Dilwale Dulhania Le Jayenge*', *Meridians: Feminism, Race, Transnationalism*, 6 (1): 58–81.

Waheed, Alia (2010), 'Katrina Kaif: How Bollywood Fell in Love with a British Unknown', *Guardian*, 19 December, online at: www.theguardian.com/film/2010/dec/19/bollywood-belly-dance-british-star (accessed 30 June 2016).

Index

Note: References in **bold** denote in-depth discussion of a topic, whilst references in *italics* denote a poster, photograph or other illustration. Footnotes are indicated by lower case *n* (if more than one footnote is present on the page they will be numbered, eg. 50*n*4).

Aadmi (1940) 16*n*
Aadmi Aur Insaan (1969) 77
Aan (1952) 74
Aandhi Toofan (1985) 169
Aankhen (1966) 74, 85
Aap ki Adaalat (TV, 2004–) 199–200
Aaraam Thampuran (1997) 99, 106, 107
Aaya Toofan (1964) 156
Abbas Ajmeri 112, 114
Abhimaan (1973) 74
The Affair see Dillagi
Afsana (1951) 110
Agent Vinod (1977) 159
Agneepath (2012) 162, 226
Ahmed, Ali Nobil 141, 162
Aikya Kerala (political group) 46
Akashdeep (1965) 77
Akhtar, Farhan 225
Akkare (1984) 102
Akkare Akkare Akkare (1990) 105, 106
Ali, Somy 194
Alien see Begaana
Aman, Zeenat 161, 166, 224
Amar Akbar Anthony (1977) 74
Amar Jyoti (1936) 15, 16, 17, *18*
The Amazing Spider-Man (2012) 3
Ambujam. Cherai 48
American Bandstand (TV, 1952–89) 131, *131*
Amrit Manthan (1933) 18
Amrohi, Kamal 168
Anakh Jattan Di (1990) *141*
Anand, Dev 73, 80, 83, 167
 education 77
Ananthaswami, B. 166
Anari (1959) 83, 84, 155
Anavalarthiya Vanambadi (1960) 49, *50*
Anavalarthiya Vanambadiyude Makan (1971) 50
Andaaz (1949) 80, 87*n*2

Anderson, Benedict 95
Andha Kanoon (1983) 169
Anhonee (1952) 80
Aniyatti (1955) 48
Anjaam (1994) 196
Anjaneyulu, C.S.R. 49
Anpadh (1962) 79
Anupama (1966) 74, 77, 79, 82
Apne (2007) 220
Apocalypse see Qayamat
Appu (1990) 105
Apte, Narayan Hari; *Na Patnari Goshta* 22
Apte, Nayana 27
Apte, Shanta 6, **15–29**, *17*, *18*, *23*, *27*, *28*
 critical praise 16, *25*
 vs Durga Khote 16–17
 early career 16
 hit songs 21
 hunger strike 24–6
 Jau mi cinemat 28
 legal battles 27
 personal life 26, 27–8
 rise to stardom 18
 voice training 20
Aram + Aram = Kinnaram (1985) 103
Arnaz, Desi Jr. 132
Arnaz, Desi Sr. 132
Arnaz, Lucie Desirée 132
As Long As I Live see Jab Tak Hai Jaan
Asa Nu Maan Watna Da (2004) 138
Ashraf, Syed Firdus 198–9
Athavale, Shantaram 17
Atmasakhi (1952) 48
Auzaar (1997) 197
Avakasi (1954) 48
Awaara (1951) 80, 84, 95
Awakening see Bedari; Jagriti
The Awakening see Jaagruti

Index

Aya Sawan Jhoom Ke (1969) 74
Ayodhyecha Raja (1932) 15, 17, 19
Ayyapan, Shree Amma Yanger *see* Sridevi
Azaad (1955) 74

Baaghi: A Rebel for Love (1990) 197, 197*n*
Baahubali: The Beginning (2015) 4
Baazi (1951) 60
Baazigar (1993) 196, 207
Baba Kalyani (2006) 107
Babar, Raj 142
Babi, Praveen 161, 166
Babul (1950) 87
Bachchan, Amitabh 1, 74, 74*n*2, 75, 85, 161, *162*, 163*n*1, 166, 169–70, 173, 182, 191*n*, 195
Baghdad (1952) 110
Baharen Phir Bhi Aayengi (1966) 77
Baharon Ki Manzil (1968) 77
Bahut Din Hue (1954) 110
Baiju Bawra (1952) 110
Bajpai, Shailaja 194
Bajrangi Bhaijaan (2015) 202–3
Bala, Kanan *see* Devi, Kanan
Ball, Lucille 132
Balyasakhi (1954) 48
Bandini (1963) 74, 77, 82
Banerjee, Maya 152
Bang Bang! (2014) 219, 228
Bangarada Manushya (1972) 94, 95
Barnouw, Erik & Krishnaswamy, S.; *Indian Film* 2
Barsaat (1949) 84
Barua, P.C. 32, 39
Basu, Anustup 152, 161, 182, 226
Batwara (1989) 85*n*
Baywatch (2017) 4
Bedara Kannappa (1954) 90–1
Bedari (1957) 109, 114, 115, 117–22
   lyrics 119–20
Begaana (1963) 77, 79, 80–1
Being Bhaijaan (2014) 199
Belli Moda (1967) 87*n*2
The Beloved see *Saawariyan*
Belton, John 19
Beltrán, Mary 220
Bend It Like Beckham (2002) 3
Benjamin, Walter 77
Berlant, Lauren 134
Betab, Narayan Prasad 40
Beyas, Felix J.H. 47
Beyond the Horizon see Vahan
Bhagavatar, Sebastian Kunju 47
Bhakta Vijaya (1956) 91

Bhaktakuchela (1949) 49
Bhaktha Kanakadasa (1960) 92
Bharatham (1991) 102
Bhattacharya, Abhi 115, 117
Bhole, Keshav Rao 18, 20
Bhookailasa (1958) 92
Bhosle, Asha 182
Bhosle, Keshavrao 19
Bhowani Junction (1956) 129
Bhushan, Bharat 77
Big Brother (UK TV, 2000–18) 210
Bikhre Moti (1971) 155
Bilet Pherat (1921) 34*n*7
Billig, Michael 187–8, 190
Billu (2009) 205, 214–16, *215*
Black Market see Kalabazaar
Bland Law see Andha Kanoon
Blast 3 see Dhoom 3
The Bluebird see Neelakuyil
Bodyguard (2011) 196
Boeing Boeing (1985) 103
The Bombay Chronicle 15
Bombay Talkies (2013) 228–9, *229*
Bombay Talkies (studio) 18
Boot Polish (1954) 110, 112, 128
Bose, Modhu 34*n*7
Bose, Subhash Chandra 117
Brahanandam 1–2
Branded Oath see Ayodhyecha Raja
Brave Man see Himmatwala
The Brave-Hearted Will Take Away the Bride see Dilwale Dulhania Le Jayenge
Bride and Prejudice (2004) 3, 4
Bride for a Night see Dulhan ek Raat Ki
Brooks, Peter 80*n*14
Brother Bajrangi see Bajrangi Bhaijaan
Brother-in-law see Devar
Brynner, Yul 76
Butler, Jeremy G. 4–5

Call of War see Elaan- E-Jung
Came the Typhoon see Aaya Toofan
Caravan (1971) 160, 161
Cartwright, Angela 132
Casanova (2012) 103
Cawelti, John 24
Chaalbaaz (1989) 184, 185, 187, 188
Chacha Bhatija (1977) 75
Chak De! India (2007) 212, 213
Chakravarty, Jaya 166, 175–6, 175*n*50
Chakravarty, Mithun 1*n*2, 73
Chakravarty, Sumita S. 5

Chakravarty, V.S. Ramanujam 176*n*51
Chandan Ka Palna (1967) 79
Chandavaliya Thota (1964) 94
Chandni (1989) 182
Chandrolsavam (2005) 104
Chaplin, Charlie 60, 185
Chatterjee, Gayatri 40
Chatterjee, Partha 34*n*6, 38
Chatterjee, Sarat Chandra 33
Chechi (1950) 54
Chennai Express (2013) 207
Cherian, P.J. 46*n*1
Childhood Friend see Balyasakhi
China Town (1962) 159
Chion, Michel 188
Chiranjeevi 1
Chiranjeevi (1936) 92
Chithram (1988) 102
Chithram, Mithunam (1993) 105
Chitnis, Leela 18
Chopra, Anupama 196, 208
Chopra, Priyanka 4, 162, 226
Chopra, Radhika 141
Chopra, Yash 182, 209
Chotta Mumbai (2007) 104
Chupke Chupke (1975) 75, 77
The Churning of Nectar see Amrit Manthan
CID (1955) 49, 69
Claimant see Avakasi
Clarion Call see Lalkaar
Clifford, James 144, 153
Consequences see Anjaam
Conviction see Yakeen
Cook, Pam 210–11
The Coronation of Lord Ram see Sreeramapattabhisekham
Courteousness see Sharafat
Courtney, Alan D. 129–30
Crawford, Joan 125
The Crazed Lover see Deewana
The Crown see Kireedam
Cruise, Tom 4*n*7, 208

Dabangg (2010) 193, 195–6, 197, 199
Dabangg 2 (2012) 162, 196, 197
Daera (1953) 23*n*
Daku Bhairav Singh (2001) 86
Dancing Lady (1933) 125
Daniel, J.C. 56
The Darjeeling Limited (2007) 3
Darr: A Violent Love Story (1993) 196, 207, 212, 216
Daru, Leena 187
Das, Srijana Mitra 140*n*

The Dating Game (TV, 1965–74) 131
Davidson, Sara 127, 131
Davis, Bette 87*n*1
De, Shobha 172
DeCordova, Richard 4
Deewana (1992) 205–6
Deewar (1975) 85, 95
Deleuze, Gilles 202
Dennis the Menace (TV, 1959–63) 127, 131–2
Deol, Abhay 225
Deol, Dharmendra Singh 7, **73–86**
    box office success 74
    career 73
    vs contemporaries 77, 85
    diminishing stardom 85–6
    discovery 75
    early life 75–6
    lack of screen persona 73
    vs Raj Kapoor 84
    in 'reform socials' 78–82
    screen image 77
    sexualization 84
    tabloid gossip 78
    versatility 74–5
Deol, Esha 174*n*43
Desai, Manmohan 165, 169
Destiny see Naseeb
Devar (1966) 74, 79
Devasuram (1993) 99, 106, 107
Devdas (1935) 3, 15, 23*n*, 37
Devdas (2002) 5, 9, 205, 213–14
Devi, Aruna 152
Devi, B. Saroja 93
Devi, Chandravati 35
Devi, Kanan 6, **31–43**
    advertising work 31
    autobiographical writing 38–41
    awards 33
    background 38
    break with studios 32, 37
    death 41
    vs Durga Khote 39
    early career 32
    and Indian national identity 31
    name change and identity 36–8
    as 'new woman' 33–4
    rise to stardom 32
    Shobare Ami Nomi 32
    singing career 32–3
    transition from silent to talkies 32
Devi, Rashundari 40
Devi, Sabita 35

Devi, Thavamani 49
The Devil Wears Prada (2006) *228*
Dhaiber, Keshavrao 17
Dharam Veer (1977) 74
Dharmendra 163–4, 167, 168, 172–4, 176–7, 178
Dhool Ka Phool (1959) 92
Dhoom 3 (2013) 224, 226, 230
Diamond of the Heart see Dil Kaa Heera
Dil Apna Punjabi (2006) 138
Dil Daulat Duniya (1972) 156–7
Dil Kaa Heera (1979) 77
Dil To Pagal Hai (1997) 207
Dillagi (1968) 77
Dilwale Dulhania Le Jayenge (1995) 143–5, 196, 206, 212–13, 222–3
Diwana (1967) 84
Dixit, Madhuri 189, 219
Dixon, Simon 104
Do Bigha Zameen (1953) 54, 110, 111
 awards 110*n*
Doane, Mary Ann 188
Don (1978) 162, *162*
Don (2006) 162, 196
Don 2 (2011) 196
Donga (1985) 1
Dost (1974) 79, 83
Douglas, Kirk 76
Dr. Madhurika (1935) 24
Dragon Flies in a Drizzle see Thoovaanathumbikal
Dream Girl (1977) 74, 169
Dream Merchant see Sapnon Ka Saudagar
The Drum (1938) 127
Dulhan ek Raat Ki (1967) 79, 82
Dulla Bhatti (1938) 119
Dum Maaro Dum (2011) 162
Duniya Na Mane see Kunku
Dutt, Guru 78
Dutt, Nargis *see* Nargis
Dutt, Sanjay 198
Dutt, Sunil 78, 156
 education 77
Dutta, J.P. 85*n*
Duty see Kartavya
Dwelling see Kidappadam
Dyer, Richard 4, 104, 110, 112, 125, 130, 206, 216
 Stars 5*n*10

East is East (1999) 3
Ego of Jats see Anakh Jattan Di
Ek Mahal Ho Sapnon Ka (1975) 77
Ek Tha Tiger (2013) 196, 197–8, 202, 219
Ekadashi (1955) 110

Elaan- E-Jung (1969) 75
Elephant Boy (1937) 127
Eleventh Lunar Day see Ekadashi
Elsaesser, Thomas 80*n*14
Embers see Pratigya; Sholay; Sholay
England Returned see Bilet Pherat
Estate see Jagir
The Eternal Flame see Amar Jyoti
Evans, Mary Ann *see* Fearless Nadia
Eyes see Aankhen

Faith and Law see Immaan Dharam
Fake Currency see Jaali Note
Fakhri, Nargis 220
FAN (2016) 206, 207, 215, 216
Farrell, Gerry 20–1
The Fearless see Dabangg
Fearless Nadia 5, 45, 152, 168, 169, 169*n*14
Female Ascetic see Jogan
Fernandes, Jacqueline 220
Fields, Danny 132
Film Hayat 118
Film India (journal) 15
Filmfare (journal) 76, 112, *113*, 116
Filmland (journal) 15
The Flower and the Stone see Phool Aur Patthar
Flower of Dust see Dhool Ka Phool
For Your Love see Tere Pyar Mein
Friday Night with Jonathan Ross (UK TV, 2001–10) 205, 212
Friend see Dost

Gaandharvam (1993) 107
Gadar Ek Prem Katha see Bajrangi Bhaijaan
Gaines, Jane 114
Gair Kanooni (1989) 186–7
The Gambler see Baazigar
Gandharva, Bal 15, 16, 19
Gandhi (1982) 3
Gandhi, Mahatma 117, 120
Gandhinagar Second Street (1986) 102, 105
Gandhy, Behroze 182
Ganga Jumna (1961) 87, 155
Ganga Ki Lehren (1964) 79
Garland of the Forest see Vanamala
Garner, Jennifer 228
Garv: Pride and Honour (2004) 197, 200
Gehlawat, Ajay 225–6
Genesan, Shivaji 50
Gentleman Cheat see Shree 420
Ghosh, Pronoti 115, 117
Ghulami (1985) 85*n*

Giddens, Anthony 106
Gill, Guggu *141*, 142
Gledhill, Christine 4, 80*n*14
Gnanamika (1940) 46*n*1
Go For It! India see Chak De! India
The God-Demon see Devasuram
Golden Man see Bangarada Manushya
Gole 15–16
Goliyon Ki Raasleela: Ram-Leela (2013) 162
Gopal Krishna (1937) 16*n*
Gopal, Sangita 4*n*7
Gopalakrishnan, Chelangatt 56
Gopinath, Gayatri 144
Govil, Nitin 4*n*7
Govinda 186
The Great Gatsby (2013) 1
Greenbaum, Andrea 186–7
Grewal, Inderpal 140
Guddi (1970) 74*n*4, 76
Gumnaam (1965) 157–8
Gunasagari (1953) 93
Gupta, Raj Kumar 117
Gupte, Sumati 24
Gurudev (1993) 184, 188
Gyllenhaal, Jake 210

Hail Goddess Mahalaxmi see Jai Mahalaxmi
Hail, Holy Mother see Jai Mata Ki
Half Acre Land see Do Bigha Zameen
Hallo (2007) 104
Hansen, Kathryn 40, 168
Happening '68 (TV, 1968) 131
Happy New Year (2014) 209, 210, 212
Haqeeqat (1964) 74, 85
Hardy, Thomas; *Tess of the d'Urbervilles* 82
Harischchandra (1955) 48
Hathaway, Anne 228
Hathyar (1989) 75, 85*n*
Hayakawa, Sessue 130
The Heart is Crazy see Dil To Pagal Hai
Heart, Wealth, World see Dil Daulat Duniya
Heer Ranjha (2009) 138
Helen 8, **151–62**, *158*, *162*, 182, 226, 230
  vs predecessors 152
  race and heritage 153
Here's Lucy (TV, 1968–74) 132
Himmatwala (1983) 183–4, 184*n*2
His Highness Abdullah (1990) 105–6, 107
Hitchcock, Alfred 80
Hollinger, Karen 5*n*10
Honor see Izzat
Howrah Bridge (1958) 154

Hum Hindustani (1960) 156
Hum Saath Saath Hain (1998) 194*n*1
Hum Tere Aashiq Hain (1979) 169
The Hunt see Shikaar
Hunterwali (1935) 169*n*14
Hurricane see Aandhi Toofan
Hyder Ali 88

I Am Your Lover see Hum Tere Aashiq Hain
I Love Lucy (TV, 1951–57) 132
Illegal see Gair Kanooni
The Illiterate see Anpadh
Illusion see Maya Machchindra
Immaan Dharam (1977) 160–1
In Your Name see Tere Naam
Indiana Jones and the Temple of Doom (1984) 3
Indira MA (1934) 24
Indira, M.K. 95
Iniyengilum (1983) 102
Inkaar (1971) 155–6
Innocent see Masoom (1957)
Intoxicating Youthfulness see Nashilee Jawani
Irani, Aruna 161
Iron Man see Loh Purush
Irupatham Noottandu (1987) 99
Issar, Punit 163
Iyengar, Gorur Ramaswamy 95
Izzat (1968) 79

Jaagruti (1992) 197
Jaali Note (1960) 129
Jab Tak Hai Jaan (2012) 219, 224, 227, 228, 229
Jackson, Amy 220
Jaffrey, Saeed 3
Jag Jeondeyan De Mele (2009) 138, 147
Jagdish 156
Jagir (1984) 75
Jagriti (1954) 109, 114, 115, *116*, 117–22
  lyrics 119–20
Jagte Raho (1956) 83, 84
Jai Ho (2014) 197, 198–9
Jai Mahalaxmi (1951) 110
Jai Mata Ki (TV, 1999) 163
Jassi (audience member) 147
Jawab see Sesh Uttar
Jedara Bale (1968) 94
Jee Aayan Nu (2002) 138, 144–5, 146
Jeet (1996) 197
Jeetendra 168, 170*n*18, 172–3
Jeevan Mrityu (1968) 77
Jewel Thief (1967) 129
Jhingan, Shikha 41

Jinnah, M.A. 117–18, 120
Jis Desh Mein Ganga Behti Hai (1960) 83, 84
Jogan (1950) 87
John, Barry 211
Johnny Gaddar (2007) 73
Johnson, Dwayne 'The Rock' 4
Johny Is My Name see Johny Mera Naam
Johny Mera Naam (1970) 167
Jones, Davy 133
Jore Barat (1931) 32
Joydeb (1926) 32
Jugnu (1973) 74
The Jungle Book (1942) 127
Junglee (1960) 155
Jurassic World (2015) 3
Jwar Bhata (1973) 82, 83
Jyoti (1981) 164, 169

Kab? Kyoon? Aur Kahan? (1970) 74
Kabhi Khushi Khabhie Gham (2001) 207
Kabli Khan (1963) 156
Kaif, Katrina 9, 162, 219–30, **219–31**, *229*
Kaivara Mahathme (1961) 92
Kajol 223
Kakar, Sudhir 103
Kal Ho Naa Ho (2003) 212–13, 222–3
Kalabazaar (1960) 83
Kalyan, Pawan 3
Kanagal, Puttanna 95
Kandhan Karunai (1967) 189
Kapadia, Dimple 182
Kaplan, Caren 140
Kapoor, Anil 4, 4n7, 188
Kapoor, Kareena 162, 226
Kapoor, Raj 1n2, 26, 64, 73, 75, 83, 163, 166
    break with Nargis 84
    vs Dharmendra Singh Deol 84
    education 77
    vs Rajkumar 96
Kapoor, Rishi 85, 170n17
Kapoor, Shakti 3, 185
Kapoor, Shammi 75, 155, 158
Kapoor, Shashi 73
    stage work 77
Kapur, Anuradha 21
Kapur, Shekhar 185
Karishma Kudrat Kaa (1985) 77
Karmakar, Raj 26
Karnad, Girish 170n18
Kartavya (1979) 77
Kasturi Nivasa (1971) 94, 95
Kattathe Kilikkoodu (1983) 102

Kazi, Jamaluddin *see* Walker, Johnny
Keemat (1973) 74
Kelly, Gene 87n1, 188
Kerala Progressive Writers Association (KPAC) 53
Khan, Aamir 193, 196–7, 199
    advertising 196
Khan, Ali (film writer) 141
Khan, Ali Akbar (musician) 128–9
Khan, Amjad 155, 184
Khan, Irrfan 3, 4n7, 216
Khan, Mehboob 126–7, 129, 130
Khan, Sajid 8, **125–36**, *126*, *131*
    adoption 126–7
    early life 125
    in the US 129–30
Khan, Salman 8–9, **193–203**, *196*
    controversy 193
    early career 195
    prison sentence 193–4
    religion 198–202
    vs 'the other Khans' 196–7
Khan, Shah Rukh 5n11, 9, 75, 193, 195, 196–7, **205–18**, *209*, *215*, 223, 228
    branding 196, 206–10
    early career 196
    early life 205–6
    wealth 205
Khanna, Rajesh 3, 75, 77, 156
Khanna, Vinod 85, 178
Khatron ke Khiladi (1988) 74
Kher, Anupam 3
Khote, Durga 15, 16, *18*, 152
    on her singing 20
    vs Kanan Devi 39, 39n
Kick (2014) 196, 197
Kidappadam (1955) 54
Kidman, Nicole 210–11
Kim 170n17
The King and I (1956) 130, 133–4
The King and I (stage musical) 133–4
King, Barry 76n8
King Brothers 127, 128, 129, 130
The King of the Khyber Rifles (1953) 129
Kipling, Rudyard 127, 128
Kireedam (1989) 102, 107
Kittur Channamma (1961) 93, 95
Klein, Christina 133–4
Kohinoor (1960) 74
Kolhatkar, Bhaurao 19
Kosambi, Meera 16
Koshy, K.K. 46n2, 57
Koshy, K.V. 48

Kothari, Rajni 83
Kranti (1981) 164, 168–9
Krishna the Devout **see** *Krishnakuchel*
Krishnakuchel (1961) 49
Krishnamurthi, P.N. 89
Krishnamurthy, Kavita 189
Kuch Kuch Hota Hai (1998) 196, 207
Kuchela the Devout **see** *Bhaktakuchela*
Kumar, Akshay 227
Kumar, Ashok 32, 154
    art 77
Kumar, Dilip 62, 74, 75, 207
    education 77
    vs Rattan Kumar 111*n*
    typecasting 87
Kumar, Inder 201
Kumar, Manoj 73, 156, 157, 169
Kumar, Raj 78*n*10
Kumar, Rattan 7–8, **109–23**, *116*
    appearance 110
    audience appeal 112
    background 111
    childhood stardom 110–12
    vs Dilip Kumar 111*n*
    education 112
    marketing of 115
    migration to Pakistan 109, 112
    Pakistani remakes 114–15, 115–22
    press coverage 112–14, *113*
    religion 112
    star image 109, 121–2
Kumar, Sanjeev 170*n*18, 176
Kumari, Meena 79, 82, 84, 182
Kumari, Miss 6–7, **45–58**, *50*
    appearance 52
    attitude to fame 51
    background 48
    briefness of career 54
    criticism of 51
    death 55, 56–7
    early career 47–8
    independence from studios 52–3
    'jungle films' 49–50
    marriage 52, 54–5
    Merryland fims 48–9
    name and identity 48, 55
    obituaries 52, 56
    off-screen persona 54
    politics 53–4
    posthomous legacy 55–6
    religion 51
    visibility and fame 50–1

Kumkum 68, 69, 183
Kunchacko 46
Kunku (1937) 19, 21–4, *23*

Laila Majnu (1953) 110
Lal, Chatur 128–9
Lal Salam (1990) 102
Lalkaar (1972) 74, 85
Lamhe (1991) 184, 187
Land of the Ganges **see** *Jis Desh Mein Ganga Behti Hai*
Lang, Fritz 80
L'Arroseur arrosé (1895) 114
The Last Legion (2007) 4
Laughing Sinners (1931) 125
Lawrence, Michael 127
Leone, Sonny 220, 226
Let There be a Mansion of Dreams **see** *Ek Mahal Ho Sapnon Ka*
Life in a Metro (2007) 73
Life of Pi (2012) 3
Light **see** *Jyoti*
The Lion Man **see** *Narasimham*
Loh Purush (1999) 86
Long Da Lishkara (1986) 142–3, 145
The Long Kiss Goodnight (1996) 200
Long Live **see** *Jai Ho*
Lore **see** *Afsana*
Loren, Sophia 56
Lost in Space (TV, 1965–68) 132
Luck by Chance (2009) 212
Lucky: No Time for Love (2005) 197, 197*n*

Maa (1934) 32
Maan, Gurdas 142
Maan, Haminder Kaur *138*, *139*
Maan, Harbhajan 8, **137–49**, *138*
    advertising 137
    early life 138
    on-screen persona 139
Mad Lover **see** *Diwana*
Madambi (2008) 107
Mader, Elke 206
Madhubala 41, 69, 183
Mafia (1996) 86
Mageshkar, Lata 27
Mahabharata 128
Mahakavi Kalidasa (1955) 91
Maharashtra Film Company 17
Mahishasura Mardhini (1959) 92
Maine Pyar Kiya (1989) 195
Majhli Didi (1967) 74, 82
Majumdar, Neepa 26, 34, 54, 76*n*8, 111, 128, 181–2

Wanted Cultured Ladies Only! Female Stardom and Cinema in India, 1930s–1950s 5
Make Room for Daddy (TV, 1957–64) 132
Malashri 3
Malini, Hema 8, **163–79**, *164*
    early career 166
    gossip and private life 172–8
    longevity 163–4
    and Raj Kapoor 163
    screen persona 166
Mammooty 3, 105
Mamta (1966) 77, 79
Man see Aadmi (1940)
Man and Humanity see Aadmi Aur Insaan
The Man Who Would Be King (1975) 3
Mangeshkar, Lata 41, 182, 188
Manjil Virinja Pookkal (1980) 101–2
Mankekar, Purnima 140
Manmoyee Girls' School (1935) 32
Marcuse, Herbert 76*n*8
Mariakutty (1958) 48
Marriage see Shaadi
Marthanda Varma (1933) 46*n*1
Martin, Dean/Dean Paul 132
Masoom (1957) 114
The Master's Daughter-in-law see Rayara Sose
Maya (film, 1966) 125, *126*, 127–8, 130
Maya (TV, 1966) 128
Maya Machchindra (1933) 17
Mazumdar, Ranjani 197
McCarthy, Anna 128
Meera (1979) 174–5
Mehta, Asok 53
Menon, Thakazhi Sivasankara 53
Mera Gaon Mera Desh (1971) 74, 85
Mera Pind (2008) 138
Merciful Kandhan see Kandhan Karunai
Mere Brother Ki Dulhan (2011) 224
Mere Hamdam Mere Dost (1968) 77
Merryland (studio) 45
    'jungle films' 49–50
    vs Udaya 47
The Middle Sister see Majhli Didi
Minnaram (1994) 106
Miracle of Nature see Karishma Kudrat Kaa
Mirza, Diya 200
Mishra, Vijay 126, 153
Mission Impossible: Ghost Protocol (2011) 4
The Mistress of Spices (2005) 4
Mitchum, Robert 76
Mitti Wajaan Maardi (2007) 138, 145–6
Miyao, Daisuke 130

Modak, Shahu 16, *17*
Modi, Narendra 198
Mohammad Iqbal 118
Mohanlal 7, **99–108**, *100*
    advertising 104–5
    character traits 102
    early films 101
    eroticism 106–7
    masculinity 103, 105–6
    off-screen persona 104
    politics 102
    private vs public persona 104
    reputation as performer 102–3
    star persona 101
The Monkees 133
Monroe, Marilyn 56
Monsoons see Aya Sawan Jhoom Ke
Monteiro, Giselli 220
Mooney, Nicola 142
Mother India (1957) 8, 95, 125–6, *127*
Mr and Mrs 55 (1955) 69–70
Mr India (1987) 184*n*1, 185, *185*, 187
Mr Truthteller see Shriman Satyawadi
Mudiyanaya Putran (1961) 53
Mukerjee, Hrishikesh 74
Mukesh, Neil Nitin 223
Mukherjee, Joy 156
Mukunndetta Sumithra Vilikkunnu (1988) 106
Music see Sargam
The Mute see Padatha Painkili
My Beautiful Launderette (1984) 3
My Brother's Bride see Mere Brother Ki Dulhan
My Name Is Khan (2010) 213
My Son the Fanatic (1997) 3
My Village see Mera Pind
My Village, My Country see Mera Gaon Mera Desh

Naadodikkattu (1987) 102, 106
Nadia see Fearless Nadia
Nagara Haavu (1972) 95
Nair, Mohanlal Viswanathan *see* Mohanlal
Nair, P.K. 24*n*
Nair, Vasudevan 51
Nalla Thanka (1950) 48
Namastey London (2007) 220, 222–3, 224, 227
Namukku Parkkaan Munthirithoppukal (1986) 102
Nanda 157
Narasimham (2000) 99, 106
Naremore, James 212
Nargis 1*n*2, 5, 87*n*2, 178
Naseeb (1981) 164, 165, 167*n*11, 169–72, 173, 178
Nashilee Jawani (1986) 184*n*1

Naughty Boy (1962) 129
Naukar Biwi Ka (1983) 75
Nava, Mica 134
Navalokam (1951) 53
Naya Daur (1957) 59, 62–4, *63*
Naya Zamana (1971) 74, 77, 79
Nazir, Prem 49, 49*n*, 50
Neelakuyil (1954) 53, 54
Negra, Diane 226
Nehru, Jawaharlal 27, 117
A Nest in the Wind see Kattathe Kilikkoodu
Never Will I Forget You see Tumko Na Bhool Payenge
New Age see Naya Daur
New Theatres (studio) 32, 37
New Times see Naya Daur
The New World see Navalokam
New York (2009) 223–4
Night in London (1967) 159
Nightingale Brought Up by the Elephant see Anavalarthiya Vanambadi
Nirmala (1948) 46*n*1
North, Jay 127

O'Connor, Jane 109
Octopussy (1983) 3
Oil Lamp in the Wind see Toofan aur Diya
Olivier, Laurence 1
Om Shanti Om (2007) 207, 208–9, *209*, 210, 212, 227
Omanakuttan, C.R. 56
Omnibus (US TV, 1952–61) 128–9
Once There Was a Tiger see Ek Tha Tiger
Once Upon A Time see Bahut Din Hue
Our Heart is Punjabi see Dil Apna Punjabi
Owaisi, Asaduddin 198

Paap Ki Aandhi (1991) 77
Pacino, Al 211
Padatha Painkili (1957) 48
Padukone, Deepika 162, 207
Pagnis, Vishnupant 19
Paniparambil, Muhammad Kutty Ismail *see* Mammooty
Paranjape, Shankutala 22
Parekh, Asha 158
Paribartan (1949) 115
Partner (2007) 220
A Passage to India (1984) 3
The Path of Fire see Agneepath
Pather Panchali (1955) 2, 128–9
Pawar, Lalita 70
Phagun (1973) 77
Phool Aur Patthar (1966) 74, 79, 82, 84
The Picture see Chithram

The Pink Panther 2 (2009) 4
Pinney, Christopher 107
Pinto, Jerry 152
Pitt, Brad 210
A Play of Bullets see Goliyon Ki Raasleela: Ram-Leela
Play with Danger see Khatron ke Khiladi
Politics see Raajneeti
Ponnamma, Kaviyoor 107
Prabhas 4
Prabhatche Prabhatnagar (1935) 18
Prahlada (1941) 46*n*1
Prakash, Chinni 187
Prakash, Om 157, 207
Pran *158*
The Prank see Chupke Chupke
Prasad, Madhava 64, 78*n*10
Pratap, Mahrana 118
Pratigya (1975) 74, 77, 85
Price see Keemat
Pride see Abhimaan
Prince of Persia: The Sands of Time (2010) 210
Prism see Spadikam
Prisoner see Bandini
Procession of Memories see Yaadon ki Baraat
The Prodigal Son see Mudiyanaya Putran
The Provoked (2006) 4
Puri, Amirsh 3, 85
Puri, Om 3
Purnima (1965) 79
Putt Jattan De (1981) 141
Pyaasa (1957) 65–7, *66*, 69

Qayamat (1983) 75
Quaid-i-Azam see Jinnah, M.A.
Qurbaani (1980) 224

Raajneeti (2010) 220
Raakhee 165*n*5, 168
Raavanaprabhu (2001) 99, 105, 106
Race (2008) 220
Radha Kirshna (1954) 110
Radha Studio 32
Radio Ceylon 115
Rafiq Riazvi 118
Ragini 119
Rai(-Bachchan), Aishwarya 194, 213, 226
Rai Bachchan, Aishwarya 3, 4, 5
The Rains of Ranchipur (1955) 129
Raja Jani (1972) 167
Rajadhyaksha, Ashish 2, 17, 20
Rajadhyaksha, Ashish & Willeman, Paul
    Encyclopaedia of Indian Cinema 6

Rajavinte Makan (1986) 99
Rajkumar 7, **87–97**
    early life 91
    entry into cinema 90–1
    and Kannada cinema 91–2
    mythological films 92
    vs Raj Kapoor 96
    star persona 96
Rajnikanth 3
Rajput Ramani (1936) 16
Ram Aur Shyam (1967) 80
Rama Rao, N.T. 78*n*10
Ramachandran, M.G. 78*n*10, 96
Ramachandran, T.K. 101
Ramaswamy, Sumathi 115–17
Ranadheera Kanteerava (1960) 93
Randidangazhi (1958) 53
Rani, Devika 15, 33*n*4
Rank, Otto 121
Rao, A.N. Krishna 95
Rao, K. Ragavendra 183
Rao, Kanta 49
Rao, N.T. Rama 2, 96
Rao, Shanta 128–9
Rao, T.R. Subba 95
Rau, Santha Rama 134
Ravana the Lord **see** *Raavanaprabhu*
Ray, Satyajit 128–9, 128*n*
Rayara Sose (1957) 93–4
Razia Sultan (1983) 164, 168
Reality **see** *Haqeeqat*
Red Salute **see** *Lal Salam*
Reflection of the Nose Ring **see** *Long Da Lishkara*
The Refusal **see** *Inkaar*
Rehman, Waheeda 65, 79
Reisfeld, Randi 132
Rekha 166
Resham Ki Dori (1974) 77, 82
Revolution **see** *Kranti*
Richardson, Helen Jairag **see** Helen
The Risk-taker **see** *Baazigar*
Roop Ki Rani Choron Ka Raja (1993) 186, *186*
Roshan, Hritik 225
Roy, Bimal 74, 111
Roy, Reena 170*n*17
Rushton, Richard 202

Saawariyan (2007) 200
Sabu 127–8
Sadhana 156
Sadma (1983) 187, 188–9
Sahni, Balraj 78–9

Saigal, K.L. 2, 32, 33*n*3, 37
Sajid-Wajid 199
Saladdin 118
Sampoorna Ramayana (1961) 159
Samraat (1982) 168*n*12
Sanam Bewafa (1991) 200
The Sandalwood Castle **see** *Chandan Ka Palna*
Sanmanassullavarkku Samadhanam (1986) 106
Sapnon Ka Saudagar (1968) 84
Sapnon ka Saudager (1968) 163, 166
Sargam (1950) 110
Sarkar, Bhaskar 79
Sarkar, Tanika 35–6
Sattar, Abdul 65
Satyakam (1969) 77, 79, 83, 84
Satyamev Jayate (TV, 2012–) 197
Saussure, Ferdinand de 153
Savage Princess **see** *Aan*
Savitri (1941) 27, *28*
Scattered Pearls **see** *Bikhre Moti*
School Master (1958) 93–4
Seeta aur Geeta (1972) 163, 167, 169
Seidman, Steve 187, 190
Seller of Dreams **see** *Sapnon ka Saudager*
Sen, Meheli 184–5
Sen, Suchitra 3
Sen, Sushmita 201
Sesh Uttar (1942) 32
Shaadi (1962) 79
Shakeela 3
Shakuntula (1943/47) 128
Shantaram, V. 18, 20, 21
    on Shanta Apte 25–6
Sharafat (1970) 79
Sharpe, Jenny 144
Shetty, Shilpa 210–11
Shikaar (1968) 74
Shingler, Martin 4, 5
Ship of Theseus (2013) 211
Shivaji 118
Sholay (1975) 74, 85, 142, 167–8, 184
Shree 420 (1955) 80, 83, 84
Shriman Satyawadi (1960) 83
Shurtleff, Michael 212
Shyam Sundar (1932) 16, *17*
Silver Linings Playbook (2012) 3
Silver Star **see** *Vellinakshatram*
The Simpleton **see** *Anari*
The Simpleton **see** *Anari*
Singapore (1960) 155
Singh, Dara 3, 142
Singh is Kinng (2008) 146–7

Singh, Yograj *141*, 142
Singin' in the Rain (1952) 188
Sinha, Mala 79
Sinha, Shatrugan 170
Sinha, Shatrughan 85
Sippy, Ramesh 163, 167
Sister see Aniyatti; Chechi
The Sixth Lord see Aaraam Thampuran
Slumdog Millionaire (2008) 3, 4
Smitha, Silk 3
The Soil Beckons see Mitti Wajaan Maardi
Something Is Happening see Kuch Kuch Hota Hai
Sometimes Happiness, Sometimes Sadness see Kabhi Khushi Khabhie Gham
Son of India (1962) 125–6, 129
The Son of the King see Rajavinte Makan
Son of the Nightingale Who Was Brought Up by the Elephant see Anavalarthiya Vanambadiyude Makan
Sons of Jat Farmers see Putt Jattan De
Soulmate see Atmasakhi
Spadikam (1995) 99, 104
Spark see Jugnu
Spider's Web see Jedara Bale (1968)
Springs Still Return see Baharen Phir Bhi Aayengi
The Sprinkler Sprinkled see L'Arroseur arrosé
Sree Gouranga (1933) 32
Sreeramapattabhisekham (1962) 52
Sridevi 8, **181–92**, *185*, *186*, 219
  breakthrough roles 183–4
  star persona 187–90
Stanislavski, Constantin 210
Stanwyck, Barbara 87*n*1
Stavers, Gloria 133
Stay Awake see Jagte Raho
Storm see Samraat
Storm of Sin see Paap Ki Aandhi
Stowe, Harriet Beecher, *Uncle Tom's Cabin* 134
Style see Andaaz
Subbulakshmi, M.S. 27, *28*
Subhash, Babbar 169
Subramanyam, P. 46, 49
Sulochana 45, 152, 169*n*15
Sultan (2016) 200
Sundaram, T.R. 46*n*1
Swades: We, the People (2004) 212
Swayamsiddha (1949) 27
Syed Nazir Ali *see* Kumar, Rattan

Tagore, Rabindranath 117
Take a Shot see Dum Maaro Dum
Tanveer, Sapna 3
Tarkhad, Nalini 18

Tasker, Yvonne 193
Taylor, Elizabeth 56
Teen Devian (1965) 80
Tees Maar Khan (2010) 226, 227–8, 230
Teesri Kasam (1966) 84
Teesri Manzil (1966) 129, 158–60
Tembe, Govind Rao 16, 19
Temple, Shirley 190
Tere Naam (2003) 197
Tere Pyar Mein (2000) 197
Thaazhvaaram (1990) 102
Thandavam (2002) 102, 106
Thankal, Nalla 48
The Third Storey see Teesri Manzil
The Third Vow see Teesri Kasam
The Thirsty One see Pyaasa
13 going on 30 (2004) 228
Thomas, Rosie 182
Thoovaanathumbikal (1987) 102
The Thread of Silk see Resham Ki Dori
Three Ladies see Teen Devian
Thressiama *see* Kumari, Miss
'Thrikkodi Thrikkodi' 47
The Tides see Jwar Bhata
The Tides of the Ganges see Ganga Ki Lehren
The Times of India 15
  cartoons *25*
Tipu Sultan 88, 93
To Meet and Celebrate While Alive see Jag Jeondeyan De Mele
Tomorrow May Never Come see Kal Ho Naa Ho
Toofan aur Diya (1956) 114
Tork, Peter 133
Transformation see Paribartan
Trauma see Sadma
Treacherous Lover see Sanam Bewafa
Trickster see Chaalbaaz
Triumph of Faith see Bhakta Vijaya
Triveni 95
Troy (2004) 210
Truth Alone Prevails see Satyamev Jayate
Tumko Na Bhool Payenge (2002) 197, 200–2
Tuntun 183
The Turbulence: A Love Story see Gadar Ek Prem Katha
A Turn of Dice 60
Turner, Lana 75
Twentieth Century see Irupatham Noottandu
Two Measures see Randidangazhi

Udaya Pictures Private Limited 46, 46*n*2
  vs Merryland 47
The Uncanny see Anhonee
Uncle and Nephew see Chacha Bhatija

The Unexpected **see** *Kunku*
Unnamed **see** *Gumnaan*
Urs, D. Devaraj 96

Vagabond **see** *Awaara* (1951)
The Vagabond Wind **see** *Naadodikkattu*
Vahan (1936) 18
Valentino, Rudolph 132–3
Valicha, Kishore 207–8
The Valley **see** *Thaazhvaaram*
Valyettan (2000) 105
Vanamala (1951) 49
Varavelpu (1989) 102, 105
Vasanthi 18
Vasudevan, Ravi 184*n*1, 212–13
Vasudevan, T.E. 47*n*4
Veeranna, Gubbi 91
Vellinakshatram (1949) 47, 48
Verendra 142
The Victory **see** *Jeet*
Vidyapati (1937) 32
Vietnam Colony (1992) 107
Vigatakumaran (1930) 46*n*1, 56
Vineyards for Us to Dwell in **see** *Namukku Parkkaan Munthirithoppukal*
Virdi, Jyotika 182
Visveswaraiya, M., Sir 89, 94

Walker, Johnny 7, **59–71**, *63*, *66*, *69*
    background and early life 59–60
    romantic leads 68–70
    screen persona 60

The Wall **see** *Deewar*
Wanted (2009) 195, 197
Warrier, Manju 107
Wayne, John 87*n*1
We Are Indians **see** *Hum Hindustani*
We Are Proud of Our Nation **see** *Asa Nu Maan Watna Da*
Weapon **see** *Hathyar* (1989)
The Weapon **see** *Auzaar*
Weinstein, Harvey 205
Welcome **see** *Varavelpu* (1989)
Welcome **see** *Jee Aayan Nu*
Welcome (2007) 220
When, Why? and Where? **see** *Kab? Kyoon? Aur Kahan?*
Who Was She? **see** *Woh Kaun Thi*
The Wife's Servant **see** *Naukar Biwi Ka*
Wildcat of Bombay (1927) 169*n*15
Willemen, Paul 2, 17, 20
Woh Kaun Thi (1964) 156

Yaadon ki Baraat (1973) 73–4
Yakeen (1969) 74, 85
You Will Meet a Tall Dark Stranger (2010) 3
You Won't Get Another Life **see** *Zindagi Na Milegi Dobarra*
Yuvraaj (2008) 220

Zindagi Na Milegi Dobarra (2011) 225–6, 228
Zinta, Preity 223